Discourses of Epictetus

Education of Barristers.

THE FATES

From a painting by Paul Thumann

Discourses of Epictet

Translated by
George Long

With a Critical and Biographical Introduction
by John Lancaster Spalding

Illustrated

New York
D. Appleton and Company
1904

EPICTETUS

O F the life of Epictetus little need be said. His biography is his character, and this lies open in his books, where the fine spirit of an earnest and noble soul still breathes. He was born in Phrygia, about the middle of the first century. His mother was a slave; his father is unknown. Epictetus is not his name, but is a Greek word which denotes his servile condition. In his youth he became the property of Epaphroditus, a freed-man of Nero's, who permitted him to attend the lectures of Musonius Rufus, one of the most celebrated teachers in Rome. Having acquired freedom, he began himself to give lessons; but he was soon sent into exile, together with the other philosophers, by the Emperor Domitian.

Settling at Nicopolis, in Epirus (the modern Albania), he opened a school, and continued to teach the doctrines of stoicism to the time of his death, at the age, it is sup-posed, of nearly a hundred years. He was feeble in body, lame, poor, and unmarried, living alone until he took an old woman into his house to care for an orphan whom he had adopted. He wrote nothing, but talked with his pupils in a familiar way of whatever concerns the conduct of life. Arrian, his favourite disciple, took notes of his conversations, not with a view to publication, but for his own use. When, however, without his knowledge, they had fallen into the hands of several, he edited them himself Thus we owe to an accident the existence of these "Discourses," which form one of the world's vital books. The "Manual" is a collection of aphorisms taken substantially from the larger work.

Epictetus was not the founder of a new philosophy. Zeno, the originator of the Stoic system, was his master, and Zeno himself derived his fundamental principles from Antisthenes, the author of the cynic school and the friend of Socrates.

The Greeks are the creators of philosophy, and their earliest attempt at systematic thought was an effort to understand Nature. But they soon learned that it was necessary to begin from within, since to know anything man must first know himself. Thus the problem of the conduct of life forced itself upon them. This is the constant preoccupation of Socrates, who was born five hundred years before Epictetus. He taught that the good is to be sought not in outward things, nor in the indulgence of appetite, but in virtue, which for him, however, is an intellectual rather than a moral habit. His calm and rational temper led him to the belief that man always acts in accordance with his knowledge, does what insight shows him to be useful to himself. He who does evil, does it from a mistake of judgment. Sin is error. Virtue, then, being chiefly knowledge, may be taught, and to teach it is the philosopher's life work. But Socrates moved in a circle from which there was no escape. To know the useful is virtue. But what is the useful? That which makes for virtue.

Antisthenes does not attempt to determine the meaning of the good. He simply declares that virtue is the only good, and, in his view, virtue is the intelligent conduct of life. Right life is the essential good; virtue is its own reward, and one need not look to its results. It is, in the midst of whatever vicissitudes, a sure possession. The virtuous man is independent of events, and stands

secure against fate and fortune. The world is full of things
he does not need; he seeks not wealth, nor fame, nor honour, nor pleasure.

Zeno, the Stoic, born in Cyprus about 340 B. C., is the
heir of the Cynics. The sage, as he conceives the truly
wise and virtuous man, is first of all independent of the
world, since only on this condition can he be free and find
happiness in himself alone; and as what is external is but
little subject to human will, he must overcome the world
within himself by gaining the mastery over the feelings
and desires which it excites. To be self-contained and
self-sufficient, to remain unmoved in the presence of good
or of evil fortune, imperturbable though the universe be
shattered, is the goal he must strive to reach. If he can
not defend himself against the excitations of feeling, he
will at least refuse his assent, and thereby prevent them
from becoming passions. His ideal is apathy, absence of
emotion. The course of things may bring him pleasure
and pain, but since he holds that the one is not a good,
the other not an evil, he retains his equanimity. Virtue
is his sole good, and the only evil is to permit passion to
conquer reason. This withdrawal of the individual within
himself, however it may be modified and supplemented, is
an essential element in the Stoic's conception of life.
Reason, from his point of view, is not only man's nature,
but that of the universe, while the impulses of the senses
are irrational. The soul, as part of the World-Reason,
must therefore exclude from itself all excitation of feeling.
To live in harmony with Nature is to rise into a sphere
where the senses cease to trouble; it is to live in communion with the cosmic power, from which all things
proceed, in cheerful obedience to the eternal destiny,
which, being the will of God, is the divine law. The wise
man accepts this life as his first and highest duty. It is
the task which Reason imposes upon him. The Stoics,

however, holding that man is by nature social, require
that he lead a social life. The social ideal of the sage is
that of a universal ethical community, and he is indifferent to forms of government and to actually existing states.
He is a citizen of the world, demands justice and sympathy
for all, and refuses to recognise the division of mankind
into Greeks and barbarians.

The chief stress is laid upon the worth of moral personality, upon the paramount value of the good that lies
within, though the duty of co-operating with one's fellow-
men for the general welfare is inculcated. The metaphysical principle is pantheistic, and involves fatalism; but the
Stoics, preoccupied exclusively with moral ideas and interests, cared little for logical consistency, and stoutly asserted the freedom of the will, holding fast to liberty of
choice and to the universality of causation.

Though of Greek origin, stoicism attained its highest
practical significance in Rome, where its doctrines seemed
to be suited to the character of the people. Those stern,
self-controlled, and brave men were attracted by a system
which emphasized the value of independence, courage, and
imperturbability. They found in it a source of the moral
enthusiasm which the pagan religions had no power to
inspire. They were drawn to the society of the philosophers, received them into their houses, and became their
disciples. By daily intercourse with these earnest and
austere teachers, such men as Scipio and Lælius, as Brutus,
Cato, and Cicero, were formed. The prestige and authority
of the preachers of stoicism were heightened by the general
corruption which was undermining the state, and the public
calamities which were becoming more and more frequent.

The noblest souls, despairing of the cause of liberty,
withdrew from politics, and sought consolation in a philosophy which taught them how to bear the ills of life
and how to die. In Rome, where only what is practical

was rightly appreciated, little attention was given to the metaphysical presuppositions of stoicism, and the great teachers, losing sight of the logical requirements of the system, took what seemed to them true and to the purpose wherever it was found. Indeed, contradiction and inconsistency did not repel, as we have seen, the early Stoics, and in its Roman development the philosophy became more and more eclectic.

Epictetus, Seneca, and Marcus Aurelius are the three famous names of this later school of stoicism, and they are all teachers of the conduct of life, in love with inner perfection, and comparatively heedless of mere speculation. In the midst of the general decadence and threatening collapse of the civilized world, they sought to rouse conscience; and as the pagan religion could do nothing for them, they strove to give a kind of sacredness to human wisdom. To derive profit from their works it is not necessary to understand their theories. All that is required is an open mind and a tractable heart. What is speculative disappears in the presence of the practical worth of the truths they utter. To read them aright we need an attentive and devout spirit rather than an acute and curious intellect.

Of these three teachers of the later stoicism, Epictetus is the noblest character and the greatest authority. His life is more completely in harmony with his doctrine. He rises in moral elevation to the level of his maxims and precepts. His purity equals his insight. He is the venerable sage. He is the saint of a philosophical religion, a man who from an abject condition raised himself to the worthiest dispositions of mind and heart, who in the midst of a corrupt society remained unstained and faithful, his thought fixed on the highest moral ideals, and following to the end his vocation as a preacher of righteousness—a slave, a cripple, a pauper, as his epitaph declares, but dear to the gods. He has drawn for us an ideal of the Stoic sage, in

which his own character is portrayed. He accuses neither
God nor man; he controls desire; he knows not anger, nor
resentment, nor envy, nor pity; he fences himself with virtuous shame. He has nothing to conceal; he does not fear
exile or death, for wherever and however he is there also
is God. But it is not enough that he be good in and for
himself. He is a messenger sent by Zeus to instruct men
concerning good and evil, to point out to them that they
walk in wrong ways. He must cry out: " Oh, mortals,
whither are ye hasting? Why do ye tumble about, like
the blind? The good is not in the body; it is not in wealth,
or power, or empire; it lies in yourselves. God has sent
you one to teach you by his example. Take notice of me
that I am without a country, without a house, without an
estate, without a servant: I lie on the ground; have no
wife, no children, no coat, but have only earth and heaven
and one poor cloak. - And what need I? Am I not without sorrow, without fear? Am I not free? Did I ever
blame God or man? Did I ever accuse any one? Have
any of you seen me look discontented? " Epictetus is
direct, plain, and earnest in his speech. His style is bare
of ornament, vigorous, and incisive. He is always serious,
often stern, and at times pathetic. He does not deliver
finished discourses, is heedless of rhetorical ornament, and
wholly intent on improving his hearers by inciting them
to the love and practice of virtue. He is not so much an
orator as a brave, genuine man, whose whole being vibrates
in his words, which are vital and electric. They are the
honest and fearless expression of what he thinks in his
heart, of what he feels and lives. They are the utterance
of what is deepest and permanent in man, and therefore
they never lose the power to stimulate and nourish faith in
the worth of a life led in obedience to the divine commands. The simple and straightforward manner in which
he speaks the highest truth has made him a favourite not

with scholars merely, but with all classes of readers. Whoever is persuaded that life is chiefly conduct may derive help from him. Only the learned can read Plato with profit, and the fewest of these study him, but an ordinary mind may find in Epictetus a friend and teacher, for his philosophy is of the most practical character and easily understood. Wisdom consists in knowing how to distinguish between what is our own and what is not ours. Our will, our opinions, desires, inclinations, and aversions are ours; the rest—body, possessions, honour, and reputation—is not ours. The divine law bids us hold fast to what is our own, and make no claim to what is not ours. God in endowing us with free will gives us control over what is ours, but other things he has not placed in our power. A man's business is with himself, with learning to think rightly and will wisely. Here he is master, here he has full control. Let him give heed to this, and in other things resign himself with a cheerful heart to the guidance of the all-wise Father, who rules the whole. Since we can not determine the course of Nature, it is our duty to accept with courage and resignation whatever befalls. Is money, or friend, or wife, or child taken from us, let us remember that they never were ours; they were but lent to us, and have been returned to the owner. Shall we complain when he asks us to restore what belongs to him? But it lies with us to have an independent soul and a victorious will, to remain imperturbable, serene, reverent, and thankful, despite disgrace and misfortune, which can not touch our inmost being or deprive us of freedom and virtue. These are the sole good, and so long as they are ours all else is unimportant. Will that things happen as they do, and nothing shall happen contrary to thy will. But how shall I bear the wrongs which the wicked inflict? May not God choose his agents to demand of thee what he has lent. Thou art but a player to whom a rôle has

been assigned. Take cheerfully whatever character is given
thee, whether it be that of a beggar or that of a king. Thy
sole business is to act well the part to which God has appointed thee. Think of him as often as thou breathest, and
let thy whole study and desire be to know and do his will.
For Epictetus a virtuous life is not a means, but an
end. The sage does right not from the hope of prosperity
and good name, not that he may have health of body and
mind, not because wise hehaviour produces a contented
and happy temper, but he does what is just, avoids what
is base, without thought of reward or punishment, im-
pelled solely by a sense of duty. He clings to virtue
though virtue be his death sentence, and though he have
no expectation of a future life. He makes no sacrifice in
abandoning all things for virtue, for virtue is his only
good. He who wishes to please men, who desires to be
known and praised even for his virtue, is not a lover of
virtue, as he who loves money or pleasure or glory is not
a lover of mankind. The wise man's will rolls like a wheel
with steady and even motion toward the one eternal goal,
to which the universe also is drawn. "If there be any
worth in thee, O man, learn to walk alone and to converse with thyself!"
In the "Manual" Epictetus appears as a stern, uncom-
promising Stoic. In the "Discourses" we find him in the
midst of his friends and disciples, where he takes a more
human and sympathetic tone. Here he infuses into his
morality the glow of religion, which makes it vital and
effective. We are not always made to feel that virtue lacks
vigour, unless it be hard and repellent, that pride heightens
truth, or that insolence is a mark of goodness, or that
harshness is zeal, or modest assertion of opinion a com-
promise with error. We almost seem to hear Thrasea
declare that he fears to hate even vice too much, lest perchance he come to hate his fellow-men. It is in the "Dis-

courses" that he tells us that the true Stoic is "the father of mankind; that all men are his sons and all women his daughters. He attends to all, takes care of all. Is it from impertinence that he rebukes those he meets? He does it as a father, as a brother, as a minister of the common parent, Zeus." He does not marry, he has no children, he accepts no office, that nothing may interfere with the work which God has given him to do. He is careful of his health and appearance, lest he repel those whom he wishes to attract. Above all, he is clean of heart, for how, if he is himself guilty, shall he reprove others? He watches and labours for men, becomes purer day by day; he rules all his thoughts as the friend, as the minister of the gods, as a partner in the empire of Zeus. He has, besides, so much patience as to appear to the vulgar insensible and like a stone; "for there is this fine circumstance connected with the character of a Cynic: that he must be beaten like an ass, and yet when beaten must love those who beat him as the father, as the brother of all."

Epictetus does not reject the pantheism of the Stoics nor the polytheism of his age, but whatever his theological opinions, which seem to have been vague, he does not think of God as an indeterminate somewhat, but as a person to whom he is bound by ties of obedience, reverence, and love; and though he often speaks of the gods, the Supreme Being is never absent from his mind. He is the creator of the world and the ruler of all things. He can not conceive that the universe should have come into existence or should continue without God. The glory and harmony of the creation fill him with devout enthusiasm. "What can I, a lame old man, do other than praise God? Were I a nightingale, I should perform the office of a nightingale; were I a swan, that of a swan; but as I am a rational being, I must praise God. This is my work, this I do, nor shall I cease from the task while life is left me. And upon you also I call to intone this hymn." With his last breath he hopes still to continue his sacred song: " Nothing but thanks to thee do I utter, because thou hast deemed me worthy to partake with thee of life's feast, to behold thy works, and to follow thy government of the world." Day and night he is mindful of the divine commands; his thoughts are raised to Heaven, and in earthly things he sees God, not as the Creator alone, but also as the Father who watches over his children and has care of even the least among them.

Epictetus takes what seems to him true and good wherever it be found. He has no respect for mere theory, and prizes only the knowledge which is brought to bear on the conduct of life. The beginning of philosophy, he says, is the turning from intellectual conceit and the recognition of one's own helplessness in the most indispensable things. To talk like a Stoic is easy; to live like one is difficult. He challenges his hearers to show him one whose life is in harmony with his principles. And yet all that is needed is the will. Will, and thou art free. From within come salvation and ruin. If the heart is set upon external things, a god can not rescue thee. But let us forget the past, he cries, and begin anew. God has placed us in the midst of the battle of life; we have sworn to be true to him, our king and leader, to defend at whatever cost the post he has assigned us. " I am thine. Where will'st thou that I live—in Rome, or Athens, or Thebes, or on the desert island of Gyara? Only, be mindful of me there."

Epictetus is not a Christian: he knows nothing of God's anger and mercy, of guilt and punishment, of redemption and forgiveness. In contradiction with his doctrine of providence, he holds to the old Stoic tradition which permits suicide, and in certain cases makes it a duty. He who can live content wherever God places him is ready to quit the tabernacle of the soul if the house is too full of smoke. Though not a Christian, he certainly knew something of the Christian religion. He lived in Rome as student and teacher of philosophy from the year 73 to 95, and at this time Christianity had penetrated even the higher circles of Roman society; and the charge of atheism which caused Domitian to send the philosophers into exile led him also to banish the Christians, many of whom suffered martyrdom while Epictetus was delivering his discourses at Nicopolis. He takes occasion to mention the heroism with which these Galileans, as he calls them, met death. They die without fear, he says, not from ignorance of the danger, nor from weariness of life, nor from madness, nor yet from philosophic conviction, but from habit. Galileans is not the name by which the Roman writers of this period designate the Christians. They did not call themselves Galileans, and to the Jews they were known as Nazarenes. It is probable, therefore, that Epictetus found the word in the New Testament writings, where the epithet is not infrequently applied to the followers of Jesus. Galen, who was educated in the Stoic philosophy and who lived but a short time after Epictetus, speaks of the contempt for death shown by "those men who are called Christians." He goes on to say that their doctrines are delivered in parables, which are more easily understood than abstruse arguments, and that their lives are in many respects like to that of the true philosophers. In fact, while the world view of the Stoic differs radically from the Christian, the moral teaching of the pagan philosopher and of the follower of Christ is often much the same. Both attach the highest importance to religious faith and sentiment; both hold that virtue is the chief good; both emphasize the principle of liberty, and draw from it that of free personality; both declare that man holds his earthly possessions as a steward of the divine owner, to whom he is responsible for the use he makes of them.

The early Stoics had taught in a general way that men are the children of God, but in Epictetus the doctrine is developed with a fulness which is found in no writer before the birth of Christ. He preaches with fiery zeal that all men are children of God, and that even slaves must be considered and treated as brothers. For him, as in the Gospel, every human being is one's neighbour. His ideal of the Cynic or perfect Stoic is that of a Christian apostle; his view of celibacy seems to have been taken from St. Paul. The portrait he draws of Hercules, as a conscious son of God and saviour of the world, is very like the character of the divine Master as revealed in the New Testament, and unlike that of the traditional Hercules, who stands at the parting of the ways.

But Epictetus—though he certainly knew something of the Christian faith, and though his " Manual " was a favourite book of some of the early Christians, and became, with simply a change of certain words, a kind of rule for St. Nilus and the anchorets of Mount Sinai—remains a Stoic. For him God is not love, but the eternal destiny, and his enthusiasm for humanity is dominated by his resignation to fate. His religion is a philosophical piety founded on self-surrender to the inexorable laws of Nature. He is, nevertheless, one of those who have had the clearest insight into the duties of man, and his utterances have now for eighteen hundred years been a source of patience, courage, and strength to minds of widely varying opinions and beliefs. He is a genuine man, whose true image looks out upon us from these " Discourses." In reading him we lose sight of his metaphysical theories, and are mindful only of the great principles which he expresses with rare force and which underlie all right human life.

JOHN LANCASTER SPALDING.

THE AUTHOR'S PREFACE

———•◆•———

ARRIAN *to* LUCIUS GELLIUS, *with wishes for his happiness·* I neither‘ wrote these " Discourses [1] of Epictetus " in the way in which a man might write such things; nor did I make them public myself, inasmuch as I declare that I did not even write them. But whatever I heard him say, the same I attempted to write down in his own words as nearly as possible, for the purpose of preserving them as memorials to myself afterward of the thoughts and the freedom of speech of Epictetus. Accordingly, the " Discourses " are naturally such as a man would address without preparation to another, not such as a man would write with the view of others reading them Now, being such, I do not know how they fell into the hands of the public, without either my consent or my knowledge. But it concerns me little if I shall be considered incompetent to write; and it concerns Epictetus not at all if any man shall despise his words; for at the. time when he uttered them it was plain that he had no other purpose than to move the minds of his hearers to the best things. If, indeed, these " Discourses " should produce this effect, they will have, I think, the result which the words of philosophers ought to have. But if they shall not, let those who read them know that, when Epictetus delivered them, the hearer could not avoid being affected in the way that Epictetus wished him to be. But if the

B   xv

" Discourses " themselves, as they are written, do not effect this result, it may be that the fault is mine, or, it may be, that the thing is unavoidable.

Farewell!   ·

[1] A. Gellius (i, 2, and xvii, 19) speaks of the " Discourses of Epictetus " as arranged by Arrian, Gellius (xix, 1) speaks of a fifth book of these " Discourses," but only four are extant and some fragments.   The whole number of books was eight, as Photius (Cod. 58) says.   There is also an " Encheiridion " or " Manual," consisting of short pieces selected from the " Discourses of Epictetus," and the valuable commentary on the " Encheiridion " written by Simplicius in the sixth century A. D., in the reign of Justinian.

Arrian explains in a manner what he means by saying that he did not write these " Discourses of Epictetus "; but he does not explain his meaning when he says that he did not make them public.   He tells us that he did attempt to write down in the words of Epictetus what the philosopher said, but how it happened that they were first published, without his knowledge or consent, Arrian does not say.   It appears, however, that he did see the " Discourses " when they were published, and as Schweig-häuser remarks, he would naturally correct any errors that he detected, and so there would be an edition revised by himself.   Schweighäuser has a note (i, ch. 26, 13) on the difficulties which we now find in the " Discourses."

CONTENTS

BOOK I

BOOK III

LIST OF ILLUSTRATIONS

MEDITATIONS

DISCOURSES

———◆———

BOOK I

———

CHAPTER I

OF THE THINGS WHICH ARE IN OUR POWER, AND NOT IN OUR
POWER

OF all the faculties (except that which I shall soon
mention), you will find not one which is capable of
contemplating itself, and, consequently, not capable either of approving or disapproving. How far
does the grammatic art possess the contemplating power?
As far as forming a judgment about what is written and
spoken. And how far music? As far as judging about
melody. Does either of them then contemplate itself? By
no means. But when you must write something to your
friend, grammar will tell you what words you should write;
but whether you should write or not, grammar will not tell
you. And so it is with music as to musical sounds; but
whether you should sing at the present time and play on the
lute, or do neither, music will not tell you. What faculty
then will tell you? That which contemplates both itself
and all other things. And what is this faculty? The
rational faculty; for this is the only faculty that we have received which examines itself, what it is, and what power it
has, and what is the value of this gift, and examines all other
faculties: for what else is there which tells us that golden

things are beautiful, for they do not say so themselves? Evidently it is the faculty which is capable of judging of appearances.[1] What else judges of music, grammar, and the other faculties, proves their uses, and points out the occasions for using them? Nothing else.

As then it was fit to be so, that which is best of all and supreme over all is the only thing which the gods have placed in our power, the right use of appearances; but all other things they have not placed in our power. Was it because they did not choose? I indeed think that, if they had been able, they would have put these other things also in our power, but they certainly could not.[2] For as we exist on the earth, and are bound to such a body and to such companions, how was it possible for us not to be hindered as to these things by externals?

But what says Zeus? Epictetus, if it were possible, I would have made both your little body and your little property free and not exposed to hindrance. But now be not ignorant of this: this body is not yours, but it is clay finely tempered. And since I was not able to do for you what I have mentioned, I have given you a small portion of us,[3] this faculty of pursuing an object and avoiding it, and the faculty of desire and aversion, and, in a word, the faculty of using the appearances of things; and if you will take care of this faculty and consider it your only possession, you will never be hindered, never meet with impediments; you will not lament, you will not blame, you will not flatter any person

Well, do these seem to you small matters? I hope not. Be content with them then and pray to the gods. But now when it is in our power to look after one thing, and to attach ourselves to it, we prefer to look after many things, and to be bound to many things, to the body and to property, and to brother and to friend, and to child and to slave. Since then we are bound to many things, we are depressed by them and dragged down. For this reason, when the weather is not fit for sailing, we sit down and torment ourselves, and continually look out to see what wind is blowing. It is north. What is that to us? When will the west wind blow? When it shall choose, my good man, or when it shall please Æolus; for God has not made you the manager of the winds, but Æolus. What then? We must make the best use that we can of the things which are in our power, and use the rest according to their nature. What is their nature then? As God may please.

Must I then alone have my head cut off? What, would you have all men lose their heads that you may be consoled? Will you not stretch out your neck as Lateranus[4] did at Rome when Nero ordered him to be beheaded? For when he had stretched out his neck, and received a feeble blow, which made him draw it in for a moment, he stretched it out again. And a little before, when he was visited by Epaphroditus,[5] Nero's freedman, who asked him about the cause of offence which he had given, he said, "If I choose to tell anything, I will tell your master."

What then should a man have in readiness in such circumstances? What else than this? What is mine, and what is not mine; and what is permitted to me, and what is not permitted to me. I must die Must I then die lamenting? I must be put in chains. Must I then also lament? I must go into exile. Does any man then hinder me from going with smiles and cheerfulness and contentment? Tell me the secret which you possess. I will not, for this is in my power. But I will put you in chains.[6] Man, what are you talking about? Me in chains? You may fetter my leg, but my will not even Zeus himself can overpower. I will throw you into prison. My poor body, you mean. I will cut your head off. When then have I told you that my head alone can not be cut off? These are the things which philosophers should meditate on, which they should write daily, in which they should exercise themselves.

Thrasea[7] used to say, I would rather be killed to-day than be banished to-morrow. What then did Rufus[8] say to him? If you choose death as the heavier misfortune, how great is the folly of your choice? But if, as the lighter, who has given you the choice? Will you not study to be content with that which has been given to you?

What then did Agrippinus[9] say? He said, "I am not a hindrance to myself." When it was reported to him that his trial was going on in the Senate, he said, "I hope it may turn out well; but it is the fifth hour of the day"—this was the time when he was used to exercise himself and then take the cold bath—"let us go and take our exercise." After he had taken his exercise, one comes and tells him, "You have been condemned." "To banishment," he replies, "or to death?" "To banishment." "What about my property?" "It is not taken from you." "Let us go to Aricia, then,"[10] he said, "and dine."

This it is to have studied what a man ought to study; to have made desire, aversion, free from hindrance, and free from all that a man would avoid. I must die. If now, I am ready to die. If, after a short time, I now dine because it is the dinner-hour; after this I will then die. How? Like a man who gives up what belongs to another.

NOTES

[1] The Stoics gave the name of appearances (φαντασίαι) to all impressions received by the senses, and to all emotions caused by external things.

[2] Compare Antoninus, ii. 3 Epictetus does not intend to limit the power of the gods, but he means that the constitution of things being what it is, they can not do contradictories. They have so constituted things that man is hindered by externals How then could they give to man a power of not being hindered by externals? Seneca (De Providentia) says: "But it may be said, many things happen which cause sadness, fear, and are hard to bear. Because (God says) I could not save you from them, I have armed your minds against all." This is the answer to those who imagine that they have disproved the common assertion of the omnipotence of God, when they ask whether He can combine inherent contradictions, whether He can cause two and two to make five. This is indeed a very absurd way of talking.

[3] Schweighauser observes that these faculties of pursuit and avoidance, and of desire and aversion, and even the faculty of using appearances, belong to animals as well as to man; but animals in using appearances are moved by passion only, and do not understand what they are doing, while in man these passions are under his control. Salmasius proposed to change ἡμέτερον into ὑμέτερον, to remove the difficulty about these animal passions being called "a small portion of us (the gods)." Schweighauser, however, though he sees the difficulty, does not accept the emendation. Perhaps Arrian has here imperfectly represented what his master said, and perhaps he did not.

[4] Plautius Lateranus, consul-elect, was charged with being engaged in Piso's conspiracy against Nero. He was hurried to execution without being allowed to see his children; and though the tribune who executed him was privy to the plot, Lateranus said nothing. (Tacit. Ann. xv. 49, 60.)

[5] Epaphroditus was a freedman of Nero, and once the master of Epictetus. He was Nero's secretary. One good act is recorded of him: he helped Nero to kill himself, and for this act he was killed by Domitian (Suetonius, Domitian, c. 14).

⁸ This is an imitation of a passage in the Bacchæ of Euripides (v. 492, etc.), which is also imitated by Horace (Epp. i. 16).

⁷ Thrasea Pætus, a Stoic philosopher, who was ordered in Nero's time to put himself to death (Tacit. Ann xvi 21-35) He was the husband of Arria, whose mother Arria, the wife of Cæcina Pætus, in the time of the Emperor Claudius, heroically showed her husband the way to die (Plinius, Letters, iii. 16). Martial has immortalised the elder Arria in a famous epigram (i 14) :—

"When Arria to her Pætus gave the sword
Which her own hand from her chaste bosom drew,
'This wound,' she said, 'believe me, gives no pain,
But that will pain me which thy hand will do.'"

⁸ C. Musonius Rufus, a Tuscan by birth, of equestrian rank, a philosopher and Stoic (Tacit Hist iii 81)

⁹ Paconius Agrippinus was condemned in Nero's time. The charge against him was that he inherited his father's hatred of the head of the Roman state (Tacit Ann xvi 28). The father of Agrippinus had been put to death under Tiberius (Suetonius, Tib c 61)

¹⁰ Aricia, about twenty Roman miles from Rome, on the Via Appia.

CHAPTER II

TO the rational animal only is the irrational intolerable; but that which is rational is tolerable. Blows are not naturally intolerable. How is that? See how the Lacedæmonians[1] endure whipping when they have learned that whipping is consistent with reason. To hang yourself is not intolerable. When then you have the opinion that it is rational, you go and hang yourself. In short, if we observe, we shall find that the animal man is pained by nothing so much as by that which is irrational; and, on the contrary, attracted to nothing so much as to that which is rational.

But the rational and the irrational appear in a different way to different persons, just as the good and the bad, the profitable and the unprofitable. For this reason, particularly, we need discipline, in order to learn how to adapt the preconception of the rational and the irrational to the several things comformably to nature. But in order to determine the rational and the irrational, we use not only the estimates of external things, but we consider also what is appropriate to each person. For to one man it is consistent with reason to hold a chamber pot for another, and to look to this only, that if he does not hold it, he will receive stripes, and he will not receive his food: but if he shall hold the pot, he will not suffer anything hard or disagreeable But to another man not only does the holding of a chamber pot appear intolerable for himself, but intolerable also for him to allow another to do this office for him. If then you ask me whether you should hold the chamber pot or not, I shall say to you that the receiving of food is worth more than the not receiving of it, and the being scourged is a greater indignity than not being scourged; so that if you measure your interests by these things, go and hold the chamber pot. "But this," you say, "would not be worthy of me." Well then, it is you who must introduce this consideration into the inquiry, not I; for it is you who know yourself, how much you are worth to yourself, and at what price you sell yourself; for men sell themselves at various prices.

For this reason, when Florus was deliberating whether he should go down to Nero's[2] spectacles, and also perform in them himself, Agrippinus said to him, "Go down": and when Florus asked Agrippinus, "Why do not you go down?" Agrippinus replied, "Because I do not even deliberate about the matter." For he who has once brought himself to deliberate about such matters, and to calculate the value of external things, comes very near to those who have forgotten their own character. For why do you ask me the question, whether death is preferable or life? I say life. Pain or pleasure? I say pleasure. "But if I do not take a part in the tragic acting, I shall have my head struck off." Go then and take a part, but I will not. "Why?" Because you consider yourself to be only one thread of those which are in the tunic. Well then it was fitting for you to take care how you should be like the rest of men, just as the thread has no design to be anything superior to the other threads. But I wish to be purple,[3] that small part which is bright, and makes all the rest appear graceful and beautiful. Why then do you tell me to make myself like the many? and if I do, how shall I still be purple?

Priscus Helvidius[4] also saw this, and acted conformably. For when Vespasian sent and commanded him not to go into the senate, he replied, "It is in your power not to allow me to be a member of the senate, but so long as I am, I must go in." "Well, go in then," says the emperor, "but say nothing." "Do not ask my opinion, and I will be silent." "But I must ask your opinion." "And I must say what I think right." "But if you do, I shall put you to death." "When then did I tell you that I am immortal? You will do your part, and I will do mine· it is your part to kill; it is mine to die, but not in fear: yours to banish me; mine to depart without sorrow."

What good then did Priscus do, who was only a single person? And what good does the purple do for the toga? Why, what else than this, that it is conspicuous in the toga as purple, and is displayed also as a fine example to all other things? But in such circumstances another would have replied to Cæsar who forbade him to enter the senate, "I thank you for sparing me." But such a man Vespasian would not even have forbidden to enter the senate, for he knew that he would either sit there like an earthen vessel, or, if he spoke, he would say what Cæsar wished and add even more.

In this way an athlete also acted who was in danger of dying unless his private parts were amputated. His brother came to the athlete, who was a philosopher, and said, "Come, brother, what are you going to do? Shall we amputate this member and return to the gymnasium?" But the athlete persisted in his resolution and died. When some one asked Epictetus, how he did this, as an athlete or a philosopher? "As a man," Epictetus replied, "and a man who had been proclaimed among the athletes at the Olympic games and had contended in them, a man who had been familiar with such a place, and not merely anointed in Baton's [5] school." Another would have allowed even his head to be cut off, if he could have lived without it. Such is that regard to character which is so strong in those who have been accustomed to introduce it of themselves and conjoined with other things into their deliberations.

"Come then, Epictetus, shave[6] yourself" If I am a philosopher, I answer, I will not shave myself. "But I will take off your head?" If that will do you any good, take it off.

Some person asked, how then shall every man among us perceive what is suitable to his character? "How," he replied, "does the bull alone, when the lion has attacked, discover his own powers and put himself forward in defence of the whole herd? It is plain that with the powers the perception of having them is immediately conjoined: and, therefore, whoever of us has such powers will not be ignorant of them. Now a bull is not made suddenly, nor a brave man; but we must discipline ourselves in the winter for the summer campaign, and not rashly run upon that which does not concern us."

Only consider at what price you sell your own will: if for no other reason, at least for this, that you sell it not for a small sum. But that which is great and superior perhaps belongs to Socrates and such as are like him. Why then, if we are naturally such, are not a very great number of us like him? Is it true then that all horses become swift, that all dogs are skilled in tracking footprints? What then, since I am naturally dull, shall I, for this reason, take no pains? I hope not. Epictetus is not superior to Socrates; but if he is not inferior, this is enough for me; for I shall never be a Milo,[7] and yet I do not neglect my body; nor shall I be a Crœsus, and yet I do not neglect my property; nor, in a word, do we neglect looking after anything because we despair of reaching the highest degree.

NOTES

[1] The Spartan boys used to be whipped at the altar of Artemis Orthia till blood flowed abundantly, and sometimes till death; but they never uttered even a groan (Cicero, Tuscul. ii. 14; v. 27).

[2] Nero was passionately fond of scenic representations, and used to induce the descendants of noble families, whose poverty made them consent, to appear on the stage (Tacitus, Annals, xiv. 14, Suetonius, Nero, 21).

[3] The "purple" is the broad purple border on the toga named the *toga prætexta*, worn by certain Roman magistrates and some others, and by senators, it is said, on certain days (Cic Phil. ii. 43).

[4] Helvidius Priscus, a Roman senator and a philosopher, is commended by Tacitus (Hist. iv. 4, 5) as an honest man: "He followed the philosophers who considered those things only to be good which are virtuous, those only to be bad which are foul; and he reckoned power, rank, and all other things which are external to the mind as neither good nor bad." Vespasian, probably in a fit of passion, being provoked by Helvidius, ordered him to be put to death, and then revoked the order when it was too late (Suetonius, Vespasianus, 15)

[5] Baton was elected for two years gymnasiarch or superintendent of a gymnasium in or about the time of Marcus Aurelius Antoninus.

[6] This is supposed, as Casaubon says, to refer to Domitian's order to the philosophers to go into exile Some of them, in order to conceal their profession of philosophy, shaved their beards. Epictetus would not take off his beard.

[7] Milo of Croton, a great athlete.

2

CHAPTER III

IF a man should be able to assent to this doctrine as he ought, that we are all sprung from God[1] in an especial manner, and that God is the father of both men and of gods, I suppose that he would never have any ignoble or mean thoughts about himself. But if Cæsar (the emperor) should adopt you, no one could endure your arrogance; and if you know that you are the son of Zeus, will you not be elated? Yet we do not so; but since these two things are mingled in the generation of man, body in common with the animals, and reason and intelligence in common with the gods, many incline to this kinship, which is miserable and mortal; and some few to that which is divine and happy. Since then it is of necessity that every man uses everything according to the opinion which he has about it, those, the few, who think that they are formed for fidelity and modesty and a sure use of appearances, have no mean or ignoble thoughts about themselves; but with the many it is quite the contrary. For they say, What am I? A poor, miserable man, with my wretched bit of flesh. Wretched, indeed; but you possess something better than your bit of flesh. Why then do you neglect that which is better, and why do you attach yourself to this?

Through this kinship with the flesh, some of us inclining to it become like wolves, faithless and treacherous and mischievous; some become like lions, savage and bestial and untamed; but the greater part of us become foxes, and other worse animals. For what else is a slanderer and a malignant man than a fox, or some other more wretched and meaner animal? See[2] then and take care that you do not become some one of these miserable things.

[1] Epictetus speaks of God (ὁ θεός) and the gods. Also conformably

to the practice of the people, he speaks of God under the name of Zeus. The gods of the people were many, but his God was perhaps one. "Father of men and gods," says Homer of Zeus, and Virgil says of Jupiter, "Father of gods and king of men." Salmasius proposed ἀπὸ τοῦ θεοῦ.

¹ Ὁρᾶτε καὶ προσέχετε μή τι τούτων ἀποβῆτε τῶν ἀτυχημάτων. Upton compares Matthew xvi. 6; ὁρᾶτε καὶ προσέχετε ἀπὸ τῆς ζύμης, etc. Upton remarks that many expressions in Epictetus are not unlike the style of the Gospels, which were written in the same period in which Epictetus was teaching. Schweighauser also refers to Wetstein's New Testament.

CHAPTER IV

OF PROGRESS OR IMPROVEMENT

HE who is making progress, having learned from philosophers that desire means the desire of good things, and aversion means aversion from bad things; having learned too that happiness and tranquillity are not attainable by man otherwise than by not failing to obtain what he desires, and not falling into that which he would avoid; such a man takes from himself desire altogether and defers it, and he employs his aversion only on things which are dependent on his will. For if he attempts to avoid anything independent of his will, he knows that sometimes he will fall in with something which he wishes to avoid, and he will be unhappy. Now if virtue promises good fortune and tranquillity and happiness, certainly also the progress towards virtue is progress towards each of these things. For it is always true that to whatever point the perfecting of anything leads us, progress is an approach towards this point.

How then do we admit that virtue is such as I have said, and yet seek progress in other things and make a display of it? What is the product of virtue? Tranquillity. Who then makes improvement? Is it he who has read many books of Chrysippus?[1] But does virtue consist in having understood Chrysippus? If this is so, progress is clearly nothing else than knowing a great deal of Chrysippus. But now we admit that virtue produces one thing, and we declare that approaching near to it is another thing, namely, progress or improvement. Such a person says one, is already able to read Chrysippus by himself. Indeed, sir, you are making great progress. What kind of progress? But why do you mock the man? Why do you draw him away from the perception of his own misfortunes? Will you not show him the effect of virtue that he may learn where to look for improvement? Seek it there, wretch, where your work lies And where is your work? In desire and in aversion, that you may not be disappointed in your desire, and that you may not fall into that which you would avoid; in your pursuit and avoiding, that you commit no error; in assent and suspension of assent, that you be not deceived. The first things, and the most necessary, are those which I have named. But if with trembling and lamentation you seek not to fall into that which you avoid, tell me how you are improving.

Do you then show me your improvement in these things? If I were talking to an athlete, I should say, Show me your shoulders; and then he might say, "Here are my Halteres." You and your Halteres² look to that. I should reply, I wish to see the effect of the Halteres. So, when you say: "Take the treatise on the active powers (ὁρμή), and see how I have studied it." I reply, Slave, I am not inquiring about this, but how you exercise pursuit and avoidance, desire and aversion, how you design and purpose and prepare yourself, whether conformably to nature or not. If conformably, give me evidence of it, and I will say that you are making progress: but if not conformably, be gone, and not only expound your books, but write such books yourself; and what will you gain by it? Do you not know that the whole book costs only five denarii? Does then the expounder seem to be worth more than five denarii? Never then look for the matter itself in one place, and progress towards it in another.

Where then is progress? If any of you, withdrawing himself from externals, turns to his own will (προαίρεσις) to exercise it and to improve it by labour, so as to make it conformable to nature, elevated, free, unrestrained, unimpeded, faithful, modest; and if he has learned that he who desires or avoids the things which are not in his power can neither be faithful nor free, but of necessity he must change with them and be tossed about with them as in a tempest, and of necessity must subject himself to others who have the power to procure or prevent what he desires or would avoid; finally, when he rises in the morning, if he observes and keeps these rules, bathes as a man of fidelity, eats as a modest man; in like manner, if in every matter that occurs he works out his chief principles (τὰ προηγούμενα) as the runner does with

reference to running, and the trainer of the voice
with reference to the voice—this is the man who
has not travelled in vain. But if he has strained
his efforts to the practice of reading books, and
labours only at this, and has travelled for this, I tell him to
return home immediately, and not to neglect his affairs
there; for this for which he has travelled is nothing. But
the other thing is something, to study how a man can rid
his life of lamentation and groaning, and saying, "Woe to
me," and, "Wretched that I am," and to rid it also of misfortune and disappointment, and to learn what death is, and
exile, and prison, and poison, that he may be able to say
when he is in fetters, "Dear Crito, if it is the will of the
gods that it be so, let it be so"; and not to say, "Wretched
am I, an old man; have I kept my grey hairs for this?"
Who is it that speaks thus? Do you think that I shall name
some man of no repute and of low condition? Does not
Priam say this? Does not Œdipus say this? Nay, all
kings say it![3] For what else is tragedy than the perturbations (πάθη) of men who value externals, exhibited in this
kind of poetry? But if a man must learn by fiction that no
external things which are independent of the will concern
us, for my part I should like this fiction, by the aid of which
I should live happily and undisturbed. But you must consider for yourselves what you wish.

What then does Chrysippus teach us? The reply is, to
know that these things are not false, from which happiness
comes and tranquillity arises. Take my books, and you will
learn how true and conformable to nature are the things
which make me free from perturbations. O great good fortune! O the great benefactor who points out the way! To
Triptolemus all men have erected temples and altars, because
he gave us food by cultivation; but to him who discovered
truth and brought it to light and communicated it to all, not
the truth which shows us how to live, but how to live well,
who of you for this reason has built an altar, or a temple, or
has dedicated a statue, or who worships God for this? Because the gods have given the vine, or wheat, we sacrifice to
them but because they have produced in the human mind

that fruit by which they designed to show us the truth which relates to happiness, shall we not thank God for this?

NOTES

[1] Diogenes Laertius (Chrysippus, lib. vii) states that Chrysippus wrote seven hundred and five books, or treatises, or whatever the word συγγράμματα means. He was born at Soli, in Cilicia, or at Tarsus, in B.C. 280, as it is reckoned, and on going to Athens he became a pupil of the Stoic Cleanthes.

[2] Halteres are gymnastic instruments, literally "leapers." They are said to have been masses of lead, used for exercise and in making jumps. The effect of such weights in taking a jump is well known to boys who have used them. A couple of bricks will serve the purpose. Martial says (XIV. 49) :—

"Quid pereunt stulto fortes haltere lacerti?
Exercet melius vinea fossa viros."

Juvenal (vi. 421) writes of a woman who uses dumb-bells till she sweats, and is then rubbed dry by a man,

"Quum lassata gravi ceciderunt brachia massa."

[3] So kings and such personages speak in the Greek tragedies. Compare what Marcus Aurelius (XI. 6) says of Tragedy.

CHAPTER V

AGAINST THE ACADEMICS

IF a man, said Epictetus, opposes evident truths, it is not easy to find arguments by which we shall make him change his opinion. But this does not arise either from the man's strength or the teacher's weakness; for when the man, though he has been confuted, is hardened like a stone, how shall we then be able to deal with him by argument?

Now there are two kinds of hardening, one of the understanding, the other of the sense of shame, when a man is resolved not to assent to what is manifest nor to desist from contradictions. Most of us are afraid of mortification of the body, and would contrive all means to avoid such a thing, but we care not about the soul's mortification. And indeed with regard to the soul, if a man be in such a state as not to apprehend anything, or understand at all, we think that he is in a bad condition: but if the sense of shame and modesty are deadened, this we call even power (or strength).

Do you comprehend that you are awake? "I do not," the man replies, "for I do not even comprehend when in my sleep I imagine that I am awake." Does this appearance then not differ from the other? "Not at all," he replies. Shall I still argue with this man? And what fire or what iron shall I apply to him to make him feel that he is deadened? He does perceive, but he pretends that he does not. He is even worse than a dead man. He does not see the contradiction: he is in a bad condition. Another does see it, but he is not moved, and makes no improvement: he is even in a worse condition. His modesty is extirpated, and his sense of shame; and the rational faculty has not been cut off from him, but it is brutalised. Shall I name this strength of mind? Certainly not, unless we also name it such in catamites, through which they do and say in public whatever comes into their head.

CHAPTER VI

FROM everything which is or happens in the world, it is easy to praise Providence, if a man possesses these two qualities, the faculty of seeing what belongs and happens to all persons and things, and a grateful disposition. If he does not possess these two qualities, one man will not see the use of things which are and which happen: another will not be thankful for them, even if he does know them. If God had made colours, but had not made the faculty of seeing them, what would have been their use? None at all. On the other hand, if He had made the faculty of vision, but had not made objects such as to fall under the faculty, what in that case also would have been the use of it? None at all. Well, suppose that He had made both, but had not made light? In that case, also, they would have been of no use. Who is it then who has fitted this to that and that to this? And who is it that has fitted the knife to the case and the case to the knife? Is it no one?[1] And, indeed, from the very structure of things which have attained their completion, we are accustomed to show that the work is certainly the act of some artificer, and that it has not been constructed without a purpose. Does then each of these things demonstrate the workman, and do not visible things and the faculty of seeing and light demonstrate Him? And the existence of male and female, and the desire of each for conjunction, and the power of using the parts which are constructed, do not even these declare the workman? If they do not, let us consider the constitution of our understanding according to which, when we meet with sensible objects, we do not simply receive impressions from them, but we also select something from them, and subtract something, and add, compound by means of them these things or those, and, in fact, pass from some to other things which, in a manner, resemble them: is not even this sufficient to move some men, and to induce them not to forget the workman? If not so,

let them explain to us what it is that makes each several
thing, or how it is possible that things so wonderful and like
the contrivances of art should exist by chance and from their
own proper motion?

What, then, are these things done in us only?   Many,
indeed, in us only, of which the rational animal had peculiarly need; but you will find many common to us with irrational animals.   Do they then understand what is done?   By
no means.   For use is one thing, and understanding is another.   God had need of irrational animals to make use of
appearances, but of us to understand the use of appearances.
It is therefore enough for them to eat and drink, and to sleep
and to copulate, and to do all the other things which they
severally do.   But for us, to whom He has given also the
intellectual faculty, these things are not sufficient; for unless
we act in a proper and orderly manner, and conformably to
the nature and constitution of each thing, we shall never attain our true end.   For where the constitutions of living beings are different, there also the acts and the ends are different.   In those animals then whose constitution is adapted
only to use, use alone is enough: but in an animal (man),
which has also the power of understanding the use, unless
there be the due exercise of the understanding, he will never
attain his proper end.   Well then God constitutes every animal, one to be eaten, another to serve for agriculture, another to supply cheese, and another for some like use; for
which purposes what need is there to understand appearances and to be able to distinguish them?   But God has
introduced man to be a spectator of God and of His works;
and not only a spectator of them, but an interpreter.   For
this reason it is shameful for man to begin and to end where
irrational animals do; but rather he ought to begin where
they begin, and to end where nature ends in us; and nature
ends in contemplation and understanding, and in a way of
life conformable to nature.   Take care then not to die without having been spectators of these things.

But you take a journey to Olympia to see the work of
Phidias,[2] and all of you think it a misfortune to die without
having seen such things.   But when there is no need to take
a journey, and where a man is, there he has the works (of

God) before him, will you not desire to see and understand them? Will you not perceive either what you are, or what you were born for, or what this is for which you have received the faculty of sight? But you may say, there are some things disagreeable and troublesome in life. And are there none at Olympia? Are you not scorched? Are you not pressed by a crowd? Are you not without comfortable means of bathing? Are you not wet when it rains? Have you not abundance of noise, clamour, and other disagreeable things? But I suppose that setting all these things off against the magnificence of the spectacle, you bear and endure. Well then and have you not received faculties by which you will be able to bear all that happens? Have you not received greatness of soul? Have you not received manliness? Have you not received endurance? And why do I trouble myself about anything that can happen if I possess greatness of soul? What shall distract my mind or disturb me, or appear painful? Shall I not use the power for the purposes which I received it, and shall I grieve and lament over what happens?

Yes, but my nose runs. For what purpose then, slave, have you hands? Is it not that you may wipe your nose?—Is it then consistent with reason that there should be running of noses in the world?—Nay, how much better it is to wipe your nose than to find fault. What do you think Hercules would have been if there had not been such a lion, and hydra, and stag, and boar, and certain unjust and bestial men, whom Hercules used to drive away and clear out? And what would he have been doing if there had been nothing of the kind? Is it not plain that he would have wrapped himself up and have slept? In the first place then he would not have been a Hercules, when he was dreaming away all his life in such luxury and ease; and even if he had been one, what would have been the use of him? and what the use of his arms, and of the strength of the other parts of his body, and his endurance and noble spirit, if such circumstances and occasions had not roused and exercised him? Well then must a man provide for himself such means of exercise, and seek to introduce a lion from some place into his country, and a boar, and a hydra? This would be folly and madness: but as they did not exist, and were found, they were useful for showing what Hercules was and for exercising him. Come then do you also having observed these things look to the faculties which you have, and when you have looked at them, say. Bring now, O Zeus, any difficulty that thou pleasest, for I have means given to me by thee and powers[3] for honouring myself through the things which happen. You do not so: but you sit still, trembling for fear that some things will happen, and weeping, and lamenting, and groaning for what does happen: and then you blame the gods For what is the consequence of such meanness of spirit but impiety? And yet God has not only given us these faculties; by which we shall be able to bear everything that happens without being depressed or broken by it; but, like a good king and a true father, He has given us these faculties free from hindrance, subject to no compulsion, unimpeded, and has put them entirely in our own power, without even having reserved to Himself any power of hindering or impeding. You, who have received these powers free and as your own, use them not: you do not even see what you have received, and from whom; some of you being blinded to the giver, and not even acknowledging your benefactor, and others, through meanness of spirit, betaking yourselves to fault-finding and making charges against God. Yet I will show to you that you have powers and means for greatness of soul and manliness · but what powers you have for finding fault and making accusations, do you show me.

NOTES

[1] Goethe has a short poem, entitled "Gleich und Gleich" (Like and Like):

> " Ein Blumenglöckchen
> Vom Boden hervor
> War früh gesprosset
> In lieblichem Flor;
> Da kam ein Bienchen
> Und naschte fein:—
> Die müssen wohl beyde
> Für einander seyn "

[2] This work was the colossal chryselephantine statue of Zeus (Jupiter) by Phidias, which was at Olympia

[3] Antoninus (ix. 1) Epictetus says that the powers which man has were given by God. Antoninus says, from nature They mean the same thing See Schweighäuser's note.

CHAPTER VII

THE handling of sophistical and hypothetical arguments, and of those which derive their conclusions
from questioning, and in a word the handling of
all such arguments, relates to the duties of life,
though the many do not know this truth. For in every
matter we inquire how the wise and good man shall discover
the proper path and the proper method of dealing with it
Let then people either say that the grave man will not descend into the contest of question and answer, or, that if he
does descend into the contest, he will take no care about not
conducting himself rashly or carelessly in questioning and
answering. But if they do not allow either the one or the
other of these things, they must admit that some inquiry
ought to be made into those topics (τόπων) on which questioning and answering are particularly employed. For what
is the end proposed in reasoning? To establish true propositions, to remove the false, to withhold assent from those
which are not plain. Is it enough then to have learned only
this? It is enough, a man may reply. Is it then also
enough for a man, who would not make a mistake in the
use of coined money, to have heard this precept, that he
should receive the genuine drachmæ and reject the spurious? It is not enough. What then ought to be added to
this precept? What else than the faculty which proves and
distinguishes the genuine and the spurious drachmæ? Consequently also in reasoning what has been said is it not
enough; but is it necessary that a man should acquire the
faculty of examining and distinguishing the true and the
false, and that which is not plain? It is necessary. Besides this, what is proposed in reasoning? That you should
accept what follows from that which you have properly
granted. Well, is it then enough in this case also to know
this? It is not enough; but a man must learn how one thing

is a consequence of other things, and when one thing follows from one thing, and when it follows from several collectively. Consider then if it be not necessary that this power should also be acquired by him who purposes to conduct himself skilfully in reasoning, the power of demonstrating himself the several things which he has proposed, and the power of understanding the demonstrations of others, and of not being deceived by sophists, as if they were demonstrating. Therefore there has arisen among us the practice and exercise of conclusive arguments and figures, and it has been shown to be necessary.

But in fact in some cases we have properly granted the premises or assumptions, and there results from them something; and though it is not true, yet none the less it does result. What then ought I to do? Ought I to admit the falsehood? And how is that possible? Well, should I say that I did not properly grant that which we agreed upon? But you are not allowed to do even this. Shall I then say that the consequence does not arise through what has been conceded? But neither is this allowed. What then must be done in this case? Consider if it is not this · as to have borrowed is not enough to make a man still a debtor,¹ but to this must be added the fact that he continues to owe the money and that the debt is not paid, so it is not enough to compel you to admit the inference that you have granted the premises (τὰ λήμματα), but you must abide by what you have granted. Indeed, if the premises continue to the end such as they were when they were granted, it is absolutely necessary for us to abide by what we have granted, and we must accept their consequences: but if the premises do not remain such as they were when they were granted, it is absolutely necessary for us also to withdraw from what we granted, and from accepting what does not follow from the words in which our concessions were made. For the inference is now not our inference, nor does it result with our assent, since we have withdrawn from the premises which we granted. We ought then both to examine such kinds of premises, and such change and variation of them (from one meaning to another), by which in the course of questioning or answering, or in making the syllogistic conclusion, or in any other such way, the premises undergo variations, and give occasion to the foolish to be confounded, if they do not see what conclusions (consequences) are. For what reason ought we to examine? In order that we may not in this matter be employed in an improper manner nor in a confused way.

And the same in hypotheses and hypothetical arguments; for it is necessary sometimes to demand the granting of some hypothesis as a kind of passage to the argument which follows. Must we then allow every hypothesis that is proposed, or not allow every one? And if not every one, which should we allow? And if a man has allowed an hypothesis, must he in every case abide by allowing it? or must he sometimes withdraw from it, but admit the consequences and not admit contradictions? Yes; but suppose that a man says, "If you admit the hypothesis of a possibility, I will draw you an impossibility." With such a person shall a man of sense refuse to enter into a contest, and avoid discussion and conversation with him? But what other man than the man of sense can use argumentation and is skilful in questioning and answering, and incapable of being cheated and deceived by false reasoning? And shall he enter into the contest, and yet not take care whether he shall engage in argument not rashly and not carelessly? And if he does not take care, how can he be such a man as we conceive him to be? But without some such exercise and preparation, can he maintain a continuous and consistent argument? Let them show this; and all these speculations (θεωρήματα) become superfluous, and are absurd and inconsistent with our notion of a good and serious man.

Why are we still indolent and negligent and sluggish, and why do we seek pretences for not labouring and not being watchful in cultivating our reason? If then I shall make a mistake in these matters may I not have killed my father? Slave, where was there a father in this matter that you could kill him? What then have you done? The only fault that was possible here is the fault which you have committed. This is the very remark which I made to Rufus[1] when he blamed me for not having discovered the one thing omitted in a certain syllogism: I suppose, I said, that I have burnt the Capitol. "Slave," he replied, "was the thing omitted here the Capitol? Or are these the only crimes, to burn the Capitol and to kill your father?" But for a man to use the appearances presented to him rashly and foolishly and carelessly, and not to understand argument, nor demonstration, nor sophism, nor, in a word, to see in questioning and answering what is consistent with that which we have granted or is not consistent; is there no error in this?

NOTE

[1] Rufus is Musonius Rufus (i. 1). To kill a father and to burn the Roman Capitol are mentioned as instances of the greatest crimes Comp. Horace, Épode, iii; Cicero, De Amicit. 11; Plutarch, Tib. Gracchus, c. 20.

CHAPTER VIII

IN as many ways as we can change things which are equivalent to one another, in just so many ways we can change the forms of arguments (ἐπιχειρήματα) and enthymemes (ἐνθυμήματα), in argumentation. This is an instance: if you have borrowed and not repaid, you owe me the money: you have not borrowed and you have not repaid; then you do not owe me the money. To do this skilfully is suitable to no man more than to the philosopher; for if the enthymeme is an imperfect syllogism, it is plain that he who has been exercised in the perfect syllogism must be equally expert in the imperfect also.

Why then do we not exercise ourselves and one another in this manner? Because, I reply, at present, though we are not exercised in these things and not distracted from the study of morality, by me at least, still we make no progress in virtue. What then must we expect if we should add this occupation? and particularly as this would not only be an occupation which would withdraw us from more necessary things, but would also be a cause of self-conceit and arrogance, and no small cause. For great is the power of arguing and the faculty of persuasion, and particularly if it should be much exercised, and also receive additional ornament from language: and so universally, every faculty acquired by the uninstructed and weak brings with it the danger of these persons being elated and inflated by it. For by what means could one persuade a young man who excels in these matters, that he ought not to become an appendage[1] to them, but to make them an appendage to himself? Does he not trample on all such reasons, and strut before us elated and inflated, not enduring that any man should reprove him and remind him of what he has neglected and to what he has turned aside?

What then was not Plato a philosopher?[2] I reply, and was not Hippocrates a physician? but you see how Hippo-

crates speaks.   Does Hippocrates then speak thus in respect
of being a physician?   Why do you mingle things which
have been accidentally united in the same men?   And if
Plato was handsome and strong, ought I also to set to work
and endeavour to become handsome or strong, as if this was
necessary for philosophy, because a certain philosopher was
at the same time handsome and a philosopher?   Will you
not choose to see and to distinguish in respect to what men
become philosophers, and what things belong to them in
other respects?   And if I were a philosopher, ought you
also to be made lame?[3]   What then?   Do I take away these
faculties which you possess?   By no means; for neither do
I take away the faculty of seeing.   But if you ask me what
is the good of man, I can not mention to you anything else
than that it is a certain disposition of the will with respect
to appearances.

NOTES

[1] A man, as Wolf explains it, should not make oratory, or the art of
speaking, his chief excellence. He should use it to set off something
which is superior.

[2] Plato was eloquent, and the adversary asks, if that is a reason for
not allowing him to be a philosopher. To which the rejoinder is that
Hippocrates was a physician, and eloquent too, but not as a physician.

[3] Epictetus was lame.

CHAPTER IX

HOW FROM THE FACT THAT WE ARE AKIN TO GOD A MAN MAY PROCEED TO THE CONSEQUENCES

IF the things are true which are said by the philosophers about the kinship between God and man, what else remains for men to do than what Socrates did? Never in reply to the question, to what country you belong, say that you are an Athenian or a Corinthian, but that you are a citizen of the world (κόσμιος). For why do you say that you are an Athenian, and why do you not say that you belong to the small nook only into which your poor body was cast at birth? Is it not plain that you call yourself an Athenian or a Corinthian from the place which has a greater authority and comprises not only that small nook itself and all your family, but even the whole country from which the stock of your progenitors is derived down to you? He then who has observed with intelligence the administration of the world, and has learned that the greatest and supreme and the most comprehensive community is that which is composed of men and God, and that from God have descended the seeds not only to my father and grandfather, but to all beings which are generated on the earth and are produced, and particularly to rational beings—for these only are by their nature formed to have communion with God, being by means of reason conjoined with him—why should not such a man call himself a citizen of the world, why not a son of God,[1] and why should he be afraid of anything which happens among men? Is kinship with Cæsar (the emperor) or with any other of the powerful in Rome sufficient to enable us to live in safety, and above contempt, and without any fear at all? and to have God for your maker (ποιητήν), and father and guardian, shall not this release us from sorrows and fears?

But a man may say, "Whence shall I get bread to eat when I have nothing?"

And how do slaves, and runaways—on what do they rely when they leave their masters? Do they rely on their lands

or slaves, or their vessels of silver? They rely on nothing
but themselves; and food does not fail them.[2]   And shall it
be necessary for one among us who is a philosopher to travel
into foreign parts, and trust to and rely on others, and not
to take care of himself; and shall he be inferior to irrational
animals and more cowardly, each of which being self-sufficient, neither fails to get its proper food, nor to find a suitable way of living, and one conformable to nature?[1]

I indeed think that the old man[3] ought to be sitting here,
not to contrive how you may have no mean thoughts nor
mean and ignoble talk about yourselves, but to take care that
there be not among us any young men of such a mind, that
when they have recognised their kinship to God, and that we
are fettered by these bonds—the body, I mean, and its po-
sessions, and whatever else on account of them is necessary
to us for the economy and commerce of life—they should intend to throw off these things as if they were burdens painful and intolerable, and to depart to their kinsmen.   But this
is the labour that your teacher and instructor ought to be
employed upon, if he really were what he should be.   You
should come to him and say, "Epictetus, we can no longer
endure being bound to this poor body, and feeding it, and
giving it drink, and rest, and cleaning it, and for the sake of
the body complying with the wishes of these and of those.[4]
Are not these things indifferent and nothing to us; and is
not death no evil?   And are we not in a manner kinsmen of
God, and did we not come from him?   Allow us to depart
to the place from which we came; allow us to be released at
last from these bonds by which we are bound and weighed
down.   Here there are robbers and thieves and courts of
justice, and those who are named tyrants, and think that they
have some power over us by means of the body and its possessions.   Permit us to show them that they have no power
over any man."   And I on my part would say, "Friends,
wait for God: when He shall give the signal and release you
from this service, then go to Him; but for the present endure
to dwell in this place where He has put you: short indeed
is this time of our dwelling here, and easy to bear for those
who are so disposed: for what tyrant or what thief, or what
courts of justice, are formidable to those who have thus con-

sidered as things of no value the body and the possessions of the body? Wait then, do not depart without a reason."

Something like this ought to be said by the teacher to ingenuous youths. But now what happens? The teacher is a lifeless body, and you are lifeless bodies. When you have been well filled to-day, you sit down and lament about the morrow, how you shall get something to eat. Wretch, if you have it, you will have it; if you have it not, you will depart from life. The door is open.[5] Why do you grieve? where does there remain any room for tears? and where is there occasion for flattery? why shall one man envy another? why should a man admire the rich or the powerful, even if they be both very strong and of violent temper? for what will they do to us? We shall not care for that which they can do; and what we do care for, that they can not do. How did Socrates behave with respect to these matters? Why, in what other way than a man ought to do who was convinced that he was a kinsman of the gods? "If you say to me now," said Socrates to his judges,[6] "we will acquit you on the condition that you no longer discourse in the way in which you have hitherto discoursed, nor trouble either our young or our old men, I shall answer, you make yourselves ridiculous by thinking that, if one of our commanders has appointed me to a certain post, it is my duty to keep and maintain it, and to resolve to die a thousand times rather than desert it; but if God has put us in any place and way of life, we ought to desert it." Socrates speaks like a man who is really a kinsman of the gods. But we think about ourselves, as if we were only stomachs, and intestines, and shameful parts; we fear, we desire; we flatter those who are able to help us in these matters, and we fear them also.

A man asked me to write to Rome about him, a man who, as most people thought, had been unfortunate, for formerly he was a man of rank and rich, but had been stripped of all, and was living here. I wrote on his behalf in a submissive manner; but when he had read the letter, he gave it back to me and said, "I wished for your help, not your pity: no evil has happened to me."

Thus also Musonius Rufus, in order to try me, used to say: This and this will befall you from your master; and

when I replied that these were things which happen in the ordinary course of human affairs. Why then, said he, should I
ask him anything when I can obtain it from you? For, in
fact, what a man has from himself, it is superfluous and foolish to receive from another? Shall I then, who am able
to receive from myself greatness of soul and a generous
spirit, receive from you land and money or a magisterial
office? I hope not: I will not be so ignorant about my own
possessions. But when a man is cowardly and mean, what
else must be done for him than to write letters as you would
about a corpse. Please to grant us the body of a certain person and a sextarius of pure blood. For such a person is, in
fact, a carcase and a sextarius (a certain quantity) of blood
and nothing more. But if he were anything more, he would
know that one man is not miserable through the means of
another.

NOTES

[1] So Jesus said, "Our Father which art in heaven" Cleanthes, in his
hymn to Zeus, writes, ἐκ σοῦ γὰρ γένος ἐσμέν. Compare Acts of
the Apostles, xvii. 28, where Paul quotes these words. It is not true
then that the "conception of a parental deity," as it has been asserted,
was unknown before the teaching of Jesus, and, after the time of
Jesus, unknown to those Greeks who were unacquainted with His teaching.

[2] In our present society there are thousands who rise in the morning
and know not how they shall find something to eat Some find their
food by fraud and theft, some receive it as a gift from others, and some
look out for any work that they can find and get their pittance by
honest labour. You may see such men everywhere, if you will keep
your eyes open Such men, who live by daily labour, live an heroic life,
which puts to shame the well-fed philosopher and the wealthy Christian.

Epictetus has made a great misstatement about irrational animals.
Millions die annually for want of sufficient food; and many human
beings perish in the same way. We can hardly suppose that he did
not know these facts

Compare the passage in Matthew vi. 25-34 It is said, v. 26: "Behold the fowls of the air: for they sow not, neither do they reap, nor
gather into barns; yet your heavenly Father feedeth them Are ye not
much better than they?" The expositors of this passage may be consulted.

[3] The old man is Epictetus.

[4] He means, as Wolf says, "on account of the necessities of the body
seeking the favour of the more powerful by disagreeable compliances"

[5] Compare Matthew vi. 31: "Therefore take no thought, saying, What
shall we eat? or, What shall we drink? or, Wherewithal shall we be
clothed? (For after all these things do the Gentiles seek), for your
heavenly Father knoweth that ye have need of all these things," etc.

[6] This passage is founded on and is in substance the same as that in
Plato's "Apology," 17.

CHAPTER X.

AGAINST THOSE WHO EAGERLY SEEK PREFERMENT AT ROME

IF we applied ourselves as busily to our own work as the old men at Rome do to those matters about which they are employed, perhaps we also might accomplish something. I am acquainted with a man older than myself, who is now superintendent of corn[1] at Rome, and I remember the time when he came here on his way back from exile, and what he said as he related the events of his former life, and how he declared that with respect to the future after his return he would look after nothing else than passing the rest of his life in quiet and tranquillity. "For how little of life," he said, "remains for me." I replied, you will not do it, but as soon as you smell Rome, you will forget all that you have said; and if admission is allowed even into the imperial palace, he[2] will gladly thrust himself in and thank God. "If you find me, Epictetus," he answered, "setting even one foot within the palace, think what you please." Well, what then did he do? Before he entered the city, he was met by letters from Cæsar, and as soon as he received them, he forgot all, and ever has added one piece of business to another. I wish that I were now by his side to remind him of what he said when he was passing this way, and to tell him how much better a seer I am than he is.

Well then do I say that man is an animal made for doing nothing?[3] Certainly not. But why are we not active?[4] (We are active.) For example, as to myself, as soon as day comes, in a few words I remind myself of what I must read over to my pupils; then forthwith I say to myself, But what is it to me how a certain person shall read? the first thing for me is to sleep. And indeed what resemblance is there between what other persons do and what we do? If you observe what they do, you will understand. And what else do they do all day long than make up accounts, enquire among themselves, give and take advice about some small quantity of grain, a bit of land, and such kind of profits? Is

31

it then the same thing to receive a petition and to read in it:
I intreat you to permit me to export[5] a small quantity of
corn; and one to this effect: "I intreat you to learn from
Chrysippus what is the administration of the world, and
what place in it the rational animal holds; consider also who
you are, and what is the nature of your good and bad." Are
these things like the other, do they require equal care, and
is it equally base to neglect these and those? Well then are
we the only persons who are lazy and love sleep? No; but
much rather you young men are. For we old men when we
see young men amusing themselves are eager to play with
them; and if I saw you active and zealous, much more should
I be eager myself to join you in your serious pursuits.

NOTES

[1] A "Præfectus Annonæ," or superintendent of the supply of corn
at Rome is first mentioned by Livy (iv 12) as appointed during a
scarcity At a later time this office was conferred on Cneius Pompeius
for five years. Mæcenas advised Augustus to make a Præfectus
Annonæ or permanent officer over the corn market and all other markets. He would thus have the office formerly exercised by the ædiles.

[2] I can not explain why the third person is used here instead of the
second

[3] The Stoics taught that man is adapted by his nature for action He
ought not therefore to withdraw from human affairs, and indulge in a
lazy life, not even a life of contemplation and religious observances only.

[4] Schweighauser proposes a small alteration in the Greek text, but
I do not think it necessary. When Epictetus says, "Why are we not
active?" He means, Why do some say that we are not active? And
he intends to say that, We are active, but not in the way in which some
people are active. I have therefore added in (   ) what is necessary
to make the text intelligible.

[5] A plain allusion to restraints put on the exportation of grain.

CHAPTER XI

OF NATURAL AFFECTION

WHEN he was visited by one of the magistrates, Epictetus inquired of him about several particulars, and asked if he had children and a wife. The man replied that he had; and Epictetus inquired further, how he felt under the circumstances "Miserable," the man said. Then Epictetus asked, In what respect, for men do not marry and beget children in order to be wretched, but rather to be happy. "But I," the man replied, "am so wretched about my little children that lately, when my little daughter was sick and was supposed to be in danger, I could not endure to stay with her, but I left home till a person sent me news that she had recovered." Well, then, said Epictetus, do you think that you acted right? "I acted naturally," the man replied. But convince me of this that you acted naturally, and I will convince you that everything which takes place according to nature takes place rightly. "This is the case," said the man, "with all or at least most fathers." I do not deny that: but the matter about which we are inquiring is whether such behaviour is right; for in respect to this matter we must say that tumours also come for the good of the body, because they do come; and generally we must say that to do wrong is natural, because nearly all or at least most of us do wrong. Do you show me then how your behaviour is natural. "I can not," he said; "but do you rather show me how it is not according to nature, and is not rightly done."

Well, said Epictetus, if we were inquiring about white and black, what criterion should we employ for distinguishing between them? "The sight," he said. And if about hot and cold, and hard and soft, what criterion? "The touch." Well then, since we are inquiring about things which are according to nature, and those which are done rightly or not rightly, what kind of criterion do you think that we should employ? "I do not know," he said. And yet not to know the criterion of colours and smells, and also of tastes, is perhaps no great harm; but if a man do not know the criterion of good and bad, and of things according to nature and contrary to nature, does this seem to you a small harm? "The greatest harm (I think)." Come tell me, do all things which seem to some persons to be good and becoming, rightly appear such; and at present as to Jews and Syrians and Egyptians and Romans, is it possible that the opinions of all of them in respect to food are right? "How is it possible?" he said. Well, I suppose, it is absolutely necessary that, if the opinions of the Egyptians are right, the opinions of the rest must be wrong: if the opinions of the Jews are right, those of the rest can not be right. "Certainly." But where there is ignorance, there also there is want of learning and training in things which are necessary. He assented to this. You then, said Epictetus, since you know this, for the future will employ yourself seriously about nothing else, and will apply your mind to nothing else than to learn the criterion of things which are according to nature, and by using it also to determine each several thing. But in the present matter I have so much as this to aid you towards what you wish. Does affection to those of your family appear to you to be according to nature and to be good? "Certainly." Well, is such affection natural and good, and is a thing consistent with reason not good? "By no means." Is then that which is consistent with reason in contradiction with affection? "I think not." You are right, for if it is otherwise, it is necessary that one of the contradictions being according to nature, the other must be contrary to nature. Is it not so? "It is," he said. Whatever then we shall discover to be at the same time affectionate and also consistent with reason, this we confidently declare to be right and good. "Agreed." Well then to leave your sick child and to go away is not reasonable, and I suppose that you will not say that it is; but it remains for us to inquire if it is consistent with affection. "Yes, let us consider." Did you then, since you had an affectionate disposition to your child, do right when you ran off and left her; and has the mother no affection for the child? "Certainly, she has." Ought then the mother also to have left her, or ought she not? "She ought not."

And the nurse, does she love her? "She does." Ought then she also to have left her? "By no means." And the peda-gogue.[1] Does he not love her? "He does love her." Ought then he also to have deserted her? and so should the child have been left alone and without help on account of the great affection of you the parents and of those about her, or should she have died in the hands of those who neither loved her nor cared for her? "Certainly not." Now this is unfair and un-reasonable, not to allow those who have equal affection with yourself to do what you think to be proper for yourself to do because you have affection. "It is absurd." Come then, if you were sick, would you wish your relations to be so affec-tionate, and all the rest, children and wife, as to leave you alone and deserted? "By no means." And would you wish to be so loved by your own that through their excessive affec-tion you would always be left alone in sickness? or for this reason would you rather pray, if it were possible, to be loved by your enemies and deserted by them? But if this is so, it results that your behaviour was not at all an affectionate act. Well then, was it nothing which moved you and in-duced you to desert your child?

"How is that possible?" But it might be something of the kind which moved a man at Rome to wrap up his head while a horse was running which he favoured; and when contrary to expectation the horse won, he required sponges to recover from his fainting fit. "What then was the motive?" The exact discussion of this does not belong to the present occasion perhaps; but it is enough to be convinced of this, if what the philoso-phers say is true, that we must not look for it anywhere with-out, but in all cases it is one and the same thing which is the cause of our doing or not doing something, of saying or not saying something, of being elated or depressed, of avoiding any thing or pursuing: the very thing which is now the cause to me and to you, to you of coming to me and sitting and hearing, and to me of saying what I do say. "And what is this?" Is it any other than our will to do so? "No other." But if we had willed otherwise, what else should we have been doing than that which we willed to do? This then was the cause of Achilles' lamentation, not the death of Patroclus; for another man does not behave thus on the death of his companion; but it was because he chose to do so. And to you this was the very cause of your then running away, that you chose to do so; and on the other side, if you should (hereafter) stay with her, the reason will be the same. And now you are going to Rome because you choose; and if you should change your mind, you will not go hither. And in a word, neither death nor exile nor pain nor anything of the kind is the cause of our doing anything or not doing; but our own opinions and our wills (δόγματα).

Do I convince you of this or not? "You do convince me." Such then as the causes are in each case, such also are the effects. When then we are doing anything not rightly from this day we shall impute it to nothing else than to the will (δόγμα or opinion), from which we have done it; and it is that which we shall endeavour to take away and to extirpate more than the tumours and abscesses out of the body. And in like manner we shall give the same account of the cause of the things which we do right; and we shall no longer allege as causes of any evil to us, either slave or neighbour, or wife or children, being persuaded, that if we do not think things to be what we do think them to be, we do not the acts which follow from such opinions; and as to thinking or not thinking, that is in our power and not in externals. "It is so," he said. From this day then we shall inquire into and examine nothing else, what its quality is, or its state, neither land nor slaves nor horses nor dogs—nothing else than opinions. "I hope so." You see than that you must become a Scholasticus,[2] an animal whom all ridicule, if you really intend to make an examination of your own opinions: and that this is not the work of one hour or day, you know yourself.

NOTES

[1] "When we are children our parents put us in the hands of a pedagogue to see on all occasions that we take no harm."—Epictetus, Frag. 97

[2] A Scholasticus is one who frequents the schools; a studious and literary person, who does not engage in the business of active life.

CHAPTER XII

OF CONTENTMENT

WITH respect to gods, there are some who say that a divine being does not exist: others say that it exists, but is inactive and careless, and takes no forethought about any thing; a third class say that such a being exists and exercises forethought, but only about great things and heavenly things, and about nothing on the earth; a fourth class say that a divine being exercises forethought both about things on the earth and heavenly things, but in a general way only, and not about things severally. There is a fifth class to whom Ulysses and Socrates belong,. who say: "I move not without thy knowledge."[1]

Before all other things then it is necessary to inquire about each of these opinions, whether it is affirmed truly or not truly. For if there are no gods, how is it our proper end to follow them? And if they exist, but take no care of anything, in this case also how will it be right to follow them? But if indeed they do exist and look after things, still if there is nothing communicated from them to men, nor in fact to myself, how even so is it right (to follow them)? The wise and good man then after considering all these things, submits his own mind to him who administers the whole, as good citizens do to the law of the state. He who is receiving instruction ought to come to be instructed with this intention, "How shall I follow the gods in all things, how shall I be contented with the divine administration, and how can I become free?" For he is free to whom every thing happens according to his will, and whom no man can hinder. What then is freedom, madness?" Certainly not: for madness and freedom do not consist. "But, you say, I would have every thing result just as I like, and in whatever way I like" You are mad, you are beside yourself. Do you not know that freedom is a noble and valuable thing? But for me inconsiderately to wish for things to happen as I inconsiderately like, this appears to be not only not noble, but even most base. For how do we proceed in the matter of writing? Do I wish to write the name of Dion as I choose? No, but I am taught to choose to write it as it ought to be written. And how with respect to music? In the same manner. And what universally in every art or science? Just the same. If it were not so, it would be of no value to know anything, if knowledge were adapted to every man's whim. Is it then in this alone, in this which is the greatest and the chief thing, I mean freedom, that I am permitted to will inconsiderately? By no means; but to be instructed is this, to learn to wish that every thing may happen as it does. And how do things happen? As the disposer has disposed them? And he has appointed summer and winter, and abundance and scarcity, and virtue and vice, and all such opposites for the harmony of the whole; and to each of us he has given a body, and parts of the body, and possessions, and companions.

Remembering then this disposition of things, we ought to go to be instructed, not that we may change the constitution of things,—for we have not the power to do it, nor is it better that we should have the power,—but in order that, as the things around us are what they are and by nature exist, we may maintain our minds in harmony with the things which happen. For can we escape from men? and how is it possible? And if we associate with them, can we change them? Who gives us the power? What then remains, or what method is discovered of holding commerce with them? Is there such a method by which they shall do what seems fit to them, and we not the less shall be in a mood which is conformable to nature? But you are unwilling to endure and are discontented: and if you are alone, you call it solitude; and if you are with men, you call them knaves and robbers; and you find fault with your own parents and children, and brothers and neighbours. But you ought when you are alone to call this condition by the name of tranquillity and freedom, and to think yourself like to the gods; and when you are with many, you ought not to call it crowd, nor trouble, nor uneasiness, but festival and assembly, and so accept all contentedly.

What then is the punishment of those who do not accept? It is to be what they are Is any person dissatisfied with being alone? let him be alone. Is a man dissatisfied with his parents? let him be a bad son, and lament. Is he dissatisfied with his children? let him be a bad father. Cast him into prison. What prison? Where he is already, for he is there against his will; and where a man is against his will, there he is in prison. So Socrates was not in prison, for he was there willingly.

"Must my leg then be lamed?" Wretch, do you then on account of one poor leg find fault with the world? Will you not willingly surrender it for the whole? Will you not withdraw from it? Will you not gladly part with it to him who gave it? And will you be vexed and discontented with the things established by Zeus, which he with the Moiræ (fates) who were present and spinning the thread of your generation, defined and put in order? Know you not how small a part you are compared with the whole.   I mean with respect to the body, for as to intelligence you are not inferior to the gods nor less; for the magnitude of intelligence is not measured by length nor yet by height, but by thoughts. Will you not then choose to place your good in that in which you are equal to the gods?

"Wretch that I am to have such a father and mother."— What then, was it permitted to you to come forth and to select and to say: "Let such a man at this moment unite with such a woman that I may be produced?" It was not permitted, but it was a necessity for your parents to exist first, and then for you to be begotten. Of what kind of parents? Of such as they were Well then, since they are such as they are, is there no remedy given to you? Now if you did not know for what purpose you possess the faculty of vision, you would be unfortunate and wretched if you closed your eyes when colours were brought before them; but in that you possess greatness of soul and nobility of spirit for every event that may happen, and you know not that you possess them, are you not more unfortunate and wretched? Things are brought close to you which are proportionate to the power which you possess, but you turn away this power most particularly at the very time when you ought to maintain it open and discerning. Do you not rather thank the gods that they have allowed you to be above these things which they have not placed in your power, and have made you accountable only for those which are in your power? As to your parents, the gods have left you free from responsibility; and so with respect to your brothers, and your body, and possessions, and death and life. For what then have they made you responsible? For that which alone is in your power, the proper use of appearances. Why then do you draw on yourself the things for which you are not responsible? It is, indeed, a giving of trouble to yourself.

NOTE

[1] The line is from the prayer of Ulysses to Athena· "Hear me child of Zeus, thou who standest by me always in all dangers, nor do I even move without thy knowledge." Iliad, x. 278 Socrates said that the gods know everything, what is said and done and thought (Xenophon, Mem. i 1, 19) Compare Cicero, De Nat Deorum, i 1, 2; and Dr Price's Dissertation on Providence, sect. i. Epictetus enumerates the various opinions about the gods in ancient times. The reader may consult the notes in Schweighauser's edition The opinions about God among modern nations, who are called civilized, and are so more or less, do not seem to be so varied as in ancient times; but the contrasts in modern opinions are striking. These modern opinions vary between denial of a God, though the number of those who deny is perhaps not large, and the superstitious notions about God and his administration of the world, which are taught by teachers, learned and ignorant, and exercise a great power over the minds of those who are unable or do not dare to exercise the faculty of reason.

CHAPTER XIII

HOW EVERYTHING MAY BE DONE ACCEPTABLY TO THE GODS

WHEN some one asked, how may a man eat acceptably to the gods, he answered: If he can eat justly and contentedly, and with equanimity, and temperately and orderly, will it not be also acceptably to the gods? But when you have asked for warm water and the slave has not heard, or if he did hear has brought only tepid water, or he is not even found to be in the house, then not to be vexed or to burst with passion, is not this acceptable to the gods?—"How then shall a man endure such persons as this slave?" Slave yourself, will you not bear with your own brother, who has Zeus for his progenitor, and is like a son from the same seeds and of the same descent from above? But if you have been put in any such higher place, will you immediately make yourself a tyrant? Will you not remember who you are, and whom you rule? that they are kinsmen, that they are brethren by nature, that they are the offspring of Zeus?[1]—"But I have purchased them, and they have not purchased me." Do you see in what direction you are looking, that it is towards the earth, towards the pit, that it is towards these wretched laws of dead men?[2] but towards the laws of the gods you are not looking.

NOTES

[1] Mrs Carter compares Job xxxi. 15: "Did not he that made me in the womb make him (my man-servant)? And did not one fashion us in the womb?"

[2] I suppose he means human laws, which have made one man a slave to another, and when he says "dead men," he may mean mortal men, as contrasted with the gods or God, who has made all men brothers.

CHAPTER XIV.

THAT THE DEITY OVERSEES ALL THINGS

WHEN a person asked him how a man could be convinced that all his actions are under the inspection of God, he answered, Do you not think that all things are united in one? "I do," the person replied. Well, do you not think that earthly things have a natural agreement and union with heavenly things? "I do." And how else so regularly as if by God's command, when He bids the plants to flower, do they flower? when He bids them to send forth shoots, do they shoot? when He bids them to produce fruit, how else do they produce fruit? when He bids the fruit to ripen, does it ripen? when again He bids them to cast down the fruits, how else do they cast them down? and when to shed the leaves, do they shed the leaves? and when He bids them to fold themselves up and to remain quiet and rest, how else do they remain quiet and rest? And how else at the growth and the wane of the moon, and at the approach and recession of the sun, are so great an alteration and change to the contrary seen in earthly things? But are plants and our bodies so bound up and united with the whole, and are not our souls much more? and our souls so bound up and in contact with God as parts of Him and portions of Him; and does not God perceive every motion of these parts as being his own motion connate with himself? Now are you able to think of the divine administration, and about all things divine, and at the same time also about human affairs, and to be moved by ten thousand things at the same time in your senses and in your understanding, and to assent to some, and to dissent from others, and again as to some things to suspend your judgment; and do you retain in your soul so many impressions from so many and various things, and being moved by them, do you fall upon notions similar to those first impressed, and do you retain numerous arts and the memories of ten thousand things; and is not God able to oversee all things, and to be present with all, and to receive from all a certain communication? And is the sun able to illuminate so large a part of the All, and to leave so little not illuminated, that part only which is occupied by the earth's shadow; and He who made the sun itself and makes it go round, being a small part of himself compared with the whole, can not He perceive all things?

"But I can not," the man may reply, "comprehend all these things at once." But who tells you that you have equal power with Zeus? Nevertheless he has placed by every man a guardian, every man's Dæmon, to whom he has committed the care of the man, a guardian who never sleeps, is never deceived For to what better and more careful guardian could He have intrusted each of us? When then you have shut the doors and made darkness within, remember never to say that you are alone, for you are not; but God is within, and your Dæmon is within, and what need have they of light to see what you are doing? To this God you ought to swear an oath just as the soldiers do to Cæsar. But they who are hired for pay swear to regard the safety of Cæsar before all things; and you who have received so many and such great favours, will you not swear, or when you have sworn, will you not abide by your oath? And what shall you swear? Never to be disobedient, never to make any charges, never to find fault with any thing that he has given, and never unwillingly to do or to suffer any thing that is necessary. Is this oath like the soldier's oath? The soldiers swear not to prefer any man to Cæsar: in this oath men swear to honour themselves before all.

CHAPTER XV

WHEN a man was consulting him how he should persuade his brother to cease being angry with him, Epictetus replied, Philosophy does not propose to secure for a man any external thing   If it did (or, if it were not, as I say), Philosophy would be allowing something which is not within its province. For as the carpenter's material is wood, and that of the statuary is copper, so the matter of the art of living is each man's life.—"What then is my brother's life?"—That again belongs to his own art; but with respect to yours, it is one of the external things, like a piece of land, like health, like reputation. But Philosophy promises none of these. In every circumstance I will maintain, she says, the governing part conformable to nature. Whose governing part? His in whom I am, she says.

"How then shall my brother cease to be angry with me?" Bring him to me and I will tell him. But I have nothing to say to you about his anger.

When the man, who was consulting him, said, "I seek to know this, How, even if my brother is not reconciled to me, shall I maintain myself in a state conformable to nature?" Nothing great, said Epictetus, is produced suddenly, since not even the grape or the fig is   If you say to me now that you want a fig, I will answer to you that it requires time: let it flower[1] first, then put forth fruit, and then ripen. Is then the fruit of a fig-tree not perfected suddenly and in one hour, and would you possess the fruit of a man's mind in so short a time and so easily? Do not expect it, even if I tell you.

NOTE

[1] " The philosopher had forgot that fig-trees do not blossom" (Mrs. Carter) The flowers of a fig are inside the fleshy receptacle which becomes the fruit.

CHAPTER XVI

OF PROVIDENCE

D O not wonder if for other animals than man all things are provided for the body, not only food and drink, but beds also, and they have no need of shoes nor bed materials, nor clothing; but we require all these additional things. For animals not being made for themselves, but for service, it was not fit for them to be made so as to need other things. For consider what it would be for us to take care not only of ourselves, but also about cattle and asses, how they should be clothed, and how shod, and how they should eat and drink. Now as soldiers are ready for their commander, shod, clothed, and armed: but it would be a hard thing for the chiliarch (tribune) to go round and shoe or clothe his thousand men: so also nature has formed the animals which are made for service, all ready, prepared, and requiring no further care. So one little boy with only a stick drives the cattle.

But now we, instead of being thankful that we need not take the same care of animals as of ourselves, complain of God on our own account; and yet, in the name of Zeus and the gods, any one thing of those which exist would be enough to make a man perceive the providence of God, at least a man who is modest and grateful. And speak not to me now of the great things, but only of this, that milk is produced from grass, and cheese from milk, and wool from skins. Who made these things or devised them? No one, you say. O amazing shamelessness and stupidity!

Well, let us omit the works of nature, and contemplate her smaller (subordinate, πάρεργα) acts. Is there anything less useful than the hair on the chin? What then, has not nature used this hair also in the most suitable manner possible? Has she not by it distinguished the male and the female? does not the nature of every man forthwith proclaim from a distance, I am a man· as such approach me, as such speak to me; look for nothing else; see the signs? Again, in

45

the case of women, as she has mingled something softer in the voice, so she has also deprived them of hair (on the chin). You say, not so: the human animal ought to have been left without marks of distinction, and each of us should have been obliged to proclaim, "I am a man." But how is not the sign beautiful and becoming and venerable? how much more beautiful than the cock's comb, how much more becoming than the lion's mane? For this reason we ought to preserve the signs which God has given, we ought not to throw them away, nor to confound, as much as we can, the distinctions of the sexes.

Are these the only works of providence in us? And what words are sufficient to praise them and set them forth according to their worth? For if we had understanding, ought we to do any thing else both jointly and severally than to sing hymns and bless the deity, and to tell of his benefits? Ought we not when we are digging and ploughing and eating to sing this hymn to God? "Great is God, who has given us such implements with which we shall cultivate the earth: great is God who has given us hands, the power of swallowing, a stomach, imperceptible growth, and the power of breathing while we sleep" This is what we ought to sing on every occasion, and to sing the greatest and most divine hymn for giving us the faculty of comprehending these things and using a proper way. Well then, since most of you have become blind, ought there not to be some man to fill this office, and on behalf of all to sing the hymn to God? For what else can I do, a lame old man, than sing hymns to God? If then I was a nightingale, I would do the part of a nightingale, if I were a swan, I would do like a swan. But now I am a rational creature, and I ought to praise God: this is my work; I do it, nor will I desert this post, so long as I am allowed to keep it; and I exhort you to join in this same song.

CHAPTER XVII

THAT THE LOGICAL ART IS NECESSARY

SINCE reason is the faculty which analyses[1] and perfects the rest, and it ought itself not to be unanalysed, by what should it be analysed? for it is plain that this should be done either by itself or by another thing. Either then this other thing also is reason, or something else superior to reason; which is impossible. But if it is reason, again who shall analyse that reason? For if that reason does this for itself, our reason also can do it. But if we shall require something else, the thing will go on to infinity and have no end.[2] Reason therefore is analysed by itself. Yes: but it is more urgent to cure (our opinions[3]) and the like. Will you then hear about those things? Hear. But if you should say, "I know not whether you are arguing truly or falsely," and if I should express myself in any way ambiguously, and you should say to me "Distinguish," I will bear with you no longer, and I shall say to you, "It is more urgent."[4] This is the reason, I suppose, why they (the Stoic teachers) place the logical art first, as in the measuring of corn we place first the examination of the measure. But if we do not determine first what is a modius, and what is a balance, how shall we be able to measure or weigh anything?

In this case then if we have not fully learned and accurately examined the criterion of all other things, by which the other things are learned, shall we be able to examine accurately and to learn fully anything else? How is this possible? Yes; but the modius is only wood, and a thing which produces no fruit.—But it is a thing which can measure corn.—Logic also produces no fruit.—As to this indeed we shall see: but then even if a man should grant this, it is enough that logic has the power of distinguishing and examining other things, and, as we may say, of measuring and weighing them. Who says this? Is it only Chrysippus, and Zeno, and Cleanthes? And does not Antisthenes say

47

so?[5] And who is it that has written that the examination of names is the beginning of education? And does not Socrates say so? And of whom does Xenophon write, that he began with the examination of names, what each name signified?[6] Is this then the great and wondrous thing to understand or interpret Chrysippus? Who says this?—What then is the wondrous thing?—To understand the will of nature. Well then do you apprehend it yourself by your own power? and what more have you need of? For if it is true that all men err involuntarily, and you have learned the truth, of necessity you must act right.—But in truth I do not apprehend the will of nature. Who then tells us what it is? —They say that it is Chrysippus.—I proceed, and I inquire what this interpreter of nature says. I begin not to understand what he says: I seek an interpreter of Chrysippus.— Well, consider how this is said, just as if it were said in the Roman tongue.[7]—What then is the superciliousness of the interpreter? There is no superciliousness which can justly be charged even to Chrysippus, if he only interprets the will of nature, but does not follow it himself; and much more is this so with his interpreter. For we have no need of Chrysippus for his own sake, but in order that we may understand nature. Nor do we need a diviner (sacrificer) on his own acount, but because we think that through him we shall know the future and understand the signs given by the gods; nor do we need the viscera of animals for their own sake, but because through them signs are given; nor do we look with wonder on the crow or raven, but on God, who through them gives signs?

I go then to the interpreter of these things and the sacrificer, and I say, "Inspect the viscera for me, and tell me what signs they give." The man takes the viscera, opens them, and interprets: "Man," he says, "you have a will free by nature from hindrance and compulsion; this is written here in the viscera." I will show you this first in the matter of assent. Can any man hinder you from assenting to the truth? No man can. Can any man compel you to receive what is false. No man can. You see that in this matter you have the faculty of the will free from hindrance, free from compulsion, unimpeded. Well, then, in the matter of desire and pursuit of an object, is it otherwise? And what can overcome pursuit except another pursuit? And what can overcome desire and aversion (ἔκκλισιν) except another desire and aversion? But, you object: "If you place before me the fear of death, you do compel me." No, it is not what is placed before you that compels, but your opinion that it is better to do so and so than to die. In this matter then it is your opinion that compellèd you: that is, will compelled will. For if God had made that part of himself, which he took from himself and gave to us, of such a nature as to be hindered or compelled either by himself or by another, he would not then be God nor would he be taking care of us as he ought. This, says the diviner, I find in the victims: these are the things which are signified to you. If you choose, you are free; if you choose, you will blame no one: you will charge no one. All will be at the same time according to your mind and the mind of God. For the sake of this divination I go to this diviner and to the philosopher, not admiring him for this interpretation, but admiring the things which he interprets.

NOTES

¹ Λόγος ἐστὶν ὁ διαρθρῶν. Διαρθοῦν means "to divide a thing into its parts or members "The word "analyse" seems to be the nearest equivalent
² This is obscure The conclusion, "Reason therefore is analysed by itself" is not in Epictetus; but it is implied. Antoninus writes: "These are the properties of the rational soul; it sees itself, analyses itself." If reason, our reason, requires another reason to analyse it, that other reason will require another reason to analyse that other reason, and so on to infinity. If reason then, our reason, can be analysed, it must be analysed by itself.
³ "Our opinions " There is some defect in the text, as Wolf remarks. "The opponent," he says, "disparages Logic (Dialectic) as a thing which is not necessary to make men good, and he prefers moral teaching to Logic: but Epictetus informs him, that a man who is not a Dialectician will not have a sufficient perception of moral teaching."
⁴ He repeats the words of the supposed opponent; and he means that his adversary's difficulty shows the necessity of Dialectic.
⁵ Antisthenes who professed the Cynic philosophy, rejected Logic and Physic
⁶ Epictetus knew what education ought to be. We learn language, and we ought to learn what it means. When children learn words, they should learn what the thing is which is signified by the word. In the case of children this can only be done imperfectly as to some words, but it may be done even then in some degree; and it must be done, or the word signifies nothing, or, what is equally bad, the word is misunder-

stood. All of us pass our lives in ignorance of many words which we
use; some of us in greater ignorance than others, but all of us in ignorance to some degree.

    ' The supposed interpreter says this. When Epictetus says "the Ro-
man tongue," perhaps he means that the supposed opponent is a Roman
and does not know Greek well.

CHAPTER XVIII

THAT WE OUGHT NOT TO BE ANGRY WITH THE ERRORS (FAULTS) OF OTHERS

IF what philosophers say is true, that all men have one principle, as in the case of assent the persuasion that a thing is so, and in the case of dissent the persuasion that a thing is not so, and in the case of a suspense of judgment the persuasion that a thing is uncertain, so also in the case of a movement towards any thing the persuasion that a thing is for a man's advantage, and it is impossible to think that one thing is advantageous and to desire another, and to judge one thing to be proper and to move towards another, why then are we angry with the many?[1] They are thieves and robbers, you may say. What do you mean by thieves and robbers? They are mistaken about good and evil. Ought we then to be angry with them, or to pity them? But show them their error, and you will see how they desist from their errors. If they do not see their errors, they have nothing superior to their present opinion.

Ought not then this robber and this adulterer to be destroyed? By no means say so, but speak rather in this way: This man who has been mistaken and deceived about the most important things, and blinded, not in the faculty of vision which distinguishes white and black, but in the faculty which distinguishes good and bad, should we not destroy him? If you speak thus, you will see how inhuman this is which you say, and that it is just as if you would say, "Ought we not to destroy this blind and deaf man?" But if the greatest harm is in the privation of the greatest things, and the greatest thing in every man is the will or choice such as it ought to be, and a man is deprived of this will, why are you also angry with him? Man, you ought not to be affected contrary to nature by the bad things of another. Pity him rather: drop this readiness to be offended and to hate, and these words which the many utter: "these accursed and odious fellows." How have you been made so wise at once? and how are you so peevish? Why then are we angry? Is it because we value so much the things of which these men rob us? Do not admire your clothes, and then you will not be angry with the thief. Do not admire the beauty of your wife, and you will not be angry with the adulterer. Learn that a thief and an adulterer have no place in the things which are yours, but in those which belong to others and which are not in your power. If you dismiss these things and consider them as nothing, with whom are you still angry? But so long as you value these things, be angry with yourself rather than with the thief and the adulterer. Consider the matter thus: you have fine clothes, your neighbour has not: you have a window; you wish to air the clothes. The thief does not know wherein man's good consists, but he thinks that it consists in having fine clothes, the very thing which you also think. Must he not then come and take them away? When you show a cake to greedy persons, and swallow it all yourself, do you expect them not to snatch it from you? Do not provoke them: do not have a window: do not air your clothes. I also lately had an iron lamp placed by the side of my household gods: hearing a noise at the door, I ran down, and found that the lamp had been carried off. I reflected that he who had taken the lamp had done nothing strange. What then? To-morrow, I said, you will find an earthen lamp: for a man only loses that which he has. "I have lost my garment." The reason is that you had a garment. "I have pain in my head." Have you any pain in your horns? Why then are you troubled? for we only lose those things, we have only pains about those things which we possess.[2]

But the tyrant will chain—what? the leg. He will take away—what? the neck. What then will he not chain and not take away? the will. This is why the ancients taught the maxim, Know thyself. Therefore we ought to exercise ourselves in small things, and beginning with them to proceed to the greater. "I have pain in the head." Do not say, alas! "I have pain in the ear." Do not say, alas! And I do not say, that you are not allowed to groan, but do not groan inwardly; and if your slave is slow in bringing a bandage, do not cry out and torment yourself, and say, "Everybody hates me" : for who would not hate such a man?   For the future, relying on these opinions, walk about upright, free; not trusting to the size of your body, as an athlete, for a man ought not to be invincible in the way that an ass is.[3]

Who then is the invincible?   It is he whom none of the things disturb which are independent of the will.   Then examining one circumstance after another I observe, as in the case of an athlete; he has come off victorious in the first contest: well then, as to the second? and what if there should be great heat? and what, if it should be at Olympia?   And the same I say in this case: if you should throw money in his way, he will despise it.   Well, suppose you put a young girl in his way, what then? and what, if it is in the dark?[4] what if it should be a little reputation, or abuse; and what, if it should be praise; and what if it should be death?   He is able to overcome all.   What then if it be in heat, and what if it is in the rain, and what if he be in a melancholy (mad) mood, and what if he be asleep?   He will still conquer.   This is my invincible athlete.

NOTES

[1] Mrs. Carter says   "The most ignorant persons often practice what they know to be evil; and they, who voluntarily suffer, as many do, their inclinations to blind their judgment, are not justified by following it. (Perhaps she means "them," "their inclinations.")   The doctrine of Epictetus therefore, here and elsewhere, on this head, contradicts the voice of reason and conscience, nor is it less pernicious than illgrounded   It destroys all guilt and merit, all punishment and reward, all blame of ourselves or others, all sense of misbehaviour towards our fellow-creatures, or our Creator   No wonder that such philosophers did not teach repentance towards God."

Mrs Carter has not understood Epictetus; and her censure is misplaced   It is true that "the most ignorant persons often practise what they know to be evil," as she truly says. But she might have said more   It is also true that persons, who are not ignorant, often do what they know to be evil, and even what they would condemn in another, at least before they had fallen into the same evil themselves; for when they have done what they know to be wrong, they have a fellow-feeling with others who are bad as themselves Nor does he say, as Mrs Carter seems to imply that he does, for her words are ambiguous, that they who voluntarily suffer their inclinations to blind their judgment are justified by following them   He says that men will do as they do, so long as they think as they think   He only traces to their origin the bad acts which bad men do; and he says that we should pity them and try to mend them.   Now the best man in the world, if he sees the origin and direct cause of bad acts in men, may pity them for their wickedness, and he will do right. He will pity, and still he will punish severely, if the interests of society require the guilty to be punished: but he will not punish in anger. Epictetus says nothing about legal penalties; and I assume that he would not say that the penalties are always unjust, if I understand his principles. His discourse is to this effect, as the title tells us, that we ought not to be angry with the errors of others: the matter of the discourse is the feeling and disposition which we ought to have towards those who do wrong, "because they are mistaken about good and evil."

He does not discuss the question of the origin of these men's mistake further than this: men think that a thing or act is advantageous, and it is impossible for them to think that one thing is advantageous and to desire another thing. Their error is in their opinion   Then he tells us to show them their error, and they will desist from their errors. He is not here examining the way of showing them their error; by which I suppose that he means convincing them of their error. He seems to admit that it may not be possible to convince them of their errors, for he says, "if they do not see their errors, they have nothing superior to their present opinion."

This is the plain and certain meaning of Epictetus which Mrs. Carter in her zeal has not seen

[2] The conclusion explains what precedes. A man can have no pain in his horns, because he has none. A man can not be vexed about the loss of a thing if he does not possess it.

[3] That is obstinate, as this animal is generally; and sometimes very obstinate. The meaning then is, as Schweighauser says· "a man should be invincible, not with a kind of stupid obstinacy or laziness and slowness in moving himself like an ass, but he should be invincible through reason, reflection, meditation, study, and diligence."

[4] "From the rustics came the old proverb, for when they commend a man's fidelity and goodness they say he is a man with whom you may play the game with the fingers in the dark." Cicero, "De Officiis," iii. 19.

CHAPTER XIX

HOW WE SHOULD BEHAVE TO TYRANTS

IF a man possesses any superiority, or thinks that he does, when he does not, such a man, if he is uninstructed, will of necessity be puffed up through it. For instance, the tyrant says, "I am master of all!" And what can you do for me? Can you give me desire which shall have no hindrance? How can you? Have you the infallible power of avoiding what you would avoid? Have you the power of moving towards an object without error? And how do you possess this power? Come, when you are in a ship, do you trust to yourself or to the helmsman? And when you are in a chariot, to whom do you trust but to the driver? And how is it in all other arts? Just the same. In what then lies your power? "All men pay respect to me." Well, I also pay respect to my platter, and I wash it and wipe it; and for the sake of my oil flask, I drive a peg into the wall "Well then, are these things superior to me?" No, but they supply some of my wants, and for this reason I take care of them. Well, do I not attend to my ass? Do I not wash his feet? Do I not clean him? Do you not know that every man has regard to himself, and to you just the same as he has regard to his ass? For who has regard to you as a man? Show me. Who wishes to become like you? Who imitates you, as he imitates Socrates? "But I can cut off your head." You say right. I had forgotten that I must have regard to you, as I would to a fever and the bile, and raise an altar to you, as there is at Rome an altar to Fever.

What is it then that disturbs and terrifies the multitude? is it the tyrant and his guards? [By no means.] I hope that it is not so. It is not possible that what is by nature free can be disturbed by anything else, or hindered by any other thing than by itself. But it is a man's own opinions which disturb him: for when the tyrant says to a man, "I will chain your leg," he who values his leg says, "Do not; have pity:" but he who values his own will says, "If it appears more advan-

tageous to you, chain it." Do you not care? "I do not care."
I will show you that I am master. You can not do that,
Zeus has set me free; do you think that he intended to allow
his own son to be ashamed? But you are master of my
carcase: take it. "So when you approach me, you have no
regard to me?" No, but I have regard to myself; and if you
wish me to say that I have regard to you also, I tell you that
I have the same regard to you that I have to my pipkin.

This is not a perverse self-regard, for the animal is constituted so as to do all things for itself. For even the sun
does all things for itself; nay, even Zeus himself. But when
he chooses to be the Giver of rain and the Giver of fruits, and
the Father of Gods and men, you see that he can not obtain
these functions and these names, if he is not useful to man;
and, universally, he has made the nature of the rational
animal such that it can not obtain any one of its own proper
interests, if it does not contribute something to the common
interest. In this manner and sense it is not unsociable for a
man to do everything for the sake of himself. For what do
you expect? that a man should neglect himself and his own
interest? And how in that case can there be one and the
same principle in all animals, the principle of attachment
(regard) to themselves?

What then? when absurd notions about things independent of our will, as if they were good and (or) bad, lie at the
bottom of our opinions, we must of necessity pay regard to
tyrants; for I wish that men would pay regard to tyrants
only, and not also to the bedchamber men. How is it that
the man becomes all at once wise, when Cæsar has made him
superintendent of the close stool? How is it that we say immediately, "Felicion spoke sensibly to me." I wish he were
ejected from the bedchamber, that he might again appear to
you to be a fool.

Epaphroditus[2] had a shoemaker whom he sold because he
was good for nothing. This fellow by some good luck was
bought by one of Cæsar's men, and became Cæsar's shoemaker. You should have seen what respect Epaphroditus
paid to him: "How does the good Felicion do, I pray?"
Then if any of us asked, "What is master (Epaphroditus)
doing?" the answer was, "He is consulting about something

with Felicion." Had he not sold the man as good for nothing? Who then made him wise all at once? This is an instance of valuing something else than the things which depend on the will.

Has a man been exalted to the tribuneship? All who meet him offer their congratulations: one kisses his eyes, another the neck, and the slaves kiss his hands.[3] He goes to his house, he finds torches lighted. He ascends the Capitol: he offers a sacrifice on the occasion. Now who ever sacrificed for having had good desires? for having acted conformably to nature? For in fact we thank the gods for those things in which we place our good.

A person was talking to me to-day about the priesthood of Augustus.[4] I say to him: "Man, let the thing alone · you will spend much for no purpose" But he replies, "Those who draw up agreements will write my name." Do you then stand by those who read them, and say to such persons, "It is I whose name is written there"? And if you can now be present on all such occasions, what will you do when you are dead? My name will remain.—Write it on a stone, and it will remain. But come, what remembrance of you will there be beyond Nicopolis?—But I shall wear a crown of gold —If you desire a crown at all, take a crown of roses and put it on, for it will be more elegant in appearance.

NOTES

[1] Such a man was named in Greek κοιτωνίτης in Latin "cubicularius," a lord of the bedchamber, as we might say Seneca, "De Constantia Sapientis," speaks "of the pride of the nomenclator (the announcer of the name), of the arrogance of the bedchamber man "

[2] Once the master of Epictetus.

[3] Hand-kissing was in those times of tyranny the duty of a slave, not of a free man. This servile practice still exists among men called free.

[4] Casaubon, in a learned note on Suetonius, "Augustus," c. 18, informs us that divine honours were paid to Augustus at Nicopolis, which town he founded after the victory at Actium. The priesthood of Augustus at Nicopolis was a high office, and the priest gave his name to the year; that is, when it was intended in any writing to fix the year, either in any writing which related to public matters, or in instruments used in private affairs, the name of the priest of Augustus was used, and this was also the practice in most Greek cities. In order to establish the sense of this passage, Casaubon changed the text from τὰς φωνάς into τὰ σύμφωνα, which emendation Schweighauser has admitted into his text.

CHAPTER XX

EVERY art and faculty contemplates certain things especially. When then it is itself of the same kind with the objects which it contemplates, it must of necessity contemplate itself also: but when it is of an unlike kind, it can not contemplate itself. For instance, the shoemaker's art is employed on skins, but itself is entirely distinct from the material of skins: for this reason it does not contemplate itself. Again, the grammarian's art is employed about articulate speech; is then the art also articulate speech? By no means. For this reason it is not able to contemplate itself. Now reason, for what purpose has it been given by nature? For the right use of appearances. What is it then itself? A system (combination) of certain appearances So by its nature it has the faculty of contemplating itself also. Again, sound sense, for the contemplation of what things does it belong to us? Good and evil, and things which are neither. What is it then itself? Good. And want of sense, what is it? Evil. Do you see then that good sense necessarily contemplates both itself and the opposite? For this reason it is the chief and the first work of a philosopher to examine appearances, and to distinguish them and to admit none without examination. You see even in the matter of coin, in which our interest appears to be somewhat concerned, how we have invented an art, and how many means the assayer uses to try the value of coin, the sight, the touch, the smell, and lastly the hearing. He throws the coin (denarius) down, and observes the sound, and he is not content with its sounding once, but through his great attention he becomes a musician. In like manner, where we think that to be mistaken and not to be mistaken make a great difference, there we apply great attention to discovering the things which can deceive. But in the matter of our miserable ruling faculty, yawning and sleeping, we carelessly admit every appearance, for the harm is not noticed.

When then you would know how careless you are with respect to good and evil, and how active with respect to things which are indifferent (neither good nor evil), observe how you feel with respect to being deprived of the sight of the eyes, and how with respect to being deceived, and you will discover that you are far from feeling as you ought to do in relation to good and evil.   But this is a matter which requires much preparation, and much labour and study.   Well then do you expect to acquire the greatest of arts with small labour?   And yet the chief doctrine of philosophers is very brief.   If you would know, read Zeno's[2] writings and you will see.   For how few words it requires to say that man's end (or object) is to follow the gods, and that the nature of good is a proper use of appearances.   But if you say What is God, what is appearance, and what is particular and what is universal[3] nature? then indeed many words are necessary. If then Epicurus should come and say, that the good must be in the body; in this case also many words become necessary, and we must be taught what is the leading principle in us, and the fundamental and the substantial, and as it is not probable that the good of a snail is in the shell, is it probable that the good of a man is in the body?   But you yourself, Epicurus, possess something better than this.   What is that in you which deliberates, what is that which examines every thing, what is that which forms a judgment about the body itself, that it is the principal part? and why do you light your lamp and labour for us, and write so many books? is it that we may not be ignorant of the truth, who we are, and what we are with respect to you?   Thus the discussion requires many[4] words.

NOTES

[1] A comparison of lib. i. chap 1, will help to explain this chapter. Compare also lib i chap 17.

[2] Zeno, a native of Citium, in the island of Cyprus, is said to have come when he was young to Athens, where he spent the rest of a long life in the study and teaching of Philosophy. He was the founder of the Stoic sect, and a man respected for his ability and high character He wrote many philosophical works. Zeno was succeeded in his school by Cleanthes.

[3] Epictetus never attempts to say what God is   He was too wise to attempt to do what man can not do   But man does attempt to do it, and only shows the folly of his attempts, and, I think, his presumption also.

[4] Epicurus is said to have written more than any other person, as

many as three hundred volumes ($\kappa\dot{v}\lambda\iota\nu\delta\rho o\iota$, rolls). Chrysippus was his rival in this respect. For if Epicurus wrote anything, Chrysippus vied with him in writing as much; and for this reason he often repeated himself, because he did not read over what he had written, and he left his writings uncorrected in consequence of his hurry.

CHAPTER XXI

AGAINST THOSE WHO WISH TO BE ADMIRED

WHEN a man holds his proper station in life, he does not gape after things beyond it. Man, what do you wish to happen to you?

I am satisfied if I desire and avoid conformably to nature, if I employ movements towards and from an object as I am by nature formed to do; and purpose and design and assent."

Why then do you strut before us as if you had swallowed a spit?

"My wish has always been that those who meet me should admire me, and those who follow me should exclaim O the great philosopher."

Who are they by whom you wish to be admired? Are they not those of whom you are used to say, that they are mad? Well then do you wish to be admired by madmen?

CHAPTER XXII

ON PRAECOGNITIONS[1]

PRÆCOGNITIONS are common to all men, and præcognition is not contradictory to præcognition. For who of us does not assume that Good is useful and eligible, and in all circumstances that we ought to follow and pursue it? And who of us does not assume that Justice is beautiful and becoming? When then does the contradiction arise? It arises in the adaptation of the præcognitions to the particular cases. When one man says, "He has done well: he is a brave man," and another says, "Not so; but he has acted foolishly;" then the disputes arise among men. This is the dispute among the Jews and the Syrians and the Egyptians and the Romans; not whether holiness should be preferred to all things and in all cases should be pursued, but whether it is holy to eat pig's flesh or not holy. You will find this dispute also between Agamemnon and Achilles;[2] for call them forth. What do you say, Agamemnon? ought not that to be done which is proper and right? "Certainly." Well, what do you say, Achilles? do you not admit that what is good ought to be done? "I do most certainly." Adapt your præcognitions then to the present matter. Here the dispute begins. Agamemnon says, "I ought not to give up Chryseis to her father." Achilles says, "You ought." It is certain that one of the two makes a wrong adaptation of the præcognition of "ought" or "duty." Further, Agamemnon says, "Then if I ought to restore Chryseis, it is fit that I take his prize from some of you." Achilles replies, "Would you then take her whom I love?" "Yes, her whom you love." "Must I then be the only man who goes without a prize? and must I be the only man who has no prize?" Thus the dispute begins.[3]

What then is education? Education is the learning how to adapt the natural præcognitions to the particular things conformably to nature; and then to distinguish that of things some are in our power, but others are not: in our power are will and all acts which depend on the will; things not in our power are the body, the parts of the body, possessions, parents, brothers, children, country and generally, all with whom we live in society. In what then should we place the good? To what kind of things (οὐσία) shall we adapt it? To the things which are in our power? Is not health then a good thing, and soundness of limb, and life? and are not children and parents and country? Who will tolerate you if you deny this?

Let us then transfer the notion of good to these things. Is it possible then, when a man sustains damage and does not obtain good things, that he can be happy? It is not possible. And can he maintain towards society a proper behaviour? He can not. For I am naturally formed to look after my own interest If it is my interest to have an estate in land, it is my interest also to take it from my neighbour. If it is my interest to have a garment, it is my interest also to steal it from the bath.⁴ This is the origin of wars, civil commotions, tyrannies, conspiracies. And how shall I be still able to maintain my duty towards Zeus? for if I sustain damage and am unlucky, he takes no care of me; and what is he to me if he can not help me; and further, what is he to me if he allows me to be in the condition in which I am? I now begin to hate him. Why then do we build temples, why set up statues to Zeus, as well as to evil dæmons, such as to Fever; and how is Zeus the Saviour, and how the giver of rain, and the giver of fruits? And in truth if we place the nature of Good in any such things, all this follows.

What should we do then? This is the inquiry of the true philosopher who is in labour. Now I do not see what the Good is nor the Bad. Am I not mad? Yes. But suppose that I place the good somewhere among the things which depend on the will: all will laugh at me. There will come some greyhead wearing many gold rings on his fingers, and he will shake his head and say, "Hear, my child. It is right that you should philosophize; but you ought to have some brains also: all this that you are doing is silly. You learn the syllogism from philosophers; but you know how to act better than philosophers do."—Man, why then do you blame me, if I know? What shall I say to this slave? If I am silent, he will burst. I must speak in this way: "Excuse me, as you would excuse lovers; I am not my own master; I am mad."

NOTES

[1] Præcognitions (*προλήψεις*) is translated Præcognita by John Smith, Select Discourses, p. 4 Cicero says (Topica, 7): "Notionem appello quod Graeci tum *ἔννοιαν*, tum *πρόληψιν* dicunt. Ea est insita et ante percepta cujusque formæ cognitio, enodationis indigens." In the De Natura Deorum (i 16) he says: "Quæ est enim gens aut quod genus hominum, quod non habeat sine doctrina anticipationem quandam deorum, quam appellat *πρόληψιν* Epicurus? id est, anteceptam animo rei quandam informationem, sine qua nec intelligi quidquam nec quæri nec disputari potest." Epicurus, as Cicero says in the follow-ing chapter (17), was the first who used *πρόληψις* in this sense, which Cicero applies to what he calls the ingrafted or rather innate cognitions of the existence of gods, and these cognitions he supposes to be universal; but whether this is so or not, I do not know. See i. c. 2; Tuscul. i 24; De Fin iii. 6, and *πρόληψις* in iv 8. 6

[2] Horace, Epp. i. 2.

[3] Iliad, i The quarrel of Achilles and Agamemnon about giving up Chryseis to her father.

[4] The bath was a place of common resort, where a thief had the opportunity of carrying off a bather's clothes From men's desires to have what they have not, and do not choose to labour for, spring the disorders of society, as it is said in the epistle of James, c. iv., v. 1, to which Mrs. Carter refers

CHAPTER XXIII

AGAINST EPICURUS

EVEN Epicurus perceives that we are by nature social, but having once placed our good in the husk he is no longer able to say anything else. For on the other hand he strongly maintains this, that we ought not to admire nor to accept any thing which is detached from the nature of good; and he is right in maintaining this. How then are we [suspicious], if we have no natural affection to our children? Why do you advise the wise man not to bring up children? Why are you afraid that he may thus fall into trouble? For does he fall into trouble on account of the mouse which is nurtured in the house? What does he care if a little mouse in the house makes lamentation to him? But Epicurus knows that if once a child is born, it is no longer in our power not to love it nor care about it. For this reason, Epicurus says, that a man who has any sense also does not engage in political matters; for he knows what a man must do who is engaged in such things; for indeed, if you intend to behave among men as you would among a swarm of flies, what hinders you? But Epicurus, who knows this, ventures to say that we should not bring up children. But a sheep does not desert its own offspring, nor yet a wolf; and shall a man desert his child? What do you mean? that we should be as silly as sheep? but not even do they desert their offspring: or as savage as wolves, but not even do wolves desert their young. Well, who would follow your advice, if he saw his child weeping after falling on the ground? For my part I think that even if your mother and your father had been told by an oracle, that you would say what you have said, they would not have cast you away.

CHAPTER XXIV

HOW WE SHOULD STRUGGLE WITH CIRCUMSTANCES

IT is circumstances (difficulties) that show what men are. Therefore when a difficulty falls upon you, remember that God, like a trainer of wrestlers, has matched you with a rough young man. For what purpose? you may say. Why that you may become an Olympic conqueror; but it is not accomplished without sweat. In my opinion no man has had a more profitable difficulty than you have had, if you choose to make use of it as an athlete would deal with a young antagonist. We are now sending a scout to Rome;[1] but no man sends a cowardly scout, who, if he only hears a noise and sees a shadow any where, comes running back in terror and reports that the enemy is close at hand. So now if you should come and tell us, Fearful, is the state of affairs at Rome, terrible is death, terrible is exile; terrible is calumny; terrible is poverty; fly, my friends; the enemy is near—we shall answer, Be gone, prophesy for yourself, we have committed only one fault, that we sent such a scout.

Diogenes,[2] who was sent as a scout before you, made a different report to us. He says that death is no evil, for neither is it base: he says that fame (reputation) is the noise of madmen. And what has this spy said about pain, about pleasure, and about poverty? He says that to be naked is better than any purple robe, and to sleep on the bare ground is the softest bed; and he gives as a proof of each thing that he affirms his own courage, his tranquillity, his freedom, and the healthy appearance, and compactness of his body. "There is no enemy near," he says; "all is peace." How so, Diogenes? "See," he replies, "if I am struck, if I have been wounded, if I have fled from any man." This is what a scout ought to be But you come to us and tell us one thing after another. Will you not go back, and you will see clearer when you have laid aside fear?

What then shall I do? What do you do when you leave a

DIOGENES

ship? Do you take away the helm or the oars? What then do you take away? You take what is your own, your bottle and your wallet; and now if you think of what is your own, you will never claim what belongs to others. The emperor (Domitian) says, "Lay aside your laticlave.[3]" See, I put on the angusticlave. "Lay aside this also." See, I have only my toga. "Lay aside your toga." See, I am now naked. "But you still raise my envy." Take then all my poor body· when, at a man's command, I can throw away my poor body, do I still fear him?

But a certain person will not leave to me the succession to his estate. What then? had I forgotten that not one of these things was mine. How then do we call them mine? Just as we call the bed in the inn. If then the innkeeper at his death leaves you the beds; all well; but if he leaves them to another, he will have them, and you will seek another bed. If then you shall not find one, you will sleep on the ground. only sleep with a good will and snore, and remember that tragedies have their place among the rich and kings and tyrants, but no poor man fills a part in a tragedy, except as one of the Chorus. Kings indeed commence with prosperity: "ornament the palace with garlands": then about the third or fourth act they call out, "Oh, Cithæron,[4] why didst thou receive me"? Slave, where are the crowns, where the diadem? The guards help thee not at all. When then you approach any of these persons, remember this that you are approaching a tragedian, not the actor, but Œdipus himself. But you say, such a man is happy; for he walks about with many, and I also place myself with the many and walk about with many. In sum remember this· the door is open;[5] be not more timid than little children, but as they say, when the thing does not please them, "I will play no longer," so do you, when things seem to you of such a kind, say "I will no longer play," and be gone: but if you stay, do not complain.

NOTES

[3] In the time of Domitian philosophers were banished from Rome and Italy by a Senatusconsultum (Sueton. Domitian, c 10; Dion, 67, c. 13), and at that time Epictetus. as Gellius says (xv. 11). went from Rome to Nicopolis in Epirus, where he opened a school. We may sup-

pose that Epictetus is here speaking of some person who had gone from
Nicopolis to Rome to inquire about the state of affairs there under the
cruel tyrant Domitian. (Schweighauser.)

 Diogenes was brought to King Philip after the battle of Chæronea
as a spy (iii. 22, 24). Plutarch in the treatise, Quomodo assentator ab
amico dignoscatur, c. 30, states that when Philip asked Diogenes if he
was a spy, he replied, "Certainly I am a spy, Philip, of your want of
judgment and of your folly, which lead you without any necessity to
put to the hazard your kingdom and your life in one single hour"

 The garment with the broad border, the laticlave, was the dress of a
senator, the garment with the narrow border, the angusticlave, was the
dress of a man of the equestrian order.

 The exclamation of Œdipus in the Œdipus Tyrannus of Sopho-
cles, v. 1391.

 This means "you can die when you please" Comp i c. 9. The
power of dying when you please is named by Plinius (N. H. ii. c. 7)
the best thing that God has given to man amidst all the sufferings of
life. Horace, Epp. ii. 2, 213,—

> " Vivere si recte nescis, decede peritis:
> Lusisti satis, edisti satis atque bibisti;
> Tempus abire tibi."

CHAPTER XXV.

IF these things are true, and if we are not silly, and are not acting hypocritically when we say that the good of man is in the will, and the evil too, and that everything else does not concern us, why are we still disturbed, why are we still afraid? The things about which we have been busied are in no man's power: and the things which are in the power of others, we care not for. What kind of trouble have we still?

"But give me directions." Why should I give you directions? has not Zeus given you directions? Has he not given to you what is your own free from hindrance and free from impediment, and what is not your own subject to hindrance and impediment? What directions then, what kind of orders did you bring when you came from him? Keep by every means what is your own; do not desire what belongs to others. Fidelity (integrity) is your own, virtuous shame is your own; who then can take these things from you? who else than yourself will hinder you from using them? But how do you act? when you seek what is not your own, you lose that which is your own. Having such promptings and commands from Zeus, what kind do you still ask from me? Am I more powerful than he, am I more worthy of confidence? But if you observe these, do you want any others besides? Well, but he has not given these orders, you will say. Produce your præcognitions ($\pi\rho o\lambda\acute{\eta}\psi\epsilon\iota\varsigma$), produce the proofs of philosophers, produce what you have often heard, and produce what you have said yourself, produce what you have read, produce what you have meditated on; and you will then see that all these things are from God. "How long then is it fit to observe these precepts from God, and not to break up the play?" As long as the play is continued with propriety. In the Saturnalia[1] a king is chosen by lot, for it has been the custom to play at this game. The king commands: "Do you drink,

Do you mix wine with me, Do you sing, Do you go, Do you come." I obey that the game may not be broken up through me.—But if he says, "Think that you are in evil plight:" I answer, I do not think so; and who will compel me to think so? Further, we agreed to play Agamemnon and Achilles. He who is appointed to play Agamemnon says to me, "Go to Achilles and tear from him Briseis." I go. He says, "Come," and I come.

For as we behave in the matter of hypothetical arguments, so ought we to do in life. Suppose it to be night. I suppose that it is night. Well then; is it day? No, for I admitted the hypothesis that it was night. Suppose that you think that it is night? Suppose that I do. But also think that it is night. That is not consistent with the hypothesis. So in this case also: Suppose that you are unfortunate. Well, suppose so. Are you then unhappy? Yes. Well then are you troubled with an unfavourable dæmon (fortune)? Yes. But think also that you are in misery. This is not consistent with the hypothesis· and another (Zeus) forbids me to think so

How long then must we obey such orders? As long as it is profitable; and this means as long as I maintain that which is becoming and consistent. Further, some men are sour and of bad temper, and they say, "I can not sup with this man to be obliged to hear him telling daily how he fought in Mysia": "I told you, brother, how I ascended the hill: then I began to be besieged again." But another says, "I prefer to get my supper and to hear him talk as much as he likes." And do you compare these estimates (judgments): only do nothing in a depressed mood, nor as one afflicted, nor as thinking that you are in misery, for no man compels you to that.—Has it smoked in the chamber? If the smoke is moderate, I will stay; if it is excessive; I go out: for you must always remember this and hold it fast, that the door is open.—Well, but you say to me, "Do not live in Nicopolis." I will not live there "Nor in Athens." I will not live in Athens. "Nor in Rome." I will not live in Rome. "Live in Gyarus."[2] I will live in Gyarus, but it seems like a great smoke to live in Gyarus; and I depart to the place where no man will hinder me from living, for that dwelling place is open to all; and as to the last garment, that is the poor body, no one has any power over me beyond this. This was the reason why Demetrius[3] said to Nero, "You threaten me with death, but nature threatens you." If I set my admiration on the poor body, I have given myself up to be a slave: if on my little possessions, I also make myself a slave: for I immediately make it plain with what I may be caught, as if the snake draws in his head, I tell you to strike that part of him which he guards; and do you be assured that whatever part you choose to guard, that part your master will attack. Remembering this whom will you still flatter or fear?

"But I should like to sit where the Senators sit."[4] Do you see that you are putting yourself in straits, you are squeezing yourself. "How then shall I see well in any other way in the amphitheatre?" Man, do not be a spectator at all, and you will not be squeezed. Why do you give yourself trouble? Or wait a little, and when the spectacle is over, seat yourself in the place reserved for the Senators and sun yourself. For remember this general truth, that it is we who squeeze ourselves, who put ourselves in straits, that is our opinions squeeze us and put us in straits. For what is it to be reviled? Stand by a stone and revile it; and what will you gain? If then a man listens like a stone, what profit is there to the reviler? But if the reviler has as a stepping-stone (or ladder) the weakness of him who is reviled, then he accomplishes something. "Strip him." What do you mean by him? "Lay hold of his garment, strip it off. I have insulted you." Much good may it do you.

This was the practice of Socrates: this was the reason why he always had one face. But we choose to practise and study any thing rather than the means by which we shall be unimpeded and free. You say, Philosophers talk paradoxes.[5] But are there no paradoxes in the other arts? and what is more paradoxical than to puncture a man's eye in order that he may see? If any one said this to a man ignorant of the surgical art, would he not ridicule the speaker? Where is the wonder then if in philosophy also many things which are true appear paradoxical to the inexperienced?

[1] A festival at Rome in December, a season of jollity and license (Livy, xxii. 1). Compare the passage in Tacitus, Ann xiii. 15, in which Nero is chosen by lot to be king. and Seneca, De Constant. Sapient c. 12, "Illi (pueri) inter ipsos magistratus gerunt, et prætextam fascesque ac tribunal imitantur."

[2] Gyarus or Gyara a wretched island in the Ægean sea, to which criminals were sent under the empire at Rome. Juvenal, Sat. i 73.

[3] Demetrius was a Cynic philosopher, of whom Seneca says: "He was in my opinion a great man, even if he is compared with the greatest." One of his sayings was: "You gain more by possessing a few precepts of philosophy, if you have them ready and use them, than by learning many if you have them not at hand" Seneca often mentions Demetrius. The saying in the text is also attributed to Anaxagoras (Life by Diogenes Lærtius) and to Socrates by Xenophon (Apologia, 27)

[4] At Rome, and probably in other towns, there were seats reserved for the different classes of men at the public spectacles.

[5] Paradoxes ($\pi\alpha\rho\acute{\alpha}\delta o\xi\alpha$), "things contrary to opinion," are contrasted with paralogies ($\pi\alpha\rho\acute{\alpha}\lambda oy\alpha$), "things contrary to reason." Cicero says (Prœmium to his Paradoxes), that paradoxes are "something which cause surprise and contradict common opinion;" and in another place he says that the Romans gave the name of "admirabilia" to the Stoic paradoxes.—The puncture of the eye is the operation for cataract.

CHAPTER XXVI

WHAT THE LAW OF LIFE IS

WHEN a person was reading hypothetical arguments, Epictetus said, This also is an hypothetical law that we must accept what follows from the hypothesis. But much before this law is the 'aw of life, that we must act conformably to nature. For if in every matter and circumstance we wish to observe what is natural, it is plain that in every thing we ought to make it our aim that neither that which is consequent shall escape us, and that we do not admit the contradictory. First then philosophers exercise us in theory[1] (contemplation of things), which is easier; and then next they lead us to the more difficult things; for in theory, there is nothing which draws us away from following what is taught, but in the matters of life, many are the things which distract us. He is ridiculous then who says that he wishes to begin with the matters of real life, for it is not easy to begin with the more difficult things; and we ought to employ this fact as an argument to those parents who are vexed at their children learning philosophy: Am I doing wrong then my father, and do I not know what is suitable to me and becoming? If indeed this can neither be learned nor taught, why do you blame me? but if it can be taught, teach me; and if you can not, allow me to learn from those who say that they know how to teach. For what do you think? do you suppose that I voluntarily fall into evil and miss the good? I hope that it may not be so. What is then the cause of my doing wrong? Ignorance. Do you not choose then that I should get rid of my ignorance? Who was ever taught by anger the art of a pilot or music? Do you think that by means of your anger I shall learn the art of life? He only is allowed to speak in this way who has shown such an intention.[2] But if a man only intending to make a display at a banquet and to show that he is acquainted with hypothetical arguments reads them and attends the philosophers, what

6

other object has he than that some man of senatorial rank who sits by him may admire? For there (at Rome) are the really great materials (opportunities), and the riches here (at Nicopolis) appear to be trifles there. This is the reason why it is difficult for a man to be master of the appearances, where the things which disturb the judgment are great. I know a certain person who complained, as he embraced the knees of Epaphroditus, that he had only one hundred and fifty times ten thousand denarii[3] remaining. What then did Epaphroditus do? Did he laugh at him, as we slaves of Epaphroditus did? No, but he cried out with amazement, "Poor man, how then did you keep silence, how did you endure it?"

When Epictetus had reproved (called) the person who was reading the hypothetical arguments, and the teacher who had suggested the reading was laughing at the reader, Epictetus said to the teacher, "You are laughing at yourself: you did not prepare the young man nor did you ascertain whether he was able to understand these matters; but perhaps you are only employing him as a reader." Well then said Epictetus, if a man has not ability enough to understand a complex (syllogism), do we trust him in giving praise, do we trust him in giving blame, do we allow that he is able to form a judgment about good or bad? and if such a man blames any one, does the man care for the blame? and if he praises any one, is the man elated, when in such small matters as an hypothetical syllogism he who praises can not see what is consequent on the hypothesis?

This then is the beginning of philosophy, a man's perception of the state of his ruling faculty; for when a man knows that it is weak, then he will not employ it on things of the greatest difficulty. But at present, if men can not swallow even a morsel, they buy whole volumes and attempt to devour them; and this is the reason why they vomit them up or suffer indigestion: and then come gripings, defluxes, and fevers.[4] Such men ought to consider what their ability is. In theory it is easy to convince an ignorant person; but in the affairs of real life no one offers himself to be convinced, and we hate the man who has convinced us. But

Socrates advised us not to live a life which is not subjected to examination.

[1] This is a profound and useful remark of Epictetus. General principles are most easily understood and accepted. The difficulty is in the application of them. What is more easy, for example, than to understand general principles of law which are true and good? But in practice cases are presented to us which as Bacon says, are "immersed in matter;" and it is this matter which makes the difficulty of applying the principles, and requires the ability and study of an experienced man. It is easy, and it is right, to teach the young the general principles of the rules of life; but the difficulty of applying them is that in which the young and the old too often fail So if you ask whether virtue can be taught, the answer is that the rules for a virtuous life can be delivered; but the application of the rules is the difficulty, as teachers of religion and morality know well, if they are fit to teach. If they do not know this truth, they are neither fit to teach the rules, nor to lead the way to the practice of them by the only method which is possible; and this method is by their own example, assisted by the example of those who direct the education of youth, and of those with whom young persons live.

[2] "Such an intention" appears to mean "the intention of learning." "The son alone can say this to his father, when the son studies philosophy for the purpose of living a good life, and not for the purpose of display."—Wolf.

[3] This was a large sum. He is speaking of drachmæ, or of the Roman equivalents denarii In Roman language the amount would be briefly expressed by "sexagies centena millia H. S.," or simply by "sexagies."

[4] Seneca, "De Tranquillitate animi," says: "What is the use of countless books and libraries, when the owner scarcely reads in his whole life the tables of contents? The number only confuses a learner, does not instruct him. It is much better to give yourself up to a few authors than to wander through many."

CHAPTER XXVII

IN HOW MANY WAYS APPEARANCES EXIST, AND WHAT AIDS WE SHOULD PROVIDE AGAINST THEM

APPEARANCES are to us in four ways: for either things appear as they are; or they are not, and do not even appear to be; or they are, and do not appear to be; or they are not, and yet appear to be. Further, in all these cases to form a right judgment (to hit the mark) is the office of an educated man. But whatever it is that annoys (troubles) us, to that we ought to apply a remedy. If the sophisms of Pyrrho[1] and of the Academics are what annoys (troubles), we must apply the remedy to them. If it is the persuasion of appearances, by which some things appear to be good, when they are not good, let us seek a remedy for this. If it is habit which annoys us, we must try to seek aid against habit. What aid then can we find against habit? The contrary habit. You hear the ignorant say: "That unfortunate person is dead: his father and mother are overpowered with sorrow;[2] he was cut off by an untimely death and in a foreign land." Hear the contrary way of speaking: Tear yourself from these expressions: oppose to one habit the contrary habit; to sophistry oppose reason, and the exercise and discipline of reason; against persuasive (deceitful) appearances we ought to have manifest præcognitions ($\pi\rho o\lambda\acute{\eta}\psi\varepsilon\iota\varsigma$), cleared of all impurities and ready to hand.

When death appears an evil, we ought to have this rule in readiness, that it is fit to avoid evil things, and that death is a necessary thing. For what shall I do, and where shall I escape it? Suppose that I am not Sarpedon, the son of Zeus, nor able to speak in this noble way: I will go and I am resolved either to behave bravely myself or to give to another the opportunity of doing so; if I can not succeed in doing any thing myself, I will not grudge another the doing of something noble.—Suppose that it is above our power to act thus; is it not in our power to reason thus? Tell me where I can escape death: discover for me the country, show me the men to whom I must go, whom death does not visit. Discover to me a charm against death. If I have not one, what do you wish me to do? I can not escape from death. Shall I not escape from the fear of death, but shall I die lamenting and trembling? For the origin of perturbation is this, to wish for something, and that this should not happen. Therefore if I am able to change externals according to my wish, I change them; but if I can not, I am ready to tear out the eyes of him who hinders me   For the nature of man is not to endure to be deprived of the good, and not to endure the falling into evil.   Then at last, when I am neither able to change circumstances nor to tear out the eyes of him who hinders me, I sit down and groan and abuse whom I can, Zeus and the rest of the gods.   For if they do not care for me, what are they to me?—Yes, but you will be an impious man —In what respect then will it be worse for me than it is now?—To sum up, remember this that unless piety and your interest be in the same thing, piety can not be maintained in any man.   Do not these things seem necessary (true)?

Let the followers of Pyrrho and the Academics come and make their objections.   For I, as to my part, have no leisure for these disputes, nor am I able to undertake the defence of common consent (opinion).   If I had a suit even about a bit of land, I would call in another to defend my interests. With what evidence then am I satisfied?   With that which belongs to the matter in hand.[3]   How indeed perception is effected, whether through the whole body or any part, perhaps I can not explain: for both opinions perplex me.   But that you and I are not the same, I know with perfect certainty.   How do you know it?   When I intend to swallow anything, I never carry it to your mouth, but to my own. When I intend to take bread, I never lay hold of a broom, but I always go to the bread as to a mark.   And you yourselves (the Pyrrhonists), who take away the evidence of the senses, do you act otherwise?   Who among you, when he intended to enter a bath, ever went into a mill?

What then?   Ought we not with all our power to hold to this also, the maintaining of general opinion, and fortifying ourselves against the arguments which are directed against it? Who denies that we ought to do this? Well, he should do it who is able, who has leisure for it; but as to him who trembles and is perturbed and is inwardly broken in heart (spirit), he must employ his time better on something else.

NOTES

[1] Pyrrho was a native of Elis, in the Peloponnesus. He is said to have accompanied Alexander the Great in his Asiatic expedition. The time of his birth is not stated, but it is said that he lived to the age of ninety.

Ἀπώλετο does not mean that the father is dead, and that the mother is dead. They survive and lament. Compare Euripides, Alcestis, v 825.

ἀπωλόμεσθα πάντες, οὐ κείνη μόν

[2] " The chief question which was debated between the Pyrrhonists and the Academics on one side, and the Stoics on the other, was this whether there is a criterion of truth; and in the first place, the question is about the evidence of the senses, or the certainty of truth in those things which are perceived by the senses."—Schweighäuser

The strength of the Stoic system was that "it furnishes a groundwork of common sense, and the universal belief of mankind, on which to found sufficient certitude for the requirements of life on the other hand, the real question of knowledge, in the philosophical sense of the word, was abandoned." Levin's Six Lectures, p. 70.

CHAPTER XXVIII

WHAT is the cause of assenting to anything? The fact that it appears to be true. It is not possible then to assent to that which appears not to be true. Why? Because this is the nature of the understanding, to incline to the true, to be dissatisfied with the false, and in matters uncertain to withhold assent. What is the proof of this? Imagine (persuade yourself), if you can, that it is now night. It is not possible. Take away your persuasion that it is day. It is not possible. Persuade yourself or take away your persuasion that the stars are even in number.[2] It is impossible. When then any man assents to that which is false, be assured that he did not intend to assent to it as false, for every soul is unwillingly deprived of the truth, as Plato says; but the falsity seemed to him to be true. Well, in acts what have we of the like kind as we have here truth or falsehood? We have the fit and the not fit (duty and not duty), the profitable and the unprofitable, that which is suitable to a person and that which is not, and whatever is like these. Can then a man think that a thing is useful to him and not choose it? He can not. How says Medea?[3]—

> "'Tis true I know what evil I shall do,
> But passion overpowers the better counsel."

She thought that to indulge her passion and take vengeance on her husband was more profitable than to spare her children. It was so; but she was deceived. Show her plainly that she is deceived, and she will not do it; but so long as you do not show it, what can she follow except that which appears to herself (her opinion)? Nothing else. Why then are you angry with the unhappy woman that she has been bewildered about the most important things, and is become a viper instead of a human creature? And why not, if

79

it is possible, rather pity, as we pity the blind and the lame. so those who are blinded and maimed in the faculties which are supreme?

Whoever then clearly remembers this, that to man the measure of every act is the appearance (the opinion),—whether the thing appears good or bad: if good, he is free from blame; if bad, himself suffers the penalty, for it is impossible that he who is deceived can be one person, and he who suffers another person—whoever remembers this will not be angry with any man, will not be vexed at any man, will not revile or blame any man, nor hate nor quarrel with any man.

So then all these great and dreadful deeds have this origin, in the appearance (opinion)? Yes, this origin and no other. The Iliad is nothing else than appearance and the use of appearances. It appeared[4] to Alexander to carry off the wife of Menelaus: it appeared to Helene to follow him. If then it had appeared to Menelaus to feel that it was a gain to be deprived of such a wife, what would have happened? Not only would the Iliad have been lost, but the Odyssey also. On so small a matter then did such great things depend? But what do you mean by such great things? Wars and civil commotions, and the destruction of many men and cities. And what great matter is this? Is it nothing?—But what great matter is the death of many oxen, and many sheep, and many nests of swallows or storks being burnt or destroyed? Are these things then like those? Very like. Bodies of men are destroyed, and the bodies of oxen and sheep; the dwellings of men are burnt, and the nests of storks. What is there in this great or dreadful? Or show me what is the difference between a man's house and a stork's nest, as far as each is a dwelling; except that man builds his little houses of beams and tiles and bricks, and the stork builds them of sticks and mud Are a stork and a man then like things? What say you?—In body they are very much alike.

Does a man then differ in no respect from a stork? Don't suppose that I say so; but there is no difference in these matters (which I have mentioned). In what then is the difference? Seek and you will find that there is a difference in another matter. See whether it is not in a man the understanding of what he does, see if it is not in social community, in fidelity, in modesty, in steadfastness, in intelligence. Where then is the great good and evil in men? It is where the difference is. If the difference is preserved and remains fenced round, and neither modesty is destroyed, nor fidelity, nor intelligence, then the man also is preserved; but if any of these things is destroyed and stormed like a city, then the man too perishes; and in this consist the great things. Alexander, you say, sustained great damage then when the Hellenes invaded and when they ravaged Troy, and when his brothers perished. By no means; for no man is damaged by an action which is not his own; but what happened at that time was only the destruction of stork's nests: now the ruin of Alexander was when he lost the character of modesty, fidelity, regard to hospitality, and to decency. When was Achilles ruined? Was it when Patroclus died? Not so. But it happened when he began to be angry, when he wept for a girl, when he forgot that he was at Troy not to get mistresses, but to fight. These things are the ruin of men, this is being besieged, this is the destruction of cities, when right opinions are destroyed, when they are corrupted.

When then women are carried off, when children are made captives, and when the men are killed, are these not evils? How is it then that you add to the facts these opinions? Explain this to me also.—I shall not do that; but how is it that you say that these are not evils?—Let us come to the rules; produce the præcognitions (προλήψεις).: for it is because this is neglected that we can not sufficiently wonder at what men do. When we intend to judge of weights, we do not judge by guess: where we intend to' judge of straight and crooked, we do not judge by guess. In all cases where it is our interest to know what is true in any matter, never will any man among us do anything by guess. But in things which depend on the first and on the only cause of doing right or wrong, of happiness or unhappiness, of being unfortunate or fortunate, there only we are inconsiderate and rash. There is then nothing like scales (balance), nothing like a rule: but some appearance is presented, and straightway I act according to it. Must I then suppose that I am superior to Achilles or Agamemnon, so that they by following appearances do and suffer so many evils: and shall not the appearance be sufficient for me?— And what tragedy has any other beginning? The Atreus of Euripides, what is it? An appearance. The Œdipus of Sophocles, what is it? An appearance. The Phœnix? An appearance. The Hippolytus? An appearance. What kind of a man then do you suppose him to be who pays no regard to this matter? And what is the name of those who follow every appearance? They are called madmen. Do we then act at all differently?

NOTES

' See Chapter 18 of this book.

' We can not conceive that the number of stars is either even or odd. The construction of the word ἀποπάσχειν is uncertain, for says Schweighäuser, the word is found only here

' The Medea of Euripides, 1079

' This is the literal version. It does not mean "that it appeared right," as Mrs. Carter translates it Alexander never thought whether it was right or wrong. All that appeared to him was the possessing of Helene, and he used the means for getting possession of her, as a dog who spies and pursues some wild animal.

CHAPTER XXIX

ON CONSTANCY (OR FIRMNESS)

THE being (nature) of the Good is a certain Will; the being of the Bad is a certain kind of Will. What then are externals? Materials for the Will, about which the will being conversant shall obtain its own good or evil. How shall it obtain the good. If it does not admire (overvalue) the materials; for the opinions about the materials, if the opinions are right, make the will good: but perverse and distorted opinions make the will bad. God has fixed this law, and says, "If you would have any thing good, receive it from yourself." You say, No, but I will have it from another.—Do not so: but receive it from yourself. Therefore when the tyrant threatens and calls me, I say, Whom do you threaten? If he says, I will put you in chains, I say, You threaten my hands and my feet. If he says, I will cut off your head, I reply, You threaten my head. If he says, I will throw you into prison, I say, You threaten the whole of this poor body. If he threatens me with banishment, I say the same. Does he then not threaten you at all? If I feel that all these things do not concern me, he does not threaten me at all; but if I fear any of them, it is I whom he threatens. Whom then do I fear? the master of what? The master of things which are in my own power? There is no such master. Do I fear the master of things which are not in my power? And what are these things to me?

Do you philosophers then teach us to despise kings? I hope not. Who among us teaches to claim against them the power over things which they possess? Take my poor body, take my property, take my reputation, take those who are about me. If I advise any persons to claim these things, they may truly accuse me.—Yes, but I intend to command your opinions also.—And who has given you this power? How can you conquer the opinion of another man? By applying terror to it, he replies, I will conquer it. Do you not know that opinion conquers itself, and is not conquered by another? But nothing else can conquer Will except the Will itself. For this reason too the law of God is most powerful and most just, which is this: Let the stronger always be superior to the weaker. Ten are stronger than one For what? For putting in chains, for killing, for dragging whither they choose, for taking away what a man has. The ten therefore conquer the one in this in which they are stronger. In what then are the ten weaker? If the one possesses right opinions and the others do not. Well then, can the ten conquer in this matter? How is it possible? If we were placed in the scales, must not the heavier draw down the scale in which it is.

How strange then that Socrates should have been so treated by the Athenians. Slave, why do you say Socrates? Speak of the thing as it is: how strange that the poor body of Socrates should have been carried off and dragged to prison by stronger men, and that any one should have given hemlock to the poor body of Socrates, and that it should breathe out the life. Do these things seem strange, do they seem unjust, do you on account of these things blame God? Had Socrates then no equivalent for these things? Where then for him was the nature of good? Whom shall we listen to, you or him? And what does Socrates say? Anytus and Melitus[1] can kill me, but they can not hurt me: and further, he says, "If it so pleases God, so let it be"

But show me that he who has the inferior principles overpowers him who is superior in principles. You will never show this, nor come near showing it; for this is the law of nature and of God that the superior shall always overpower the inferior. In what? In that in which it is superior. One body is stronger than another: many are stronger than one: the thief is stronger than he who is not a thief. This is the reason why I also lost my lamp, because in wakefulness the thief was superior to me. But the man bought the lamp at this price: for a lamp he became a thief, a faithless fellow, and like a wild beast. This seemed to him a good bargain. Be it so. But a man has seized me by the cloak, and is drawing me to the public place: then others bawl out,

"Philosopher, what has been the use of your opinions? see you are dragged to prison, you are going to be beheaded." And what system of philosophy (εἰσαγωγήν) could I have made so that, if a stronger man should have laid hold of my cloak, I should not be dragged off; that if ten men should have laid hold of me and cast me into prison, I should not be cast in? Have I learned nothing else then? I have learned to see that everything which happens, if it be independent of my will, is nothing to me. I may ask, if you have not gained by this. Why then do you seek advantage in any thing else than in that in which you have learned that advantage is?

Then sitting in prison I say: The man who cries out in this way neither hears what words mean, nor understands what is said, nor does he care at all to know what philosophers say or what they do. Let him alone.

But now he says to the prisoner, Come out from your prison.—If you have no further need of me in prison, I come out: if you should have need of me again, I will enter the prison.—How long will you act thus?—So long as reason requires me to be with the body: but when reason does not require this, take away the body, and fare you well. Only we must not do it inconsiderately, nor weakly, nor for any slight reason; for, on the other hand, God does not wish it to be done, and he has need of such a world and such inhabitants in it. But if he sounds the signals for retreat, as he did to Socrates, we must obey him who gives the signal, as if he were a general.[2]

Well then, ought we to say such things to the many? Why should we? Is it not enough for a man to be persuaded himself? When children come clapping their hands and crying out, "To-day is the good Saturnalia," do we say, "The Saturnalia are not good"? By no means, but we clap our hands also. Do you also then, when you are not able to make a man change his mind, be assured that he is a child, and clap your hands with him; and if you do not choose to do this, keep silent.

A man must keep this in mind; and when he is called to any such difficulty, he should know that the time is come for showing if he has been instructed. For he who is come

into a difficulty is like a young man from a school who has
practised the resolution of syllogisms; and if any person proposes to him an easy syllogism, he says, rather propose to
me a syllogism which is skilfully complicated that I may
exercise myself on it. Even athletes are dissatisfied with
slight young men, and say, "He can not lift me."—"This is
a youth of noble disposition." [You do not so]; but when
the time of trial is come, one of you must weep and say, "I
wish that I had learned more." A little more of what? If
you did not learn these things in order to show them in practice, why did you learn them? I think that there is some
one among you who are sitting here, who is suffering like a
woman in labour, and saying, "Oh, that such a difficulty
does not present itself to me as that which has come to this
man; oh, that I should be wasting my life in a corner, when
I might be crowned at Olympia. When will any one an-
·nounce to me such a contest?" Such ought to be the disposition of all of you. Even among the gladiators of Cæsar
(the Emperor) there are some who complain grievously that
they are not brought forward and matched, and they offer
up prayers to God and address themselves to their superintendents intreating that they may fight.[3] And will no one
among you show himself such? I would willingly take a
voyage [to Rome] for this purpose and see what my athlete
is doing, how he is studying his subject.—I do not choose
such a subject, he says. Why, is it in your power to take
what subject you choose? There has been given to you
such a body as you have, such parents, such brethren, such
a country, such a place in your country :—then you come to
me and say, Change my subject. Have you not abilities
which enable you to manage the subject which has been
given to you? [You ought to say] : It is your business to
propose; it is mine to exercise myself well. However, you
do not say so, but you say, "Do not propose to me such a
tropic,[4] but such [as I would choose] : do not urge against me
such an objection, but such [as I would choose]." There
will be a time perhaps when tragic actors will suppose that
they are [only] masks and buskins and the long cloak.[5] I
say, these things, man, are your material and subject Utter
something that we may know whether you are a tragic actor

or a buffoon; for both of you have all the rest in common. If any one then should take away the tragic actor's buskins and his mask, and introduce him on the stage as a phantom, is the tragic actor lost, or does he still remain? If he has voice, he still remains.

An example of another kind. "Assume the governorship of a province." I assume it, and when I have assumed it, I show how an instructed man behaves. "Lay aside the laticlave (the mark of senatorial rank), and clothing yourself in rags, come forward in this character." What then have I not the power of displaying a good voice (that is, of doing something that I ought to do)? How then do you now appear (on the stage of life)? As a witness summoned by God. "Come forward,[6] you, and bear testimony for me, for you are worthy to be brought forward as a witness by me: is any thing external to the will good or bad? Do I hurt any man? have I made every man's interest dependent on any man except himself? What testimony do you give for God?"—I am in a wretched condition, Master[7] (Lord), and I am unfortunate; no man cares for me, no man gives me anything; all blame me, all speak ill of me.—Is this the evidence that you are going to give, and disgrace his summons, who has conferred so much honour on you, and thought you worthy of being called to bear such testimony?

But suppose that he who has the power has declared, "I judge you to be impious and profane." What has happened to you? I have been judged to be impious and profane? Nothing else? Nothing else. But if the same person had passed judgment on an hypothetical syllogism (συνημμένου), and had made a declaration, "the conclusion that, if it is day, it is light, I declare to be false," what has happened to the hypothetical syllogism? who is judged in this case? who has been condemned? the hypothetical syllogism, or the man who has been deceived by it? Does he then who has the power of making any declaration about you know what is pious or impious? Has he studied it, and has he learned it? Where? From whom? Then is it the fact that a musician pays no regard to him who declares that the lowest chord in the lyre is the highest; nor yet a geometrician, if he declares that the lines from the centre of a circle to the circumference are not equal; and shall he who is really instructed pay any regard to the uninstructed man when he pronounces judgment on what is pious and what is impious, on what is just and unjust? Oh, the signal wrong done by the instructed. Did they learn this here?

Will you not leave the small arguments (λογάρια) about these matters to others, to lazy fellows, that they may sit in a corner and receive their sorry pay, or grumble that no one gives them any thing: and will you not come forward and make use of what you have learned? For it is not these small arguments that are wanted now · the writings of the Stoics are full of them. What then is the thing which is wanted? A man who shall apply them, one who by his acts shall bear testimony to his words. Assume, I intreat you, this character, that we may no longer use in the schools the examples of the ancients, but may have some example of our own.

To whom then does the contemplation of these matters (philosophical inquiries) belong? To him who has leisure, for man is an animal that loves contemplation. But it is shameful to contemplate these things as runaway slaves do: we should sit, as in a theatre, free from distraction, and listen at one time to the tragic actor, at another time to the lute-player; and not do as slaves do. As soon as the slave has taken his station he praises the actor and at the same time looks round · then if any one calls out his master's name, the slave is immediately frightened and disturbed. It is shameful for philosophers thus to contemplate the works of nature. For what is a master? Man is not the master of man; but death is, and life and pleasure and pain; for if he comes without these things, bring Cæsar to me and you will see how firm I am. But when he shall come with these things, thundering and lightning,[8] and when I am afraid of them, what do I do then except to recognize my master like the runaway slave? But so long as I have any respite from these terrors, as a runaway slave stands in the theatre, so do I · I bathe, I drink, I sing; but all this I do with terror and uneasiness. But if I shall release myself from my masters, that is from those things by means of which masters are formidable, what further trouble have I, what master have I still?

What then, ought we to publish these things to all men? No, but we ought to accommodate ourselves to the ignorant⁹ (τοῖς ἰδιώταις) and to say: "This man recommends to me that which he thinks good for himself: I excuse him." For Socrates also excused the jailor, who had the charge of him in prison and was weeping when Socrates was going to drink the poison, and said, "How generously he laments over us."[11] Does he then say to the jailor that "for this reason we have sent away the women?" No, but he says it to his friends who were able to hear (understand) it; and he treats the jailor as a child.

NOTES

[1] The two chief prosecutors of Socrates (Plato, Apology, c 18; Epictetus, ii 2, 15).

[2] Socrates was condemned by the Athenians to die, and he was content to die, and thought that it was a good thing; and this was the reason why he made such a defence as he did, which brought on him condemnation; and he preferred condemnation to escaping it by entreating the dicasts (judges), and lamenting, and saying and doing things unworthy of himself, as others did.—Plato, Apology, cc. 29-33

[3] The Roman emperors kept gladiators for their own amusement and that of the people (Lipsius, Saturnalia, ii. 16). Seneca says (De Provid c 4), "I have heard a mirmillo (a kind of gladiator) in the time of C. Cæsar (Caligula) complaining of the rarity of gladiatorial exhibitions: 'What a glorious period of life is wasting.'" "Virtue," says Seneca, "is eager after dangers; and it considers only what it seeks, not what it may suffer."—Upton.

[4] Tropic (τροπικόν) a logical term used by Stoics, which Schweighauser translates "propositio connexa in syllogismo hypothetico"

The meaning of the whole is this. You do not like the work which is set before you· as we say, you are not content "to do your duty in that state of life unto which it shall please God to call you" Now this is as foolish, says Wolf, as for a man in any discussion to require that his adversary should raise no objection except such as may serve the man's own case.

[5] There will be a time when Tragic actors shall not know what their business is, but will think that it is all show. So, says Wolf, philosophers will be only beard and cloak, and will not show by their life and morals what they really are, or they will be like false monks, who only wear the cowl, and do not show a life of piety and sanctity.

[6] God is introduced as speaking.—Schweighäuser.

[7] The word is Κύριος, the name by which a slave in Epictetus addresses his master (dominus), a physician is addressed by his patient, and in other cases also it is used. It is also used by the Evangelists They speak of the angel of the Lord (Matt. i 24), and Jesus is addressed by the same term (Matt. viii. 2), Lord or master.

Mrs Carter has the following note. "It hath been observed that this manner of expression is not to be met with in the heathen anthors before Christianity, and therefore it is one instance of Scripture language coming early into common use."

But the word (κύριος) is used by early Greek writers to indicate one who has power or authority, and in a sense like the Roman "dominus" as by Sophocles for instance The use of the word then by Epictetus was not new, and it may have been used by the Stoic writers long before his time. The language of the Stoics was formed at least two centuries before the Christian era, and the New Testament writers would use the Greek word which was current in their age The notion of "Scripture language coming early into common use" is entirely unfounded, and is even absurd. Mrs. Carter's remark implies that Epictetus used the Scripture language, whereas he used the particular language of the Stoics, and the general language of his age, and the New Testament writers would do the same There are resemblances between the language of Epictetus and the New Testament writers, such as the expression μὴ γένοιτο of Paul, which Epictetus often uses; but this is a slight matter The words of Peter (Ep. ii 1, 4), "that by these ye might be partakers of the divine nature," are a Stoic expression, and the writer of this Epistle, I think, took them from the language of the Stoics.

⁸ Upton supposes that Epictetus is alluding to the verse of Aristophanes (Acharn. 531), where it is said of Pericles:

"He flashed, he thundered, and confounded Hellas."

⁹ He calls the uninstructed and ignorant by the Greek word "Idiotæ," "idiots," which we now use in a peculiar sense. An Idiota was a private individual as opposed to one who filled some public office, and thence it had generally the sense of one who was ignorant of any particular act, as, for instance, one who had not studied philosophy.

¹⁰ Compare the Phædon of Plato (p. 116). The children of Socrates were brought in to see him before he took the poison by which he died; and also the wives of the friends of Socrates who attended him to his death Socrates had ordered his wife Xanthippe to be led home before he had his last conversation with his friends, and she was taken away lamenting and bewailing.

CHAPTER XXX

WHAT WE OUGHT TO HAVE READY IN DIFFICULT CIRCUM-STANCES[1]

WHEN you are going in to any great personage, remember that another also from above sees what is going on, and that you ought to please him rather than the other. He then who sees from above asks you: "In the schools what used you to say about exile and bonds and death and disgrace?" I used to say that they are things indifferent (neither good nor bad). "What then do you say of them now? Are they changed at all?" No. "Are you changed then?" No. "Tell me then what things are indifferent?" The things which are independent of the will "Tell me, also, what follows from this." The things which are independent of the will are nothing to me. "Tell me also about the Good, what was your opinion?" A will such as we ought to have and also such a use of appearances. "And the end (purpose), what is it?" To follow thee. "Do you say this now also?" I say the same now also.

Then go in to the great personage boldly and remember these things; and you will see what a youth is who has studied these things when he is among men who have not studied them. I indeed imagine that you will have such thoughts as these: Why do we make so great and so many preparations for nothing? Is this the thing which men name power? Is this the antechamber? this the men of the bed-chamber? this the armed guards? Is it for this that I listened to so many discourses? All this is nothing: but I have been preparing myself as for something great.

NOTE

[1] The reader may understand why Epictetus gave such a lesson as this, if he will remember the tyranny under which men at that time lived.

BOOK II

CHAPTER I

THAT COURAGE IS NOT INCONSISTENT WITH CAUTION

THE opinion of the philosophers perhaps seems to some to be a paradox; but still let us examine as well as we can, if it is true that it is possible to do everything both with caution and with confidence. For caution seems to be in a manner contrary to confidence, and contraries are in no way consistent. That which seems to many to be a paradox in the matter under consideration in my opinion is of this kind: if we asserted that we ought to employ caution and confidence in the same things, men might justly accuse us of bringing together things which can not be united. But now where is the difficulty in what is said? for if these things are true, which have been often said and often proved, that the nature of good is in the use of appearances, and the nature of evil likewise, and that things independent of our will do not admit either the nature of evil nor of good, what paradox do the philosophers assert if they say that where things are not dependent on the will, there you should employ confidence, but where they are dependent on the will, there you should employ caution? For if the bad consists in a bad exercise of the will, caution ought only to be used where things are dependent on the will. But if things independent of the will and not in our power are nothing to us, with respect to these we must employ confidence; and thus we shall both be cautious and confident, and indeed confident because of our caution. For by employing caution towards things which are really bad, it will result that we shall have confidence with respect to things which are not so.

We are then in the condition of deer,[1] when they flee from the huntsmen's feathers in fright, whither do they turn and in what do they seek refuge as safe? They turn to the nets, and thus they perish by confounding things which are objects of fear with things that they ought not to fear. Thus we also act: in what cases do we fear? In things which are independent of the will. In what cases on the contrary do we behave with confidence, as if there were no danger? In things dependent on the will. To be deceived then, or to act rashly, or shamelessly or with base desire to seek something, does not concern us at all, if we only hit the mark in things which are independent of our will. But where there is death, or exile or pain or infamy, there we attempt to run away, there we are struck with terror. Therefore as we may expect it to happen with those who err in the greatest matters, we convert natural confidence (that is, according to nature, into audacity, desperation, rashness, shamelessness; and we convert natural caution and modesty into cowardice and meanness, which are full of fear and confusion. For if a man should transfer caution to those things in which the will may be exercised and the acts of the will, he will immediately by willing to be cautious have also the power of avoiding what he chooses: but if he transfer it to the things which are not in his power and will, and attempt to avoid the things which are in the power of others, he will of necessity fear, he will be unstable, he will be disturbed. For death or pain is not formidable, but the fear of pain or death. For this reason we commend the poet[2] who said

"Not death is evil, but a shameful death."

Confidence (courage) then ought to be employed against death, and caution against the fear of death. But now we do the contrary, and employ against death the attempt to escape; and to our opinion about it we employ carelessness, rashness and indifference. These things Socrates properly used to call tragic masks; for as to children masks appear terrible and fearful from inexperience, we also are affected in like manner by events (the things which happen in life) for no other reason than children are by masks. For what is a child? Ignorance. What is a child? Want of knowledge. For when a child knows these things, he is in no way inferior to us. What is death? A tragic mask. Turn it and examine it. See, it does not bite. The poor body must be separated[3] from the spirit either now or later as it was separated from it before. Why then are you troubled, if it be separated now? for if it is not separated now, it will be separated afterwards. Why? That the period of the universe may be completed,[4] for it has need of the present, and of the future, and of the past. What is pain? A mask. Turn it and examine it. The poor flesh is moved roughly, then on the contrary smoothly. If this does not satisfy (please) you, the door is open: if it does, bear (with things). For the door ought to be open for all occasions; and so we have no trouble.

What then is the fruit of these opinions? It is that which ought to be the most noble and the most becoming to those who are really educated; release from perturbation, release from fear, freedom. For in these matters we must not believe the many, who say that free persons only ought to be educated, but we should rather believe the philosophers who say that the educated only are free. How is this? In this manner. Is freedom any thing else than the power of living as we choose? Nothing else. Tell me then, ye men, do you wish to live in error? We do not. No one then who lives in error is free. Do you wish to live in fear? Do you wish to live in sorrow? Do you wish to live in perturbation? By no means. No one then who is in a state of fear or sorrow or perturbation is free; but whoever is delivered from sorrows and fears and perturbations, he is at the same time also delivered from servitude. How then can we continue to believe you, most dear legislators, when you say, We only allow free persons to be educated? For philosophers say we allow none to be free except the educated; that is, God does not allow it. When then a man has turned[5] round before the prætor his own slave, has he done nothing? He has done something. What? He has turned round his own slave before the prætor. Has he done nothing more? Yes: he is also bound to pay for him the tax called the twentieth. Well then, is not the man who has gone through this

ceremony become free? No more than he is become free
from perturbations. Have you who are able to turn round
(free) others no master? is not money your master, or a girl
or a boy, or some tyrant, or some friend of the tyrant? why
do you tremble then when you are going off to any trial
(danger) of this kind? It is for this reason that I often
say, study and hold in readiness these principles by which
you may determine what those things are with reference to
which you ought to have confidence (courage), and those
things with reference to which you ought to be cautious:
courageous in that which does not depend on your will; cautious in that which does depend on it.

Well have I not read to you,[6] and do you not know what
I was doing? In what? In my little dissertations.—Show me
how you are with respect to desire and aversion (ἔκκλισιν):
and show me if you do not fail in getting what you wish,
and if you do not fall into the things which you would avoid:
but as to these long and laboured sentences you will take
them and blot them out.

What then did not Socrates write? And who wrote so
much?[7]—But how? As he could not always have at hand
one to argue against his principles or to be argued against
in turn, he used to argue with and examine himself, and he
was always treating at least some one subject in a practical
way. These are the things which a philosopher writes. But
little dissertations and that method, which I speak of, he
leaves to others, to the stupid, or to those happy men who
being free from perturbations[8] have leisure, or to such as
are too foolish to reckon consequences.

And will you now, when the opportunity invites, go and
display those things which you possess, and recite them, and
make an idle show, and say, See how I make dialogues? Do
not so, my man; but rather say; See how I am not disappointed of that which I desire: See how I do not fall into
that which I would avoid. Set death before me, and you
will see. Set before me pain, prison, disgrace and condemnation. This is the proper display of a young man who is
come out of the schools. But leave the rest to others, and
let no one ever hear you say a word about these things; and
if any man commends you for them, do not allow it; but

think that you are nobody and know nothing. Only show
that you know this, how never to be disappointed in your
desire and how never to fall into that which you would
avoid. Let others labour at forensic causes, problems and
syllogisms do you labour at thinking about death,[9] chains,
the rack, exile ;[10] and do all this with confidence and reliance
on him who has called you to these sufferings, who has
judged you worthy of the place in which being stationed
you will show what things the rational governing power
can do when it takes its stand against the forces which are
not within the power of our will. And thus this paradox
will no longer appear either impossible or a paradox, that a
man ought to be at the same time cautious and courageous :
courageous towards the things which do not depend on the
will, and cautious in things which are within the power of
the will.

NOTES

[1] It was the fashion of hunters to frighten deer by displaying feathers
of various colours on ropes or strings and thus frightening them towards
the nets Virgil, Georg iii. 372—

Puniceæve agitant pavidos formidine pennæ.

[2] Euripides, Fragments.
[3] It was the opinion of some philosophers that the soul was a portion
of the divinity sent down into human bodies.
[4] This was a doctrine of Heraclitus and of Zeno. Zeno (Diog. Laert.
vii 137) speaks of God as "in certain periods or revolutions of time
exhausting into himself the universal substance (οὐσία) and again
generating it out of himself" Antoninus (xi. 1) speaks of the periodical renovation of all things. For man, whose existence is so short, the
doctrine of all existing things perishing in the course of time and then
being renewed, is of no practical value. The present is enough for most
men But for the few who are able to embrace in thought the past, the
present and the future, the contemplation of the perishable nature of
all existing things may have a certain value by elevating their minds
above the paltry things which others prize above their worth.
[5] This is an allusion to one of the Roman modes of manumitting a
slave before the prætor.
[6] The sum paid on manumission was a tax of five per cent., established
in B C. 356 and paid by the slave. Epictetus here speaks of the tax
being paid by the master; but in iii 26, he speaks of it as paid by the
enfranchised slave.
[7] These are the words of some pupil who is boasting of what he has
written
[8] No other author speaks of Socrates having written any thing It
is therefore very difficult to explain this passage in which Arrian, who
took down the words of Epictetus, represents him as saying that Soc-

rates wrote so much. Socrates talked much, and Epictetus may have spoken of talking as if it were writing; for he must have known that Socrates was not a writer.

⁸The word is ὑπὸ ἀταραξίας. Mrs. Carter thinks that the true reading is ὑπὸ ἀπραξίας, 'through idleness' or 'having nothing to do'; and she remarks that 'freedom from perturbations' is the very thing that Epictetus had been recommending through the whole chapter and is the subject of the next chapter, and therefore can not be well supposed to be the true reading in a place where it is mentioned with contempt. It is probable that Mrs. Carter is right Upton thinks that Epictetus is alluding to the Sophists, and that we should understand him as speaking ironically; and this may also be right. Schweighäuser attempts to explain the passage by taking 'free from perturbations' in the ordinary simple sense; but I doubt if he has succeeded.

⁹"The whole life of philosophers," says Cicero (Tusc. i. 30), following Plato, "is a reflection upon death"

¹⁰"Some English readers, too happy to comprehend how chains, torture, exile and sudden executions, can be ranked among the common accidents of life, may be surprised to find Epictetus so frequently endeavouring to prepare his hearers for them. But it must be recollected that he addressed himself to persons who lived under the Roman emperors, from whose tyranny the very best of men were perpetually liable to such kind of dangers."—Mrs. Carter. All men even now are exposed to accidents and misfortunes against which there is no security, and even the most fortunate of men must die at last. The lessons of Epictetus may be as useful now as they were in his time.

CHAPTER II

CONSIDER, you who are going into court, what you wish to maintain and what you wish to succeed in. For if you wish to maintain a will conformable to nature, you have every security, every facility, you have no troubles. For if you wish to maintain what is in your own power and is naturally free, and if you are content with these, what else do you care for? For who is the master of such things? Who can take them away? If you choose to be modest and faithful, who shall not allow you to be so? If you choose not to be restrained or compelled, who shall compel you to desire what you think that you ought not to desire? who shall compel you to avoid what you do not think fit to avoid? But what do you say? The judge will determine against you something that appears formidable; but that you should also suffer in trying to avoid it, how can he do that? When then the pursuit of objects and the avoiding of them are in your power, what else do you care for? Let this be your preface,[1] this your narrative, this your confirmation, this your victory, this your peroration, this your applause (or the approbation which you will receive).

Therefore Socrates said to one who was reminding him to prepare for his trial,[2] "Do you not think then that I have been preparing for it all my life?" By what kind of preparation? "I have maintained that which was in my own power." How then? "I have never done anything unjust either in my private or in my public life."

But if you wish to maintain externals also, your poor body, your little property and your little estimation, I advise you to make from this moment all possible preparation, and then consider both the nature of your judge and your adversary. If it is necessary to embrace his knees, embrace his knees; if to weep, weep; if to groan, groan. For when you have subjected to externals what is your own, then be a slave and do not resist, and do not sometimes choose to be a slave, and sometimes not choose, but with all your mind be one or the other, either free or a slave, either instructed or uninstructed, either a well bred cock or a mean one, either endure to be beaten until you die or yield at once; and let it not happen to you to receive many stripes and then to yield. But if these things are base, determine immediately. Where is the nature of evil and good? It is where truth is: where truth is and where nature is, there is caution: where truth is, there is courage where nature is.

For what do you think? do you think that, if Socrates had wished to preserve externals, he would have come forward and said: "Anytus and Melitus can certainly kill me, but to harm me they are not able?" Was he so foolish as not to see that this way leads not to the preservation of life and fortune, but to another end? What is the reason then that he takes no account of his adversaries, and even irritates them? Just in the same way my friend Heraclitus, who had a little suit in Rhodes about a bit of land, and had proved to the judges (δικασταῖς) that his case was just, said when he had come to the peroration of his speech, "I will neither intreat you nor do I care what judgment you will give, and it is you rather than I who are on your trial." And thus he ended the business. What need was there of this? Only do not intreat; but do not also say, "I do not intreat;" unless there is a fit occasion to irritate purposely the judges, as was the case with Socrates. And you, if you are preparing such a peroration, why do you wait, why do you obey the order to submit to trial? For if you wish to be crucified, wait and the cross will come: but if you choose to submit and to plead your cause as well as you can, you must do what is consistent with this object, provided you maintain what is your own (your proper character).

For this reason also it is ridiculous to say, Suggest something to me[3] (tell me what to do). What should I suggest to you? Well, form my mind so as to accommodate itself to any event. Why that is just the same as if a man who is ignorant of letters should say, "Tell me what to write when any name is proposed to me." For if I should tell him to write Dion, and then another should come and propose to him not the name of Dion but that of Theon, what will be

done? what will he write?   But if you have practised writing, you are also prepared to write (or to do) any thing that
is required.   If[4] you are not, what can I now suggest?   For
if circumstances require something else, what will you say,
or what will you do?   Remember then this general precept
and you will need no suggestion.   But if you gape after externals, you must of necessity ramble up and down in obedience to the will of your master.   And who is the master?
He who has the power over the things which you seek to
gain or try or avoid.

NOTES

[1] Epictetus refers to the rhetorical divisions of a speech.

[2] Xenophon has reported this saying of Socrates on the authority of
Hermogenes.

[3] "The meaning is, You must not ask for advice when you are come
into a difficulty, but every man ought to have such principles as to be
ready on all occasions to act as he ought; just as he who knows how
to write can write any name which is proposed to him."—Wolf

[4] "The reader must know that these dissertations were spoken ex-
tempore, and that one thing after another would come into the thoughts
of the speaker.   So the reader will not be surprised that when the discourse is on the maintenance of firmness or freedom from perturbations, Epictetus should now speak of philosophical preparation, which
is most efficient for the maintenance of firmness."—Wolf.

CHAPTER III

D IOGENES said well to one who asked from him letters of recommendation, "That you are a man, he said, he will know as soon as he sees you; and he will know whether you are good or bad, if he is by experience skilful to distinguish the good and the bad; but if he is without experience, he will never know, if I write to him ten thousand times."[1] For it is just the same as if a drachma (a piece of silver money) asked to be recommended to a person to be tested. If he is skilful in testing silver, he will know what you are, for you (the drachma) will recommend yourself. We ought then in life also to have some skill as in the case of silver coin that a man may be able to say like the judge of silver. Bring me any drachma and I will test it. But in the case of syllogisms, I would say, Bring any man that you please, and I will distinguish for you the man who knows how to resolve syllogisms and the man who does not. Why? Because I know how to resolve syllogisms. I have the power, which a man must have who is able to discover those who have the power of resolving syllogisms. But in life how do I act? At one time I call a thing good, and at another time bad. What is the reason? The contrary to that which is in the case of syllogisms, ignorance and inexperience.

NOTE

[1] Mrs. Carter says "This is one of the many extravagant refinements of the philosophers; and might lead persons into very dangerous mistakes, if it was laid down as a maxim in ordinary life." I think that Mrs. Carter has not seen the meaning of Epictetus. The philosopher will discover the man's character by trying him, as the assayer tries the silver by a test.

Cicero (De legibus, i. 9) says that the face expresses the hidden character. Euripides (Medea, 518) says better, that no mark is impressed on the body by which we can distinguish the good man from the bad. Shakespere says

"There's no art
To find the mind's construction in the face."
Macbeth, act i. sc. 4.

CHAPTER IV

AGAINST A PERSON WHO HAD ONCE BEEN DETECTED IN ADULTERY

AS Epictetus was saying that man is formed for fidelity, and that he who subverts fidelity subverts the peculiar characteristic of men, there entered one of those who are considered to be men of letters, who had once been detected in adultery in the city. Then Epictetus continued, But if we lay aside this fidelity for which we are formed and make designs against our neighbour's wife, what are we doing? What else but destroying and overthrowing? Whom, the man of fidelity, the man of modesty, the man of sanctity. Is this all? And are we not overthrowing neighbourhood, and friendship, and the community; and in what place are we putting ourselves? How shall I consider you, man? As a neighbour, as a friend? What kind of one? As a citizen? Wherein shall I trust you? So if you were an utensil so worthless that a man could not use you, you would be pitched out on the dung heaps, and no man would pick you up. But if being a man you are unable to fill any place which befits a man, what shall we do with you? For suppose that you can not hold the place of a friend, can you hold the place of a slave? And who will trust you? Are you not then content that you also should be pitched somewhere on a dung heap, as a useless utensil, and a bit of dung? Then will you say, no man cares for me, a man of letters? They do not, because you are bad and useless. It is just as if the wasps complained because no man cares for them, but all fly from them, and if a man can, he strikes them and knocks them down. You have such a sting that you throw into trouble and pain any man that you wound with it. What would you have us do with you? You have no place where you can be put.

"What then, are not women common by nature?"[1] So I say also; for a little pig is common to all the invited guests, but when the portions have been distributed, go, if you think it right, and snatch up the portion of him who reclines next to you, or slily steal it, or place your hand down by it and lay hold of it, and if you can tear away a bit of the meat, grease your fingers and lick them. A fine companion over cups, and Socratic guest indeed! Well, is not the theatre common to the citizens? When then they have taken their seats, come, if you think proper, and eject one of them. In this way women also are common by nature. When then the legislator, like the master of a feast, has disturbed them, will you not also look for your own portion and not filch and handle what belongs to another. " But I am a man of letters and understand Archedemus." [2] Understand Archedemus then, and be an adulterer, and faithless, and instead of a man, be a wolf or an ape; for what is the difference? [3]

NOTES

[1] It is not clear what is meant by women being common by nature in any rational sense. Zeno and his school said "it is their opinion also that the women should be common among the wise, so that any man should use any woman, as Zeno says in his Polity, and Chrysippus in the book on Polity, and Diogenes the Cynic, and Plato; and we shall love all the children equally like fathers, and the jealousy about adultery will be removed." These wise men knew little about human nature, if they taught such doctrines.

[2] Archedemus was a Stoic philosopher of Tarsus. We know little about him.

[3] A man may be a philosopher or pretend to be; and at the same time he may be a beast.

CHAPTER V

THINGS themselves (material) are indifferent;[1] but the use of them is not indifferent. How then shall a man preserve firmness and tranquillity, and at the same time be careful and neither rash nor negligent? If he imitates those who play at dice. The counters are indifferent; the dice are indifferent. How do I know what the cast will be? But to use carefully and dexterously the cast of the dice, this is my business.[2] Thus then in life also the chief business is this: distinguish and separate things, and say, Externals are not in my power: will is in my power. Where shall I seek the good and the bad? Within, in the things which are my own. But in what does not belong to you call nothing either good or bad, or profit or damage or any thing of the kind.

What then? Should we use such things carelessly? In no way: for this on the other hand is bad for the faculty of the will, and consequently against nature; but we should act carefully because the use is not indifferent, and we should also act with firmness and freedom from perturbations because the material is indifferent. For where the material is not indifferent, there no man can hinder me nor compel me. Where I can be hindered and compelled, the obtaining of those things is not in my power, nor is it good or bad; but the use is either bad or good, and the use is in my power. But it is difficult to mingle and to bring together these two things, the carefulness of him who is affected by the matter (or things about him) and the firmness of him who has no regard for it; but it is not impossible: and if it is, happiness is impossible. But we should act as we do in the case of a voyage. What can I do? I can choose the master of the ship, the sailors, the day, the opportunity. Then comes a storm. What more have I to care for? for my part is done. The business belongs to another, the master.—But the ship is sinking—what then have I to do? I do the only

thing that I can, not to be drowned full of fear, nor screaming nor blaming God, but knowing that what has been produced must also perish: for I am not an immortal being, but
a man, a part of the whole, as an hour is a part of the day:
I must be present like the hour, and past like the hour.
What difference then does it make to me, how I pass away,
whether by being suffocated or by a fever, for I must pass
through some such means?

This is just what you will see those doing who play at
ball skilfully. No one cares about the ball[3] as being good
or bad, but about throwing and catching it. In this therefore is the skill, in this the art, the quickness, the judgment,
so that even if I spread out my lap I may not be able to
catch it, and another, if I throw, may catch the ball. But if
with perturbation and fear we receive or throw the ball, what
kind of play is it then, and wherein shall a man be steady,
and how shall a man see the order in the game? But one
will say, "Throw;" or "Do not throw;" and another will say,
"You have thrown once." This is quarrelling, not play.

Socrates then knew how to play at ball. How? By
using pleasantry in the court where he was tried. "Tell me,"
he says, "Anytus, how do you say that I do not believe in
God. The Dæmons ($\delta\alpha\iota\mu o\nu\epsilon\varsigma$), who are they, think you? Are
they not sons of Gods, or compounded of gods and men?"
When Anytus admitted this, Socrates said, "Who then, think
you, can believe that there are mules (half asses), but not
asses." And this he said as if he were playing at ball.[4] And
what was the ball in this case? Life, chains, banishment, a
draught of poison, separation from wife and leaving children orphans. These were the things which he was playing;
but still he did play and threw the ball skilfully. So we
should do: we must employ all the care of the players, but
show the same indifference about the ball. For we ought
by all means to apply our art to some external material, not
as valuing the material, but, whatever it may be, showing our
art in it. Thus too the weaver does not make wool, but exercises his art upon such as he receives. Another gives you
food and property and is able to take them away and your
poor body also. When then you have received the material,
work on it. If then you come out (of the trial) without

8

having suffered anything, all who meet you will congratulate you on your escape; but he who knows how to look at such things, if he shall see that you have behaved properly in the matter, will commend you and be pleased with you; and if he shall find that you owe your escape to any want of proper behaviour, he will do the contrary. For where rejoicing is reasonable, there also is congratulation reasonable.

How then is it said that some external things are according to nature and others contrary to nature? It is said as it might be said if we were separated from union (or society): for to the foot I shall say that it is according to nature for it to be clean; but if you take it as a foot and as a thing not detached (independent), it will befit it both to step into the mud and tread on thorns, and sometimes to be cut off for the good of the whole body, otherwise it is no longer a foot. We should think in some such way about ourselves also. What are you? A man. If you consider yourself as detached from other men, it is according to nature to live to old age, to be rich, to be healthy. But if you consider yourself as a man and a part of a certain whole, it is for the sake of that whole that at one time you should be sick, at another time take a voyage and run into danger, and at another time be in want, and in some cases die prematurely. Why then are you troubled? Do you not know, that as a foot is no longer a foot if it is detached from the body, so you are no longer a man if you are separated from other men. For what is a man? A part of a state, of that first which consists of Gods and of men; then of that which is called next to it, which is a small image of the universal state. What then must I be brought to trial; must another have a fever, another sail on the sea, another die, and another be condemned? Yes, for it is impossible in such a body, in such a universe of things, among so many living together, that such things should not happen, some to one and others to others. It is your duty then since you are come here, to say what you ought, to arrange these things as it is fit.[5] Then some one says, "I shall charge you with doing me wrong." Much good may it do you: I have done my part; but whether you also have done yours, you must look to that; for there is some danger of this too, that it may escape your notice.

[1]The materials (ὕλαι) on which man works are neither good nor bad, and so they are, as Epictetus names them, indifferent. But the use of things, or of material, is not indifferent. They may be used well or ill, conformably to nature or not.

[2] Terence says (Adelphi, iv. 7)—

> Si illud, quod est maxime opus, jactu non cadit,
> Illud quod cecidit forte, id arte ut corrigas.

'Dexterously' is 'arte,' τεχνικῶς in Epictetus.—Upton.

[3] The word is ἁρπαστόν, which was also used by the Romans. One threw the ball and the other caught it. Chrysippus used this simile of a ball in speaking of giving and receiving (Seneca, "De Beneficiis," ii 17). Martial has the word ("Epigrams" iv. 19) "Sive harpasta manu pulverulenta rapis"; and elsewhere.

[4] In Plato's "Apology," Socrates addresses Meletus; and he says, it would be equally absurd if a man should believe that there are foals of horses and asses, and should not believe that there are horses and asses. But Socrates says nothing of mules, for the word mules in some texts of the "Apology" is manifestly wrong.

[5] He tells some imaginary person, who hears him, that since he is come into the world, he must do his duty in it.

CHATPER VI

OF INDIFFERENCE

THE hypothetical proposition is indifferent: the judgment about it is not indifferent, but it is either knowledge or opinion or error. Thus life is indifferent: the use is not indifferent. When any man then tells you that these things also are indifferent, do not become negligent; and when a man invites you to be careful (about such things), do not become abject and struck with admiration of material things. And it is good for you to know your own preparation and power, that in those matters where you have not been prepared, you may keep quiet, and not be vexed, if others have the advantage over you. For you too in syllogisms will claim to have the advantage over them; and if others should be vexed at this, you will console them by saying, "I have learned them, and you have not." Thus also where there is need of any practice, seek not that which is acquired from the need (of such practice), but yield in that matter to those who have had practice, and be yourself content with firmness of mind.

Go and salute a certain person. How? Not meanly.— But I have been shut out, for I have not learned to make my way through the window; and when I have found the door shut, I must either come back or enter through the window.—But still speak to him —In what way? Not meanly. But suppose that you have not got what you wanted. Was this your business, and not his? Why then do you claim that which belongs to another? Always remember what is your own, and what belongs to another; and you will not be disturbed. Chrysippus therefore said well, So long as future things are uncertain, I always cling to those which are more adapted to the conservation of that which is according to nature; for God himself has given me the faculty of such choice. But if I knew that it was fated (in the order of things) for me to be sick, I would even move towards it; for the foot also, if it had intelligence, would move to go into the mud. For why are ears of corn produced? Is it not that they may become dry? And do they not become dry that they may be reaped?[2] for they are not separated from communion with other things. If then they had perception, ought they to wish never to be reaped? But this is a curse upon ears of corn, to be never reaped. So we must know that in the case of men too it is a curse not to die, just the same as not to be ripened and not to be reaped. But since we must be reaped, and we also know that we are reaped, we are vexed at it; for we neither know what we are nor have we studied what belongs to man, as those who have studied horses know what belongs to horses. But Chrysantas[3] when he was going to strike the enemy checked himself when he heard the trumpet sounding a retreat: so it seemed better to him to obey the general's command than to follow his own inclination. But not one of us chooses, even when necessity summons, readily to obey it, but weeping and groaning we suffer what we do suffer, and we call them circumstances. What kind of circumstances, man? If you give the name of circumstances to the things which are around you, all things are circumstances; but if you call hardships by this name, what hardship is there in the dying of that which has been produced? But that which destroys is either a sword, or a wheel, or a sea, or a tile, or a tyrant. Why do you care about the way of going down to Hades? All ways are equal.[4] But if you will listen to the truth, the way which the tyrant sends you is shorter. A tyrant never killed a man in six months: but a fever is often a year about it. All these things are only sound and the noise of empty names.

I am in danger of my life from Cæsar. And am not I in danger who dwell in Nicopolis, where there are so many earthquakes: and when you are crossing the Hadriatic, what hazard do you run? Is it not the hazard of your life? But I am in danger also as to opinion. Do you mean your own? how? For who can compel you to have any opinion which you do not choose? But is it as to another man's opinion? and what kind of danger is yours, if others have false opinions? But I am in danger of being banished. What is it to be banished? To be somewhere else than at Rome?

Yes: what then if I should be sent to Gyara? If that suits you, you will go there; but if it does not, you can go to another place instead of Gyara, whither he also will go, who sends you to Gyara, whether he choose or not. Why then do you go up to Rome as if it were something great? It is not worth all this preparation, that an ingenuous youth should say, it was not worth while to have heard so much and to have written so much and to have sat so long by the side of an old man who is not worth much. Only remember that division by which your own and not your own are distinguished: never claim any thing which belongs to others. A tribunal and a prison are each a place, one high and the other low; but the will can be maintained equal, if you choose to maintain it equal in each. And we shall then be imitators of Socrates, when we are able to write pæans in prison.[5] But in our present disposition, consider if we could endure in prison another person saying to us, "Would you like me to read Pæans to you?" "Why do you trouble me? do you not know the evils which hold me? Can I in such circumstances (listen to pæans)?" "What circumstances?" "I am going to die." "And will other men be immortal?"

[1] This discussion is with a young philosopher who, intending to return from Nicopolis to Rome, feared the tyranny of Domitian, who was particularly severe towards philosophers.
The title "of indifference" means "of the indifference of things;" of the things which are neither good nor bad.
[2] Epictetus alludes to the verses from the Hypsipyle of Euripides. Compare Antoninus (vii. 40): "Life must be reaped like the ripe ears of corn: one man is born: another dies." Cicero (Tuscul. Disp. iii. 25) has translated six verses from Euripides, and among them are these two:

> tum vita omnibus
> Metenda ut fruges: sic jubet necessitas.

[3] The story is in Xenophon's Cyropædia (IV, near the beginning) where Cyrus says that he called Chrysantas by name Epictetus, as Upton remarks, quotes from memory.
[4] So Anaxagoras said that the road to the other world (ad inferos) is the same from all places (Cicero, Tusc. Disp i. 43.) What follows is one of the examples of extravagant assertion in Epictetus. A tyrant may kill by a slow death as a fever does I suppose that Epictetus

would have some answer to that. Except to a Stoic the ways to death are not indifferent: some ways of dying are painful, and even he who can endure with fortitude, would prefer an easy death.

* Diogenes Laertius reports in his life of Socrates that he wrote in prison a Pæan, and he gives the first line which contains an address to Apollo and Artemis.

CHAPTER VII

THROUGH an unreasonable regard to divination many of us omit many duties.[1] For what more can the diviner see than death or danger or disease, or generally things of that kind? If then I must expose myself to danger for a friend, and if it is my duty even to die for him, what need have I then for divination? Have I not within me a diviner who has told me the nature of good and of evil, and has explained to me the signs (or marks) of both? What need have I then to consult the viscera of victims or the flight of birds, and why do I submit when he says, "It is for your interest?" For does he know what is for my interest, does he know what is good; and as he has learned the signs of the viscera, has he also learned the signs of good and evil? For if he knows the signs of these, he knows the signs both of the beautiful and of the ugly, and of the just and of the unjust. Do you tell me, man, what is the thing which is signified for me; is it life or death, poverty or wealth? But whether these things are for my interest or whether they are not, I do not intend to ask you. Why don't you give your opinion on matters of grammar, and why do you give it here about things on which we are all in error and disputing with one another?[2] The woman therefore, who intended to send by a vessel a month's provisions to Gratilla[3] in her banishment, made a good answer to him who said that Domitian would seize what she sent, I would rather, she replied, that Domitian should seize all than that I should not send it.

What then leads us to frequent use of divination? Cowardice, the dread of what will happen. This is the reason why we flatter the diviners. Pray, master, shall I succeed to the property of my father? Let us see: let us sacrifice on the occasion—Yes, master, as fortune chooses.—When he has said, You shall succeed to the inheritance, we thank him as if we received the inheritance from him.   The consequence is that they play upon us.[4]

What then should we do? We ought to come (to divination) without desire or aversion, as the wayfarer asks of the man whom he meets which of two roads leads (to his journey's end), without any desire for that which leads to the right rather than to the left, for he has no wish to go by any road except the road which leads (to his end).   In the same way ought we to come to God also as a guide; as we use our eyes, not asking them to show us rather such things as we wish, but receiving the appearances of things such as the eyes present them to us.   But now we trembling take the augur (bird interpreter) by the hand, and while we invoke God we intreat the augur, and say "Master have mercy on me; suffer me to come safe out of this difficulty."   Wretch, would you have then any thing other than what is best?   Is there then any thing better than what pleases God?   Why do you, as far as in your power, corrupt your judge and lead astray your adviser?

NOTES

[1]Divination was a great part of ancient religion, and, as Epictetus says, it led men "to omit many duties" In a certain sense there was some meaning in it. If it is true that those who believe in God can see certain signs in the administration of the world by which they can judge what their behaviour ought to be, they can learn what their duties are. If these signs are misunderstood, or if they are not seen right, men may be governed by an abject superstition So the external forms of any religion may become the means of corruption and of human debasement, and the true indications of God's will may be neglected. Upton compares Lucan (ix. 572), who sometimes said a few good things.

[2]A man who gives his opinion on grammar gives an opinion on a thing of which many know something. A man who gives his opinion on divination or on future events, gives an opinion on things of which we all know nothing When then a man affects to instruct on things unknown, we may ask him to give his opinion on things which are known, and so we may learn what kind of man he is.

[3]Gratilla was a lady of rank, who was banished from Rome and Italy by Domitian.

[4]As knavish priests have often played on the fears and hopes of the superstitious.

CHAPTER VIII

GOD is beneficial. But the Good also is beneficial.[2] It is consistent then that where the nature of God is, there also the nature of the good should be. What then is the nature of God?[3] Flesh? Certainly not. An estate in land? By no means. Fame? No. Is it intelligence, knowledge, right reason? Yes. Herein then simply seek the nature of the good; for I suppose that you do not seek it in a plant. No. Do you seek it in an irrational animal? No. If then you seek it in a rational animal, why do you still seek it any where except in the superiority of rational over irrational minds?[4] Now plants have not even the power of using appearances, and for this reason you do not apply the term good to them. The good then requires the use of appearances. Does it require this use only? For if you say that it requires this use only, say that the good, and that happiness and unhappiness are in irrational animals also. But you do not say this, and you do right; for if they possess even in the highest degree the use of appearances, yet they have not the faculty of understanding the use of appearances; and there is good reason for this, for they exist for the purpose of serving others, and they exercise no superiority. For the ass, I suppose, does not exist for any superiority over others. No; but because we had need of a back which is able to bear something; and in truth we had need also of his being able to walk, and for this reason he received also the faculty of making use of appearances, for otherwise he would not have been able to walk. And here then the matter stopped. For if he had also received the faculty of comprehending the use of appearances, it is plain that consistently with reason he would not then have been subjected to us, nor would he have done us these services, but he would have been equal to us and like to us.

Will you not then seek the nature of good in the rational animal? for if it is not there, you will not choose to say that it exists in any other thing (plant or animal). What then? are not plants and animals also the works of God? They are; but they are not superior things, nor yet parts of the Gods? But you are a superior thing; you are a portion separated from the deity; you have in yourself a certain portion of him. Why then are you ignorant of your own noble descent?[5] Why do you not know whence you came? will you not remember when you are eating, who you are who eat and whom you feed? When you are in conjunction with a woman, will you not remember who you are who do this thing? When you are in social intercourse, when you are exercising yourself, when you are engaged in discussion, know you not that you are nourishing a god, that you are exercising a god? Wretch, you are carrying about a god with you, and you know it not.[6] Do you think that I mean some God of silver or of gold, and external? You carry him within yourself, and you perceive not that you are polluting him by impure thoughts and dirty deeds. And if an image of God were present, you would not dare to do any of the things which you are doing: but when God himself is present within and sees all and hears all, you are not ashamed of thinking and doing such things, ignorant as you are of your own nature and subject to the anger of God. Then why do we fear when we are sending a young man from the school into active life, lest he should do anything improperly, eat improperly, have improper intercourse with women; and lest the rags in which he is wrapped should debase him, lest fine garments should make him proud? This youth (if he acts thus) does not know his own God: he knows not with whom he sets out (into the world). But can we endure when he says " I wish I had you (God) with me." Have you not God with you? and do you seek for any other, when you have him? or will God tell you any thing else than this? If you were a statue of Phidias, either Athena or Zeus, you would think both of yourself and of the artist, and if you had any understanding (power of perception) you would try to do nothing unworthy of him who made you or of yourself, and try not to appear in an unbecoming dress (attitude) to those who look on you. But now because Zeus has made you, for this reason do you care not how you shall appear? And yet is the artist (in the one case) like the artist in the other? or the work in the one case like the other? And what work of an artist, for instance, has in itself the faculties, which the artist shows in making it? Is it not marble or bronze, or gold or ivory? and the Athena of Phidias when she has once extended the hand and received in it the figure of Victory[7] stands in that attitude for ever. But the works of God have power of motion, they breathe, they have the faculty of using the appearances of things, and the power of examining them. Being the work of such an artist do you dishonour him? And what shall I say, not only that he made you, but also entrusted you to yourself and made you a deposit to yourself? Will you not think of this too, but do you also dishonour your guardianship? But if God had entrusted an orphan to you, would you thus neglect him? He has delivered yourself to your own care, and says, "I had no one fitter to intrust him to than yourself; keep him for me such as he is by nature, modest, faithful, erect, unterrified, free from passion and perturbation." And then you do not keep him such.

But some will say, "Whence has this fellow got the arrogance which he displays and these supercilious looks?" I have not yet so much gravity as befits a philosopher; for I do not yet feel confidence in what I have learned and in what I have assented to: I still fear my own weakness Let me get confidence and then you shall see a countenance such as I ought to have and an attitude such as I ought to have; then I will show to you the statue, when it is perfected, when it is polished. What do you expect? a supercilious countenance? Does the Zeus at Olympia[8] lift up his brow? No, his look is fixed as becomes him who is ready to say

"Irrevocable is my word and shall not fail."—Iliad, i. 526.

Such will I show myself to you, faithful, modest, noble, free from perturbation—What, and immortal too, exempt from old age, and from sickness? No, but dying as becomes a god, sickening as becomes a god. This power I possess; this I can do. But the rest I do not possess, nor can I do. I will show the nerves (strength) of a philosopher. What nerves[9] are these? A desire never disappointed, an aversion which never falls on that which it would avoid, a proper pursuit (ὁρμήν), a diligent purpose, an assent which is not rash. These you shall see.

NOTES

[1]Schweighäuser observes that the title of this chapter would more correctly be ὁ Θεὸς ἐν ὑμῖν, God in man. There is no better chapter in the book
[2] Socrates (Xenophon, Mem. iv. 6, 8) concludes "that the useful is good to him to whom it is useful."
[3] I do not remember that Epictetus has attempted any other description of the nature of God. He has done more wisely than some who have attempted to answer a question which can not be answered. But see ii. 14, 11-13.
[4] Compare Cicero, de Offic. i. 27.
[5] Noble descent. See i. 9.
The doctrine that God is in man is an old doctrine. Euripides said (Apud Theon. Soph. Progym.) : —

ʿΟ νοῦς γὰρ ἡμῖν ἐστιν ἐν ἑκάστῳ Θεός.

The doctrine became a commonplace of the poets (Ovid, Fast. vi.), " Est deus in nobis, agitante calescimus illo;" and Horace, Sat. ii. 6, 79, "Atque affigit humo divinæ particulam auræ." See i. 14, note 4
[6] Mrs. Carter has a note here. "See 1 Cor. vi: 19; 2 Cor. vi: 16; 2 Tim. 1: 14; 1 John iii: 24, iv: 12, 13. But though the simple expression of carrying God about with us may seem to have some nearly parallel to it in the New Testament, yet those represent the Almighty in a more venerable manner, as taking the hearts of good men for a temple to dwell in. But the other expressions here of feeding and exercising God, and the whole of the paragraph, and indeed of the Stoic system, show the real sense of even its more decent phrases to be vastly different from that of Scripture "
The passage in 1 Cor. vi: 19, is ("What? know ye not that your body is the temple of the Holy Ghost which is in you, which ye have of God, and ye are not your own")? This follows v. 18, which is an exhortation to "flee fornication " The passage in 2 Cor. vi: 16 is, "And what agreement hath the temple of God with idols? for ye are the temple of the living God; as God hath said, I will dwell in them and walk in them," etc. Mrs. Carter has not correctly stated the sense of these two passages.
It is certain that Epictetus knew nothing of the writers of the Epistles in the New Testament: but whence did these writers learn such forms of expression as we find in the passages cited by Mrs. Carter? I believe that they drew them from the Stoic philosophers who wrote before Epictetus and that they applied them to the new religion which they were teaching The teaching of Paul and of Epictetus does not differ: the spirit of God is in man.
Swedenborg says, "In these two faculties (rationality and liberty) the Lord resides with every man, whether he be good or evil, they being

the Lord's mansions in the human race. But the mansion of the Lord is nearer with a man, in proportion as the man opens the superior degrees by these faculties, for by the opening thereof he comes into superior degrees of love and wisdom, and consequently nearer to the Lord. Hence it may appear that as these degrees are opened, so a man is in the Lord and the Lord in him." Swedenborg, Angelic Wisdom, 240. Again, "the faculty of thinking rationally, viewed in itself, is not man's, but God's in man."

I am not quite sure in what sense the administration of the Eucharist ought to be understood in the church of England service. Some English divines formerly understood, and perhaps some now understand, the ceremony as a commemoration of the blood of Christ shed for us and of his body which was broken; as we see in T Burnet's posthumous work (de Fide et Officiis Christianorum, p. 80). It was a commemoration of the last supper of Jesus and the Apostles But this does not appear to be the sense in which the ceremony is now understood by some priests and by some members of the church of England, whose notions approach near to the doctrine of the Catholic mass. Nor does it appear to be the sense of the prayer made before delivering the bread and wine to the Communicants, for the prayer is "Grant us, gracious Lord, so to eat the flesh of thy dear son Jesus Christ and to drink his blood that our sinful bodies may be made clean by his body and our souls washed through his most precious blood and that we may evermore dwell in him and he in us" This is a different thing from Epictetus' notion of God being in man, and also different, as I understand it, from the notion contained in the two passages of Paul, for it is there said generally that the Holy Ghost is in man or God in man, not that God is in man by virtue of a particular ceremony. It should not be omitted that there is after the end of the Communion service an admonition that the sacramental bread and wine remain what they were, "and that the natural body and blood of our Saviour Christ are in heaven and not here; it being against the truth of Christ's natural body to be at one time in more places than one." It was affirmed by the Reformers and the best writers of the English church that the presence of Christ in the Eucharist is a spiritual presence, and in this opinion they followed Calvin and the Swiss divines: and yet in the Prayer book we have the language that I have quoted; and even Calvin, who only maintained a spiritual presence, said, "that the verity is nevertheless joined to the signs, and that in the sacrament we have 'true Communion in Christ's body and blood.'" (Contemporary Review, p 464, August 1874) What would Epictetus have thought of the subtleties of our days?

' The Athena of Phidias was in the Parthenon on the Athenian Acropolis, a colossal chryselephantine statue, that is, a frame work of wood, covered with ivory and gold The figure of Victory stood on the hand of the goddess, as we frequently see in coins.

° The great statue at Olympia was the work of Phidias It was a seated colossal chryselephantine statue, and held a Victory in the right hand

' An allusion to the combatants in the public exercises, who used to show their shoulders, muscles and sinews as a proof of their strength.

CHAPTER IX

THAT WHEN WE CAN NOT FULFIL THAT WHICH THE CHARACTER OF A MAN PROMISES, WE ASSUME THE CHARACTER OF A PHILOSOPHER

IT is no common (easy) thing to do this only, to fulfil the promise of a man's nature. For what is a man? The answer is, a rational and mortal being. Then by the rational faculty from whom are we separated? From wild beasts. And from what others? From sheep and like animals. Take care then to do nothing like a wild beast; but if you do, you have lost the character of a man; you have not fulfilled your promise. See that you do nothing like a sheep; but if you do, in this case also the man is lost. What then do we do as sheep? When we act gluttonously, when we act lewdly, when we act rashly, filthily, inconsiderately, to what have we declined? To sheep. What have we lost? The rational faculty. When we act contentiously and harmfully and passionately, and violently, to what have we declined? To wild beasts. Consequently some of us are great wild beasts, and others little beasts, of a bad disposition and small, whence we may say, Let me be eaten by a lion.[1] But in all these ways the promise of a man acting as a man is destroyed. For when is a conjunctive (complex) proposition maintained?[2] When it fulfils what its nature promises; so that the preservation of a complex proposition is when it is a conjunction of truths. When is a disjunctive maintained? When it fulfils what it promises. When are flutes, a lyre, a horse, a dog, preserved? (when they severally keep their promise). What is the wonder then if man also in like manner is preserved, and in like manner is lost? Each man is improved and preserved by corresponding acts, the carpenter by acts of carpentry, the grammarian by acts of grammar. But if a man accustoms himself to write ungrammatically, of necessity his art will be corrupted and destroyed. Thus modest actions preserve the modest man, and immodest actions destroy him:

119

and actions of fidelity preserve the faithful man, and the contrary actions destroy him.   And on the other hand contrary actions strengthen contrary characters: shamelessness strengthens the shameless man, faithlessness the faithless man, abusive words the abusive man, anger the man of an angry temper, and unequal receiving and giving make the avaricious man more avaricious.

For this reason philosophers admonish us not to be satisfied with learning only, but also to add study, and then practice.³   For we have long been accustomed to do contrary things, and we put in practice opinions which are contrary to true opinions.   If then we shall not also put in practice right opinions, we shall be nothing more than the expositors of the opinions of others.   For now who among us is not able to discourse according to the rules of art about good and evil things (in this fashion)?   That of things some are good, and some are bad, and some are indifferent: the good then are virtues, and the things which participate in virtues; and the bad are the contrary; and the indifferent are wealth, health, reputation.—Then, if in the midst of our talk there should happen some greater noise than usual, or some of those who are present should laugh at us, we are disturbed.   Philosopher, where are the things which you were talking about?   Whence did you produce and utter them.   From the lips, and thence only.   Why then do you corrupt the aids provided by others?   Why do you treat the weightiest matters as if you were playing a game of dice?   For it is one thing to lay up bread and wine as in a storehouse, and another thing to eat.   That which has been eaten, is digested, distributed, and is become sinews, flesh, bones, blood, healthy colour, healthy breath.   Whatever is stored up, when you choose you can readily take and show it; but you have no other advantage from it except so far as to appear to possess it.   For what is the difference between explaining these doctrines and those of men who have different opinions?   Sit down now and explain according to the rules of art the opinions of Epicurus, and perhaps you will explain his opinions in a more useful manner than Epicurus himself.⁴   Why then do you call yourself a Stoic?   Why do you deceive the many?   Why do you act the part of a Jew,⁵

when you are a Greek?   Do you not see how (why) each is
called a Jew, or a Syrian or an Egyptian? and when we see
a man inclining to two sides, we are accustomed to say, This
man is not a Jew, but he acts as one.   But when he has assumed the affects of one who has been imbued with Jewish
doctrine and has adopted that sect, then he is in fact and he
is named a Jew.⁶   Thus we too being falsely imbued (baptized), are in name Jews, but in fact we are something else.
Our affects (feelings) are inconsistent with our words; we
are far from practising what we say, and that of which we
are proud, as if we knew it.   Thus being unable to fulfil
even what the character of a man promises, we even add to
it the profession of a philosopher, which is as heavy a burden, as if a man who is unable to bear ten pounds should attempt to raise the stone which Ajax⁷ lifted.

NOTES

¹ This seems to be a proverb If I am eaten, let me be eaten by the
nobler animal.

²A conjunctive or complex (συμπεπλεγμένον)   axiom or lemma.
Gellius (xvi 8) gives an example: " P Scipio, the son of Paulus, was
both twice consul and triumphed, and exercised the censorship and was
the colleague of L Mummius in his censorship." Gellius adds, "in every
conjunctive if there is one falsehood, though the other parts are true,
the whole is said to be false," For the whole is proposed as true· therefore if one part is false, the whole is not true The disjunctive
(διεζευγμένον) is of this kind   "pleasure is either bad or good, or
neither good nor bad"

³ We often say a man learns a particular thing; and there are men
who profess to teach certain things, such as a language, or an art; and
they mean by teaching that the taught shall learn; and learning means
that they shall be able to do what they learn. He who teaches an art
professes that the scholar shall be able to practice the art, the art of
making shoes for example, or other useful things   There are men who
profess to teach religion, and morality, and virtue generally These men
may tell us what they conceive to be religion, and morality, and virtue;
and those who are said to be taught may know what their teachers have
told them But the learning of religion, and of morality and of virtue,
mean that the learner will do the acts of religion and of morality and of
virtue; which is a very different thing from knowing what the acts of
religion, of morality, and of virtue are. The teacher's teaching is in fact
only made efficient by his example, by his doing that which he teaches

⁴ "He is not a Stoic philosopher, who can only explain in a subtle and
proper manner the Stoic principles: for the same person can explain the
principles of Epicurus, of course for the purpose of refuting them, and·
perhaps he can explain them better than Epicurus himself Consequently
he might be at the same time a Stoic and an Epicurean; which is absurd."—Schweig. He means that the mere knowledge of Stoic opinions

does not make a man a Stoic, or any other philosopher. A man must
according to Stoic principles practice them in order to be a Stoic philosopher. So if we say that a man is a religious man, he must do the acts
which his religion teaches; for it is by his acts only that we can know
him to be a religious man   What he says and professes may be false,
and no man knows except himself whether his words and professions
are true. The uniformity, regularity, and consistency of his acts are evidence which can not be mistaken.

⁵ It has been suggested that Epictetus confounded under the name of
Jews those who were Jews and those who were Christians   We know
that some Jews became Christians

⁶ It is possible, as I have said, that by Jews Epictetus means Christians,
for Christians and Jews are evidently confounded by some writers, as
the first Christians were of the Jewish nation   In book iv. 7, Epictetus
gives the name of Galilæans to the Jews.   The term Galilæans points to
the country of the great teacher. Paul says (Romans, ii: 28), "For he
is not a Jew, which is one outwardly—but he is a Jew which is one inwardly," etc. His remarks (ii: 17-29) on the man "who is called a Jew,
and rests in the law and makes his boast of God" may be compared with
what Epictetus says of a man who is called a philosopher, and does not
practice that which he professes.

⁷ See ii. 24, 26; Iliad, vii. 264, etc. ; Juvenal, xv. 65.

"Nec hunc lapidem, quales et Turnus et Ajax
Vel quo Tydides percussit pondere coxam
Æneæ."—Upton.

CHAPTER X

CONSIDER who you are. In the first place, you are a man; and this is one who has nothing superior to the faculty of the will, but all other things subjected to it; and the faculty itself he possesses unenslaved and free from subjection. Consider then from what things you have been separated by reason. You have been separated from wild beasts: you have been separated from domestic animals (προβάτων). Further, you are a citizen of the world, and a part of it, not one of the subservient (serving), but one of the principal (ruling) parts, for you are capable of comprehending the divine administration and of considering the connexion of things. What then does the character of a citizen promise (profess)? To hold nothing as profitable to himself; to deliberate about nothing as if he were detached from the community, but to act as the hand or foot would do, if they had reason and understood the constitution of nature, for they would never put themselves in motion nor desire any thing otherwise than with reference to the whole. Therefore the philosophers say well, that if the good man had foreknowledge of what would happen, he would co-operate towards his own sickness and death and mutilation, since he knows[1] that these things are assigned to him according to the universal arrangement, and that the whole is superior to the part, and the state to the citizen. But now because we do not know the future, it is our duty to stick to the things which are in their nature more suitable for our choice, for we were made among other things for this.

After this remember that you are a son. What does this character promise? To consider that every thing which is the son's belongs to the father, to obey him in all things, never to blame him to another, nor to say or do any thing which does him injury, to yield to him in all things and give way, co-operating with him as far as you can. After

123

this know that you are a brother also, and that to this character it is due to make concessions; to be easily persuaded, to speak good of your brother, never to claim in opposition to him any of the things which are independent of the will, but readily to give them up, that you may have the larger share in what is dependent on the will. For see what a thing it is, in place of a lettuce, if it should so happen, or a seat, to gain for yourself goodness of disposition. How great is the advantage.[2]

Next to this, if you are a senator of any state, remember that you are a senator: if a youth, that you are a youth: if an old man, that you are an old man; for each of such names, if it comes to be examined, marks out the proper duties. But if you go and blame your brother, I say to you, You have forgotten who you are and what is your name. In the next place, if you were a smith and made a wrong use of the hammer, you would have forgotten the smith; and if you have forgotten the brother and instead of a brother have become an enemy, would you appear not to have changed one thing for another in that case? And if instead of a man, who is a tame animal and social, you are become a mischievous wild beast, treacherous, and biting, have you lost nothing? But, (I suppose) you must lose a bit of money that you may suffer damage? And does the loss of nothing else do a man damage? If you had lost the art of grammar or music, would you think the loss of it a damage? and if you shall lose modesty, moderation ($\kappa\alpha\tau\alpha\sigma\tauo\lambda\eta\nu$) and gentleness, do you think the loss nothing? And yet the things first mentioned are lost by some cause external and independent of the will, and the second by our own fault; and as to the first neither to have them nor to lose them is shameful; but as to the second, not to have them and to lose them is shameful and matter of reproach and a misfortune. What does the pathic lose? He loses the (character of) man. What does he lose who makes the pathic what he is? Many other things; and he also loses the man no less than the other. What does he lose who commits adultery? He loses the (character of the) modest, the temperate, the decent, the citizen, the neighbour. What does he lose who is angry? Something else. What does the coward lose? Something else. No man is bad without suffering some loss and damage. If then you look for the damage in the loss of money only, all these men receive no harm or damage; it may be, they have even profit and gain, when they acquire a bit of money by any of these deeds. But consider that if you refer every thing to a small coin, not even he who loses his nose is in your opinion damaged. Yes, you say, for he is mutilated in his body. Well; but does he who has lost his smell only lose nothing? Is there then no energy of the soul which is an advantage to him who possesses it, and a damage to him who has lost it?—Tell me what sort (of energy) you mean. —Have we not a natural modesty?—We have.—Does he who loses this sustain no damage? is he deprived of nothing, does he part with nothing of the things which belong to him? Have we not naturally fidelity? natural affection, a natural disposition to help others, a natural disposition to forbearance? The man then who allows himself to be damaged in these matters, can he be free from harm and uninjured. What then? shall I not hurt him, who has hurt me?[3] In the first place consider what hurt ($\beta\lambda\dot{\alpha}\beta\eta$) is, and remember what you have heard from the philosophers. For if the good consists in the will (purpose, intention, $\pi\rho o\alpha\iota\acute{\epsilon}\sigma\epsilon\iota$), and the evil also in the will, see if what you say is not this: What then, since that man has hurt himself by doing an unjust act to me, shall I not hurt myself by doing some unjust act to him? Why do we not imagine to ourselves (mentally think of) something of this kind? But where there is any detriment to the body or to our possession, there is harm there; and where the same thing happens to the faculty of the will, there is (you suppose) no harm; for he who has been deceived or he who has done an unjust act neither suffers in the head nor in the eye nor in the hip, nor does he lose his estate; and we wish for nothing else than (security to) these things. But whether we shall have the will modest and faithful or shameless and faithless, we care not the least, except only in the school so far as a few words are concerned. Therefore our proficiency is limited to these few words, but beyond them it does not exist even in the slightest degree.[4]

NOTES

¹ This may appear extravagant; but it is possible to explain it, and even to assent to it. If a man believes that all is wisely arranged in the course of human events, he would not even try to resist that which he knows it is appointed for him to suffer: he would submit and he would endure If Epictetus means that the man would actively promote the end or purpose which he foreknew, in order that his acts may be consistent with what he foreknows and with his duty, perhaps the philosopher's saying is too hard to deal with; and as it rests on an impossible assumption of foreknowledge, we may be here wiser than the philosophers, if we say no more about it.

² A lettuce is an example of the most trifling thing. A seat probably means a seat of superiority, a magistrate's seat, a Roman sella curulis.

³ Socrates—We must by no means then do an act of injustice Crito — Certainly not Socrates.—Nor yet when you are wronged must you do wrong in return, as most people think, since you must in no way do an unjust act. Plato, Crito, c. 10.

⁴ The same remark will apply to most dissertations spoken or written on moral subjects: they are exercises of skill for him who delivers or writes them, or matter for criticism and perhaps a way of spending an idle hour for him who listens; and that is all Epictetus blames our indolence and indifference as to acts, and the trifling of the schools of philosophy in disputation.

CHAPTER XI

THE beginning of philosophy to him at least who enters on it in the right way and by the door, is a consciousness of his own weakness and inability about necessary things. For we come into the world with no natural notion of a right angled triangle, or of a diesis (a quarter tone), or of a half tone; but we learn each of these things by a certain transmission according to art; and for this reason those who do not know them, do not think that they know them. But as to good and evil, and beautiful and ugly, and becoming and unbecoming, and happiness and misfortune, and proper and improper, and what we ought to do and what we ought not to do, who ever came into the world without having an innate idea of them? Wherefore we all use these names, and we endeavour to fit the preconceptions to the several cases (things) thus: he has done well, he has not done well; he has done as he ought, not as he ought; he has been unfortunate, he has been fortunate; he is unjust, he is just: who does not use these names? who among us defers the use of them till he has learned them, as he defers the use of the words about lines (geometrical figures) or sounds? And the cause of this is that we come into the world already taught as it were by nature some things on this matter (τόπον), and proceeding from these we have added to them self-conceit (οἴησιν). For why, a man says, do I not know the beautiful and the ugly? Have I not the notion of it? You have. Do I not adapt it to particulars? You do. Do I not then adapt it properly? In that lies the whole question; and conceit is added here. For beginning from these things which are admitted men proceed to that which is matter of dispute by means of unsuitable adaptation; for if they possessed this power of adaptation in addition to those things, what would hinder them from being perfect? But now since you think that you properly adapt the preconceptions to the particulars, tell me whence you derive this (assume that you do so). Because I think so. But it does not seem so to another, and he thinks that he also makes a proper adaptation; or does he not think so? He does think so. Is it possible then that both of you can properly apply the preconceptions to things about which you have contrary opinions? It is not possible. Can you then show us anything better towards adapting the preconceptions beyond your thinking that you do? Does the madman do any other things than the things which seem to him right? Is then this criterion sufficient for him also? It is not sufficient. Come then to something which is superior to seeming ($\tau o\tilde{v}$ $\delta o\kappa\epsilon\tilde{i}\nu$). What is this?

Observe, this is the beginning of philosophy, a perception of the disagreement of men with one another, and an inquiry into the cause of the disagreement, and a condemnation and distrust of that which only seems, and a certain investigation of that which seems whether it seems rightly, and a discovery of some rule ($\kappa\alpha\nu\acute{o}\nu o\varsigma$), as we have discovered a balance in the determination of weights, and a carpenter's rule (or square) in the case of straight and crooked things.—This is the beginning of philosophy. Must we say that all things are right which seem so to all? And how is it possible that contradictions can be right?—Not all then, but all which seem to us to be right.—How more to you than those which seem right to the Syrians? why more than what seem right to the Egyptians? why more than what seems right to me or to any other man? Not at all more. What then seems to every man is not sufficient for determining what is; for neither in the case of weights or measures are we satisfied with the bare appearance, but in each case we have discovered a certain rule. In this matter then is there no rule superior to what seems? And how is it possible that the most necessary things among men should have no sign (mark), and be incapable of being discovered? There is then some rule. And why then do we not seek the rule and discover it, and afterwards use it without varying from it, not even stretching out the finger without it?[1] For this, I think, is that which when it is discovered cures of their madness those who use mere seeming as a measure, and misuse it; so that for the future proceeding from certain things (principles) known and made clear we may use in the case of particular things the preconceptions which are distinctly fixed.

What is the matter presented to us about which we are inquiring? Pleasure (for example). Subject it to the rule, throw it into the balance. Ought the good to be such a thing that it is fit that we have confidence in it? Yes. And in which we ought to confide? It ought to be. Is it fit to trust to any thing which is insecure? No. Is then pleasure any thing secure? No. Take it then and throw it out of the scale, and drive it far away from the place of good things. But if you are not sharp-sighted, and one balance is not enough for you, bring another. Is it fit to be elated over what is good? Yes. Is it proper then to be elated over present pleasure? See that you do not say that it is proper; but if you do, I shall then not think you worthy even of the balance.[2] Thus things are tested and weighed when the rules are ready. And to philosophize is this, to examine and confirm the rules; and then to use them when they are known is the act of a wise and good man.[3]

NOTES

[1] Doing nothing without the rule. This is a Greek proverb.
[2] That is, so far shall I consider you from being able to judge rightly of things without a balance that I shall understand that not even with the aid of a balance can you do it, that you can not even use a balance, and consequently that you are not worth a single word from me. —Schweig
[3] This is a just conclusion. We must fix the canons or rules by which things are tried; and then the rules may be applied by the wise and good to all cases.

9

CHAPTER XII

OF DISPUTATION OR DISCUSSION

WHAT things a man must learn in order to be able to apply the art of disputation, has been accurately shown by our philosophers (the Stoics); but with respect to the proper use of the things, we are entirely without practice. Only give to any of us, whom you please, an illiterate man to discuss with, and he can not discover how to deal with the man. But when he has moved the man a little, if he answers beside the purpose, he does not know how to treat him, but he then either abuses or ridicules him, and says, "He is an illiterate man; it is not possible to do any thing with him." Now a guide, when he has found a man out of the road leads him into the right way: he does not ridicule or abuse him and then leave him. Do you also show the illiterate man the truth, and you will see that he follows. But so long as you do not show him the truth, do not ridicule him, but rather feel your own incapacity.

How then did Socrates act? He used to compel his adversary in disputation to bear testimony to him, and he wanted no other witness.[1] Therefore he could say, "I care not for other witnesses, but I am always satisfied with the evidence (testimony) of my adversary, and I do not ask the opinion of others, but only the opinion of him who is disputing with me." For he used to make the conclusion drawn from natural notions so plain that every man saw the contradiction (if it existed) and withdrew from it (thus) · Does the envious[2] man rejoice? By no means, but he is rather pained. Well, Do you think that envy is pain over evils? and what envy is there of evils? Therefore he made his adversary say that envy is pain over good things Well then, would any man envy those who are nothing to him? By no means. Thus having completed the notion and distinctly fixed it he would go away without saying to his adversary, Define to me envy; and if the adversary had defined envy, he did not say, You have defined it badly, for the terms of the

130

definition do not correspond to the thing defined—These are
technical terms, and for this reason disagreeable and hardly
intelligible to illiterate men, which terms we (philosophers)
can not lay aside. But that the illiterate man himself, who
follows the appearances presented to him, should be able to
concede any thing or reject it, we can never by the use of
these terms move him to do.   Accordingly being conscious
of our own inability, we do not attempt the thing; at least
such of us as have any caution do not.   But the greater part
and the rash, when they enter into such disputations, confuse
themselves and confuse others; and finally abusing their adversaries and abused by them, they walk away.

Now this was the first and chief peculiarity of Socrates,
never to be irritated in argument, never to utter any thing
abusive, any thing insulting, but to bear with abusive persons
and to put an end to the quarrel.   If you would know what
great power he had in this way, read the Symposium of
Xenophon,[3] and you will see how many quarrels he put an
end to.   Hence with good reason in the poets also this power
is most highly praised,

"Quickly with skill he settles great disputes."[4]

Well then; the matter is not now very safe, and particularly
at Rome; for he who attempts to do it, must not do it in a
corner, you may be sure, but must go to a man of consular
rank, if it so happen, or to a rich man, and ask him, Can you
tell me, Sir, to whose care you have entrusted your horses?
I can tell you.   Have you entrusted them to any person indifferently and to one who has no experience of horses?—By
no means.—Well then; can you tell me to whom you entrust
your gold or silver things or your vestments?   I don't entrust even these to any one indifferently.   Well; your own
body, have you already considered about entrusting the care
of it to any person?—Certainly.—To a man of experience,
I suppose, and one acquainted with the aliptic,[5] or with the
healing art?—Without doubt.—Are these the best things
that you have, or do you also possess something else which is
better than all these?—What kind of a thing do you mean?
—That I mean which makes use of these things, and tests

each of them, and deliberates.—It is the soul that you mean?
—You think right, for it is the soul that I mean.—In truth
I do think that the soul is a much better thing than all the
others which I possess.—Can you then show us in what way
you have taken care of the soul? for it is not likely that you,
who are so wise a man and have a reputation in the city, inconsiderately and carelessly allow the most valuable thing
that you possess to be neglected and to perish.—Certainly not.—But have you taken care of the soul yourself;
and have you learned from another to do this, or have you
discovered the means yourself?—Here comes the danger that
in the first place he may say, What is this to you, my good
man, who are you?   Next, if you persist in troubling him,
there is danger that he may raise his hands and give you
blows.   I was once myself also an admirer of this mode of
instruction until I fell into these dangers.⁶

NOTES

¹ This is what is said in the Gorgias of Plato.
² Socrates' notion of envy is stated by Xenophon to be this: "it is the
pain or vexation which men have at the prosperity of their friends, and
that such are the only envious persons." Bishop Butler gives a better
definition; at least a more complete description of the thing "Emulation
is merely the desire and hope of equality with or superiority over others,
with whom we may compare ourselves There does not appear to be any
other grief in the natural passion, but only that want which is implied
in desire However this may be so strong as to be the occasion of great
grief. To desire the attainment of this equality or superiority, by the particular means of others being brought down to our level, or below it, is,
I think, the distinct notion of envy.   From whence it is easy to see, that
the real end which the natural passion, emulation, and which the unlaw-
ful one, envy, aims at is the same; namely, that equality or superiority:
and consequently that to do mischief is not the end of envy, but merely
the means it makes use of to attain its end."—Sermons upon Human
Nature, I.
³ The Symposium or Banquet of Xenophon is extant.
⁴ Hesiod, Theogony, v. 87.
⁵ The aliptic is the art of anointing and rubbing, one of the best
means of maintaining a body in health The iatric or healing art is the
art of restoring to health a diseased body. The aliptic art is also equivalent to the gymnastic art, or the art of preparing for gymnastic exercises,
which are also a means of preserving the body's health, when the exercises are good and moderate.
⁶ Epictetus is speaking of himself and of his experience at Rome.

CHAPTER XIII

ON ANXIETY (SOLICITUDE)

WHEN I see a man anxious, I say, What does this man want? If he did not want some thing which is not in his power, how could he be anxious? For this reason a lute player when he is singing by himself has no anxiety, but when he enters the theatre, he is anxious even if he has a good voice and plays well on the lute; for he not only wishes to sing well, but also to obtain applause: but this is not in his power. Accordingly, where he has skill, there he has confidence. Bring any single person who knows nothing of music, and the musician does not care for him. But in the matter where a man knows nothing and has not been practised, there he is anxious. What matter is this? He knows not what a crowd is or what the praise of a crowd is. However he has learned to strike the lowest chord and the highest; but what the praise of the many is, and what power it has in life he neither knows nor has he thought about it. Hence he must of necessity tremble and grow pale. I can not then say that a man is not a lute player when I see him afraid, but I can say something else, and not one thing, but many. And first of all I call him a stranger and say, This man does not know in what part of the world he is, but though he has been here so long, he is ignorant of the laws of the State and the customs, and what is permitted and what is not; and he has never employed any lawyer to tell him and to explain the laws. But a man does not write a will, if he does not know how it ought to be written, or he employs a person who does know; nor does he rashly seal a bond or write a security. But he uses his desire without a lawyer's advice, and aversion, and pursuit (movement), and attempt and purpose. How do you mean without a lawyer? He does not know that he wills what is not allowed, and does not will that which is of necessity; and he does not know either what is his own or what is another man's; but if he did know, he would

133

never be impeded, he would never be hindered, he would not
be anxious.   How so?—Is any man then afraid about things
which are not evils?—No.—Is he afraid about things which
are evils, but still so far within his power that they may not
happen?—Certainly he is not.—If then the things which are
independent of the will are neither good nor bad, and all
things which do depend on the will are within our power,
and no man can either take them from us or give them to us,
if we do not choose, where is room left for anxiety?   But
we are anxious about our poor body, our little property,
about the will of Cæsar; but not anxious about things internal.   Are we anxious about not forming a false opinion?—
No, for this is in my power.—About not exerting our movements contrary to nature?—No, not even about this.—When
then you see a man pale, as the physician says, judging from
the complexion, this man's spleen is disordered, that man's
liver; so also say, this man's desire and aversion are disordered, he is not in the right way, he is in a fever.   For nothing else changes the colour, or causes trembling or chattering
of the teeth, or causes a man to

"Sink in his knees and shift from foot to foot."[1]—

For this reason when Zeno was going to meet Antigonus,[2]
he was not anxious, for Antigonus had no power over any
of the things which Zeno admired; and Zeno did not care for
those things over which Antigonus had power.   But Antigonus was anxious when he was going to meet Zeno, for he
wished to please Zeno; but this was a thing external (out of
his power).   But Zeno did not want to please Antigonus;
for no man who is skilled in any art wishes to please one who
has no such skill.
    Should I try to please you?   Why?   I suppose, you
know the measure by which one man is estimated by another.
Have you taken pains to learn what is a good man and what
is a bad man, and how a man becomes one or the other?
Why then are you not good yourself?—How, he replies, am
I not good?—Because no good man laments or groans or
weeps, no good man is pale and trembles, or says, How will
he receive me, how will he listen to me?—Slave, just as it

pleases him. Why do you care about what belongs to others? Is it now his fault if he receives badly what proceeds from you?—Certainly.—And is it possible that a fault should be one man's, and the evil in another?—No.—Why then are you anxious about that which belongs to others? —Your question is reasonable; but I am anxious how I shall speak to him. Can not you then speak to him as you choose? —But I fear that I may be disconcerted?—If you are going to write the name of Dion, are you afraid that you would be disconcerted?—By no means —Why? is it not because you have practised writing the name?—Certainly.—Well, if you were going to read the name, would you not feel the same? and why? Because every art has a certain strength and confidence in the things which belong to it.—Have you then not practised speaking? and what else did you learn in the school? Syllogisms and sophistical propositions? For what purpose? was it not for the purpose of discoursing skilfully? and is not discoursing skilfully the same as discoursing seasonably and cautiously and with intelligence, and also without making mistakes and without hindrance, and besides all this with confidence?—Yes.—When then you are mounted on a horse and go into a plain, are you anxious at being matched against a man who is on foot, and anxious in a matter in which you are practised, and he is not?—Yes, but that person (to whom I am going to speak) has power to kill me.[3] Speak the truth then, unhappy man, and do not brag, nor claim to be a philosopher, nor refuse to acknowledge your masters, but so long as you present this handle in your body, follow every man who is stronger than yourself. Socrates used to practise speaking, he who talked as he did to the tyrants,[4] to the dicasts (judges), he who talked in his prison. Diogenes had practised speaking, he who spoke as he did to Alexander, to the pirates, to the person who bought him. These men were confident in the things which they practised. But do you walk off to your own affairs and never leave them: go and sit in a corner, and weave syllogisms, and propose them to another. There is not in you the man who can rule a state.

[1] Iliad, xiii. 281.

[2] In Diogenes Laertius (Zeno, vii.) there is a letter from Antigonus to Zeno and Zeno's answer. Simplicius (note on the Encheiridion, c. 51) supposes this Antigonus to be the King of Syria; but Upton remarks that it is Antigonus Gonatas, king of Macedonia.

[3] The original is "but that person (ἐκεῖνος) has power to kill me." "That person" must be the person already mentioned, and Mrs. Carter has done right in adding this explanation.

[4] The Thirty tyrants of Athens, as they were called. The talk of Socrates with Critias and Charicles two of the Thirty is reported in Xenophon's "Memorabilia" (i 2, 33) The defence of Socrates before those who tried him and his conversation in prison are reported in Plato's "Apology," and in the "Phædon" and "Crito." Diogenes was captured by some pirates and sold (iv. 1, 115).

CHAPTER XIV,

TO NASO

WHEN a certain Roman entered with his son and listened to one reading, Epictetus said, This is the method of instruction; and he stopped. When the Roman asked him to go on, Epictetus said, Every art when it is taught causes labour to him who is unacquainted with it and is unskilled in it, and indeed the things which proceed from the arts immediately show their use in the purpose for which they were made; and most of them contain something attractive and pleasing. For indeed to be present and to observe how a shoemaker learns is not a pleasant thing; but the shoe is useful and also not disagreeable to look at. And the discipline of a smith when he is learning is very disagreeable to one who chances to be present and is a stranger to the art: but the work shows the use of the art. But you will see this much more in music; for if you are present while a person is learning, the discipline will appear most disagreeable; and yet the results of music are pleasing and delightful to those who know nothing of music. And here we conceive the work of a philosopher to be something of this kind: he must adapt his wish (βούλησιν) to what is going on, so that neither any of the things which are taking place shall take place contrary to our wish, nor any of the things which do not take place shall not take place when we wish that they should. From this the result is to those who have so arranged the work of philosophy, not to fail in the desire, nor to fall in with that which they should avoid; without uneasiness, without fear, without perturbation to pass through life themselves, together with their associates maintaining the relations both natural and acquired,[1] as the relation of son, of father, of brother, of citizen, of man, of wife, of neighbour, of fellow traveller, of ruler, of ruled. The work of a philosopher we conceive to be something like this. It remains next to inquire how this must be accomplished.

10

We see then that the carpenter (τέκτων) when he has learned certain things becomes a carpenter; the pilot by learning certain things becomes a pilot. May it not then in philosophy also not be sufficient to wish to be wise and good, and that there is also a necessity to learn certain things? We inquire then what these things are. The philosophers say that we ought first to learn that there is a God and that he provides for all things; also that it is not possible to conceal from him our acts, or even our intentions and thoughts.[2] The next thing is to learn what is the nature of the Gods; for such as they are discovered to be, he, who would please and obey them, must try with all his power to be like them. If the divine is faithful, man also must be faithful; if it is free, man also must be free; if beneficent, man also must be beneficent; if magnanimous, man also must be magnanimous; as being then an imitator of God he must do and say every thing consistently with this fact.

With what then must we begin? If you will enter on the discussion, I will tell you that you must first understand names (words).—So then you say that I do not now understand names.—You do not understand them —How then do I use them?—Just as the illiterate use written language, as cattle use appearances: for use is one thing, understanding is another. But if you think that you understand them, produce whatever word you please, and let us try whether we understand it.—But it is a disagreeable thing for a man to be confuted who is now old, and, it may be, has now served his three campaigns.—I too know this: for now you are come to me as if you were in want of nothing: and what could you even imagine to be wanting to you? You are rich, you have children and a wife perhaps, and many slaves: Cæsar knows you, in Rome you have many friends, you render their dues to all, you know how to requite him who does you a favour, and to repay in the same kind him who does you a wrong. What do you lack? If then I shall shew you that you lack the things most necessary and the chief things for happiness, and that hitherto you have looked after every thing rather than what you ought, and to crown all,[3] that you neither know what God is nor what man is, nor what is good nor what is bad; and as to what I have said about your ignorance of other matters, that may perhaps be endured, but if I say that you know nothing about yourself, how is it possible that you should endure me and bear the proof and stay here? It is not possible; but you immediately go off in bad humour. And yet what harm have I done you? unless the mirror also injures the ugly man because it shows him to himself such as he is; unless the physician also is supposed to insult the sick man, when he says to him, Man, do you think that you ail nothing? But you have a fever: go without food to-day; drink water. And no one says, what an insult! But if you say to a man, Your desires are inflamed, your aversions are low, your intentions are inconsistent, your pursuits (movements) are not conformable to nature, your opinions are rash and false, the man immediately goes away and says, He has insulted me.

Our way of dealing is like that of a crowded assembly. Beasts are brought to be sold and oxen; and the greater part of the men come to buy and sell, and there are some few who come to look at the market and to inquire how it is carried on, and why, and who fixes the meeting and for what purpose. So it is here also in this assembly (of life): some like cattle trouble themselves about nothing except their fodder. For to all of you who are busy about possessions and lands and slaves and magisterial offices, these are nothing except fodder. But there are a few who attend the assembly, men who love to look on and consider what is the world, who governs it. Has it no governor? And how is it possible that a city or a family can not continue to exist, not even the shortest time without an administrator and guardian, and that so great and beautiful a system should be administered with such order and yet without a purpose and by chance?[4] There is then an administrator. What kind of administrator and how does he govern? And who are we, who were produced by him, and for what purpose? Have we some connexion with him and some relation towards him, or none? This is the way in which these few are affected, and then they apply themselves only to this one thing, to examine the meeting and then to go away. What then? They are ridiculed by the many, as the spectators at the fair are by the traders; and if the beasts had any understanding, they would ridicule those who admired anything else than fodder.

ITTER### NOTES

[1] Compare iii. 2, 4, iv. 8, 20. Antoninus (viii. 27) writes: "There are three relations [between thee and other things]: the one to the body which surrounds thee; the second to the divine cause from which all things come to all; and the third to those who live with thee." This is precise, true and practical. Those who object to "the divine cause," may write in place of it "the nature and constitution of things;" for there is a constitution of things, which the philosopher attempts to discover; and for most practical purposes, it is immaterial whether we say that it is of divine origin or has some other origin, or no origin can be discovered. The fact remains that a constitution of things exists; or, if that expression be not accepted, we may say that we conceive that it exists and we can not help thinking so.

[2] When God is said to provide for all things, this is what the Greeks called πρόνοια, providence. (Epictetus, i. 16, iii. 17.) In the second of these passages there is a short answer to some objections made to Providence.

Epictetus could only know or believe what God is by the observation of phenomena; and he could only know what he supposed to be God's providence by observing his administration of the world and all that happens in it. Among other works of God is man, who possesses certain intellectual powers which enable him to form a judgment of God's works, and a judgment of man himself. Man has or is supposed to have certain moral sentiments, or a capacity of acquiring them in some way. On the supposition that all man's powers are the gift of God, man's power of judging what happens in the world under God's providence is the gift of God; and if he should not be satisfied with God's administration, we have the conclusion that man, whose powers are from God, condemns that administration which is also from God. Thus God and man, who is God's work, are in opposition to one another.

If a man rejects the belief in a deity and in a providence, because of the contradictions and difficulties involved in this belief or supposed to be involved in it, and if he finds the contradictions and difficulties such as he can not reconcile with his moral sentiments and judgments, he will be consistent in rejecting the notion of a deity and of providence. But he must also consistently admit that his moral sentiments and judgments are his own, and that he can not say how he acquired them, or how he has any of the corporeal or intellectual powers which he is daily using. By the hypothesis they are not from God. All then that a man can say is that he has such powers.

[3] The original is "to add the colophon," which is a proverbial expression and signifies to give the last touch to a thing.

[4] From the fact that man has some intelligence Voltaire concludes that we must admit that there is a greater, intelligence. Letter to Mde. Necker.

CHAPTER XV

WHEN some persons have heard these words, that a man ought to be constant (firm), and that the will is naturally free and not subject to compulsion, but that all other things are subject to hindrance, to slavery, and are in the power of others, they suppose that they ought without deviation to abide by every thing which they have determined. But in the first place that which has been determined ought to be sound (true). I require tone (sinews) in the body, but such as exists in a healthy body, in an athletic body; but if it is plain to me that you have the tone of a phrensied man and you boast of it, I shall say to you, man, seek the physician: this is not tone, but atony (deficiency in right tone). In a different way something of the same kind is felt by those who listen to these discourses in a wrong manner; which was the case with one of my companions who for no reason resolved to starve himself to death.[1] I heard of it when it was the third day of his abstinence from food and I went to inquire what had happened. I have resolved, he said.—But still tell me what it was which induced you to resolve; for if you have resolved rightly, we shall sit with you and assist you to depart; but if you have made an unreasonable resolution, change your mind.—We ought to keep to our determinations.—What are you doing, man? We ought to keep not to all our determinations, but to those which are right; for if you are now persuaded that it is night, do not change your mind, if you think fit, but persist and say, we ought to abide by our determinations. Will you not make the beginning and lay the foundation in an inquiry whether the determination is sound or not sound, and so then build on it firmness and security? But if you lay a rotten and ruinous foundation, will not your miserable little building fall down the sooner, the more and the stronger are the materials which you shall lay on it?

Without any reason would you withdraw from us out of life
a man who is a friend, and a companion, a citizen of the same
city, both the great and the small city?² Then while you are
committing murder and destroying a man who has done no
wrong, do you say that you ought to abide by your determinations? And if it ever in any way came into your head
to kill me, ought you to abide by your determinations?

Now this man was with difficulty persuaded to change his
mind. But it is impossible to convince some persons at present; so that I seem now to know, what I did not know before, the meaning of the common saying, That you can
neither persuade nor break a fool.³ May it never be my lot
to have a wise fool for my friend: nothing is more untract-
able. "I am determined," the man says. Madmen are also;
but the more firmly they form a judgment on things which
do not exist, the more ellebore⁴ they require. Will you not
act like a sick man and call in the physician?—I am sick,
master, help me; consider what I must do; it is my duty to
obey you. So it is here also: I know not what I ought to do,
but I am come to learn.—Not so; but speak to me about
other things: upon this I have determined.—What other
things? for what is greater and more useful than for you to
be persuaded that it is not sufficient to have made your determination and not to change it. This is the tone (energy)
of madness, not of health.—I will die, if you compel me to
this.—Why, man? What has happened?—I have determined—I have had a lucky escape that you have not determined to kill me—I take no money.⁵ Why?—I have determined—Be assured that with the very tone (energy) which
you now use in refusing to take, there is nothing to hinder
you at some time from inclining without reason to take
money and then saying, I have determined. As in a distem-
pered body, subject to defluxions, the humour inclines sometimes to these parts, and then to those, so too a sickly soul
knows not which way to incline: but if to this inclination and
movement there is added a tone (obstinate resolution), then
the evil becomes past help and cure.

NOTES

[1] The word is ἀποκαρτερεῖν, which Cicero (Tusc. i. 34) renders "per inediam vita discedere" The words "I have resolved" are in Epictetus, κέκρικα. Pliny (Epp. i. 12) says that Corellius Rufus, when he determined to end his great sufferings by starvation made the same answer, κέκρικα, to the physician who offered him food.

[2] The great city is the world.

[3] The meaning is that you can not lead a fool from his purpose either by words or force. "A wise fool" must mean a fool who thinks himself wise; and such we sometimes see. "Though thou shouldst bray a fool in the mortar among wheat with a pestle, yet will not his foolishness depart from him." Proverbs, xxvii. 22

[4] Ellebore was a medicine used in madness. Horace says, Sat. ii. 3. 82—

"Danda est ellebori multo pars maxima avaris."

[5] "Epictetus seems in this discussion to be referring to some professor, who had declared that he would not take money from his hearers, and then, indirectly at least, had blamed our philosopher for receiving some fee from his hearers." Schweig.

CHAPTER XVI

THAT WE DO NOT STRIVE TO USE OUR OPINIONS ABOUT GOOD AND EVIL

WHERE is the good? In the will.[1] Where is the evil? In the will. Where is neither of them? In those things which are independent of the will. Well then? Does any one among us think of these lessons out of the schools? Does any one meditate (strive) by himself to give an answer to things[2] as in the case of questions? Is it day?—Yes.—Is it night?—No.— Well, is the number of stars even?[3]—I can not say.—When money is shown (offered) to you, have you studied to make the proper answer, that money is not a good thing? Have you practised yourself in these answers, or only against sophisms? Why do you wonder then if in the cases which you have studied, in those you have improved; but in those which you have not studied, in those you remain the same? When the rhetorician knows that he has written well, that he has committed to memory what he has written, and brings an agreeable voice, why is he still anxious? Because he is not satisfied with having studied. What then does he want? To be praised by the audience? For the purpose then of being able to practise declamation he has been disciplined; but with respect to praise and blame he has not been disciplined. For when did he hear from any other what praise is, what blame is, what the nature of each is, what kind of praise should be sought, or what kind of blame should be shunned? And when did he practise this discipline which follows these words (things)?[4] Why then do you still wonder, if in the matters which a man has learned, there he surpasses others, and in those in which he has not been disciplined, there he is the same with the many. So the lute player knows how to play, sings well, and has a fine dress, and yet he trembles when he enters on the stage; for these matters he understands, but he does not know what a crowd is, nor the shouts of a crowd, nor what ridicule is. Neither does he know what anxiety is, whether it is our work or the work of another, whether it is possible to stop it or not. For this reason if he has been praised, he leaves the theatre puffed up, but if he has been ridiculed, the swollen bladder has been punctured and subsides.

This is the case also with ourselves. What do we admire? Externals. About what things are we busy? Externals. And have we any doubt then why we fear or why we are anxious? What then happens when we think the things, which are coming on us, to be evils? It is not in our power not to be afraid, it is not in our power not to be anxious. Then we say, Lord God, how shall I not be anxious? Fool, have you not hands, did not God make them for you? Sit down now and pray that your nose may not run. Wipe yourself rather and do not blame him. Well then, has he given to you nothing in the present case? Has he not given to you endurance? has he not given to you magnanimity? has he not given to you manliness? When you have such hands, do you still look for one who shall wipe your nose? But we neither study these things nor care for them. Give me a man who cares how he shall do any thing, not for the obtaining of a thing, but who cares about his own energy. What man, when he is walking about, cares for his own energy? who, when he is deliberating, cares about his own deliberation, and not about obtaining that about which he deliberates? And if he succeeds, he is elated and says, How well we have deliberated; did I not tell you, brother, that it is impossible, when we have thought about any thing, that it should not turn out thus? But if the thing should turn out otherwise, the wretched man is humbled; he knows not even what to say about what has taken place. Who among us for the sake of this matter has consulted a seer? Who among us as to his actions has not slept in indifference? Who? Give (name) to me one that I may see the man whom I have long been looking for, who is truly noble and ingenuous, whether young or old; name him.

Why then are we still surprised, if we are well practised in thinking about matters (any given subject), but in our acts are low, without decency, worthless, cowardly, impatient of labour, altogether bad? For we do not care about these

things nor do we study them.   But if we had feared not
death or banishment, but fear itself, we should have studied
not to fall into those things which appear to us evils.   Now
in the school we are irritable and wordy; and if any little
question arises about any of these things, we are able to
examine them fully.   But drag us to practice, and you will
find us miserably shipwrecked.   Let some disturbing appearance come on us, and you will know what we have been
studying and in what we have been exercising ourselves.
Consequently through want of discipline we are always adding something to the appearance and representing things to
be greater than what they are.   For instance as to myself,
when I am on a voyage and look down on the deep sea, or
look round on it and see no land, I am out of my mind and
imagine that I must drink up all this water if I am wrecked,
and it does not occur to me that three pints are enough.
What then disturbs me?   The sea?   No, but my opinion.
Again, when an earthquake shall happen, I imagine that the
city is going to fall on me; but is not one little stone enough
to knock my brains out?

What then are the things which are heavy on us and disturb us?   What else than opinions?   What else than opinions lie heavy upon him who goes away and leaves his companions and friends and places and habits of life?   Now
little children, for instance, when they cry on the nurse leaving them for a short time, forget their sorrow if they receive
a small cake.   Do you choose then that we should compare
you to little children?—No, by Zeus, for I do not wish to be
pacified by a small cake, but by right opinions.—And what
are these?   Such as a man ought to study all day, and not to
be affected by any thing that is not his own, neither by companion nor place nor gymnasia, and not even by his own
body, but to remember the law and to have it before his eyes.
And what is the divine law?   To keep a man's own, not to
claim that which belongs to others, but to use what is given,
and when it is not given, not to desire it; and when a thing is
taken away, to give it up readily and immediately, and to be
thankful for the time that a man has had the use of it, if you
would not cry for your nurse and mamma.   For what matter does it make by what thing a man is subdued, and on

what he depends?   In what respect are you better than he who cries for a girl, if you grieve for a little gymnasium, and little porticoes and young men and such places of amusement?   Another comes and laments that he shall no longer drink the water of Dirce.   Is the Marcian water worse than that of Dirce?   But I was used to the water of Dirce.[5]   And you in turn will be used to the other.   Then if you become attached to this also, cry for this too, and try to make a verse like the verse of Euripides,

> "The hot baths of Nero and the Marcian water."

See how tragedy is made when common things happen to silly men.

When then shall I see Athens again and the Acropolis? Wretch, are you not content with what you see daily? have you any thing better or greater to see than the sun, the moon, the stars, the whole earth, the sea?   But if indeed you comprehend him who administers the Whole, and carry him about in yourself, do you still desire small stones, and a beautiful rock?[6]   When then you are going to leave the sun itself and the moon, what will you do? will you sit and weep like children?   Well, what have you been doing in the school? what did you hear, what did you learn? why did you write yourself a philosopher, when you might have written the truth; as, "I made certain introductions,[7] and I read Chrysippus, but I did not even approach the door of a philosopher." For how should I possess any thing of the kind which Socrates possessed, who died as he did, who lived as he did, or any thing such as Diogenes possessed?   Do you think that any one of such men wept or grieved, because he was not going to see a certain man, or a certain woman, nor to be in Athens or in Corinth, but, if it should so happen, in Susa or in Ecbatana?   For if a man can quit the banquet when he chooses, and no longer amuse himself, does he still stay and complain, and does he not stay, as at any amusement, only so long as he is pleased?   Such a man, I suppose, would endure perpetual exile or to be condemned to death.   Will you not be weaned now, like children, and take more solid food, and not cry after mammas and nurses, which are the lamentations

of old women?—But if I go away, I shall cause them sorrow.
—You cause them sorrow? By no means; but that will
cause them sorrow which also causes you sorrow, opinion.
What have you to do then? Take away your own opinion,
and if these women are wise, they will take away their own:
if they do not, they will lament through their own fault.

My man, as the proverb says, make a desperate effort on
behalf of tranquillity of mind, freedom and magnanimity.
Lift up your head at last as released from slavery. Dare
to look up to God and say, Deal with me for the future as
thou wilt; I am of the same mind as thou art; I am thine:
I refuse nothing that pleases thee: lead me where thou wilt:
clothe me in any dress thou choosest: is it thy will that I
should hold the office of a magistrate, that I should be in the
condition of a private man, stay here or be an exile, be poor,
be rich? I will make thy defence to men in behalf of all these
conditions: I will shew the nature of each thing what it is.—
You will not do so; but sit in an ox's belly and wait for your
mamma till she shall feed you. Who would Hercules have
been, if he had sat at home? He would have been Eurystheus
and not Hercules. Well, and in his travels through the world
how many intimates and how many friends had he? But
nothing more dear to him than God. For this reason it was
believed that he was the son of God, and he was. In obedience to God then he went about purging away injustice and
lawlessness. But you are not Hercules and you are not
able to purge away the wickedness of others; nor yet are you
Theseus, able to purge away the evil things of Attica. Clear
away your own. From yourself, from your thoughts cast
away instead of Procrustes and Sciron,⁸ sadness, fear, desire,
envy, malevolence, avarice, effeminacy, intemperance. But
it is not possible to eject these things otherwise than by looking to God only, by fixing your affections on him only, by
being consecrated to his commands. But if you choose any
thing else, you will with sighs and groans be compelled to fol-
low⁹ what is stronger than yourself, always seeking tranquillity and never able to find it; for you seek tranquillity
there where it is not, and you neglect to seek it where it is.

¹ See ii. 10, 25.

² "To answer to things" means to act in a way suitable to circumstances, to be a match for them.

³ Perhaps this was a common puzzle. The man answers right; he can not say.

⁴ That is which follows praise or blame. He seems to mean making the proper use of praise or of blame.

⁵ Dirce a pure stream in Bœotia, which flows into the Ismenus. The Marcian water is the Marcian aqueduct at Rome, which was constructed B.C. 144, and was the best water that Rome had. Some of the arches of this aqueduct exist. The "bright stream of Dirce" is spoken of in the "Hercules Furens" of Euripides (v. 573). The verse in the text which we may suppose that Epictetus made, has a spondee in the fourth place, which is contrary to the rule.

⁶ The "small stones" are supposed to be the marbles which decorated Athens, and the rock to be the Acropolis.

⁷ In the original it is Εἰσαγωγαί. It was a name used for short commentaries on the principles of any art; such as we now call Introductions, Compendiums, Elements. Gellius, xvi. 8.

⁸ Procrustes and Sciron, two robbers who infested Attica and were destroyed by Theseus, as Plutarch tells in his life of Theseus.

⁹ Antoninus x. 28, "only to the rational animal is it given to follow voluntarily what happens; but simply to follow is a necessity imposed on all." Compare Seneca, Quæst. Nat. ii. 59.

CHAPTER XVII

HOW WE MUST ADAPT PRECONCEPTIONS TO PARTICULAR CASES

WHAT is the first business of him who philoso-
phizes? To throw away self conceit (οἴησις).[1]
For it is impossible for a man to begin to
learn that which he thinks that he knows. As
to things then which ought to be done and ought not
to be done, and good and bad, and beautiful and ugly,
all of us talking of them at random go to the philosophers; and on these matters we praise, we censure, we
accuse, we blame, we judge and determine about principles
honourable and dishonourable. But why do we go to the
philosophers? Because we wish to learn what we do not
think that we know. And what is this? Theorems.[2] For
we wish to learn what philosophers say as being something
elegant and acute; and some wish to learn that they may get
profit from what they learn. It is ridiculous then to think
that a person wishes to learn one thing, and will learn another; or further, that a man will make proficiency in that
which he does not learn. But the many are deceived by this
which deceived also the rhetorician Theopompus,[3] when he
blames even Plato for wishing everything to be defined.
For what does he say? Did none of us before you use the
words Good or Just, or do we utter the sounds in an unmean-
ing and empty way without understanding what they severally signify? Now who tells you, Theopompus, that we had
not natural notions of each of these things and preconceptions (προλήψεις)? But it is not possible to adapt preconceptions to their correspondent objects if we have not distinguished (analyzed) them, and inquired what object must
be subjected to each preconception. You may make the
same charge against physicians also. For who among us
did not use the words healthy and unhealthy before Hippocrates lived, or did we utter these words as empty sounds?
For we have also a certain preconception of health, but we

are not able to adapt it. For this reason one says, abstain from food; another says, give food; another says, bleed; and another says, use cupping. What is the reason? is it any other than that a man can not properly adapt the preconception of health to particulars?

So it is in this matter also, in the things which concern life. Who among us does not speak of good and bad, of useful and not useful; for who among us has not a preconception of each of these things? Is it then a distinct and perfect preconception? Show this. How shall I show this? Adapt the preconception properly to the particular things. Plato, for instance, subjects definitions to the preconception of the useful, but you to the preconception of the useless. Is it possible then that both of you are right? How is it possible? Does not one man adapt the preconception of good to the matter of wealth, and another not to wealth, but to the matter of pleasure and to that of health? For, generally, if all of us who use those words know sufficiently each of them, and need no diligence in resolving (making distinct) the notions of the preconceptions, why do we differ, why do we quarrel, why do we blame one another?

And why do I now allege this contention with one another and speak of it? If you yourself properly adapt your preconceptions, why are you unhappy, why are you hindered? Let us omit at present the second topic about the pursuits (ὅρμας) and the study of the duties which relate to them. Let us omit also the third topic, which relates to the assents (συγκαταθέσεις): I give up to you these two topics. Let us insist upon the first, which presents an almost obvious demonstration that we do not properly adapt the preconceptions. Do you now desire that which is possible and that which is possible to you? Why then are you hindered? why are you unhappy? Do you not now try to avoid the unavoidable? Why then do you fall in with any thing which you would avoid? Why are you unfortunate? Why, when you desire a thing, does it not happen, and, when you do not desire it, does it happen? For this is the greatest proof of unhappiness and misery; I wish for something, and it does not happen. And what is more wretched than I?

It was because she could not endure this that Medea came

to murder her children: an act of a noble spirit in this view
at least, for she had a just opinion what it is for a thing not
to succeed which a person wishes.   Then she says, "Thus I
shall be avenged on him (my husband) who has wronged
and insulted me; and what shall I gain if he is punished thus?
how then shall it be done?   I shall kill my children, but I
shall punish myself also; and what do I care?"[4]   This is the
aberration of soul which possesses great energy.   For she
did not know wherein lies the doing of that which we wish;
that you can not get this from without, nor yet by the alteration and new adaptation of things.   Do not desire the man
(Jason, Medea's husband), and nothing which you desire
will fail to happen: do not obstinately desire that he shall
live with you: do not desire to remain in Corinth; and in a
word desire nothing than that which God wills.—And who
shall hinder you? who shall compel you?   No man shall
compel you any more than he shall compel Zeus.

When you have such a guide and your wishes and desires
are the same as his, why do you still fear disappointment?
Give up your desire to wealth and your aversion to poverty,
and you will be disappointed in the one, you will fall into the
other.   Well give them up to health, and you will be unfortunate: give them up to magistracies, honours, country,
friends, children, in a word to any of the things which are
not in man's power (and you will be unfortunate).   But
give them up to Zeus and to the rest of the gods; surrender
them to the gods, let the gods govern, let your desire and
aversion be ranged on the side of the gods, and wherein will
you be any longer unhappy?   But if, lazy wretch, you envy,
and complain, and are jealous and fear, and never cease for a
single day complaining both of yourself and of the gods, why
do you still speak of being educated?   What kind of an
education, man?   Do you mean that you have been employed
about sophistical syllogisms (συλλογισμοὺς μεταπίπτοντας)?
Will you not, if it is possible, unlearn all these things and
begin from the beginning, and see at the same time that
hitherto you have not even touched the matter; and then
commencing from this foundation, will you not build up all
that comes after, so that nothing may happen which you do

not choose, and nothing shall fail to happen which you do choose?

Give me one young man who has come to the school with this intention, who is become a champion for this matter and says, "I give up everything else, and it is enough for me if it shall ever be in my power to pass my life free from hindrance and free from trouble, and to stretch out (present) my neck to all things like a free man, and to look up to heaven as a friend of God and fear nothing that can happen." Let any of you point out such a man that I may say, "Come, young man, into the possession of that which is your own, for it is your destiny to adorn philosophy: yours are these possessions, yours these books, yours these discourses." Then when he shall have laboured sufficiently and exercised himself in this part of the matter (τόπον), let him come to me again and say, "I desire to be free from passion and free from perturbation; and I wish as a pious man and a philosopher and a diligent person to know what is my duty to the gods, what to my parents, what to my brothers, what to my country, what to strangers." (I say) "Come also to the second matter (τόπον): this also is yours."—"But I have now sufficiently studied the second part (τόπον) also, and I would gladly be secure and unshaken, and not only when I am awake, but also when I am asleep, and when I am filled with wine, and when I am melancholy." Man, you are a god, you have great designs.

No: but I wish to understand what Chrysippus says in his treatise of the "Pseudomenos"[5] (the Liar).—Will you not hang yourself, wretch, with such your intention? And what good will it do you? You will read the whole with sorrow, and you will speak to others trembling. Thus you also do. "Do you wish me,[6] brother, to read to you, and you to me"? —You write excellently, my man; and you also excellently in the style of Xenophon, and you in the style of Plato, and you in the style of Antisthenes. Then having told your dreams to one another you return to the same things: your desires are the same, your aversions the same, your pursuits are the same, and your designs and purposes, you wish for the same things and work for the same. In the next place you do not even seek for one to give you advice, but you are vexed if

you hear such things (as I say).   Then you say, "An ill-natured old fellow: when I was going away, he did not weep
nor did he say, Into what danger you are going: if you come
off safe, my child, I will burn lights.   This is what a good
natured man would do."   It will be a great thing for you if
you do return safe, and it will be worth while to burn lights
for such a person: for you ought to be immortal and exempt
from disease.

Casting away then, as I say, this conceit of thinking that
we know something useful, we must come to philosophy as
we apply to geometry, and to music: but if we do not, we
shall not even approach to proficiency though we read all the
collections and commentaries of Chrysippus and those of
Antipater and Archedemus.

NOTES

[1] See ii. 11, 1, and iii. 14, 8.
[2] Theorems are defined by Cicero, "De Fato," c. 6, "Percepta appello
quæ dicuntur Græce θεωρήματα."
[3] This rhetorician or orator, as Epictetus names him, appears to be
the same person as Theopompus of Chios, the historian.
[4] This is the meaning of what Medea says in the "Medea" of Euripides
Epictetus does not give the words of the poet.
[5] The "Pseudomenos" was a treatise by Chrysippus. "The Pseudomenos was a famous problem among the Stoics, and it is this.   When a
person says, I lie; doth he lie, or doth he not?   If he lies, he speaks
truth: if he speaks truth, he lies.   The philosophers composed many
books on this difficulty.   Chrysippus wrote six.   Philetas wasted himself
in studying to answer it."—Mrs. Carter.
[6] Epictetus is ridiculing the men who compliment one another on their
writings.   Upton compares Horace, Epp. ii. 2, 87.

"ut alter
Alterius sermone meros audiret honores—
Discedo Alcæus puncto illius? ille meo quis?
Quis nisi Callimachus?"

CHAPTER XVIII

HOW WE SHOULD STRUGGLE AGAINST APPEARANCES

EVERY habit and faculty is maintained and increased by the corresponding actions: the habit of walking by walking, the habit of running by running. If you would be a good reader, read; if a writer, write. But when you shall not have read for thirty days in succession, but have done something else, you will know the consequence. In the same way, if you shall have lain down ten days, get up and attempt to make a long walk, and you will see how your legs are weakened. Generally then if you would make any thing a habit, do it; if you would not make it a habit, do not do it, but accustom yourself to do something else in place of it.

So it is with respect to the affections of the soul: when you have been angry, you must know that not only has this evil befallen you, but that you have also increased the habit, and in a manner thrown fuel upon fire. When you have been overcome in sexual intercourse with a person, do not reckon this single defeat only, but reckon that you have also nurtured, increased your incontinence. For it is impossible for habits and faculties, some of them not to be produced, when they did not exist before, and others not be increased and strengthened by corresponding acts.

In this manner certainly, as philosophers say, also diseases of the mind grow up. For when you have once desired money, if reason be applied to lead to a perception of the evil, the desire is stopped, and the ruling faculty of our mind is restored to the original authority. But if you apply no means of cure, it no longer returns to the same state, but being again excited by the corresponding appearance, it is inflamed to desire quicker than before: and when this takes place continually, it is henceforth hardened (made callous), and the disease of the mind confirms the love of money. For he who has had a fever, and has been relieved from it, is not in the same state that he was before, unless he has been completely cured.   Something of the kind happens also in diseases of the soul.   Certain traces and blisters are left in it, and unless a man shall completely efface them, when he is again lashed on the same places, the lash will produce not blisters (weals) but sores.   If then you wish not to be of an angry temper, do not feed the habit: throw nothing on it which will increase it: at first keep quiet, and count the days on which you have not been angry.   I used to be in passion every day; now every second day; then every third, then every fourth.   But if you have intermitted thirty days, make a sacrifice to God.   For the habit at first begins to be weakened, and then is completely destroyed.   "I have not been vexed to-day, nor the day after, nor yet on any succeeding day during two or three months; but I took care when some exciting things happened."   Be assured that you are in a good way.   To-day when I saw a handsome person, I did not say to myself, I wish I could lie with her, and Happy is her husband; for he who says this says, Happy is her adulterer also.   Nor do I picture the rest to my mind; the woman present, and stripping herself and lying down by my side. I stroke my head and say, Well done, Epictetus, you have solved a fine little sophism, much finer than that which is called the master sophism.   And if even the woman is willing, and gives signs, and sends messages, and if she also fondle me and come close to me, and I should abstain and be victorious, that would be a sophism beyond that which is named the Liar, and the Quiescent.   Over such a victory as this a man may justly be proud; not for proposing the master sophism.

How then shall this be done?   Be willing at length to be approved by yourself, be willing to appear beautiful to God, desire to be in purity with your own pure self and with God.   Then when any such appearance visits you, Plato says, "Have recourse to expiations, go a suppliant to the temples of the averting deities."   It is even sufficient if you resort to the society of noble and just men, and compare yourself with them, whether you find one who is living or dead.   Go to Socrates and see him lying down with Alcibiades, and mocking his beauty: consider what a victory he at last found that he had gained over himself; what an Olympian victory;

in what number he stood from Hercules;[1] so that, by the Gods, one may justly salute him, Hail, wondrous man, you who have conquered not these sorry boxers and pancratiasts, nor yet those who are like them, the gladiators. By placing these objects on the other side you will conquer the appearance: you will not be drawn away by it. But in the first place be not hurried away by the rapidity of the appearance, but say, Appearances, wait for me a little: let me see who you are, and what you are about: let me put you to the test. And then do not allow the appearance to lead you on and draw lively pictures of the things which will follow; for if you do, it will carry you off wherever it pleases. But rather bring in to oppose it some other beautiful and noble appearance and cast out this base appearance. And if you are accustomed to be exercised in this way, you will see what shoulders, what sinews, what strength you have. But now it is only trifling words, and nothing more.

This is the true athlete, the man who exercises himself against such appearances. Stay, wretch, do not be carried away. Great is the combat, divine is the work; it is for kingship, for freedom, for happiness, for freedom from perturbation. Remember God: call on him as a helper and protector, as men at sea call on the Dioscuri[2] in a storm. For what is a greater storm than that which comes from appearances which are violent and drive away the reason? For the storm itself, what else is it but an appearance? For take away the fear of death, and suppose as many thunders and lightnings as you please, and you will know what calm[3] and serenity there is in the ruling faculty. But if you have once been defeated and say that you will conquer hereafter, and then say the same again, be assured that you will at last be in so wretched a condition and so weak that you will not even know afterwards that you are doing wrong, but you will even begin to make apologies (defences) for your wrong doing, and then you will confirm the saying of Hesiod[4] to be true,

" With constant ills the dilatory strives."

NOTES

[1] Hercules is said to have established gymnastic contests and to have been the first victor. Those who gained the victory both in wrestling

and in the pancratium were reckoned in the list of victors as coming in the second or third place after him, and so on.

³ Castor and Pollux Horace, Carm. 1. 12:—

> "Quorum simul alba nautis
> Stella refulsit, etc."

¹ " Consider that every thing is opinion, and opinion is in thy power. Take away then, when thou choosest, thy opinion, and like a mariner, who has doubled the promontory, thou wilt find calm, every thing stable, and a waveless bay."   Antoninus, xii.

⁴ Hesiod, Works and Days, v. 411.

CHAPTER XIX

AGAINST THOSE WHO EMBRACE PHILOSOPHICAL OPINIONS
ONLY IN WORDS

T HE argument called the ruling argument (ὁ κυριεύων λόγος) appears to have been proposed from such principles as these: there is in fact a common contradiction between one another in these three propositions, each two being in contradiction to the third. The propositions are, that every thing past must of necessity be true; that an impossibility does not follow a possibility; and that a thing is possible which neither is nor will be true. Diodorus[1] observing this contradiction employed the probative force of the first two for the demonstration of this proposition. That nothing is possible which is not true and never will be. Now another will hold these two: That something is possible, which is neither true nor ever will be: and That an impossibility does not follow a possibility. But he will not allow that every thing which is past is necessarily true, as the followers of Cleanthes seem to think, and Antipater copiously defended them. But others maintain the other two propositions, That a thing is possible which is neither true nor will be true: and That everything which is past is necessarily true; but then they will maintain that an impossibility can follow a possibility. But it is impossible to maintain these three propositions, because of their common contradiction.[2]

If then any man should ask me, which of these propositions do you maintain? I will answer him, that I do not know; but I have received this story, that Diodorus maintained one opinion, the followers of Panthoides, I think, and Cleanthes maintained another opinion, and those of Chrysippus a third. What then is your opinion? I was not made for this purpose, to examine the appearances that occur to me, and to compare what others say and to form an opinion of my own on the thing. Therefore I differ not at all from the grammarian. Who was Hector's father? Priam.

Who were his brothers? Alexander and Deiphobus. Who
was their mother? Hecuba—I have heard this story. From
whom? From Homer. And Hellanicus also, I think,
writes about the same things, and perhaps others like him.
And what further have I about the ruling argument? Nothing. But, if I am a vain man, especially at a banquet I
surprise the guests by enumerating those who have written
on these matters. Both Chrysippus has written wonder-
fully in his first book about Possibilities, and Cleanthes has
written specially on the subject, and Archedemus. Antipater also has written not only in his work about Possibilities, but also separately in his work on the ruling argument.
Have you not read the work? I have not read it. Read.
And what profit will a man have from it? he will be more
trifling and impertinent than he is now; for what else have
you gained by reading it? What opinion have you formed
on this subject? none; but you will tell us of Helen and
Priam, and the island of Calypso which never was and never
will be. And in this matter indeed it is of no great importance if you retain the story, but have formed no opinion of
your own. But in matters of morality (Ethic) this happens
to us much more than in these things of which we are speaking.

Speak to me about good and evil.[3] Listen:

> "The wind from Ilium to Ciconian shores
> Brought me."[4]

Of things some are good, some are bad, and others are
indifferent. The good then are the virtues and the things
which partake of the virtues: the bad are the vices, and the
things which partake of them; and the indifferent are the
things which lie between the virtues and the vices, wealth,
health, life, death, pleasure, pain. Whence do you know
this? Hellanicus says it in his Egyptian history; for what
difference does it make to say this, or to say that Diogenes
has it in his Ethic, or Chrysippus or Cleanthes? Have you
then examined any of these things and formed an opinion of
your own? Show how you are used to behave in a storm
on shipboard? Do you remember this division (distinction
of things), when the sail rattles and a man, who knows noth-

ing of times and seasons, stands by you when you are
screaming and says, "Tell me, I ask you by the gods, what
you were saying just now, Is it a vice to suffer shipwreck:
does it participate in vice?" Will you not take up a stick and
lay it on his head? What have we to do with you, man? we
are perishing and you come to mock us? But if Cæsar send
for you to answer a charge, do you remember the distinction? If when you are going in pale and trembling, a person should come up to you and say, "Why do you tremble,
man? what is the matter about which you are engaged?
Does Cæsar who sits within give virtue and vice to those
who go in to him?" You reply, Why do you also mock me
and add to my present sorrows?—"Still tell me, philosopher,
tell me why you tremble? Is it not death of which you run
the risk, or a prison, or pain of the body, or banishment, or
disgrace? What else is there? Is there any vice or anything which partakes of vice?" What then did you use to
say of these things?—"What have you to do with me, man?
my own evils are enough for me." And you say right.
Your own evils are enough for you, your baseness, your
cowardice, your boasting which you showed when you sat
in the school. Why did you decorate yourself with what
belonged to others? Why did you call yourself a Stoic?

Observe yourselves thus in your actions, and you will find
to what sect you belong. You will find that most of you are
Epicureans, a few Peripatetics,[5] and those feeble. For
wherein will you show that you really consider virtue equal
to everything else or even superior? But show me a Stoic,
if you can. Where or how? But you can show me an
endless number who utter small arguments of the Stoics.
For do the same persons repeat the Epicurean opinions any
worse? And the Peripatetic, do they not handle them also
with equal accuracy? who then is a Stoic? As we call a
statue Phidiac, which is fashioned according to the art of
Phidias; so show me a man who is fashioned according to
the doctrines which he utters. Show me a man who is sick
and happy, in danger and happy, dying and happy, in exile
and happy, in disgrace and happy. Show him: I desire, by
the gods, to see a Stoic. You can not show me one fashioned
so; but show me at least one who is forming, who has shown

11

a tendency to be a Stoic.   Do me this favour: do not grudge
an old man seeing a sight which I have not seen yet.   Do
you think that you must show me the Zeus of Phidias or the
Athena, a work of ivory and gold?   Let any of you show
me a human soul ready to think as God does, and not to
blame[6] either God or man, ready not to be disappointed about
any thing, not to consider himself damaged by any thing, not
to be angry, not to be envious, not to be jealous; and why
should I not say it direct? desirous from a man to become
a god, and in this poor mortal body thinking of his fellowship with Zeus.[7] Show me the man. But you can not.
Why then do you delude yourselves and cheat others? and
why do you put on a guise which does not belong to you, and
walk about being thieves and pilferers of these names and
things which do not belong to you?

   And now I am your teacher, and you are instructed in my
school.   And I have this purpose, to make you free from
restraint, compulsion, hindrance, to make you free, prosperous, happy, looking to God in everything small and great.
And you are here to learn and practise these things.   Why
then do you not finish the work, if you also have such a purpose as you ought to have, and if I in addition to the purpose
also have such qualification as I ought to have?   What is
that which is wanting?   When I see an artificer and material
lying by him, I expect the work.   Here then is the artificer,
here the material; what is it that we want?   Is not the thing
one that can be taught?   It is.   Is it not then in our power?
The only thing of all that is in our power.   Neither wealth
is in our power, nor health, nor reputation, nor in a word
any thing else except the right use of appearances   This,
(right use) is by nature free from restraint, this alone is
free from impediment.   Why then do you not finish the
work? Tell me the reason.   For it is either through my
fault that you do not finish it, or through your own fault, or
through the nature of the thing.   The thing itself is possible,
and the only thing in our power.   It remains then that the
fault is either in me or in you, or, what is nearer the truth,
in both.   Well then, are you willing that we begin at last to
bring such a purpose into this school, and to take no notice of

the past? Let us only make a beginning. Trust to me, and you will see.

NOTES

[1] Diodorus, surnamed Cronus, lived at Alexandria in the time of Ptolemæus Soter. He was of the school named the Megaric, and distinguished in dialectic.

[2] If you assume any two of these three, they must be in contradiction to the third and destroy it.

[3] "Speak to me," etc, may be supposed to be said to Epictetus, who has been ridiculing logical subtleties and the grammarians' learning. When he is told to speak of good and evil, he takes a verse of the Odyssey, the first which occurs to him, and says, Listen. There is nothing to listen to, but it is as good for the hearer as anything else Then he utters some philosophical principles, and being asked where he learned them, he says, from Hellanicus, who was an historian, not a philosopher. He is bantering the hearer: it makes no matter from what author I learned them; it is all the same. The real question is, have you examined what Good and Evil are, and have you formed an opinion yourself?

[4] Odyssey, ix. 39.

[5] The Peripatetics allowed many things to be good which contributed to a happy life; but still they contended that the smallest mental excellence was superior to all other things. Cicero, De Fin. v. 5, 31.

[6] "To blame God" means to blame the constitution and order of things, for to do this appeared to Epictetus to be absurd and wicked; as absurd as for the potter's vessel to blame the potter, if that can be imagined, for making it liable to wear out and to break.

[7] "'Our fellowship is with the Father and with his son Jesus Christ,' I John i. 3 The attentive reader will observe several passages besides those which have been noticed, in which there is a striking conformity between Epictetus and the Scriptures: and will perceive from them, either that the Stoics had learned a good deal of the Christian language or that treating a subject practically and in earnest leads men to such strong expressions as we often find in Scripture and sometimes in the philosophers, especially Epictetus."—Mrs. Carter.

CHAPTER XX

T HE propositions which are true and evident are of necessity used even by those who contradict them: and a man might perhaps consider it to be the greatest proof of a thing being evident that it is found to be necessary even for him who denies it to make use of it at the same time. For instance, if a man should deny that there is anything universally true, it is plain that he must make the contradictory negation, that nothing is universally true. What, wretch, do you not admit even this? For what else is this than to affirm that whatever is universally affirmed is false? Again if a man should come forward and say: Know that there is nothing that can be known, but all things are incapable of sure evidence; or if another say, Believe me and you will be the better for it, that a man ought not to believe any thing; or again, if another should, say, Learn from me, man, that it is not possible to learn any thing; I tell you this and will teach you, if you choose. Now in what respect do these differ from those? Whom shall I name? Those who call themselves 'Academics? "Men, agree [with us] that no man agrees [with another] : believe us that no man believes anybody."

Thus Epicurus[1] also, when he designs to destroy the natural fellowship of mankind, at the same time makes use of that which he destroys. For what does he say? "Be not deceived, men, nor be led astray, nor be mistaken: there is no natural fellowship among rational animals; believe me. But those who say otherwise, deceive you and seduce you by false reasons."—What is this to you? Permit us to be deceived. Will you fare worse, if all the rest of us are persuaded that there is a natural fellowship among us, and that it ought by all means to be preserved? Nay, it will be much better and safer for you. Man, why do you trouble yourself about us? Why do you keep awake for us? Why do you light your lamp? Why do you rise early? Why do you write so many books, that no one of us may be deceived about the gods and believe that they take care of men; or that no one may suppose the nature of good to be other than pleasure? For if this is so, lie down and sleep, and lead the life of a worm, of which you judged yourself worthy: eat and drink, and enjoy women, and ease yourself, and snore.[2] And what is it to you, how the rest shall think about these things, whether right or wrong?   For what have we to do with you?   You take care of sheep because they supply us with wool and milk, and last of all with their flesh.   Would it not be a desirable thing if men could be lulled and enchanted by the Stoics, and sleep and present themselves to you and to those like you to be shorn and milked?   For this you ought to say to your brother Epicureans: but ought you not to conceal it from others, and particularly before every thing to persuade them, that we are by nature adapted for fellowship, that temperance is a good thing; in order that all things may be secure for you?[3]   Or ought we to maintain this fellowship with some and not with others?   With whom then ought we to maintain it?   With such as on their part also maintain it, or with such as violate this fellowship?   And who violate it more than you who establish such doctrines?

What then was it that waked Epicurus from his sleepiness, and compelled him to write what he did write?   What else was it than that which is the strongest thing in men, Nature, which draws a man to her own will though he be unwilling and complaining? For since, she says, you think that there is no community among mankind, write this opinion and leave it for others, and break your sleep to do this, and by your own practice condemn your own opinions.   Shall we then say that Orestes was agitated by the Erinyes (Furies) and roused from his deep sleep, and did not more savage Erinyes and Pains rouse Epicurus from his sleep and not allow him to rest, but compelled him to make known his own evils, as madness and wine did the Galli (the priests of Cybele)?   So strong and invincible is man's nature.   For how can a vine be moved not in the manner of a vine, but in the manner of an olive tree? or on the other hand how can an olive tree be moved not in the manner of an olive tree, but in the manner of a vine?   It is impossible: it can not be conceived. Neither then is it possible for a man completely to lose the movements (affects) of a man; and even those who are deprived of their genital members are not able to deprive themselves of man's desires. Thus Epicurus also mutilated all the offices of a man, and of a father of a family, and of a citizen and of a friend, but he did not mutilate human desires, for he could not; not more than the lazy Academics can cast away or blind their own senses, though they have tried with all their might to do it. What a shame is this? when a man has received from nature measures and rules for the knowing of truth, and does not strive to add to these measures and rules and to improve them, but just the contrary, endeavours to take away and destroy whatever enables us to discern the truth?

What say you philosopher? piety and sanctity, what do you think that they are? If you like, I will demonstrate that they are good things. Well, demonstrate it, that our citizens may be turned and honour the deity and may no longer be negligent about things of the highest value. Have you then the demonstrations?—I have, and I am thankful. —Since then you are well pleased with them, hear the contrary: That there are no Gods, and, if there are, they take no care of men, nor is there any fellowship between us and them; and that this piety and sanctity which is talked of among most men is the lying of boasters and sophists, or certainly of legislators for the purpose of terrifying and checking wrong doers.[4]—Well done, philosopher, you have done something for our citizens, you have brought back all the young men to contempt of things divine.—What then, does not this satisfy you? Learn now, that justice is nothing, that modesty is folly, that a father is nothing, a son nothing.—Well done, philosopher, persist, persuade the young men, that we may have more with the same opinions as you and who say the same as you. From such principles as these have grown our well constituted states; by these was Sparta founded: Lycurgus fixed these opinions in the Spartans by his laws and education, that neither is the servile condition more base than honourable, nor the condition of free men more honourable than base, and that those who died at Thermopylæ[5] died from these opinions; and through what other opinions did the Athenians leave their city?⁶ Then those who talk thus, marry and beget children, and employ themselves in public affairs and make themselves priests and interpreters. Of whom? of gods who do not exist: and they consult the Pythian priestess that they may hear lies, and they report the oracles to others. Monstrous impudence and imposture.

Man what are you doing?⁷ are you refuting yourself every day; and will you not give up these frigid attempts? When you eat, where do you carry your hand to? to your mouth or to your eye? When you wash yourself, what do you go into? Do you ever call a pot a dish, or a ladle a spit? If I were a slave of any of these men, even if I must be flayed by him daily, I would rack him. If he said, "Boy, throw some olive oil into the bath," I would take pickle sauce and pour it down on his head. What is this? he would say—An appearance was presented to me, I swear by your genius, which could not be distinguished from oil and was exactly like it—Here give me the barley-drink (tisane), he says—I would fill and carry him a dish of sharp sauce—Did I not ask for the barley drink? Yes, master: this is the barley drink? Take it and smell; take it and taste. How do you know then if our senses deceive us?—If I had three or four fellow-slaves of the same opinion, I should force him to hang himself through passion or to change his mind. But now they mock us by using all the things which nature gives, and in words destroying them.

Grateful indeed are men and modest, who, if they do nothing else, are daily eating bread and yet are shameless enough to say, we do not know if there is a Demeter or her daughter Persephone or a Pluto:⁸ not to mention that they are enjoying the night and the day, the seasons of the year, and the stars, and the sea and the land and the co-operation of mankind, and yet they are not moved in any degree by these things to turn their attention to them; but they only seek to belch out their little problem (matter for discussion), and when they have exercised their stomach to go off to the bath. But what they shall say, and about what things or to what persons, and what their hearers shall learn from this talk, they care not even in the least degree, nor do they care if any

generous youth after hearing such talk should suffer any
harm from it, nor after he has suffered harm should lose all
the seeds of his generous nature; nor if we should give an
adulterer help towards being shameless in his acts; nor if a
public peculator should lay hold of some cunning excuse
from these doctrines; nor if another who neglects his parents
should be confirmed in his audacity by this teaching.—What
then in your opinion is good or bad?   This or that?—Why
then should a man say any more in reply to such persons as
these, or give them any reason or listen to any reason from
them, or try to convince them?   By Zeus one might much
sooner expect to make catamites change their mind than
those who are become so deaf and blind to their own evils.[9]

NOTES

[1] Cicero, de Fin. ii. 30. 31, speaking of the letter, which Epicurus wrote
to Hermarchus when he was dying, says "that the actions of Epicurus
were inconsistent with his sayings," and "his writings were confuted
by his probity and morality."
[2] Paul says, 1 Cor 15:32 "If after the manner of men I have fought
with beasts at Ephesus, what advantageth it me, if the dead rise not?
let us eat and drink, for to-morrow we die." The words "let us eat and
drink," etc are said to be a quotation from the Thais of Menander The
meaning seems to be, that if I do not believe in the resurrection of the
dead, why should I not enjoy the sensual pleasures of life only? This
is not the doctrine of Epictetus, as we see in the text
[3] It would give security to the Epicureans, that they would enjoy all
that they value, if other men should be persuaded that we are all made
for fellowship, and that temperance is a good thing
[4] Polybius when he is speaking of the Roman state, commends the men
of old time, who established in the minds of the multitude the opinions
about the gods and Hades, wherein, he says, they acted more wisely than
those in his time who would destroy such opinions.
[5] Epictetus alludes to the Spartans who fought at Thermopylæ B. C.
480 against Xerxes and his army. Herodotus has recorded the inscrip-
tion placed over the Spartans:—

> "Stranger go tell the Spartans, Here we lie
> Obedient to those who bade us die."

[6] When Xerxes was advancing on Athens, the Athenians left the city
and embarked on their vessels before the battle of Salamis, B.C. 480
[7] He is now attacking the Academics, who asserted that we can know
nothing.
[8] Epictetus is speaking according to the popular notions To deny
Demeter and to eat the bread which she gives is the same thing in the
common notions of the Greeks, as it would be for Epictetus to deny the
existence of God and to eat the bread which he gives.
[9] "This resembles what our Saviour said to the Jewish rulers: Verily

I say unto you, that the publicans and the harlots go into the kingdom of God before you." Matthew, xxi. 31.—Mrs. Carter

To an Academic who said he comprehended nothing, the Stoic Ariston replied, "Do you not see even the person who is sitting near you?" When the Academic denied it, Ariston said, "Who made you blind? who stole your power of sight?" (Diogenes Laertius, vii. 163.)

CHAPTER XXI

OF INCONSISTENCY

SOME things men readily confess, and other things they do not. No one then will confess that he is a fool or without understanding; but quite the contrary you will hear all men saying, I wish that I had fortune equal to my understanding. But men readily confess that they are timid, and they say: I am rather timid, I confess; but as to other respects you will not find me to be foolish. A man will not readily confess that he is intemperate; and that he is unjust, he will not confess at all. He will by no means confess that he is envious or a busy body. Most men will confess that they are compassionate. What then is the reason?—The chief thing (the ruling thing) is inconsistency and confusion in the things which relate to good and evil. But different men have different reasons; and generally what they imagine to be base, they do not confess at all. But they suppose timidity to be a characteristic of a good disposition, and compassion also; but silliness to be the absolute characteristic of a slave. And they do not at all admit (confess) the things which are offences against society. But in the case of most errors for this reason chiefly they are induced to confess them, because they imagine that there is something involuntary in them as in timidity and compassion; and if a man confess that he is in any respect intemperate, he alleges love (or passion) as an excuse for what is involuntary. But men do not imagine injustice to be at all involuntary. There is also in jealousy, as they suppose, something involuntary; and for this reason they confess to jealousy also.

Living then among such men, who are so confused, so ignorant of what they say, and of the evils which they have or have not, and why they have them, or how they shall be relieved of them, I think it is worth the trouble for a man to watch constantly (and to ask) whether I am also one of them, what imagination I have about myself, how I conduct

myself, whether I conduct myself as a prudent man, whether
I conduct myself as a temperate man, whether I ever say
this, that I have been taught to be prepared for everything
that may happen.   Have I the consciousness, which a man
who knows nothing ought to have, that I know nothing?
Do I go to my teacher as men go to oracles, prepared to
obey? or do I like a snivelling boy go to my school to learn
history and understand the books which I did not understand before, and, if it should happen so, to explain them
also to others?—Man, you have had a fight in the house with
a poor slave, you have turned the family upside down, you
have frightened the neighbours, and you come to me as if
you were a wise man, and you take your seat and judge how
I have explained some word, and how I have babbled whatever came into my head. You come full of envy, and humbled, because you bring nothing from home; and you sit
during the discussion thinking of nothing else than how
your father is disposed towards you and your brother.
"What are they saying about me there? now they think that
I am improving, and are saying, He will return with all
knowledge.   I wish I could learn every thing before I return: but much labour is necessary, and no one sends me
any thing, and the baths at Nicopolis are dirty; every thing
is bad at home, and bad here."
    Then they say, no one gains any profit from the school.
—Why, who comes to the school? who comes for the purpose of being improved? who comes to present his opinions
to be purified? who comes to learn what he is in want of?
Why do you wonder then if you carry back from the school
the very things which you bring into it?   For you come not
to lay aside (your principles) or to correct them or to receive other principles in place of them.   By no means, nor
any thing like it.   You rather look to this, whether you possess already that for which you come.   You wish to prattle
about theorems?   What then?   Do you not become greater
triflers? Do not your little theorems give you some opportunity of display?   You solve sophistical syllogisms.   Do
you not examine the assumptions of the syllogism named the
Liar?   Do you not examine hypothetical syllogisms?   Why
then are you still vexed if you receive the things for which

you come to the school? Yes; but if my child die or my
brother, or if I must die or be racked, what good will these
things do me?—Well, did you come for this? for this do
you sit by my side? did you ever for this light your lamp or
keep awake? or, when you went out to the walking place,
did you ever propose any appearance that had been presented
to you instead of a syllogism, and did you and your friends
discuss it together? Where and when? Then you say,
Theorems are useless. To whom? To such as make a bad
use of them. For eye-salves are not useless to those who
use them as they ought and when they ought. Fomenta-
tions are not useless. Dumb-bells are not useless; but they
are useless to some, useful to others. If you ask me now if
syllogisms are useful, I will tell you that they are useful, and
if you choose, I will prove it.—How then will they in any
way be useful to me? Man, did you ask if they are useful
to you, or did you ask generally? Let him who is suffering from dysentery, ask me if vinegar is useful; I will say
that it is useful.—Will it then be useful to me?—I will say,
no. Seek first for the discharge to be stopped and the ulcers
to be closed. And do you, O men, first cure the ulcers and
stop the discharge; be tranquil in your mind, bring it free
from distraction into the school, and you will know what
power reason has.

CHAPTER XXII

ON FRIENDSHIP[1]

WHAT a man applies himself to earnestly, that he naturally loves. Do men then apply themselves earnestly to the things which are bad? By no means. Well, do they apply themselves to things which in no way concern themselves? not to these either. It remains then that they employ themselves earnestly only about things which are good; and if they are earnestly employed about things, they love such things also. Whoever then understands what is good, can also know how to love: but he who can not distinguish good from bad, and things which are neither good nor bad from both, how can he possess the power of loving? To love then is only in the power of the wise.

How is this? a man may say; I am foolish, and yet I love my child.—I am surprised indeed that you have begun by making the admission that you are foolish. For what are you deficient in? Can you not make use of your senses? do you not distinguish appearances? do you not use food which is suitable for your body, and clothing and habitation? Why then do you admit that you are foolish? It is in truth because you are often disturbed by appearances and perplexed, and their power of persuasion often conquers you; and sometimes you think these things to be good, and then the same things to be bad, and lastly neither good nor bad; and in short you grieve, fear, envy, are disturbed, you are changed. This is the reason why you confess that you are foolish. And are you not changeable in love? But wealth, and pleasure and in a word things themselves, do you sometimes think them to be good, and sometimes bad? and do you not think the same men at one time to be good, at another time bad? and have you not at one time a friendly feeling towards them, and at another time the feeling of an enemy? and do you not at one time praise them, and at another time blame them? Yes; I have these feelings also.

Well then, do you think that he who has been deceived about a man is his friend? Certainly not. And he who has selected a man as his friend and is of a changeable dispostion, has he good-will towards him? He has not. And he who now abuses a man, and afterwards admires him? This man also has no good-will to the other. Well then, did you never see little dogs caressing and playing with one another, so that you might say, there is nothing more friendly? but that you may know what friendship is, throw a bit of flesh among them, and you will learn. Throw between yourself and your son a little estate, and you will know how soon he will wish to bury you and how soon you wish your son to die. Then you will change your tone and say, what a son I have brought up! He has long been wishing to bury me. Throw a pretty girl between you; and do you the old man love her, and the young one will love her too. If a little fame intervene or dangers, it will be just the same. You will utter the words of the father of Admetus!

"Life gives you pleasure: and why not your father?" [2]   .

Do you think that Admetus did not love his own child when he was little? that he was not in agony when the child had a fever? that he did not often say, I wish I had the fever instead of the child? then when the test (the thing) came and was near, see what words they utter. Were not Eteocles and Polynices from the same mother and from the same father? Were they not brought up together, had they not lived together, drunk together, slept together, and often kissed one another? So that, if any man, I think, had seen them, he would have ridiculed the philosophers for the paradoxes which they utter about friendship. But when a quarrel rose between them about the royal power, as between dogs about a bit of meat, see what they say

Polynices. Where will you take your station before the towers?
Eteocles. Why do you ask me this?
Pol. I will place myself opposite and try to kill you.
Et. I also wish to do the same. [3]

Such are the wishes that they utter.

For universally, be not deceived, every animal is attached to nothing so much as to its own interest.[4] Whatever then appears to it an impediment to this interest, whether this be a brother, or a father, or a child, or beloved, or lover, it hates, spurns, curses: for its nature is to love nothing so much as its own interest; this is father, and brother, and kinsman, and country, and God. When then the gods appear to us to be an impediment to this, we abuse them and throw down their statues and burn their temples, as Alexander ordered the temples of Æsculapius to be burned when his dear friend died.[5]

For this reason if a man put in the same place his interest, sanctity, goodness, and country, and parents, and friends, all these are secured: but if he puts in one place his interest, in another his friends, and his country and his kinsmen and justice itself, all these give way being borne down by the weight of interest. For where the I and the Mine are placed, to that place of necessity the animal inclines: if in the flesh, there is the ruling power: if in the will, it is there: and if it is in externals, it is there.[6] If then I am there where my will is, then only shall I be a friend such as I ought to be, and son, and father; for this will be my interest, to maintain the character of fidelity, of modesty, of patience, of abstinence, of active co-operation, of observing my relations (towards all). But if I put myself in one place, and honesty in another, then the doctrine of Epicurus becomes strong, which asserts either that there is no honesty or it is that which opinion holds to be honest (virtuous).

It was through this ignorance that the Athenians and the Lacedæmonians quarrelled, and the Thebans with both; and the great king quarrelled with Hellas, and the Macedonians with both; and the Romans with the Getæ.[7] And still earlier the Trojan war happened for these reasons. Alexander was the guest of Menelaus; and if any man had seen their friendly disposition, he would not have believed any one who said that they were not friends. But there was cast between them (as between dogs) a bit of meat, a handsome woman, and about her war arose. And now when you see brothers to be friends appearing to have one mind, do not conclude from this any thing about their friendship, not even if they swear it and say that it is impossible for them to be separated from one another. For the ruling principle of a bad man can not be trusted, it is insecure, has no certain rule by which it is directed, and is overpowered at different times by different appearances. But examine, not what other men examine, if they are born of the same parents and brought up together, and under the same pedagogue; but examine this only, wherein they place their interest, whether in externals or in the will. If in externals, do not name them friends, no more than name them trustworthy or constant, or brave or free: do not name them even men, if you have any judgment. For that is not a principle of human nature which makes them bite one another, and abuse one another, and occupy deserted places or public places, as if they were mountains,[8] and in the courts of justice display the acts of robbers; nor yet that which makes them intemperate and adulterers and corrupters, nor that which makes them do whatever else men do against one another through this one opinion only, that of placing themselves and their interests in the things which are not within the power of their will. But if you hear that in truth these men think the good to be only there, where will is, and where there is a right use of appearances, no longer trouble yourself whether they are father or son, or brothers, or have associated a long time and are companions, but when you have ascertained this only, confidently declare that they are friends, as you declare that they are faithful, that they are just. For where else is friendship than where there is fidelity, and modesty, where there is a communion of honest things and of nothing else?

But you may say, such a one treated me with regard so long; and did he not love me? How do you know, slave, if he did not regard you in the same way as he wipes his shoes with a sponge, or as he takes care of his beast? How do you know, when you have ceased to be useful as a vessel, he will not throw you away like a broken platter? But this woman is my wife, and we have lived together so long. And how long did Eriphyle live with Amphiaraus, and was the mother of children and of many? But a necklace[9] came between them: and what is a necklace? It is the opinion about such things. That was the bestial principle, that was the thing which broke asunder the friendship between husband and wife, that which did not allow the woman to be a wife, nor the mother to be a mother. And let every man among you who has seriously resolved either to be a friend himself or have another for his friend, cut out these opinions, hate them, drive them from his soul. And thus first of all he will not reproach himself, he will not be at variance with himself, he will not change his mind, he will not torture himself. In the next place, to another also, who is like himself, he will be altogether and completely a friend. But he will bear with the man who is unlike himself, he will be kind to him, gentle, ready to pardon on account of his ignorance, on account of his being mistaken in things of the greatest importance; but he will be harsh to no man, being well convinced of Plato's doctrine that every mind is deprived of truth unwillingly. If you can not do this, yet you can do in all other respects as friends do, drink together, and lodge together, and sail together, and you may be born of the same parents; for snakes also are: but neither will they be friends nor you, so long as you retain these bestial and cursed opinions.

NOTES

[1] " In this dissertation is expounded the Stoic principle that friendship is only possible between the good." Schweig. He also says that there was another discourse by Epictetus on this subject, in which he expressed some of the opinions of Musonius Rufus (1 1, note 12). Schweig. draws this conclusion from certain words of Stobæus; and he supposes that this dissertation of Epictetus was in one of the last four books of Epictetus' discourses by Arrian, which have been lost.
Cicero (de Amicit. c. 5) says "nisi in bonis amicitiam esse non posse," and c. 18
[2] The first verse is from the "Alcestis" of Euripides, v. 691. The second in Epictetus is not in Euripides.
[3] From the "Phœnissæ" of Euripides, v. 723, etc.
[4] Compare Euripides, "Hecuba," v. 846, etc.

δεινόν γε θνητοῖς ὡς ἅπαντα ὄυμπίτνει:
καὶ τὰς ἀνάγκας ὡς νόμοι διώρισαν,
φίλους τιθέντες τούς γε πολεμιωτάτους
ἐχθρούς τε τοὺς πρὶν εὐμενεῖς ποιούμενοι.

[5] Alexander did this when Hephæstion died. Arrian, Expedition of Alexander, vii. 14.
[6] Matthew vi. 21, "for where your treasure is, there will your heart be also."

¹ The quarrels of the Athenians with the Lacedæmonians appear chiefly in the history of the Peloponnesian war. (Thucydides, ı. ı.) The quarrel of the great king, the king of Persia, ıs the subject of the history of Herodotus (i ı). The great quarrel of the Macedonians with the Persians is the subject of Arrian's expedition of Alexander. The Romans were at war with the Getæ or Dacı in the tıme of Trajan, and we may assume that Epictetus was stıll lıving then.

⁸ Schweıg. thınks that thıs is the plaın meaning. "as wıld beasts in the mountains lie in waıt for men, so men lie ın wait for men, not only ın deserted places, but even in the forum "

⁹ The old story about Eriphyle who betrayed her husband for a necklace.

CHAPTER XXIII

ON THE POWER OF SPEAKING

EVERY man will read a book with more pleasure or even with more ease, if it is written in fairer characters. Therefore, every man will also listen more readily to what is spoken, if it is signified by appropriate and becoming words. We must not say then that there is no faculty of expression: for this affirmation is the characteristic of an impious and also of a timid man. Of an impious man, because he undervalues the gifts which come from God, just as if he would take away the commodity of the power of vision, or of hearing, or of seeing. Has then God given you eyes to no purpose? and to no purpose has he infused into them a spirit[1] so strong and of such skilful contrivance as to reach a long way and to fashion the forms of things which are seen? What messenger is so swift and vigilant? And to no purpose has he made the interjacent atmosphere so efficacious and elastic that the vision penetrates through the atmosphere which is in a manner moved? And to no purpose has he made light, without the presence of which there would be no use in any other thing?

Man, be neither ungrateful for these gifts nor yet forget the things which are superior to them. But indeed for the power of seeing and hearing, and indeed for life itself, and for the things which contribute to support it, for the fruits which are dry, and for wine and oil give thanks to God: but remember that he has given you something else better than all these, I mean the power of using them, proving them and estimating the value of each. For what is that which gives information about each of these powers, what each of them is worth? Is it each faculty itself? Did you ever hear the faculty of vision saying any thing about itself? or the faculty of hearing? or wheat, or barley, or a horse, or a dog? No; but they are appointed as ministers and slaves to serve the faculty which has the power of making use of the appear-

ances of things. And if you inquire what is the value of
each thing, of whom do you inquire? who answers you?
How then can any other faculty be more powerful than this,
which uses the rest as ministers and itself proves each and
pronounces about them? for which of them knows what itself
is, and what is its own value? which of them knows when
it ought to employ itself and when not? what faculty is it
which opens and closes the eyes, and turns them away from
objects to which it ought not to apply them and does apply
them to other objects? Is it the faculty of vision? No;
but it is the faculty of the will. What is that faculty
which closes and opens the ears? what is that by which
they are curious and inquisitive, or on the contrary unmoved
by what is said? is it the faculty of hearing? It is no other
than the faculty of the will. Will this faculty then, seeing
that it is amidst all the other faculties which are blind and
dumb and unable to see any thing else except the very acts
for which they are appointed in order to minister to this
(faculty) and serve it, but this faculty alone sees sharp and
sees what is the value of each of the rest; will this faculty
declare to us that any thing else is the best, or that itself is?
And what else does the eye do when it is opened than see?
But whether we ought to look on the wife of a certain person, and in what manner, who tells us? The faculty of the
will. And whether we ought to believe what is said or not
to believe it, and if we do believe, whether we ought to be
moved by it or not, who tells us? Is it not the faculty of
the will? But this faculty of speaking and of ornamenting
words, if there is indeed any such peculiar faculty, what else
does it do, when there happens to be discourse about a thing,
than to ornament the words and arrange them as hair-dress-
ers do the hair? But whether it is better to speak or to be
silent, and better to speak in this way or that way, and
whether this is becoming or not becoming, and the season
for each and the use, what else tells us than the faculty of
the will? Would you have it then to come forward and
condemn itself?

What then? it (the will) says,[2] if the fact is so, can that
which ministers be superior to that to which it ministers, can
the horse be superior to the rider, or the dog to the hunts-

man, or the instrument to the musician, or the servants to
the king? What is that which makes use of the rest? The
will. What takes care of all? The will. What destroys
the whole man, at one time by hunger, at another time by
hanging, and at another time by a precipice? The will.
Then is any thing stronger in men than this? and how is it
possible that the things which are subject to restraint are
stronger than that which is not? What things are naturally
formed to hinder the faculty of vision? Both will and
things which do not depend on the faculty of the will. It
is the same with the faculty of hearing, with the faculty of
speaking in like manner. But what has a natural power of
hindering the will? Nothing which is independent of the
will; but only the will itself, when it is perverted. Therefore this (the will) is alone vice or alone virtue.

Then being so great a faculty and set over all the rest, let
it (the will) come forward and tell us that the most excellent of all things is the flesh. Not even if the flesh itself declared that it is the most excellent, would any person bear
that it should say this. But what is it, Epicurus, which pronounces this, which wrote about the End (purpose) of our
Being,[3] which wrote on the Nature of Things, which wrote
about the Canon (rule of truth), which led you to wear a
beard, which wrote when it was dying that it was spending
the last and a happy day?[4] Was this the flesh or the will?
Then do you admit that you possess any thing superior to
this (the will)? and are you not mad? are you in fact so
blind and deaf?

What then? does any man despise the other faculties? I
hope not. Does any man say that there is no use or excellence in the speaking faculty? I hope not. That would be
foolish, impious, ungrateful towards God. But a man renders to each thing its due value. For there is some use even
in an ass, but not so much as in an ox: there is also use in
a dog, but not so much as in a slave: there is also some use
in a slave, but not so much as in citizens: there is also some
use in citizens, but not so much as in magistrates. Not indeed because some things are superior, must we undervalue
the use which other things have. There is a certain value in
the power of speaking, but it is not so great as the power

of the will. When then I speak thus, let no man think that I ask you to neglect the power of speaking, for neither do I ask you to neglect the eyes, nor the ears nor the hands nor the feet, nor clothing nor shoes. But if you ask me what then is the most excellent of all things, what must I say? I can not say the power of speaking, but the power of the will, when it is right (ὀρθή). For it is this which uses the other (the power of speaking), and all the other faculties both small and great. For when this faculty of the will is set right, a man who is not good becomes good: but when it fails, a man becomes bad. It is through this that we are unfortunate, that we are fortunate, that we blame one another, are pleased with one another. In a word, it is this which if we neglect it makes unhappiness, and if we carefully look after it, makes happiness.

But to take away the faculty of speaking and to say that there is no such faculty in reality, is the act not only of an ungrateful man towards those who gave it, but also of a cowardly man: for such a person seems to me to fear, if there is any faculty of this kind, that we shall not be able to despise it. Such also are those who say that there is no difference between beauty and ugliness. Then it would happen that a man would be affected in the same way if he saw Thersites and if he saw Achilles. in the same way, if he saw Helen and any other woman. But these are foolish and clownish notions, and the notions of men who know not the nature of each thing, but are afraid, if a man shall see the difference, that he shall immediately be seized and carried off vanquished. But this is the great matter; to leave to each thing the power (faculty) which it has, and leaving to it this power to see what is the worth of the power, and to learn what is the most excellent of all things, and to pursue this always, to be diligent about this, considering all other things of secondary value compared with this, but yet, as far as we can, not neglecting all those other things. For we must take care of the eyes also, not as if they were the most excellent thing, but we must take care of them on account of the most excellent thing, because it will not be in its true natural condition, if it does not rightly use the other faculties, and prefer some things to others.

What then is usually done? Men generally act as a traveller would do on his way to his own country, when he enters a good inn, and being pleased with it should remain there. Man, you have forgotten your purpose: you were not travelling to this inn, but you were passing through it.—But this is a pleasant inn.—And how many other inns are pleasant? and how many meadows are pleasant? yet only for passing through. But your purpose is this, to return to your country, to relieve your kinsmen of anxiety, to discharge the duties of a citizen, to marry, to beget children, to fill the usual magistracies.[5] For you are not come to select more pleasant places, but to live in these where you were born and of which you were made a citizen. Something of the kind takes place in the matter which we are considering. Since by the aid of speech and such communication as you receive here you must advance to perfection, and purge your will and correct the faculty which makes use of the appearances of things; and since it is necessary also for the teaching (delivery) of theorems to be effected by a certain mode of expression and with a certain variety and sharpness, some persons captivated by these very things abide in them, one captivated by the expression, another by syllogisms, another again by sophisms, and still another by some other inn (πανδοκείου) of this kind; and there they stay and waste away as if they were among Sirens.

Man, your purpose (business) was to make yourself capable of using conformably to nature the appearances presented to you, in your desires not to be frustrated, in your aversion from things not to fall into that which you would avoid, never to have no luck (as one may say), nor ever to have bad luck, to be free, not hindered, not compelled, conforming yourself to the administration of Zeus, obeying it, well satisfied with this, blaming no one, charging no one with fault, able from your whole soul to utter these verses

"Lead me, O Zeus, and thou too Destiny."

Then having this purpose before you, if some little form of expression pleases you, if some theorems please you, do you abide among them and choose to dwell there, forgetting the

things at home, and do you say, These things are fine?
Who says that they are not fine? but only as being a way
home, as inns are.   For what hinders you from being an
unfortunate man, even if you speak like Demosthenes? and
what prevents you, if you can resolve syllogisms like Chrysippus,[6] from being wretched, from sorrowing, from envy-
ing, in a word, from being disturbed, from being unhappy?
Nothing.   You see then that these were inns, worth nothing; and that the purpose before you was something else.
When I speak thus to some persons, they think that I am rejecting care about speaking or care about theorems. But
I am not rejecting this care, but I am rejecting the abiding
about these things incessantly and putting our hopes in them.
If a man by this teaching does harm to those who listen to
him, reckon me too among those who do this harm: for I
am not able, when I see one thing which is most excellent
and supreme, to say that another is so, in order to please you.

NOTES

[1] The word for "spirit" is πνεῦμα, a vital spirit, an animal spirit,
a nervous fluid, as Schweighauser explains it, or as Plutarch says
(De Placit. Philosoph. iv. 15), "the spirit which has the power of vision,
which permeates from the chief faculty of the mind to the pupil of the
eye;" and in another passage of the same treatise (iv. 8), "the instruments of perception said to be intelligent spirits (πνεύματα νοερά)
have a motion from the chief faculty of the mind to the organs."

[2] On the Greek text Upton remarks that, "there are many passages in
these dissertations which are ambiguous or rather confused on account
of the small questions, and because the matter is not expanded by
oratorical copiousness, not to mention other causes"

[3] This appears to be the book which Cicero (Tuscul iii 18) entitles
on the "supreme good" (de summo bono), which, as Cicero says, contains all the doctrine of Epicurus. The book on the Canon or Rule is
mentioned by Velleius in Cicero de Nat. Decorum i c. 16, as "that celestial volume of Epicurus on the Rule and Judgment." See also De Fin.
i. 19.

[4] This is said in a letter written by Epicurus, when he was dying in
great pain (Diog. Laert. x. 22); Cicero (De Fin. ii. c. 30) quotes this
letter.

[5] The Stoics taught that a man should lead an active life. Horace
(Ep i. 1, 16) represents himself as sometimes following the Stoic principles:

"Nunc agilis fio et mersor civilibus undis"

but this was only talk. The Stoic should discharge all the duties of
a citizen, says Epictetus, he should even marry and beget children.
But the marrying may be done without any sense of duty; and the continuance of the human race is secured by the natural love of the male

and of the female for conjunction. Still it is good advice, which the Roman censor Metellus gave to his fellow citizens, that, as they could not live without women, they should make the best of this business of marriage   (Gellius, i. 6.)

* Chrysippus wrote a book on the resolution of Syllogisms. Diogenes Laertius (vii.) says of Chrysippus that he was so famous among Dialecticians that most persons thought, if there was Dialectic among the Gods, it would not be any other than that of Chrysippus.

CHAPTER XXIV

TO (OR AGAINST) A PERSON WHO WAS ONE OF THOSE WHO WERE NOT VALUED (ESTEEMED) BY HIM

A CERTAIN person said to him (Epictetus): Frequently I desired to hear you and came to you, and you never gave me any answer: and now, if it is possible, I intreat you to say something to me. Do you think, said Epictetus, that as there is an art in any thing else, so there is also an art in speaking, and that he who has the art, will speak skilfully, and he who has not, will speak unskilfully?—I do think so.—He then who by speaking receives benefit himself, and is able to benefit others, will speak skilfully: but he who is rather damaged by speaking and does damage to others, will he be unskilled in this art of speaking? And you may find that some are damaged and others benefited by speaking. And are all who hear benefited by what they hear? Or will you find that among them also some are benefited and some damaged?—There are both among these also, he said.—In this case also then those who hear skilfully are benefited, and those who hear unskilfully are damaged? He admitted this. Is there then a skill in hearing also, as there is in speaking?—It seems so —If you choose, consider the matter in this way also. The practice of music, to whom does it belong? To a musician. And the proper making of a statue, to whom do you think that it belongs? To a statuary. And the looking at a statue skilfully, does this appear to you to require the aid of no art?—This also requires the aid of art.—Then if speaking properly is the business of the skilful man, do you see that to hear also with benefit is the business of the skilful man? Now as to speaking and hearing perfectly, and usefully,[1] let us for the present, if you please, say no more, for both of us are a long way from every thing of the kind. But I think that every man will allow this, that he who is going to hear philosophers requires some amount of practice in hearing. Is it not so?

Tell me then about what I should talk to you: about what matter are you able to listen?—About good and evil.—Good and evil in what? In a horse? No. Well, in an ox? No. What then? In a man? Yes. Do we know then what a man is, what the notion is which we have of him, or have we our ears in any degree practised about this matter? But do you understand what nature is? or can you even in any degree understand me' when I say, I shall use demonstration to you? How? Do you understand this very thing, what demonstration is, or how any thing is demonstrated, or by what means; or what things are like demonstration, but are not demonstration? Do you know what is true or what is false? What is consequent on a thing, what is repugnant to a thing, or not consistent, or inconsistent? But must I excite you to philosophy, and how? Shall I show to you the repugnance in the opinions of most men, through which they differ about things good and evil, and about things which are profitable and unprofitable, when you know not this very thing, what repugnance (contradiction) is? Show me then what I shall accomplish by discoursing with you: excite my inclination to do this. As the grass which is suitable, when it is presented to a sheep, moves its inclination to eat, but if you present to it a stone or bread, it will not be moved to eat; so there are in us certain natural inclinations also to speak, when the hearer shall appear to be somebody, when he himself shall excite us: but when he shall sit by us like a stone or like grass, how can he excite a man's desire (to speak)? Does the vine say to the husbandman, "Take care of me?" No, but the vine by showing in itself that it will be profitable to the husbandman, if he does take care of it, invites him to exercise care. When children are attractive and lively, whom do they not invite to play with them, and crawl with them, and lisp with them? But who is eager to play with an ass or to bray with it? for though it is small, it is still a little ass.

Why then do you say nothing to me? I can only say this to you, that he who knows not who he is, and for what purpose he exists, and what is this world, and with whom he is associated, and what things are the good and the bad, and the beautiful and the ugly, and who neither understands discourse nor demonstration, nor what is true nor what is false, and who is not able to distinguish them, will neither desire according to nature nor turn away nor move towards, nor intend (to act), nor assent, nor dissent nor suspend his judgment: to say all in a few words, he will go about dumb and blind, thinking that he is somebody, but being nobody. Is this so now for the first time? Is it not the fact that ever since the human race existed, all errors and misfortunes have arisen through this ignorance? Why did Agamemnon and Achilles quarrel with one another? Was it not through not knowing what things are profitable and not profitable? Does not the one say it is profitable to restore Chryseis to her father, and does not the other say that it is not profitable? does not the one say that he ought to take the prize of another, and does not the other say that he ought not? Did they not for these reasons forget, both who they were and for what purpose they had come there? Oh, man, for what purpose did you come? to gain mistresses or to fight? To fight. With whom? the Trojans or the Hellenes? With the Trojans. Do you then leave Hector alone and draw your sword against your own king? And do you, most excellent Sir, neglect the duties of the king, you who are the people's guardian and have such cares; and are you quarrelling about a little girl with the most warlike of your allies, whom you ought by every means to take care of and protect? and do you become worse than (inferior to) a well behaved priest who treats you these fine gladiators with all respect? Do you see what kind of things ignorance of what is profitable does?

But I also am rich. Are you then richer than Agamemnon? But I am also handsome. Are you then more handsome than Achilles? But I have also beautiful hair. But had not Achilles more beautiful hair and gold coloured? and he did not comb it elegantly nor dress it. But I am also strong. Can you then lift so great a stone as Hector or Ajax? But I am also of noble birth. Are you the son of a goddess mother? are you the son of a father sprung from Zeus? What good then do these things do to him, when he sits and weeps for a girl? But I am an orator. And was he not? Do you not see how he handled the most skil-

ful of the Hellenes in oratory, Odysseus and Phœnix? how
he stopped their mouths?[2]

This is all that I have to say to you; and I say even this
not willingly. Why? Because you have not roused me.
For what must I look to in order to be roused, as men who
are expert in riding are roused by generous horses? Must
I look to your body? You treat it disgracefully. To your
dress? That is luxurious. To your behaviour, to your
look? That is the same as nothing. When you would
listen to a philosopher, do not say to him, "You tell me nothing;" but only show yourself worthy of hearing or fit for
hearing; and you will see how you will move the speaker.

NOTES

[1] "That is, let us not now consider whether I am perfect in the art
of speaking, and you have a mind well prepared to derive real advantage
from philosophical talk. Let us consider this only, whether your ears
are sufficiently prepared for listening, whether you can understand a
philosophical discussion." Schweig

[2] In the ninth book of the Iliad, where Achilles answers the messen-
gers sent to him by Agamemnon. The reply of Achilles is a wonderful
example of eloquence.

CHAPTER XXV

THAT LOGIC IS NECESSARY

WHEN one of those who were present said, "Persuade me that logic is necessary," he replied, Do you wish me to prove this to you?—The answer was "Yes"—Then I must use a demonstrative form of speech.—This was granted.—How then will you know if I am cheating you by my argument? The man was silent. Do you see, said Epictetus, that you yourself are admitting that logic is necessary, if without it you can not know so much as this, whether logic is necessary or not necessary?

CHAPTER XXVI

WHAT IS THE PROPERTY OF ERROR

EVERY error comprehends contradiction: for since he who errs does not wish to err, but to be right, it is plain that he does not do what he wishes. For what does the thief wish to do? That which is for his own interest. If then the theft is not for his own interest, he does not do that which he wishes. But every rational soul is by nature offended at contradiction, and so long as it does not understand this contradiction, it is not hindered from doing contradictory things: but when it does understand the contradiction, it must of necessity avoid the contradiction and avoid it as much as a man must dissent from the false when he sees that a thing is false; but so long as this falsehood does not appear to him, he assents to it as to truth.

He then is strong in argument and has the faculty of exhorting and confuting, who is able to show to each man the contradiction through which he errs and clearly to prove how he does not do that which he wishes and does that which he does not wish. For if any one shall show this, a man will himself withdraw from that which he does; but so long as you do not show this, do not be surprised if a man persists in his practice; for having the appearance of doing right, he does what he does. For this reason Socrates also trusting to this power used to say, "I am used to call no other witness of what I say, but I am always satisfied with him with whom I am discussing and I ask him to give his opinion and call him as a witness, and though he is only one, he is sufficient in the place of all." For Socrates knew by what the rational soul is moved, just like a pair of scales, and then it must incline, whether it chooses or not. Show the rational governing faculty a contradiction, and it will withdraw from it; but if you do not show it, rather blame yourself than him who is not persuaded.

BOOK III

CHAPTER I

A CERTAIN young man, a rhetorician, came to see Epictetus, with his hair dressed more carefully than was usual and his attire in an ornamental style; whereùpon Epictetus said, Tell me if you do not think that some dogs are beautiful and some horses, and so of all other animals. "I do think so," the youth replied. Are not then some men also beautiful and others ugly? "Certainly." Do we then for the same reason call each of them in the same kind beautiful, or each beautiful for something peculiar? And you will judge of this matter thus. Since we see a dog naturally formed for one thing, and a horse for another, and for another still, as an example, a nightingale, we may generally and not improperly declare each of them to be beautiful then when it is most excellent according to its nature; but since the nature of each is different, each of them seems to me to be beautiful in a different way. Is it not so? He admitted that it was. That then which makes a dog beautiful, makes a horse ugly; and that which makes a horse beautiful, makes a dog ugly, if it is true that their natures are different. "It seems to be so." For I think that what makes a Pancratiast beautiful, makes a wrestler to be not good, and a runner to be most ridiculous; and he who is beautiful for the Pentathlon, is very ugly for wrestling.[1] It is so said he. What then makes a man beautiful? Is it that which in its kind makes both a dog and a horse beautiful? "It is," he said. What then makes a dog beautiful? The possession of the excellence of a dog. And what makes a horse beautiful? The possession of the excellence of a horse. What then makes a man beautiful? Is it not the possession of the excellence of a man? And do you then, if you wish to be beautiful, young man, labour at this, the acquisition of human excellence. But what is this? Observe whom you yourself praise, when you praise many persons without partiality: do you praise the just or the unjust? "The just." Whether do you praise the moderate or the immoderate? "The moderate." And the temperate or the intemperate? "The temperate." If then you make yourself such a person, you will know that you make yourself beautiful. but so long as you neglect these things, you must be ugly (αἰσχρόν), even though you contrive all you can to appear beautiful.

Further I do not know what to say to you: for if I say to you what I think, I shall offend you, and you will perhaps leave the school and not return to it: and if I do not say what I think, see how I shall be acting, if you come to me to be improved, and I shall not improve you at all, and if you come to me as to a philosopher, and I shall say nothing to you as a philosopher. And how cruel it is to you to leave you uncorrected. If at any time afterwards you shall acquire sense, you will with good reason blame me and say, What did Epictetus observe in me that when he saw me in such a plight coming to him in such a scandalous condition, he neglected me and never said a word? did he so much despair of me? was I not young? was I not able to listen to reason? and how many other young men at this age commit many like errors? I hear that a certain Polemon from being a most dissolute youth underwent such a great change. Well, suppose that he did not think that I should be a Polemon;[2] yet he might have set my hair right, he might have stripped off my decorations, he might have stopped me from plucking the hair out of my body; but when he saw me dressed like—what shall I say?—he kept silent. I do not say like what; but you will say when you come to your senses, and shall know what it is, and what persons use such a dress.

If you bring this charge against me hereafter, what defence shall I make? Why, shall I say that the man will not be persuaded by me? Was Laius persuaded by Apollo?

13

Did he not go away and get drunk and show no care for the oracle?[3] Well then for this reason did Apollo refuse to tell him the truth? I indeed do not know, whether you will be persuaded by me or not: but Apollo knew most certainly that Laius would not be persuaded and yet he spoke. But why did he speak? I say in reply, But why is he Apollo, and why does he deliver oracles, and why has he fixed himself in this place as a prophet and source of truth and for the inhabitants of the world to resort to him? and why are the words "Know yourself" written in front of the temple, though no person takes any notice of them?

Did Socrates persuade all his hearers to take care of themselves? Not the thousandth part. But however, after he had been placed in this position by the deity, as he himself says, he never left it. But what does he say even to his judges? "If you acquit me on these conditions that I no longer do that which I do now, I will not consent and I will not desist; but I will go up both to young and old, and, to speak plainly, to every man whom I meet, and I will ask the questions which I ask now; and most particularly will I do this to you my fellow citizens, because you are more nearly related to me."[4]—Are you so curious, Socrates, and such a busy-body? and how does it concern you how we act? and what is it that you say? Being of the same community and of the same kin, you neglect yourself, and show yourself a bad citizen to the state, and a bad kinsman to your kinsmen, and a bad neighbour to your neighbours. Who then are you?—Here it is a great thing to say, "I am he whose duty it is to take care of men; for it is not every little heifer which dares to resist a lion; but if the bull comes up and resists him, say to the bull, if you choose, 'and who are you,' and what business have you here?' " Man, in every kind there is produced something which excels; in oxen, in dogs, in bees, in horses. Do not then say to that which excels, "Who then are you?" If you do, it will find a voice in some way and say, "I am such a thing as the purple in a garment: do not expect me to be like the others, or blame my nature that it has made me different from the rest of men."

What then? am I such a man? Certainly not. And are

you such a man as can listen to the truth? I wish you were. But however since in a manner I have been condemned to wear a white beard and a cloak, and you come to me as to a philosopher, I will not treat you in a cruel way nor yet as if I despaired of you, but I will say, Young man, whom do you wish to make beautiful? In the first place, know who you are and then adorn yourself appropriately. You are a human being; and this is a mortal animal which has the power of using appearances rationally. But what is meant by "rationally"? Conformably to nature[5] and completely. What then do you possess which is peculiar? Is it the animal part? No. Is it the condition of mortality? No. Is it the power of using appearances?[6] No. You possess the rational faculty as a peculiar thing: adorn and beautify this; but leave your hair to him who made it as he chose. Come, what other appellations have you? Are you man or woman? Man. Adorn yourself then as man, not as woman. Woman is naturally smooth and delicate; and if she has much hair (on her body), she is a monster and is exhibited at Rome among monsters. And in a man it is monstrous not to have hair; and if he has no hair, he is a monster; but if he cuts off his hairs and plucks them out, what shall we do with him? where shall we exhibit him? and under what name shall we show him? I will exhibit to you a man who chooses to be a woman rather than a man. What a terrible sight! There is no man who will not wonder at such a notice. Indeed I think that the men who pluck out their hairs do what they do without knowing what they do. Man what fault have you to find with your nature? That it made you a man? What then? was it fit that nature should make all human creatures women? and what advantage in that case would you have had in being adorned? for whom would you have adorned yourself, if all human creatures were women? But you are not pleased with the matter: set to work then upon the whole business. Take away—what is its name?—that which is the cause of the hairs: make yourself a woman in all respects, that we may not be mistaken: do not make one half man, and the other half woman. Whom do you wish to please? The women? Please them as a man. Well; but they like smooth men. Will you not hang yourself? and if women took delight in catamites, would you become one? Is this your business? were you born for this purpose, that dissolute women should delight in you? Shall we make such a one as you a citizen of Corinth and perchance a prefect of the city, or chief of the youth, or general or superintendent of the games? Well, and when you have taken a wife, do you intend to have your hairs plucked out? To please whom and for what purpose? And when you have begotten children, will you introduce them also into the state with the habit of plucking their hairs? A beautiful citizen, and senator and rhetorician. We ought to pray that such young men be born among us and brought up.

Do not so, I intreat you by the Gods, young man: but when you have once heard these words, go away and say to yourself, "Epictetus has not said this to me: for how could he? but some propitious God through him: for it would never have come into his thoughts to say this, since he is not accustomed to talk thus with any person. Come then let us obey God, that we may not be subject to his anger." You say, No. But (I say), if a crow by his croaking signifies any thing to you, it is not the crow which signifies, but God through the crow; and if he signifies any thing through a human voice, will he not cause the man to say this to you, that you may know the power of the divinity, that he signifies to some in this way, and to others in that way, and concerning the greatest things and the chief he signifies through the noblest messenger? What else is it which the poet says:

> "For we ourselves have warned him, and have sent
> Hermes the careful watcher, Argus' slayer,
> The husband not to kill nor wed the wife"[7]

Was Hermes going to descend from heaven to say this to him (Ægisthus)? And now the gods say this to you and send the messenger, the slayer of Argus, to warn you not to pervert that which is well arranged, nor to busy yourself about it, but to allow a man to be a man, and a woman to be a woman, a beautiful man to be as a beautiful man; and an ugly man as an ugly man, for you are not flesh and hair, but you are will ($\pi\rho o\alpha i\rho\epsilon\sigma\iota\varsigma$); and if your will is beautiful, then you will be beautiful. But up to the present time I dare not tell you that you are ugly, for I think that you are readier to hear anything than this. But see what Socrates says to the most beautiful and blooming of men Alcibiades: "Try then to be beautiful." What does he say to him? Dress your hair and pluck the hairs from your legs? Nothing of that kind. But adorn your will, take away bad opinions. How with the body? Leave it as it is by nature. Another has looked after these things: intrust them to him. What then, must a man be uncleaned? Certainly not; but what you are and are made by nature, cleanse this. A man should be cleanly as a man, a woman as a woman, a child as a child. You say no: but let us also pluck out the lion's mane, that he may not be uncleaned, and the cock's comb for he also ought to be cleaned. Granted, but as a cock, and the lion as a lion, and the hunting dog as a hunting dog.

NOTES

[1] A Pancratiast is a man who is trained for the Pancratium, that is, both for boxing and wrestling. The Pentathlon comprised five exercises, which are expressed by one Greek line,

Leaping, running, the quoit, throwing the javelin, wrestling.

[2] Comp. Horace, Sat ii 3, v. 253.

Quæro, faciasne quod olim
Mutatus Polemon? etc.

The story of Polemon is told by Diogenes Laertius. He was a dissolute youth. As he was passing one day the place where Xenocrates was lecturing, he and his drunken companions burst into the school, but Polemon was so affected by the words of the excellent teacher that he came out quite a different man, and ultimately succeeded Xenocrates in the school of the Academy See Epictetus, iv. 11, 30

[3] Laius consulted the oracle at Delphi how he should have children. The oracle told him not to beget children, and even to expose them if he did. Laius was so foolish as to disobey the god in both respects, for he begot children and brought them up. He did indeed order his child Œdipus to be exposed, but the boy was saved and became the murderer of Laius

[4] Plato, Apology, i. 9, and 17.

[5] Cicero, de Fin. ii. 11; Horace, Epp i 10,12. This was the great principle of Zeno, to live according to nature. Bishop Butler in the Preface to his Sermons says of this philosophical principle, that virtue consisted in following nature, that it is "a manner of speaking not loose and undeterminate, but clear and distinct, strictly just and true."

[6] The bare use of objects (appearances) belongs to all animals; a rational use of them is peculiar to man Mrs. Carter, Introd. sec 7.

[7] From the Odyssey, i, 37, where Zeus is speaking of Ægisthus.

CHAPTER II

IN WHAT A MAN OUGHT TO BE EXERCISED WHO HAS MADE
PROFICIENCY; AND THAT WE NEGLECT THE CHIEF THINGS

THERE are three things (topics, τόποι) in which a man
ought to exercise himself who would be wise and
good.[1] The first concerns the desires and the aversions, that a man may not fail to get what he desires, and that he may not fall into that which he does not
desire. The second concerns the movements (towards an
object) and the movements from an object, and generally
in doing what a man ought to do, that he may act according
to order, to reason, and not carelessly. The third thing concerns freedom from deception and rashness in judgment, and
generally it concerns the assents (ὀυγκαταθέσεις). Of these
topics the chief and the most urgent is that which relates to
the affects (τὰ πάθη, perturbations); for an affect is produced in no other way than by a failing to obtain that which
a man desires or falling into that which a man would wish
to avoid. This is that which brings in perturbations, disorders, bad fortune, misfortunes, sorrows, lamentations, and
envy; that which makes men envious and jealous; and by
these causes we are even unable to listen to the precepts of
reason. The second topic concerns the duties of a man; for
I ought not to be free from affects (ἀπαθῆ) like a statue, but
I ought to maintain the relations (ὀχέσεις) natural and acquired, as a pious man; as a son, as a father, as a citizen.

The third topic is that which immediately concerns those
who are making proficiency, that which concerns the security
of the other two, so that not even in sleep any appearance
unexamined may surprise us, nor in intoxication, nor in
melancholy This, it may be said, is above our power. But
the present philosophers neglecting the first topic and the
second (the affects and duties), employ themselves on
the third, using sophistical arguments (μεταπίπτοντας), making conclusions from questioning, employing hypotheses,
lying. For a man must, as it is said, when employed on

these matters, take care that he is not deceived. Who must?
The wise and good man. This then is all that is wanting
to you. Have you successfully worked out the rest? Are
you free from deception in the matter of money? If you see
a beautiful girl, do you resist the appearance? If your
neighbour obtains an estate by will, are you not vexed?
Now there is nothing else wanting to you except unchangeable firmness of mind (ἀμεταπτωσία)? Wretch, you hear
these very things with fear and anxiety that some person
may despise you, and with inquiries about what any person
may say about you. And if a man come and tell you that in
a certain conversation in which the question was, Who is
the best philosopher, a man who was present said that a certain person was the chief philosopher, your little soul which
was only a finger's length stretches out to two cubits. But if
another who is present says, You are mistaken; it is not
worth while to listen to a certain person, for what does he
know? he has only the first principles, and no more? then you
are confounded, you grow pale, you cry out immediately, I
will show him who I am, that I am a great philosopher.—It
is seen by these very things: why do you wish to show it by
others? Do you not know that Diogenes pointed out one of
the sophists in this way by stretching out his middle finger?[2]
And then when the man was wild with rage, "This," he said,
"is the certain person; I have pointed him out to you." For a
man is not shown by the finger, as a stone or a piece of wood;
but when any person shows the man's principles, then he
shows him as a man.

Let us look at your principles also. For is it not plain
that you value not at all your own will (προαίρεσις), but
you look externally to things which are independent of your
will? For instance, what will a certain person say? and what
will people think of you? will you be considered a man of
learning; have you read Chrysippus or Antipater? for if you
have read Archedemus[3] also, you have every thing [that you
can desire]. Why are you still uneasy lest you should not
show us who you are? Would you let me tell you what manner of man you have shown us that you are? You have exhibited yourself to us as a mean fellow, querulous, passionate, cowardly, finding fault with every thing, blaming every

body, never quiet, vain: this is what you have exhibited to us. Go away now and read Archedemus; then if a mouse should leap down and make a noise, you are a dead man. For such a death awaits you as it did[4]—what was the man's name?—Crinis; and he too was proud, because he understood Archedemus.

Wretch, will you not dismiss these things that do not concern you at all? These things are suitable to those who are able to learn them without perturbation, to those who can say: "I am not subject to anger, to grief, to envy: I am not hindered, I am not restrained. What remains for me? I have leisure, I am tranquil. let us see how we must deal with sophistical arguments; let us see how when a man has accepted an hypothesis he shall not be led away to any thing absurd." To them such things belong. To those who are happy it is appropriate to light a fire, to dine; if they choose, both to sing and to dance. But when the vessel is sinking, you come to me and hoist the sails.[5]

NOTES

[1] Καλὸς καὶ ἀγαθός is the usual Greek expression to signify a perfect man The Stoics, according to Stobæus, absurdedly called "virtue," καλόν (beautiful), because it naturally "calls" (καλεῖ) to itself those who desire it. The Stoics also said that every thing good was beautiful (καλός), and that the good and the beautiful were equivalent. The Roman expression is "Vir bonus et sapiens" Perhaps the phrase καλὸς καὶ ἀγαθός arose from the notion of beauty and goodness being the combination of a perfect human being

[2] To point out a man with the middle finger was a way of showing the greatest contempt for him

[3] As to Archedemus, see ii 4, 11. ἀπέχεις ἄπαντα: this expression is compared by Upton with Matthew vi. 2, ἀπέχουσι μισθὸν.

[4] Crinis was a Stoic philosopher mentioned by Diogenes Laertius. We may suppose that he was no real philosopher, and that he died of fright.

[5] The philosopher is represented as being full of anxiety about things which do not concern him, and which are proper subjects for those only who are free from disturbing passions and are quite happy, which is not the philosopher's condition. He is compared to a sinking ship, and at this very time he is supposed to be employed in the useless labour of hoisting the sails.

CHAPTER III

THE material for the wise and good man is his own
ruling faculty: and the body is the material for the
physician and the aliptes (the man who oils persons); the land is the matter for the husbandman.
The business of the wise and good man is to use appearances
conformably to nature: and as it is the nature of every soul
to assent to the truth, to dissent from the false, and to remain
in suspense as to that which is uncertain; so it is its nature to
be moved towards the desire of the good, and to aversion
from the evil; and with respect to that which is neither good
nor bad it feels indifferent. For as the money-changer
(banker) is not allowed to reject Cæsar's coin, nor the seller
of herbs, but if you show the coin, whether he chooses or not,
he must give up what is sold for the coin; so it is also in the
matter of the soul. When the good appears, it immediately
attracts to itself; the evil repels from itself. But the soul will
never reject the manifest appearance of the good, any more
than persons will reject Cæsar's coin. On this principle depends every movement both of man and God.

For this reason the good is preferred to every intimate
relationship (obligation). There is no intimate relationship between me and my father, but there is between
me and the good. Are you so hard-hearted? Yes, for such
is my nature; and this is the coin which God has given me.
For this reason if the good is something different from the
beautiful and the just, both father is gone (neglected), and
brother and country, and every thing. But shall I overlook
my own good, in order that you may have it, and shall I give
it up to you? Why? I am your father. But you are not my
good. I am your brother. But you are not my good.
But if we place the good in a right determination of
the will, the very observance of the relations of life is

good, and accordingly he who gives up any external things, obtains that which is good. Your father takes away your property. But he does not injure you. Your brother will have the greater part of the estate in land. Let him have as much as he chooses. Will he then have a greater share of modesty, of fidelity, of brotherly affection? For who will eject you from this possession? Not even Zeus, for neither has he chosen to do so; but he has made this in my own power, and he has given it to me just as he possessed it himself, free from hindrance, compulsion, and impediment. When then the coin which another uses is a different coin, if a man presents this coin, he receives that which is sold for it. Suppose that there comes into the province a thievish proconsul, what coin does he use? Silver coin. Show it to him, and carry off what you please. Suppose one comes who is an adulterer: what coin does he use? Little girls. Take, a man says, the coin, and sell me the small thing. Give, says the seller, and buy [what you want]. Another is eager to possess boys. Give him the coin, and receive what you wish. Another is fond of hunting: give him a fine nag or a dog. Though he groans and laments, he will sell for it that which you want. For another compels him from within, he who has fixed (determined) this coin.[1]

Against (or with respect to) this kind of thing chiefly a man should exercise himself. As soon as you go out in the morning, examine every man whom you see, every man whom you hear; answer as to a question, What have you seen? A handsome man or woman? Apply the rule. Is this independent of the will, or dependent? Independent. Take it away. What have you seen? A man lamenting over the death of a child. Apply the rule. Death is a thing independent of the will. Take it away. Has the proconsul met you? Apply the rule. What kind of thing is a proconsul's office? Independent of the will, or dependent on it? Independent. Take this away also: it does not stand examination: cast it away: it is nothing to you

If we practised this and exercised ourselves in it daily from morning to night, something indeed would be done. But now we are forthwith caught half asleep by every appearance, and it is only, if ever, that in the school we are

THE AUGURS

From a painting by Jean Léon Gérôme

roused a little. Then when we go out, if we see a man lamenting, we say, "He is undone." If we see a consul, we say, "He is happy." If we see an exiled man, we say, "He is miserable." If we see a poor man, we say, "He is wretched: he has nothing to eat."

We ought then to eradicate these bad opinions, and to this end we should direct all our efforts. For what is weeping and lamenting? Opinion. What is bad fortune? Opinion What is civil sedition, what is divided opinion, what is blame, what is accusation, what is impiety, what is trifling? All these things are opinions, and nothing more, and opinions about things independent of the will, as if they were good, and bad. Let a man transfer these opinions to things dependent on the will, and I engage for him that he will be firm and constant, whatever may be the state of things around him. Such as is a dish of water, such is the soul. Such as is the ray of light which falls on the water, such are the appearances. When the water is moved, the ray also seems to be moved, yet it is not moved. And when then a man is seized with giddiness, it is not the arts and the virtues which are confounded, but the spirit (the nervous power) on which they are impressed; but if the spirit be restored to its settled state, those things also are restored.

NOTE

¹ Mrs. Carter compares the Epistle to the Romans, vii. 21-23. Schweighauser says, the man either sees that the thing which he is doing is bad or unjust, or for any other reason he does not do the thing willingly; but he is compelled, and allows himself to be carried away by the passion which rules him The "another" who compels is God, Schweig says, who has made the nature of man such, that he must postpone everything else to that thing in which he places his Good: and he adds, that it is man's fault if he places his good in that thing, in which God has not placed it.

Some persons will not consider this to be satisfactory. The man is "compelled and allows himself to be carried away," etc. The notion of "compulsion" is inconsistent with the exercise of the will The man is unlucky. He is like him "who sees," as the Latin poet says, "the better things and approves of them, but follows the worse."

CHAPTER IV

AGAINST A PERSON WHO SHOWED HIS PARTISANSHIP IN AN UNSEEMLY WAY IN A THEATRE

THE governor of Epirus having shown his favour to an actor in an unseemly way and being publicly blamed on this account, and afterwards having reported to Epictetus that he was blamed and that he was vexed at those who blamed him, Epictetus said, What harm have they been doing? These men also were acting as partizans, as you were doing. The governor replied, Does then any person show his partizanship in this way? When they see you, said Epictetus, who are their governor, a friend of Cæsar and his deputy, showing partizanship in this way, was it not to be expected that they also should show their partizanship in the same way? for if it is not right to show partizanship in this way, do not do so yourself; and if it is right, why are you angry if they followed your example? For whom have the many to imitate except you, who are their superiors? to whose example should they look when they go to the theatre except yours? See how the deputy of Cæsar looks on: he has cried out, and I too then will cry out. He springs up from his seat, and I will spring up. His slaves sit in various parts of the theatre and call out. I have no slaves, but I will myself cry out as much as I can and as loud as all of them together. You ought then to know when you enter the theatre that you enter as a rule and example to the rest how they ought to look at the acting. Why then did they blame you? Because every man hates that which is a hindrance to him. They wished one person to be crowned; you wished another. They were a hindrance to you, and you were a hindrance to them. You were found to be the stronger; and they did what they could; they blamed that which hindered them. What then would you have? That you should do what you please, and they should not even say what they please? And what is the wonder? Do not the husbandmen abuse Zeus when they are hindered by him? do not the sailors abuse him? do they ever cease abusing Cæsar? What then? does not Zeus know? is not what is said reported to Cæsar? What then does he do? he knows that, if he punished all who abuse him, he would have nobody to rule over. What then? when you enter the theatre, you ought to say not, "Let Sophron (some actor) be crowned," but you ought to say this, "Come let me maintain my will in this matter, so that it shall be conformable to nature: no man is dearer to me than myself. It would be ridiculous then for me to be hurt (injured) in order that another who is an actor may be crowned. Whom then do I wish to gain the prize? Why the actor who does gain the prize; and so he will always gain the prize whom I wish to gain it."—But I wish Sophron to be crowned.—Celebrate as many games as you choose in your own house, Nemean, Pythian, Isthmian, Olympian, and proclaim him victor. But in public do not claim more than your due, nor attempt to appropriate to yourself what belongs to all. If you do not consent to this, bear being abused: for when you do the same as the many, you put yourself on the same level with them.

CHAPTER V.

AGAINST THOSE WHO ON ACCOUNT OF SICKNESS GO AWAY HOME

I AM sick here, said one of the pupils, and I wish to return home.—At home, I suppose, you were free from sickness. Do you not consider whether you are doing any thing here which may be useful to the exercise of your will, that it may be corrected? For if you are doing nothing, towards this end, it was to no purpose that you came. Go away. Look after your affairs at home. For if your ruling power can not be maintained in a state conformable to nature, it is possible that your land can, that you will be able to increase your money, you will take care of your father in his old age, frequent the public place, hold magisterial office: being bad you will do badly any thing else that you have to do. But if you understand yourself, and know that you are casting away certain bad opinions and adopting others in their place, and if you have changed your state of life from things which are not within your will to things which are within your will, and if you ever say, Alas! you are not saying what you say on account of your father, or your brother, but on account of yourself, do you still allege your sickness? Do you not know that both disease and death must surprise us while we are doing something? the husbandman while he is tilling the ground, the sailor while he is on his voyage? what would you be doing when death surprises you, for you must be surprised when you are doing something? If you can be doing anything better than this when you are surprised, do it. For I wish to be surprised by disease or death when I am looking after nothing else than my own will, that I may be free from perturbation, that I may be free from hindrance, free from compulsion, and in a state of liberty. I wish to be found practising these things that I may be able to say to God, "Have I in any respect transgressed thy commands? have I in any respect wrongly used the powers which thou gavest me? have I misused my perceptions or my preconceptions (προλήψεσι)? have I ever blamed thee? have I ever found fault with thy administration? · I have been sick, because it was thy will, and so have others, but I was content to be sick. I have been poor because it was thy will, but I was content also. I have not filled a magisterial office, because it was not thy pleasure that I should. I have never desired it. Hast thou ever seen me for this reason discontented? have I not always approached thee with a cheerful countenance, ready to do thy commands and to obey thy signals? Is it now thy will that I should depart from the assemblage of men? I depart. I give thee all thanks that thou hast allowed me to join in this thy assemblage of men and to see thy works, and to comprehend this thy administration" May death surprise me while I am thinking of these things, while I am thus writing and reading.

But my mother will not hold my head when I am sick. Go to your mother then; for you are a fit person to have your head held when you are sick.—But at home I used to lie down on a delicious bed.—Go away to your bed: indeed you are fit to lie on such a bed even when you are in health: do not then lose what you can do there (at home).

But what does Socrates say?[1] As one man, he says, is pleased with improving his land, another with improving his horse, so I am daily pleased in observing that I am growing better. Better in what? in using nice little words? Man, do not say that. In little matters of speculation (θεωρήματα)? what are you saying?—And indeed I do not see what else there is on which philosophers employ their time.—Does it seem nothing to you to have never found fault with any person, neither with God nor man? to have blamed nobody? to carry the same face always in going out and coming in? This is what Socrates knew, and yet he never said that he knew any thing or taught any thing.[2] But if any man asked for nice little words or little speculations, he would carry him to Protagoras or to Hippias; and if any man came to ask for potherbs, he would carry him to the gardener. Who then among you has this purpose (motive to action)? for if indeed you had it, you would both be content in sickness, and in hunger, and in death. If any among you has been in love with a charming girl, he knows that I say what is true.[3]

[1] Xenophon (Memorab 1 6, 14); but Epictetus does not quote the words, he only gives the meaning Antoninus' (viii 43) says, "Different things delight different people. But it is my delight to keep the ruling faculty sound without turning away either from any man or from any of the things which happen to men, but looking at and receiving all with welcome eyes, and using every thing according to its value "

[2] Socrates never professed to teach virtue, but by showing himself to be a virtuous man he expected to make his companions virtuous by imitating his example. Xenophon, Memorab 1. 2, 3.

[3] Upton explains this passage thus: "He who loves knows what it is to endure all things for love If any man then being captivated with love for a girl would for her sake endure dangers and even death, what would he not endure if he possessed the love of God, the Universal, the chief of beautiful things?"

CHAPTER VI

WHEN some person asked him how it happened that since reason has been more cultivated by the men of the present age the progress made in former times was greater. In what respect, he answered, has it been more cultivated now, and in what respect was the progress greater then? For in that in which it has now been more cultivated, in that also the progress will now be found. At present it has been cultivated for the purpose of resolving syllogisms, and progress is made. But in former times it was cultivated for the purpose of maintaining the governing faculty in a condition conformable to nature, and progress was made. Do not then mix things which are different, and do not expect, when you are labouring at one thing to make progress in another. But see if any man among us when he is intent upon this, the keeping himself in a state conformable to nature and living so always, does not make progress. For you will not find such a man.

The good man is invincible, for he does not enter the contest where he is not stronger. If you (his adversary) want to have his land and all that is on it, take the land; take his slaves, take his magisterial office, take his poor body. But you will not make his desire fail in that which it seeks, nor his aversion fall into that which he would avoid. The only contest into which he enters is that about things which are within the power of his will; how then will he not be invincible?

Some person having asked him what is Common sense, Epictetus replied, As that may be called a certain Common hearing which only distinguishes vocal sounds, and that which distinguishes musical sounds is not Common, but artificial; so there are certain things which men, who are not altogether perverted, see by the common notions which all possess. Such a constitution of the mind is named Common sense.[1]

It is not easy to exhort weak young men; for neither is it easy to hold (soft) cheese with a hook.[2] But those who have a good natural disposition, even if you try to turn them aside, cling still more to reason. Wherefore Rufus generally attempted to discourage (his pupils), and he used this method as a test of those who had a good natural disposition and those who had not. For it was his habit to say, as a stone, if you cast it upwards, will be brought down to the earth by its own nature, so the man whose mind is naturally good, the more you repel him, the more he turns towards that to which he is naturally inclined.

NOTES

[1] The Greek is κοίνος νοῦς, the Communis sensus of the Romans, and our Common sense. Horace (Sat. 1. 3, 65) speaks of a man who "communi sensu plane caret," one who has not the sense or understanding which is the common property of men.

[2] This is a proverb used by Bion, as Digenes Laertius says. The cheese was new and soft, as the ancients used it.

CHAPTER VII

TO THE ADMINISTRATOR OF THE FREE CITIES WHO WAS AN EPICUREAN

WHEN the administrator[1] came to visit him, and the man was an Epicurean, Epictetus said, It is proper for us who are not philosophers to inquire of you who are philosophers,[2] as those who come to a strange city inquire of the citizens and those who are acquainted with it, what is the best thing in the world, in order that we also after inquiry may go in quest of that which is best and look at it, as strangers do with the things in cities. For that there are three things which relate to man, soul, body, and things external, scarcely any man denies. It remains for you philosophers to answer what is the best. What shall we say to men? Is the flesh the best? and was it for this that Maximus[3] sailed as far as Cassiope in winter (or bad weather) with his son, and accompanied him that he might be gratified in the flesh? When the man said that it was not, and added, "Far be that from him." Is it not fit then, Epictetus said, to be actively employed about the best? It is certainly of all things the most fit. What then do we possess which is better than the flesh? The soul, he replied. And the good things of the best, are they better, or the good things of the worse? The good things of the best. And are the good things of the best within the power of the will or not within the power of the will? They are within the power of the will. Is then the pleasure of the soul a thing within the power of the will? It is, he replied. And on what shall this pleasure depend? On itself? But that can not be conceived: for there must first exist a certain substance or nature ($o\dot{v}\sigma\acute{\iota}\alpha$) of good, by obtaining which we shall have pleasure in the soul. He assented to this also. On what then shall we depend for this pleasure of the soul? for if it shall depend on things of the soul, the substance (nature) of the good is discovered; for good can not be one thing, and that at which we are rationally delighted another

211

thing; nor if that which precedes is not good, can that which comes after be good, for in order that the thing which comes after may be good, that which precedes must be good But you would not affirm this, if you are in your right mind, for you would then say what is inconsistent both with Epicurus and the rest of your doctrines. It remains then that the pleasure of the soul is in the pleasure from things of the body: and again that those bodily things must be the things which precede and the substance (nature) of the good.

For this reason Maximus acted foolishly if he made the voyage for any other reason than for the sake of the flesh, that is, for the sake of the best. And also a man acts foolishly if he abstains from that which belongs to others, when he is a judge (δικαστής) and able to take it. But, if you please, let us consider this only, how this thing may be done secretly, and safely, and so that no man will know it. For not even does Epicurus himself declare stealing to be bad,[4] but he admits that detection is; and because it is impossible to have security against detection, for this reason he says, Do not steal. But I say to you that if stealing is done cleverly and cautiously, we shall not be detected: further also we have powerful friends in Rome both men and women, and the Hellenes (Greeks) are weak, and no man will venture to go up to Rome for the purpose (of complaining).. Why do you refrain from your own good? This is senseless, foolish. But even if you tell me that you do refrain, I will not believe you. For as it is impossible to assent to that which appears false, and to turn away from that which is true, so it is impossible to abstain from that which appears good. But wealth is a good thing, and certainly most efficient in producing pleasure. Why will you not acquire wealth? And why should we not corrupt our neighbour's wife, if we can do it without detection? and if the husband foolishly prates about the matter, why not pitch him out of the house? If you would be a philosopher such as you ought to be, if a perfect philosopher, if consistent with your own doctrines, [you must act thus]. If you would not, you will not differ at all from us who are called Stoics; for we also say one thing, but we do another: we talk of the things which are beautiful (good), but we do what is base. But you will be perverse in the contrary way, teaching what is bad, practising what is good.

In the name of God,[5] are you thinking of a city of Epicureans? [One man says], "I do not marry."—"Nor I, for a man ought not to marry; nor ought we to beget children, nor engage in public matters." What then will happen? whence will the citizens come? who will bring them up? who will be governor of the youth, who preside over gymnastic exercises? and in what also will the teacher instruct them? will he teach them what the Lacedæmonians were taught, or what the Athenians were taught? Come take a young man, bring him up according to your doctrines. The doctrines are bad, subversive of a state, pernicious to families, and not becoming to women. Dismiss them, man. You live in a chief city: it is your duty to be a magistrate, to judge justly, to abstain from that which belongs to others; no woman ought to seem beautiful to you except your own wife, and no youth, no vessel of silver, no vessel of gold (except your own). Seek for doctrines which are consistent with what I say, and by making them your guide you will with pleasure abstain from things which have such persuasive power to lead us and overpower us. But if to the persuasive power of these things, we also devise such a philosophy as this which helps to push us on towards them and strengthens us to this end, what will be the consequence? In a piece of toreutic[6] art which is the best part? the silver or the workmanship? The substance of the hand is the flesh; but the work of the hand is the principal part (that which precedes and leads the rest). The duties then are also three: those which are directed towards the existence of a thing; those which are directed towards its existence in a particular kind; and third, the chief or leading things themselves. So also in man we ought not to value the material, the poor flesh, but the principal (leading things, τὰ προηγούμενα). What are these? Engaging in public business, marrying, begetting children, venerating God, taking care of parents, and generally, having desires, aversions (ἐκκλίνειν), pursuits of things and avoidances, in the way in which we ought to do these things, and according to our nature. And how are we constituted by nature? Free, noble, modest: for what other animal blushes? what other is capable of receiving the appearance (the impression) of shame? and we are so constituted by nature as to subject pleasure to these things, as a minister, a servant, in order that it may call forth our activity, in order that it may keep us constant in acts which are conformable to nature.

"But I am rich and I want nothing."—Why then do you pretend to be a philosopher? Your golden and your silver vessels are enough for you. What need have you of principles (opinions)? "But I am also a judge (κριτής) of the Greeks."—Do you know how to judge? Who taught you to know? "Cæsar wrote to me a codicil."[7] Let him write and give you a commission to judge of music; and what will be the use of it to you? Still how did you become a judge? whose hand did you kiss? the hand of Symphorus or Numenius? Before whose bedchamber have you slept?[8] To whom have you sent gifts? Then do you not see that to be a judge is just of the same value as Numenius is? "But I can throw into prison any man whom I please."—So you can do with a stone.—"But I can beat with sticks whom I please." —So you may an ass. This is not a governing of men. Govern us as rational animals: show us what is profitable to us, and we will follow it: show us what is unprofitable, and we will turn away from it. Make us imitators of yourself, as Socrates made men imitators of himself. For he was like a governor of men, who made them subject to him their desires, their aversion, their movements towards an object and their turning away from it.—Do this: do not do this: if you do not obey, I will throw you into prison.—This is not governing men like rational animals. But I (say): As Zeus has ordained, so act: if you do not act so, you will feel the penalty, you will be punished.—What will be the punishment? Nothing else than not having done your duty: you will lose the character of fidelity, modesty, propriety. Do not look for greater penalties than these.

NOTES

[1] The Greek is διορθωτής. The Latin word is Corrector, which occurs in inscriptions, and elsewhere

[2] The Epicureans are ironically named Philosophers, for most of them were arrogant men

[3] Maximus was appointed by Trajan to conduct a campaign against the Parthians, in which he lost his life.

Cassiope or Cassope is a city in Epirus, near the sea, and between Pandosia and Nicopolis, where Epictetus lived

⁴ Diogenes Laertius, quoted by Upton. "Injustice," says Epicurus "is not an evil in itself, but the evil is in the fear which there is on account of suspicion."

⁵ Upton compares the passage (v. 333) in the "Cyclops" of Euripides, who speaks like an Epicurean. Not to marry and not to engage in public affairs were Epicurean doctrines

⁶ The toreutic art is the art of working in metal, stone, or wood, and of making figures on them in relief or by cutting into the material.

⁷ A codicillus is a small codex and the original sense of codex is a strong stem or stump. Lastly it was used for a book, and even for a will. Codicilli were small writing-tablets, covered with wax, on which men wrote with a stylus or pointed metal. Lastly, codicillus is a book or writing generally; and a writing or letter by which the emperor conferred any office. Our word codicil has only one sense, which is a small writing added or subjoined to a will or testament, but this sense is also derived from the Roman use of the word. (Dig. 29, tit. 7, de jure codicillorum.)

⁸ Upton supposes this to mean, whose bedchamber man are you? and he compares i 19. Schweig. says that this is not the meaning here, and that the meaning is this: He who before daybreak is waiting at the door of a rich man, whose favour he seeks, is said in a derisive way to be passing the night before a man's chamber.

CHAPTER VIII

HOW WE MUST EXERCISE OURSELVES AGAINST APPEARANCES

AS we exercise ourselves against sophistical questions, so we ought to exercise ourselves daily against appearances; for these appearances also propose questions to us. A certain person's son is dead. Answer; the thing is not within the power of the will: it is not an evil. A father has disinherited a certain son. What do you think of it? It is a thing beyond the power of the will, not an evil. Cæsar has condemned a person. It is a thing beyond the power of the will, not an evil. The man is afflicted at this. Affliction is a thing which depends on the will: it is an evil. He has borne the condemnation bravely. That is a thing within the power of the will: it is a good. If we train ourselves in this manner, we shall make progress; for we shall never assent to any thing of which there is not an appearance capable of being comprehended. Your son is dead. What has happened? Your son is dead. Nothing more? Nothing. Your ship is lost. What has happened? Your ship is lost. A man has been led to prison. What has happened? He has been led to prison. But that herein he has fared badly, every man adds from his own opinion. But Zeus, you say, does not do right in these matters. Why? because he has made you capable of endurance? because he has made you magnanimous? because he has taken from that which befalls you the power of being evils? because it is in your power to be happy while you are suffering what you suffer; because he has opened the door to you, when things do not please you? Man, go out and do not complain.

Hear how the Romans feel towards philosophers, if you would like to know. Italicus, who was the most in repute of the philosophers, once when I was present being vexed with his own friends and as if he was suffering something intolerable said, "I can not bear it, you are killing me: you will make me such as that man is;" pointing to me

CHAPTER IX

TO A CERTAIN RHETORICIAN WHO WAS GOING UP TO ROME ON A SUIT

WHEN a certain person came to him, who was going up to Rome on account of a suit which had regard to his rank, Epictetus enquired the reason of his going to Rome, and the man then asked what he thought about the matter. Epictetus replied, If you ask me what you will do in Rome, whether you will succeed or fail, I have no rule (θεώρημα) about this. But if you ask me how you will fare, I can tell you: if you have right opinions (δόγματα), you will fare well; if they are false, you will fare ill. For to every man the cause of his acting is opinion. For what is the reason why you desired to be elected governor of the Cnossians? Your opinion. What is the reason that you are now going up to Rome? Your opinion. And going in winter, and with danger and expense.—I must go.—What tells you this? Your opinion. Then if opinions are the causes of all actions, and a man has bad opinions, such as the cause may be, such also is the effect. Have we then all sound opinions, both you and your adversary? And how do you differ? But have you sounder opinions than your adversary? Why? You think so. And so does he think that his opinions are better; and so do madmen. This is a bad criterion. But show to me that you have made some inquiry into your opinions and have taken some pains about them. And as now you are sailing to Rome in order to become governor of the Cnossians, and you are not content to stay at home with the honours which you had, but you desire something greater and more conspicuous, so when did you ever make a voyage for the purpose of examining your own opinions, and casting them out, if you have any that are bad? Whom have you approached for this purpose? What time have you fixed for it? What age? Go over the times of your life by yourself, if you are ashamed of me (knowing the fact), when you were a boy, did you examine your own opinions? and did you not then, as you do all things now, do as you did do? and when you were become a youth and attended' the rhetoricians, and yourself practised rhetoric, what did you imagine that you were deficient in? And when you were a young man and engaged in public matters, and pleaded causes yourself, and were gaining reputation, who then seemed your equal? And when would you have submitted to any man examining and showing that your opinions are bad? What then do you wish me to say to you?—Help me in this matter.—I have no theorem (rule) for this. Nor have you, if you came to me for this purpose, come to me as a philosopher, but as to a seller of vegetables or a shoemaker. For what purpose then have philosophers theorems? For this purpose, that whatever may happen, our ruling faculty may be and continue to be conformable to nature. 'Does this seem to you a small thing?—No; but the greatest.—What then? does it need only a short time? and is it possible to seize it as you pass by? If you can, seize it.

Then you will say, I met with Epictetus as I should meet with a stone or a statue: for you saw me, and nothing more. But he meets with a man as a 'man, who learns his opinions, and in his turn shows his own. Learn my opinions: show me yours; and then say that you·have visited me. Let us examine one another: if I have any bad opinion, take it away: if you have any, show it. This is the meaning of meeting ·with a philosopher.—Not so, (you say): but this is only a passing visit, and while we are hiring the vessel, we can also see Epictetus. Let us see what he says. Then you go away and say: Epictetus was nothing; he used solecisms and spoke in a' barbarous way. For of what else do you come as judges?—Well, but a man may say to me, if I attend to such matters (as you do), I shall have no land, as you have none; I shall have no silver cups as you have none, nor fine beasts as you have none.—In answer to this it is perhaps sufficient to say: I have no need of such things: but if you possess many things, you have need of others: whether you choose or not, you are poorer than I am. What then have I need of? Of that which you have not: of firmness, of a mind which is conformable to nature, of being free from perturbation. Whether I have a patron[1] or not, what is that to me? but it is something to you. I am richer than you: I am not anxious what Cæsar will think of me: for this reason, I flatter no man. This is what I possess instead of vessels of silver and gold. You have utensils of gold; but your discourse, your opinions, your assents, your movements (pursuits), your desires are of earthenware. But when I have these things conformable to nature, why should I not employ my studies also upon reason? for I have leisure: my mind is not distracted What shall I do, since I have no distraction? What more suitable to a man have I than this? When you have nothing to do, you are disturbed, you go to the theatre or you wander about without a purpose. Why should not the philosopher labour to improve his reason? You employ yourself about crystal vessels: I employ myself about the syllogism named the lying:[2] you about myrrhine[3] vessels; I employ myself about the syllogism named the denying (τοῦ ἀποφάσκοντος). To you every thing appears small that you possess: to me all that I have appears great. Your desire is insatiable: mine is satisfied. To (children) who put their hand into a narrow-necked earthen vessel and bring out figs and nuts, this happens; if they fill the hand, they can not take it out, and then they cry. Drop a few of them and you will draw things out. And do you part with your desires: do not desire many things and you will have what you want.

NOTES

[1] The Roman word "patronus," which at that time had the sense of a protector.
[2] On the syllogism named lying (ψευδόμενος) see Epict ii 17, 34.
[3] "Murrhina vasa" were reckoned very precious by the Romans, and they gave great prices for them. It is not certain of what material they were made.

CHAPTER X

IN WHAT MANNER WE OUGHT TO BEAR SICKNESS

WHEN the need of each opinion comes, we ought to have it in readiness:[1] on the occasion of breakfast, such opinions as relate to breakfast; in the bath, those that concern the bath; in bed, those that concern bed.

> "Let sleep not come upon thy languid eyes,
> Before each daily action thou hast scann'd:
> What's done amiss, what done, what left undone;
> From first to last examine all, and then
> Blame what is wrong, in what is right rejoice"[2]

And we ought to retain these verses in such way that we may use them, not that we may utter them aloud, as when we exclaim "Pæan Apollo."[3] Again in fever we should have ready such opinions as concern a fever; and we ought not, as soon as the fever begins, to lose and forget all. (A man who has a fever) may say: If I philosophize any longer, may I be hanged: wherever I go, I must take care of the poor body, that a fever may not come. But what is philosophizing? Is it not a preparation against events which may happen? Do you not understand that you are saying something of this kind? "If I shall still prepare myself to bear with patience what happens, may I be hanged." But this is just as if a man after receiving blows should give up the Pancratium "In the Pancratium it is in our power to desist and not to receive blows." But in the other matter if we give up philosophy, what shall we gain? What then should a man say on the occasion of each painful thing? It was for this that I exercised myself, for this I disciplined myself. God says to you, "Give me a proof that you have duly practised athletics,[4] that you have eaten what you ought, that you have been exercised, that you have obeyed the aliptes (the oiler and rubber)." Then do you show yourself weak when the time for action comes? Now is the time for the fever. Let it be borne well. Now is the time for thirst, bear it well; now is the time for hunger, bear it well. Is it not in your power? who shall hinder you? The physician will hinder you from drinking; but he can not prevent you from bearing thirst well: and he will hinder you from eating; but he can not prevent you from bearing hunger well.

But I can not attend to my philosophical studies. And for what purpose do you follow them? Slave, is it not that you may be happy. that you may be constant, is it not that you be in a state conformable to nature and live so? What hinders you when you have a fever from having your ruling faculty conformable to nature? Here is the proof of the thing, here is the test of the philosopher. For this also is a part of life, like walking, like sailing, like journeying by land, so also is fever. Do you read when you are walking? No. Nor do you when you have a fever. But if you walk about well, you have all that belongs to a man who walks. If you bear a fever well, you have all that belongs to a man in a fever. What is it to bear a fever well? Not to blame God or man; not to be afflicted at that which happens, to expect death well and nobly, to do what must be done: when the physician comes in, not to be frightened at what he says; nor if he says, "You are doing well," to be overjoyed. For what good has he told you? and when you were in health, what good was that to you? And even if he says, "You are in a bad way," do not despond. For what is it to be ill? is it that you are near the severance of the soul and the body? what harm is there in this? If you are not near now, will you not afterwards be near? Is the world going to be turned upside down when you are dead? Why then do you flatter the physician?⁵ Why do you say if you please, master, I shall be well?⁵ Why do you give him an opportunity of raising his eyebrows (being proud; or showing his importance)? Do you not value a physician, as you do a shoemaker when he is measuring your foot, or a carpenter when he is building your house, and so treat the physician as to the body which is not yours, but by nature dead? He who has a fever has an opportunity of doing this: if he does these things, he has what belongs to him. For it is not the business of a philosopher to look after these externals, neither his wine nor his oil nor his poor body, but his own ruling power. But as to externals how must he act? so far as not to be careless about them. Where then is there reason for fear? where is there then still reason for anger, and of fear about what belongs to others, about things which are of no value? For we ought to have these two principles in readiness, that except the will nothing is good nor bad; and that we ought not to lead events, but to follow them.—My brother ought not to have behaved thus to me.—No; but he will see to that: and, however he may behave, I will conduct myself towards him as I ought. For this is my own business: that belongs to another; no man can prevent this, the other thing can be hindered.

NOTES

[1] "As physicians have always their instruments and knives ready for cases which suddenly require their skill, so do thou have principles ($\delta\acute{o}\gamma\mu\alpha\tau\alpha$), ready for the understanding of things divine and human, and for doing every thing, even the smallest, with a recollection of the bond which unites the divine and human to one another. For neither wilt thou do anything well which pertains to man without at the same time having a reference to things divine; nor the contrary."—Marcus Aurelius.

[2] These verses are from the Golden verses attributed to Pythagoras See iv. 6, 32.

[3] The beginning of a form of prayer, as in Macrobius, Sat i. 17: "namque Vestales Virgines ita indigitant Apollo Mædice, Apollo Pæan."

[4] $\epsilon i\ \nu o\mu\acute{\iota}\mu\omega\varsigma\ \mathring{\eta}\theta\lambda\eta\sigma\alpha\varsigma$. "St. Paul hath made use of this very expression $\dot{\epsilon}\grave{\alpha}\nu\ \mu\grave{\eta}\ \nu o\mu\acute{\iota}\mu\omega\varsigma\ \dot{\alpha}\theta\lambda\acute{\eta}\delta\eta$, 2 Tim ii. 3 "—Mrs Carter.

[5] "Et quid opus Cratero magnos promittere montes?" Persius, iii. 65. Craterus was a physician.

[6] Upton compares Matthew, viii. 2. "Lord, if thou wilt, thou canst make me clean."

CHAPTER XI

CERTAIN MISCELLANEOUS MATTERS

THERE are certain penalties fixed as by law for those who disobey the divine administration. Whoever thinks any other thing to be good except those things which depend on the will, let him envy, let him desire, let him flatter, let him be perturbed: whoever considers any thing else to be evil, let him grieve, let him lament, let him weep, let him be unhappy. And yet, though so severely punished, we can not desist.

Remember what the poet[1] says about the stranger:

"Stranger, I must not, e'en if a worse man come."

This then may be applied even to a father: I must not, even if a worse man than you should come, treat a father unworthily; for all are from paternal Zeus. And (let the same be said) of a brother, for all are from the Zeus who presides over kindred. And so in the other relations of life we shall find Zeus to be an inspector.

NOTE

[1] The poet is Homer. The complete passage is in the Odyssey, xiv. 55, et seq.
"Stranger, I must not, e'en if a worse man come,
Ill treat a stranger, for all come from Zeus,
Strangers and poor."

CHAPTER XII

ABOUT EXERCISE

WE ought not to make our exercises consist in means contrary to nature and adapted to cause admiration, for if we do so, we who call ourselves philosophers, shall not differ at all from jugglers. For it is difficult even to walk on a rope; and not only difficult, but it is also dangerous. Ought we for this reason to practise walking on a rope, or setting up a palm tree,[1] or embracing statues? By no means. Every thing which is difficult and dangerous is not suitable for practice; but that is suitable which conduces to the working out of that which is proposed to us. And what is that which is proposed to us as a thing to be worked out? To live with desire and aversion (avoidance of certain things) free from restraint. And what is this? Neither to be disappointed in that which you desire, nor to fall into any thing which you would avoid. Towards this object then exercise (practice) ought to tend. For since it is not possible to have your desire not disappointed and your aversion free from falling into that which you would avoid, without great and constant practice, you must know that if you allow your desire and aversion to turn to things which are not within the power of the will, you will neither have your desire capable of attaining your object, nor your aversion free from the power of avoiding that which you would avoid. And since strong habit leads (prevails), and we are accustomed to employ desire and aversion only to things which are not within the power of our will, we ought to oppose to this habit a contrary habit, and where there is great slipperiness in the appearances, there to oppose the habit of exercise.

I am rather inclined to pleasure: I will incline to the contrary side above measure for the sake of exercise. I am averse to pain: I will rub and exercise against this the appearances which are presented to me for the purpose of withdrawing my aversion from every such thing. For who is a practitioner in exercise? He who practises not using his desire, and applies his aversion only to things which are within the power of his will, and practises most in the things which are difficult to conquer. For this reason one man must practise himself more against one thing and another against another thing. What then is it to the purpose to set up a palm tree, or to carry about a tent of skins, or a mortar and pestle?[2] Practise, man, if you are irritable, to endure if you are abused, not to be vexed if you are treated with dishonour. Then you will make so much progress that, even if a man strikes you you will say to yourself, Imagine that you have embraced a statue: then also exercise yourself to use wine properly so as not to drink much, for in this also there are men who foolishly practise themselves; but first of all you should abstain from it, and abstain from a young girl and dainty cakes Then at last, if occasion presents itself, for the purpose of trying yourself at a proper time you will descend into the arena to know if appearances overpower you as they did formerly. But at first fly far from that which is stronger than yourself: the contest is unequal between a charming young girl and a beginner in philosophy. The earthen pitcher, as the saying is, and the rock do not agree.[3]

After the desire and the aversion comes the second topic (matter) of the movements towards action and the withdrawals from it; that you may be obedient to reason, that you do nothing out of season or place, or contrary to any propriety of the kind. The third topic concerns the assents, which is related to the things which are persuasive and attractive. For as Socrates said, we ought not to live a life without examination, so we ought not to accept an appearance without examination, but we should say, Wait, let me see what you are and whence you come; like the watch at night (who says) "Show me the pass (the Roman tessera)." Have you the signal from nature which the appearance that may be accepted ought to have? And finally whatever means are applied to the body by those who exercise it, if they tend in any way towards desire and aversion, they also may be fit means of exercise; but if they are for display, they are the indications of one who has turned himself towards something external and who is hunting for something else

`15

and who looks for spectators who will say, "Oh the great man." For this reason Apollonius said well, "When you intend to exercise yourself for your own advantage, and you are thirsty from heat, take in a mouthful of cold water, and spit it out and tell nobody."[4]

NOTES

[1] " To set up a palm tree." He does not mean a real palm tree, but something high and upright. The climbers of palm trees are mentioned by Lucian, de Dea Syria (c 29). Schweighauser has given the true interpretation when he says that on certain feast days in the country a high piece of wood is fixed in the earth and climbed by the most active youths by using only their hands and feet. In England we know what this is.

It is said that Diogenes used to embrace statues when they were covered with snow for the purpose of exercising himself. I suppose bronze statues, not marble which might be easily broken The man would not remain long in the embrace of a metal statue in winter. But perhaps the story is not true. I have heard of a general, not an English general, setting a soldier on a cold cannon; but it was as a punishment.

[4] This was done for the sake of exercise says Upton, but I don't understand the passage.

[3] There is a like fable in Æsop of the earthen pitcher and the brazen.— Upton.

[4] Schweighäuser refers to Arrian's "Expedition of Alexander" (vi: 26) for such an instance of Alexander's abstinence. There was an Apollonius of Tyana, whose life was written by Philostratus: but it may be that this is not the man who is mentioned here.

CHAPTER XIII

WHAT SOLITUDE IS, AND WHAT KIND OF PERSON A SOLITARY MAN IS

SOLITUDE is a certain condition of a helpless man, For because a man is alone, he is not for that reason also solitary; just as though a man is among numbers, he is not therefore not solitary. When then we have lost either a brother, or a son, or a friend on whom we were accustomed to repose, we say that we are left solitary, though we are often in Rome, though such a crowd meet us, though so many live in the same place, and sometimes we have a great number of slaves. For the man who is solitary, as it is conceived, is considered to be a helpless person and exposed to those who wish to harm him. For this reason when we travel, then especially do we say that we are lonely when we fall among robbers, for it is not the sight of a human creature which removes us from solitude, but the sight of one who is faithful and modest and helpful to us. For if being alone is enough to make solitude, you may say that even Zeus is solitary in the conflagration[1] and bewails himself saying, "Unhappy that I am who have neither Hera, nor Athena, nor Apollo, nor brother, nor son, nor descendant, nor kinsman." This is what some say that he does when he is alone at the conflagration.[2] For they do not understand how a man passes his life when he is alone, because they set out from a certain natural principle, from the natural desire of community and mutual love and from the pleasure of conversation among men. But none the less a man ought to be prepared in a manner for this also (being alone), to be able to be sufficient for himself and to be his own companion. For as Zeus dwells with himself, and is tranquil by himself, and thinks of his own administration and of its nature, and is employed in thoughts suitable to himself, so ought we also to be able to talk with ourselves, not to feel the want of others also, not to be unprovided with the means of passing our time; to observe the divine admin-

227

istration, and the relation of ourselves to every thing else; to consider how we formerly were affected towards things that happen and how at present; what are still the things which give us pain; how these also can be cured and how removed; if any things require improvement, to improve them according to reason.

For you see that Cæsar appears to furnish us with great peace, that there are no longer enemies nor battles nor great associations of robbers nor of pirates, but we can travel at every hour and sail from east to west. But can Cæsar give us security from fever also, can he from shipwreck, from fire, from earthquake or from lightning? well, I will say, can he give us security against love? He can not. From sorrow? He can not. From envy? He can not. In a word then he can not protect us from any of these things. But the doctrine of philosophers promises to give us security (peace) even against these things. And what does it say? Men, if you will attend to me, wherever you are, whatever you are doing, you will not feel sorrow, nor anger, nor compulsion, nor hindrance, but you will pass your time without perturbations and free from every thing. When a man has this peace, not proclaimed by Cæsar, (for how should he be able to proclaim it?), but by God through reason, is he not content when he is alone? when he sees and reflects, Now no evil can happen to me; for me there is no robber, no earthquake, every thing is full of peace, full of tranquillity: every way, every city, every meeting, neighbour, companion is harmless. One person whose business it is, supplies me with food; another with raiment; another with perceptions, and preconceptions (προλήψεις). And if he does not supply what is necessary, he (God) gives the signal for retreat, opens the door, and says to you, "Go." Go whither? To nothing terrible, but to the place from which you came, to your friends and kinsmen, to the elements: what there was in you of fire goes to fire; of earth, to earth; of air (spirit), to air; of water to water: no Hades, nor Acheron, nor Cocytus, nor Pyriphlegethon, but all is full of Gods and Dæmons. When a man has such things to think on, and sees the sun, the moon and stars, and enjoys earth and sea, he is not solitary nor even helpless. Well then, if some man should come upon me when I am alone and murder me? Fool, not murder You, but your poor body.

What kind of solitude then remains? what want? why do we make ourselves worse than children? and what do children do when they are left alone? They take up shells and ashes, and they build something, then pull it down, and build something else, and so they never want the means of passing the time. Shall I then, if you sail away, sit down and weep, because I have been left alone and solitary? Shall I then have no shells, no ashes? But children do what they do through want of thought (or deficiency in knowledge), and we through knowledge are unhappy.

Every great power (faculty) is dangerous to beginners. You must then bear such things as you are able, but conformably to nature: but not. . . . Practise sometimes a way of living like a person out of health that you may at some time live like a man in health. Abstain from food, drink water, abstain sometimes altogether from desire, in order that you may some time desire consistently with reason; and if consistently with reason, when you have anything good in you, you will desire well.—Not so; but we wish to live like wise men immediately and to be useful to men—Useful how? what are you doing? have you been useful to yourself? But, I suppose, you wish to exhort them? You exhort them! You wish to be useful to them. Show to them in your own example what kind of men philosophy makes, and don't trifle. When you are eating, do good to those who eat with you; when you are drinking, to those who are drinking with you; by yielding to all, giving way, bearing with them, thus do them good, and do not spit on them your phlegm (bad humours).

NOTES

[1] This was the doctrine of Heraclitus "that all things were composed from (had their origin in) fire, and were resolved into it," an opinion afterwards adopted by the Stoics. It is not so extravagant, as it may appear to some persons, to suppose that the earth had a beginning, is in a state of continual change, and will finally be destroyed in some way, and have a new beginning.

[2] The Latin translation is: "hoc etiam nonnulli facturum cum in conflagratione mundi . . . . aiunt." But the word is $\pi o \iota \epsilon \hat{\iota}$: and this may mean that the conflagration has happened, and will happen again. The Greek philosophers in their speculations were not troubled with

the consideration of time. Even Herodotus (ii: 11), in his speculations
on the gulf, which he supposes that the Nile valley was once, speaks of
the possibility of it being filled up in 20,000 years, or less. Modern specu-
lators have only recently become bold enough to throw aside the notion
of the earth and the other bodies in space being limited by time, as the
ignorant have conceived it.

CHAPTER XIV

CERTAIN MISCELLANEOUS MATTERS

AS bad[1] tragic actors can not sing alone, but in company with many: so some persons can not walk about alone. Man, if you are anything, both walk alone and talk to yourself, and do not hide yourself in the chorus. Examine a little at last, look around, stir yourself up, that you may know who you are.

When a man drinks water, or does anything for the sake of practice (discipline), whenever there is an opportunity he tells it to all: "I drink water." Is it for this that you drink water, for the purpose of drinking water? Man, if it is good for you to drink, drink; but if not, you are acting ridiculously. But if it is good for you and you do drink, say nothing about it to those who are displeased with water-drinkers. What then, do you wish to please these very men?

Of things that are done some are done with a final purpose ($\pi\rho o\eta\gamma o\upsilon\mu\acute{\epsilon}\nu\omega\varsigma$), some according to occasion, others with a certain reference to circumstances, others for the purpose of complying with others, and some according to a fixed scheme of life.[2]

You must root out of men these two things, arrogance (pride) and distrust. Arrogance then is the opinion that you want nothing (are deficient in nothing): but distrust is the opinion that you can not be happy when so many circumstances surround you. Arrogance is removed by confutation; and Socrates was the first who practised this. And (to know) that the thing is not impossible inquire and seek. This search will do you no harm; and in a manner this is philosophizing, to see how it is possible to employ desire and aversion ($\dot{\epsilon}\kappa\kappa\lambda\acute{\iota}\sigma\epsilon\iota$) without impediment.

I am superior to you, for my father is a man of consular rank. Another says, I have been a tribune, but you have not. If we were horses, would you say, My father was swifter? I have much barley and fodder, or elegant neck ornaments. If then while you were saying this, I said,

231

Be it so: let us run then. Well, is there nothing in a man such as running in a horse, by which it will be known which is superior and inferior? Is there not modesty ($αἰδὼς$), fidelity, justice? Show yourself superior in these, that you may be superior as a man. If you tell me that you can kick violently, I also will say to you, that you are proud of that which is the act of an ass.

NOTES

[1] All the manuscripts have "good" ($καλοί$), which the critics have properly corrected.
[2] This section is not easy to translate.

CHAPTER XV

IN every act consider what precedes and what follows, and then proceed to the act. If you do not consider, you will at first begin with spirit, since you have not thought at all of the things which follow; but afterwards when some consequences have shown themselves, you will basely desist (from that which you have begun).—I wish to conquer at the Olympic games.—[And I too, by the gods: for it is a fine thing]. But consider here what precedes and what follows; and then, if it is for your good, undertake the thing. You must act according to rules, follow strict diet, abstain from delicacies, exercise yourself by compulsion at fixed times, in heat, in cold; drink no cold water, nor wine, when there is opportunity of drinking it.[2] In a word you must surrender yourself to the trainer, as you do to a physician. Next, in the contest, you must be covered with sand,[3] sometimes dislocate a hand, sprain an ankle, swallow a quantity of dust, be scourged with the whip; and after undergoing all this, you must sometimes be conquered. After reckoning all these things, if you have still an inclination, go to the athletic practice. If you do not reckon them, observe you will behave like children who at one time play as wrestlers, then as gladiators, then blow a trumpet, then act a tragedy, when they have seen and admired such things. So you also do: you are at one time a wrestler (athlete), then a gladiator, then a philosopher, then a rhetorician; but with your whole soul you are nothing; like the ape you imitate all that you see; and always one thing after another pleases you, but that which becomes familiar displeases you. For you have never undertaken any thing after consideration, nor after having explored the whole matter and put it to a strict examination; but you have undertaken it at hazard and with a cold desire. Thus some persons having seen a philosopher and having heard one speak like Euphrates[4]—

and yet who can speak like him?—wish to be philosophers themselves.

Man, consider first what the matter is (which you propose to do), then your own nature also, what it is able to bear. If you are a wrestler, look at your shoulders, your thighs, your loins: for different men are naturally formed for different things. Do you think that, if you do (what you are doing daily), you can be a philosopher? Do you think that you can eat as you do now, drink as you do now, and in the same way be angry and out of humour? You must watch, labour, conquer certain desires, you must depart from your kinsmen, be despised by your slave, laughed at by those who meet you, in every thing you must be in an inferior condition, as to magisterial office, in honours, in courts of justice. When you have considered all these things completely, then, if you think proper, approach to philosophy, if you would gain in exchange for these things freedom from perturbations, liberty, tranquillity. If you have not considered these things, do not approach philosophy: do not act like children, at one time a philosopher, then a tax collector, then a rhetorician, then a procurator (officer) of Cæsar. These things are not consistent. You must be one man either good or bad: you must either labour at your own ruling faculty or at external things: you must either labour at things within or at external things: that is, you must either occupy the place of a philosopher or that of one of the vulgar.

A person said to Rufus[5] when Galba was murdered, "Is the world now governed by Providence?" But Rufus replied, "Did I ever incidentally form an argument from Galba that the world is governed by Providence?"

NOTES

[1] " This chapter has a great conformity to Luke xiv: 28, etc. But it is to be observed that Epictetus, both here and elsewhere, supposes some persons incapable of being philosophers; that is, virtuous and pious men: but Christianity requires and enables all to be such."—Mrs. Carter.

The passage in Luke contains a practical lesson, and so far is the same as the teaching of Epictetus: but the conclusion in v: 33 does not appear to be helped by what immediately precedes v. 28-32. The remark that Christianity "enables all to be such" is not true, unless Mrs. Carter gives to the word "enables" a meaning which I do not see.

[1] The commentators refer us to Paul, 1 Cor. c. 9, 25. Compare Horace, "Ars Poetica," 39:

> "Versate diu quid ferre recusent,
> Quid valeant humeri."

[2] Wolf thought that the word παρορύσσεσθαι might mean the loss of an eye; but other commentators give the word a different meaning
[3] In place of Euphrates the "Encheiridion" 29 had in the text "Socrates," which name the recent editors of the "Encheiridion altered to "Euphrates," and correctly. The younger Pliny (i. Ep. 10) speaks in high terms of the merits and attractive eloquence of this Syrian philosopher Euphrates, who is mentioned by M. Antoninus (x 31) and by others
[4] Rufus was a philosopher. See i: 1, i: 9. Galba is the emperor Galba, who was murdered The meaning of the passage is rather obscure, and it is evident that it does not belong to this chapter. Lord Shaftesbury remarks that this passage perhaps belongs to chapter 11 or 14, or perhaps to the end of chapter 17.

CHAPTER XVI

THAT WE OUGHT WITH CAUTION TO ENTER INTO FAMILIAR INTERCOURSE WITH MEN

IF a man has frequent intercourse with others either for talk, or drinking together, or generally for social purposes, he must either become like them, or change them to his own fashion.   For if a man places a piece of quenched charcoal close to a piece that is burning, either the quenched charcoal will quench the other, or the burning charcoal will light that which is quenched.   Since then the danger is so great, we must cautiously enter into such intimacies with those of the common sort, and remember that it is impossible that a man can keep company with one who is covered with soot without being partaker of the soot himself. For what will you do if a man speaks about gladiators, about horses, about athletes, or what is worse about men?   Such a person is bad, such a person is good: this was well done, this was done badly.   Further, if he scoff, or ridicule, or show an ill-natured disposition?   Is any man among us prepared like a lute-player when he takes a lute, so that as soon as he has touched the strings, he discovers which are discordant, and tunes the instrument? such a power as Socrates had who in all his social intercourse could lead his companions to his own purpose? How should you have this power? It is therefore a necessary consequence that you are carried about by the common kind of people.

Why then are they more powerful than you?   Because they utter these useless words from their real opinions: but you utter your elegant words only from your lips; for this reason they are without strength and dead, and it is nauseous to listen to your exhortations and your miserable virtue, which is talked of every where (up and down).   In this way the vulgar have the advantage over you: for every opinion (δόγμα) is strong and invincible.   Until then the good (κομψαί) sentiments (ὑπολήψεις) are fixed in you, and you shall have acquired a certain power for your security, I advise you to be careful in your association with common persons: if you are not, every day like wax in the sun there will be melted away whatever you inscribe on your minds in the school. Withdraw then yourselves far from the sun so long as you have these waxen sentiments. For this reason also philosophers advise men to leave their native country, because ancient habits distract them and do not allow a beginning to be made of a different habit; nor can we tolerate those who meet us and say: "See such a one is now a philosopher, who was once so and so." Thus also physicians send those who have lingering diseases to a different country and a different air; and they do right. Do you also introduce other habits than those which you have: fix your opinions and exercise yourselves in them. But you do not so: you go hence to a spectacle, to a show of gladiators, to a place of exercise (ξυστόν), to a circus; then you come back later, and again from this place you go to those places, and still the same persons. And there is no pleasing (good) habit, nor attention, nor care about self and observation of this kind. How shall I use the appearances presented to me? according to nature, or contrary to nature? how do I answer to them? as I ought, or as I ought not? Do I say to those things which are independent of the will, that they do not concern me? For if you are not yet in this state, fly from your former habits, fly from the common sort, if you intend ever to begin to be something.

CHAPTER XVII

OF PROVIDENCE

WHEN you make any charge against Providence, consider, and you will learn that the thing has happened according to reason.—Yes, but the unjust man has the advantage.—In what?—In money.—Yes, for he is superior to you in this, that he flatters, is free from shame, and is watchful. What is the wonder? But see if he has the advantage over you in being faithful, in being modest: for you will not find it to be so; but wherein you are superior, there you will find that you have the advantage. And I once said to a man who was vexed because Philostorgus was fortunate: Would you choose to lie with Sura?[1] "May it never happen," he replied, "that this day should come?" Why then are you vexed, if he receives something in return for that which he sells; or how can you consider him happy who acquires those things by such means as you abominate; or what wrong does Providence, if he gives the better things to the better men? Is it not better to be modest than to be rich?—He admitted this—Why are you vexed then, man, when you possess the better thing? Remember then always and have in readiness the truth, that this is a law of nature, that the superior has an advantage over the inferior in that in which he is superior; and you will never be vexed.

But my wife treats me badly.—Well, if any man asks you what this is, say, my wife treats me badly—Is there then nothing more? Nothing.—My father gives me nothing—[What is this? my father gives me nothing—Is there nothing else then?—Nothing] · but to say that this is an evil is something which must be added to it externally, and falsely added. For this reason we must not get rid of poverty, but of the opinion about poverty, and then we shall be happy.

NOTE

[1] Upton suggests that Sura may be Palfurius (Juvenal, iv. 53), or Palfurius Sura (Suetonius, Domitian, c. 13).

CHAPTER XVIII

WHEN any thing shall be reported to you which is of a nature to disturb, have this principle in readiness, that the news is about nothing which is within the power of your will. Can any man report to you that you have formed a bad opinion, or had a bad desire? By no means. But perhaps he will report that some person is dead. What then is that to you? He may report that some person speaks ill of you. What then is that to you? Or that your father is planning something or other. Against whom? Against your will (προαίρεσις)? How can he? But is it against your poor body, against your little property? You are quite safe: it is not against you. But the judge declares that you have committed an act of impiety. And did not the judges (δικασται) make the same declaration against Socrates? Does it concern you that the judge has made this declaration? No. Why then do you trouble yourself any longer about it? Your father has a certain duty, and if he shall not fulfill it, he loses the character of a father, of a man of natural affection, of gentleness. Do not wish him to lose any thing else on this account. For never does a man do wrong in one thing, and suffer in another. On the other side it is your duty to make your defence firmly, modestly, without anger: but if you do not, you also lose the character of a son, of a man of modest behaviour, of generous character. Well then, is the judge free from danger? No; but he also is in equal danger. Why then are you still afraid of his decision? What have you to do with that which is another man's evil? It is your own evil to make a bad defence: be on your guard against this only. But to be condemned or not to be condemned, as that is the act of another person, so it is the evil of another person. A certain person threatens you. Me? No. He blames you. Let him see how he manages his own affairs. He is going to condemn you unjustly. He is a wretched man.

CHAPTER XIX

WHAT IS THE CONDITION OF A COMMON KIND OF MAN AND OF A PHILOSOPHER

THE first difference between a common person (ἰδιώτης) and a philosopher is this: the common person says, "Woe to me for my little child, for my brother, for my father."[1] The philosopher, if he shall ever be compelled to say, Woe to me, stops and says, "but for myself." For nothing which is independent of the will can hinder or damage the will, and the will can only hinder or damage itself. If then we ourselves incline in this direction, so as, when we are unlucky, to blame ourselves and to remember that nothing else is the cause of perturbation or loss of tranquillity except our own opinion, I swear to you by all the gods that we have made progress. But in the present state of affairs we have gone another way from the beginning. For example, while we were still children, the nurse, if we ever stumbled through want of care, did not chide us, but would beat the stone. But what did the stone do? Ought the stone to have moved on account of your child's folly? Again, if we find nothing to eat on coming out of the bath, the pedagogue never checks our appetite, but he flogs the cook. Man, did we make you the pedagogue of the cook and not of the child? Correct the child, improve him. In this way even when we are grown up we are like children. For he who is unmusical is a child in music; he who is without letters is a child in learning: he who is untaught, is a child in life.

NOTE

[1] Compare iii: 5, 4.

CHAPTER XX

THAT WE CAN DERIVE ADVANTAGE FROM ALL EXTERNAL THINGS

IN the case of appearances which are objects of the vision,[1] nearly all have allowed the good and the evil to be in ourselves, and not in externals. No one gives the name of good to the fact that it is day, nor bad to the fact that it is night, nor the name of the greatest evil to the opinion that three are four. But what do men say? They say that knowledge is good, and that error is bad; so that even in respect to falsehood itself there is a good result, the knowledge that it is falsehood. So it ought to be in life also. Is health a good thing, and is sickness a bad thing? No, man. But what is it? To be healthy, and healthy in a right way, is good: to be healthy in a bad way is bad; so that it is possible to gain advantage even from sickness, I declare. For is it not possible to gain advantage even from death, and is it not possible to gain advantage from mutilation? Do you think that Menœceus gained little by death?[2] Could a man who says so, gain so much as Menœceus gained? Come, man, did he not maintain the character of being a lover of his country, a man of great mind, faithful, generous? And if he had continued to live, would he not have lost all these things? would he not have gained the opposite? would he not have gained the name of coward, ignoble, a hater of his country, a man who feared death? Well, do you think that he gained little by dying? I suppose not. But did the father of Admetus[3] gain much by prolonging his life so ignobly and miserably? Did he not die afterwards? Cease, I adjure you by the gods, to admire material things. Cease to make yourselves, slaves, first of things, then on account of things slaves of those who are able to give them or take them away.

Can advantage then be derived from these things? From all; and from him who abuses you. Wherein does the man who exercises before the combat profit the athlete? Very greatly. This man becomes my exerciser before the combat: he exercises me in endurance, in keeping my temper, in mildness. You say no: but he, who lays hold of my neck and disciplines my loins and shoulders, does me good; and the exercise master (the aliptes, or oiler) does right when he says, "Raise him up with both hands;" and the heavier he (ἐκεῖνος) is, so much the more is my advantage. But if a man exercises me in keeping my temper, does he not do me good?—This is not knowing how to gain an advantage from men. Is my neighbour bad? Bad to himself, but good to me: he exercises my good disposition, my moderation. Is my father bad? Bad to himself, but to me good. This is the rod of Hermes: touch with it what you please, as the saying is, and it will be of gold. I say not so: but bring what you please, and I will make it good.[4] Bring disease, bring death, bring poverty, bring abuse, bring trial on capital charges: all these things through the rod of Hermes shall be made profitable. What will you do with death? Why, what else than that it shall do you honour, or that it shall show you by act through it, what a man is who follows the will of nature? What will you do with disease? I will show its nature, I will be conspicuous in it, I will be firm, I will be happy, I will not flatter the physician, I will not wish to die. What else do you seek? Whatever you shall give me, I will make it happy, fortunate, honoured, a thing which a man shall seek.

You say "No: but take care that you do not fall sick: it is a bad thing." This is the same as if you should say, "Take care that you never receive the impression (appearance) that three are four: that is bad." Man, how is it bad? If I think about it as I ought, how shall it then do me any damage? and shall it not even do me good? If then I think about poverty as I ought to do, about disease, about not having office, is not that enough for me? will it not be an advantage? How then ought I any longer to look to seek evil and good in externals? What happens? these doctrines are maintained here, but no man carries them away home; but immediately every one is at war with his slave, with his neighbours, with those who have sneered at him, with those

who have ridiculed him.   Good luck to Lesbius,[5] who daily
proves that I know nothing.

NOTES

[1]The original is θεωρητικῶν φαντασιῶν which is translated in
the Latin version visa theoretica, but this does not help us.   Perhaps
the author means any appearances which are presented to us either by
the eyes or by the understanding; but I am not sure what he means.
[2]Menœceus, the son of Creon, gave up his life by which he would
save his country, as it was declared by an oracle. (Cicero, Tuscul. 1. c.
48.) Juvenal (Sat. xiv. 238) says

"Quarum Amor in te
Quantus erat patriæ Deciorum in pectore ; quantum
Dilexit Thebas, si Græcia vera, Menœceus."

Euripides, Phœnissae, v. 913.

[3] The father of Admetus was Pheres (Euripides, Alcestis).
[4] Mrs. Carter quotes the epistle to the Romans (viii 28): "and we
know that all things work together for good to them that love God";
but she quotes only the first part of the verse and omits the conclusion,
"to them who are the called according to his purpose."
[5] Some abusive fellow, known to some of the hearers of Epictetus.
We ought perhaps to understand the words as if it were said, "each of
you ought to say to himself, Good luck to Lesbius, etc." Schweig's note.

CHAPTER XXI

THEY who have taken up bare theorems ($\theta\epsilon\omega\rho\acute{\eta}\mu\alpha\tau\alpha$) immediately wish to vomit them forth, as persons whose stomachs are diseased do with food. First digest the thing, then do not vomit it up thus: if you do not digest it, the thing becomes truly an emetic, a crude food and unfit to eat. But after digestion show us some change in your ruling faculty, as athletes show in their shoulders by what they have been exercised and what they have eaten; as those who have taken up certain arts show by what they have learned. The carpenter does not come and say, Hear me talk about the carpenter's art; but having undertaken to build a house, he makes it, and proves that he knows the art. You also ought to do something of the kind; eat like a man, drink like a man, dress, marry, beget children, do the office of a citizen, endure abuse, bear with an unreasonable brother, bear with your father, bear with your son, neighbour, companion.[1] Show us these things that we may see that you have in truth learned something from the philosophers. You say, No; but come and hear me read (philosophical) commentaries. Go away, and seek somebody to vomit them on. (He replies) And indeed I will expound to you the writings of Chrysippus as no other man can: I will explain his text most clearly: I will add also, if I can, the vehemence of Antipater and Archedemus.[2]

Is it then for this that young men shall leave their country and their parents, that they may come to this place, and hear you explain words? Ought they not to return with a capacity to endure, to be active in association with others, free from passions, free from perturbation, with such a provision for the journey of life with which they shall be able to bear well the things that happen and derive honour from them?[3] And how can you give them any of these things which you do not possess? Have you done from the begin-

ning any thing else than employ yourself about the resolution of syllogisms, of sophistical arguments (οἱ μεταπίπτοντες),
and in those which work by questions? But such a man has
a school; why should not I also have a school? These
things are not done, man, in a careless way, nor just as it
may happen; but there must be a (fit) age and life, and God
as a guide. You say, No. But no man sails from a port
without having sacrificed to the gods and invoked their help;
nor do men sow without having called on Demeter; and shall
a man who has undertaken so great a work undertake it
safely without the gods? and shall they who undertake this
work come to it with success? What else are you doing,
man, than divulging the mysteries? You say, there is a
temple at Eleusis, and one here also. There is an Hierophant at Eleusis,[4] and I also will make an Hierophant: there
is a herald, and I will establish a herald: there is a torchbearer at Eleusis, and I also will establish a torchbearer;
there are torches at Eleusis, and I will have torches here.
The words are the same: how do the things done here differ
from those done there?—Most impious man, is there no difference? these things are done both in due place and in due
time; and when accompanied with sacrifice and prayers,
when a man is first purified, and when he is disposed in his
mind to the thought that he is going to approach sacred rites
and ancient rites. In this way the mysteries are useful, in
this way we come to the notion that all these things were
established by the ancients for the instruction and correction
of life But you publish and divulge them out of time, out
of place, without sacrifices, without purity; you have not
the garments which the hierophant ought to have, nor the
hair, nor the headdress, nor the voice, nor the age; nor have
you purified yourself as he has: but you have committed to
memory the words only, and you say, Sacred are the words
by themselves.[5]

You ought to approach these matters in another way: the
thing is great, it is mystical, not a common thing, nor is it
given to every man. But not even wisdom[6] perhaps is
enough to enable a man to take the care of youths: a man
must have also a certain readiness and fitness for this purpose, and a certain quality of body, and above all things he

must have God to advise him to occupy this office, as God advised Socrates to occupy the place of one who confutes error, Diogenes the office of royalty and reproof, and the office of teaching precepts. But you open a doctor's shop, though you have nothing except physic . but where and how they should be applied, you know not nor have you taken any trouble about it. "See," that man says, "I too have salves for the eyes." Have you also the power of using them? Do you know both when and how they will do good, and to whom they will do good? Why then do you act at hazard in things of the greatest importance? why are you careless? why do you undertake a thing that is in no way fit for you? Leave it to those who are able to do it, and to do it well. Do not yourself bring disgrace on philosophy through your own acts, and be not one of those who load it with a bad reputation. But if theorems please you, sit still, and turn them over by yourself; but never say that you are a philosopher, nor allow another to say it: but say: "He is mistaken, for neither are my desires different from what they were before, nor is my activity directed to other objects, nor do I assent to other things, nor in the use of appearances have I altered at all from my former condition." This you must think and say about yourself, if you would think as you ought: if not act at hazard, and do what you are doing; for it becomes you.

NOTES

[1] The practical teaching of the Stoics is contained in iii. c. 7, and it is good and wise. A modern writer says of modern practice: "If we open our eyes and if we will honestly acknowledge to ourselves what we discover, we shall be compelled to confess that all the life and efforts of the civilized people of our times is founded on a view of the world, which is directly opposed to the view of the world which Jesus had" (Strauss, " Der alte und der neue Glaube " p. 74).

[2] Cicero (Academ. Prior. ii. 47) names Antipater and Archidemus (Archedemus) the chief of dialecticians, and also opiniosissimi homines.

[3] This passage is one of those which show the great good sense of Epictetus in the matter of education; and some other remarks to the same effect follow in this chapter. A man might justly say that we have no clear notion of the purpose of education. A modern writer, who seems to belong to the school of Epictetus says : " it can not be denied that in all schools of all kinds it ought to be the first and the chief object to make children healthy, good, honest, and, if possible, sensible men and women; and if this is not done in a reasonable degree, I maintain that the education of these schools is good for nothing—I do not

propose to make children good and honest and wise by precepts and dogmas and preaching, as you will see. They must be made good and wise by a cultivation of the understanding, by the practice of the discipline necessary for that purpose, and by the example of him who governs, directs and instructs." Further, "my men and women teachers have something which the others have not: they have a purpose, an end in their system of education, and what is education? What is human life without some purpose or end which may be attained by industry, order and the exercise of moderate abilities? Great abilities are rare, and they are often accompanied by qualities which make the abilities useless to him who has them, and even injurious to society."

⁴ There was a great temple of Demeter (Ceres) at Eleusis in Attica, and solemn mysteries, and an Hierophant or conductor of the ceremonies

⁵ The reader, who has an inclination to compare religious forms ancient and modern, may find something in modern practice to which the words of Epictetus are applicable

⁶ This is a view of the fitness of a teacher which, as far as I know, is quite new; and it is also true. Perhaps there was some vague notion of this kind in modern Europe at the time when teachers of youths were only priests, and when it was supposed that their fitness for the office of teacher was secured by their fitness for the office of priest. In the present "ordering of Deacons" in the Church of England, the person, who is proposed as a fit person to be a deacon, is asked the following question by the bishop: "Do you trust that you are inwardly moved by the Holy Ghost to take upon you this office and ministration to serve God for the promotion of his glory and the edifying of his people?" "In the ordering of priests" this question is omitted, and another question only is put, which is used only in the ordering of Deacons: "Do you think in your heart that you be truly called, according to the will of our Lord Jesus Christ," etc. The teacher ought to have God to advise him to occupy the office of teacher, as Epictetus says He does not say how God will advise; perhaps he supposed that this advice might be given in the way in which Socrates said that he received it.

"Wisdom perhaps is not enough" to enable a man to take care of youths. Whatever wisdom may mean, it is true that a teacher should have a fitness and liking for the business. If he has not, he will find it disagreeable, and he will not do it well. He may and ought to gain a reasonable living by his labour: if he seeks only money and wealth, he is on the wrong track, and he is only like a common dealer in buying and selling, a butcher or a shoemaker, or a tailor, all useful members of society and all of them necessary in their several kinds. But the teacher has a priestly office, the making, as far as it is possible, children into good men and women. Should he be ordered like a Deacon or a Priest, for his office is even more useful than that of a Priest or Deacon? Some will say that this is ridiculous. Perhaps the wise will not think so.

CHAPTER XXII

ABOUT CYNICISM

WHEN one of his pupils inquired of Epictetus, and he was a person who appeared to be inclined to Cynicism, what kind of a person a Cynic ought to be and what was the notion (πρόληψις) of the thing, we will inquire, said Epictetus, at leisure: but I have so much to say to you that he who without God attempts so great a matter, is hateful to God, and has other purpose than to act indecently in public. For in any well-managed house no man comes forward, and says to himself, I ought to be manager of the house. If he does so, the master turns round, and seeing him insolently giving orders, drags him forth and flogs him. So it is also in this great city (the world); for here also there is a master of the house who orders every thing. (He says) You are the sun; you can by going round make the year and seasons, and make the fruits grow and nourish them, and stir the winds and make them remit, and warm the bodies of men properly: go, travel round, and so administer things from the greatest to the least. You are a calf; when a lion shall appear, do your proper business (*i. e.* run away): if you do not, you will suffer. You are a bull: advance and fight, for this is your business, and becomes you, and you can do it. You can lead the army against Ilium: be Agamemnon. You can fight in single combat against Hector: be Achilles. But if Thersites[1] came forward and claimed the command, he would either not have obtained it; or if he did obtain it, he would have disgraced himself before many witnesses.

Do you also think about the matter carefully: it is not what it seems to you. (You say) I wear a cloak now and I shall wear it then: I sleep hard now, and I shall sleep hard then: I will take in addition a little bag now and a staff, and I will go about and begin to beg and to abuse those whom I meet; and if I see any man plucking the hair out of his body, I will rebuke him, or if he has dressed his hair, or if he walks about in purple—If you imagine the thing to be such as this, keep far away from it: do not approach it: it is not at all for you. But if you imagine it to be what it is, and do not think yourself to be unfit for it, consider what a great thing you undertake.

In the first place in the things which relate to yourself, you must not be in any respect like what you are now: you must not blame God or man: you must take away desire altogether, you must transfer avoidance (ἔκκλισις) only to the things which are within the power of the will: you must not feel anger nor resentment nor envy nor pity; a girl must not appear handsome to you, nor must you love a little reputation, nor be pleased with a boy or a cake. For you ought to know that the rest of men throw walls around them and houses and darkness when they do any such things, and they have many means of concealment. A man shuts the door, he sets somebody before the chamber: if a person comes, say that he is out, he is not at leisure. But the Cynic instead of all these things must use modesty as his protection: if he does not, he will be indecent in his nakedness and under the open sky. This is his house, his door: this is the slave before his bedchamber: this is his darkness. For he ought not to wish to hide any thing that he does: and if he does, he is gone, he has lost the character of a Cynic, of a man who lives under the open sky, of a free man: he has begun to fear some external thing, he has begun to have need of concealment, nor can he get concealment when he chooses. For where shall he hide himself and how? And if by chance this public instructor shall be detected, this pedagogue, what kind of things will he be compelled to suffer? When then a man fears these things, is it possible for him to be bold with his whole soul to superintend men? It can not be: it is impossible.

In the first place then you must make your ruling faculty pure, and this mode of life also. Now (you should say), to me the matter to work on is my understanding, as wood is to the carpenter, as hides to the shoemaker; and my business is the right use of appearances. But the body is nothing to me: the parts of it are nothing to me. Death? Let it come when it chooses, either death of the whole or of a

part. Fly, you say. And whither; can any man eject me
out of the world? He can not. But wherever I go, there is
the sun, there is the moon, there are the stars, dreams, omens,
and the conversation (ὁμελία) with gods.

Then, if he is thus prepared, the true Cynic can not be satisfied with this; but he must know that he is sent a messenger from Zeus to men about good and bad things,[2] to show
them that they have wandered and are seeking the substance
of good and evil where it is not, but where it is, they never
think; and that he is a spy, as Diogenes was carried off to
Philip after the battle of Chæroneia as a spy. For in fact a
Cynic is a spy of the things which are good for men and
which are evil, and it is his duty to examine carefully and
to come and report truly, and not to be struck with terror so
as to point out as enemies those who are not enemies, nor
in any other way to be perturbed by appearances nor confounded.

It is his duty then to be able with a loud voice, if the occasion should arise, and appearing on the tragic stage to say
like Socrates: Men, whither are you hurrying; what are you
doing, wretches? like blind people you are wandering up and
down: you are going by another road, and have left the true
road: you seek for prosperity and happiness where they are
not, and if another shows you where they are, you do not
believe him. Why do you seek it without?[3] In the body?
It is not there. If you doubt, look at Myro, look at Ophel-
lius.[4] In possessions? It is not there. But if you do not
believe me, look at Crœsus: look at those who are now rich,
with what lamentations their life is filled. In power? It
is not there. If it is, those must be happy who have been
twice and thrice consuls; but they are not. Whom shall we
believe in these matters? You who from without see their
affairs and are dazzled by an appearance, or the men themselves? What do they say? Hear them when they groan,
when they grieve, when on account of these very consulships and glory and splendour they think that they are more
wretched and in greater danger. Is it in royal power? It
is not: if it were, Nero would have been happy, and Sardanapalus. But neither was Agamemnon happy, though he

was a better man than Sardanapalus and Nero; but while others are snoring, what is he doing?

" Much from his head he tore his rooted hair:"
Iliad, x: 15.

and what does he say himself?

" ' I am perplexed,' he says, 'and
Disturb'd I am,' and 'my heart out of my bosom
Is leaping.' "
Iliad, x: 91.

Wretch, which of your affairs goes badly? Your possessions? No. Your body? No. But you are rich in gold and copper. What then is the matter with you? That part of you, whatever it is, has been neglected by you and is corrupted, the part with which we desire, with which we avoid, with which we move towards and move from things. How neglected? He knows not the nature of good for which he is made by nature and the nature of evil; and what is his own, and what belongs to another; and when any thing that belongs to others goes badly, he says, "Woe to me, for the Hellenes are in danger." Wretched is his ruling faculty, and alone neglected and uncared for. The Hellenes are going to die destroyed by the Trojans. And if the Trojans do not kill them, will they not die? Yes; but not all at once. What difference then does it make? For if death is an evil, whether men die altogether, or if they die singly, it is equally an evil. Is any thing else then going to happen than the separation of the soul and the body? Nothing. And if the Hellenes perish, is the door closed, and is it not in your power to die? It is. Why then do you lament and say, "Oh, you who are a king and have the sceptre of Zeus!" An unhappy king does not exist more than an unhappy god. What then art thou? In truth a shepherd: for you weep as shepherds do, when a wolf has carried off one of their sheep: and these who are governed by you are sheep. And why did you come hither? Was your desire in any danger? was your aversion (ἔκκλισις)? was your movement (pursuits)? was your avoidance of things? He replies, "No; but the wife of my brother was carried off." Was it not then a great gain to be deprived of an adulterous wife? "Shall we be despised then by the Trojans?" What kind of people are the Trojans, wise or foolish? If they are wise, why do you fight with them? If they are fools, why do you care about them?

In what then is the good, since it is not in these things? Tell us, you who are lord, messenger and spy. Where you do not think that it is, nor choose to seek it: for if you chose to seek it, you would have found it to be in yourselves; nor would you be wandering out of the way, nor seeking what belongs to others as if it were your own. Turn your thoughts into yourselves: observe the preconceptions which you have. What kind of a thing do you imagine the good to be? That which flows easily, that which is happy, that which is not impeded. Come, and do you not naturally imagine it to be great, do you not imagine it to be valuable? do you not imagine it to be free from harm? In what material then ought you to seek for that which flows easily, for that which is not impeded? in that which serves or in that which is free? In that which is free. Do you possess the body then free or is it in servile condition? We do not know. Do you not know that it is the slave of fever, of gout, ophthalmia, dysentery, of a tyrant, of fire, of iron, of every thing which is stronger? Yes, it is a slave. How then is it possible that any thing which belongs to the body can be free from hindrance? and how is a thing great or valuable which is naturally dead, or earth, or mud? Well then, do you possess nothing which is free? Perhaps nothing. And who is able to compel you to assent to that which appears false? No man. And who can compel you not to assent to that which appears true? No man. By this then you see that there is something in you naturally free. But to desire or to be averse from, or to move towards an object or to move from it, or to prepare yourself, or to propose to do anything, which of you can do this, unless he has received an impression of the appearance of that which is profitable or a duty? No man. You have then in these things also something which is not hindered and is free. Wretched men, work out this, take care of this, seek for good here.

And how is it possible that a man who has nothing, who is naked, houseless, without a hearth, squalid, without a slave, without a city, can pass a life that flows easily? See, God has sent you a man to show you that it is possible.[6] Look at me, who am without a city, without a house, without possessions, without a slave; I sleep on the ground; I have no wife, no children, no prætorium, but only the earth and heavens, and one poor cloak. And what do I want? Am I not without sorrow? am I not without fear? Am I not free? When did any of you see me failing in the object of my desire? or ever falling into that which I would avoid? did I ever blame God or man?[7] did I ever accuse any man? did any of you ever see me with sorrowful countenance? And how do I meet with those you are afraid of and admire? Do not I treat them like slaves? Who, when he sees me, does not think that he sees his king and master?

This is the language of the Cynics, this their character, this is their purpose. You say No: but their characteristic is the little wallet, and staff, and great jaws: the devouring of all that you give them, or storing it up, or the abusing unreasonably all whom they meet, or displaying their shoulder as a fine thing.—Do you see how you are going to undertake so great a business? First take a mirror: look at your shoulders: observe your loins, your thighs. You are going, my man, to be enrolled as a combatant in the Olympic games, no frigid and miserable contest. In the Olympic games a man is not permitted to be conquered only and to take his departure; but first he must be disgraced in the sight of all the world, not in the sight of Athenians only, or of Lacedæmonians or of Nicopolitans; next he must be whipped also if he has entered into the contests rashly; and before being whipped, he must suffer thirst and heat, and swallow much dust.

Reflect more carefully, know thyself,[8] consult the divinity, without God attempt nothing; for if he shall advise you (to do this or anything), be assured that he intends you to become great or to receive many blows. For this very amusing quality is conjoined to a Cynic: he must be flogged like an ass, and when he is flogged, he must love those who flog him, as if he were the father of all, and the brother of all.[9]— You say No; but if a man flogs you, stand in the public place and call out, "Cæsar, what do I suffer in this state of peace under thy protection?" Let us bring the offender before the proconsul.—But what is Cæsar to a Cynic, or what is a proconsul or what is any other except him who sent the Cynic down hither, and whom he serves, namely Zeus? Does he call upon any other than Zeus? Is he not convinced that whatever he suffers, it is Zeus who is exercising him? Hercules when he was exercised by Eurystheus did not think that he was wretched, but without hesitation he attempted to execute all that he had in hand. And is he who is trained to the contest and exercised by Zeus going to call out and to be vexed, he who is worthy to bear the sceptre of Diogenes? Hear what Diogenes says to the passers by when he is in a fever. "Miserable wretches, will you not stay? but are you going so long a journey to Olympia to see the destruction or the fight of athletes; and will you not choose to see the combat between a fever and a man?" Would such a man accuse God who sent him down as if God were treating him unworthily, a man who gloried in his circumstances, and claimed to be an example to those who were passing by? For what shall he accuse him of? because he maintains a decency of behaviour, because he displays his virtue more conspicuously? Well, and what does he say of poverty, about death, about pain? How did he compare his own happiness with that of the great king (the king of Persia)? or rather he thought that there was no comparison between them. For where there are perturbations, and griefs, and fears, and desires not satisfied, and aversions of things which you can not avoid, and envies and jealousies, how is there a road to happiness there? But where there are corrupt principles, there these things must of necessity be.

When the young man asked, if when a Cynic has fallen sick, and a friend asks him to come to his house and to be taken care of in his sickness, shall the Cynic accept the invitation, he replied, And where shall you find, I ask, a Cynic's friend? For the man who invites ought to be such another as the Cynic that he may be worthy of being reckoned the Cynic's friend. He ought to be a partner in the Cynic's sceptre and his royalty, and a worthy minister, if he intends to be considered worthy of a Cynic's friendship, as Diogenes was a friend of Antisthenes, as Crates was a friend of Diogenes. Do you think that if a man comes to a Cynic and salutes him, that he is the Cynic's friend, and that the Cynic will think him worthy of receiving a Cynic into his house? So that if you please, reflect on this also: rather look round for some convenient dunghill on which you shall bear your fever and which will shelter you from the north wind that you may not be chilled. But you seem to me to wish to go into some man's house and to be well fed there for a time. Why then do you think of attempting so great a thing (as the life of a Cynic)?

But, said the young man, shall marriage and the procreation of children as a chief duty be undertaken by the Cynic?[10] If you grant me a community of wise men, Epictetus replies perhaps no man will readily apply himself to the Cynic practice. For on whose account should he undertake this manner of life? However if we suppose that he does, nothing will prevent him from marrying and begetting children; for his wife will be another like himself, and his father-in-law another like himself, and his children will be brought up like himself. But in the present state of things which is like that of an army placed in battle order, is it not fit that the Cynic should without any distraction be employed only on the ministration of God,[11] able to go about among men, not tied down to the common duties of mankind, nor entangled in the ordinary relations of life, which if he neglects, he will not maintain the character of an honourable and good man? and if he observes them he will lose the character of the messenger, and spy and herald of God. For consider that it is his duty to do something towards his father-in-law, something to the other kinsfolks of his wife, something to his wife also (if he has one). He is also excluded by being a Cynic from looking after the sickness of his own family, and from providing for their support. And to say nothing of the rest, he must have a vessel for heating water for the child that he may wash it in the bath; wool for his wife when she is delivered of a child, oil, a bed, a cup: so the furniture of the house is increased. I say nothing of his other occupa-

tions, and of his distraction.   Where then now is that king,
he who devotes himself to the public interests,

"The people's guardian and so full of cares."
Homer, Iliad ii : 25

whose duty it is to look after others, the married and those
who have children; to see who uses his wife well, who uses
her badly; who quarrels; what family is well administered,
what is not; going about as a physician does and feels
pulses?   He says to one, you have a fever, to another you
have a head-ache, or the gout: he says to one, abstain from
food; to another he says, eat; or do not use the bath: to another, you require the knife, or the cautery.   How can he
have time for this who is tied to the duties of common life?
is it not his duty to supply clothing to his children, and to
send them to the schoolmaster with writing tablets, and
styles (for writing).   Besides must he not supply them with
beds? for they can not be genuine Cynics as soon as they are
born.   If he does not do this, it would be better to expose
the children as soon as they are born than to kill them in
this way.   Consider what we are bringing the Cynic down
to, how we are taking his royalty from him.—Yes, but
Crates took a wife.—You are speaking of a circumstance
which arose from love and of a woman who was another
Crates.[12]   But we are inquiring about ordinary marriages
and those which are free from distractions, and making this
inquiry we do not find the affair of marriage in this state
of the world a thing which is especially suited to the Cynic.
How then shall a man maintain the existence of society?
In the name of God, are those men greater benefactors to
society who introduce into the world to occupy their own
places two or three grunting children, or those who superintend as far as they can all mankind, and see what they do,
how they live, what they attend to, what they neglect contrary to their duty?   Did they who left little children to the
Thebans do them more good than Epaminondas who died
childless?   And did Priamus who begat fifty worthless sons
or Danaus or Æolus contribute more to the community than
Homer?   Then shall the duty of a general or the business of
a writer exclude a man from marriage or the begetting of

children, and such a man shall not be judged to have accepted the condition of childlessness for nothing; and shall not the royalty of a Cynic be considered an equivalent for the want of children? Do we not perceive his grandeur and do we not justly contemplate the character of Diogenes; and do we instead of this turn our eyes to the present Cynics who are dogs that wait at tables, and in no respect imitate the Cynics of old except perchance in breaking wind, but in nothing else? For such matters would not have moved us at all nor should we have wondered if a Cynic should not marry or beget children. Man, the Cynic is the father of all men; the men are his sons, the women are his daughters: he so carefully visits all, so well does he care for all Do you think that it is from idle impertinence that he rebukes those whom he meets? He does it as a father, as a brother, and as the minister of the father of all, the minister of Zeus.

If you please, ask me also if a Cynic shall engage in the administration of the state. Fool, do you seek a greater form of administration than that in which he is engaged? Do you ask if he shall appear among the Athenians and say something about the revenues and the supplies, he who must talk with all men, alike with Athenians, alike with Corinthians, alike with Romans, not about supplies, nor yet about revenues, nor about peace or war, but about happiness and unhappiness, about good fortune and bad fortune, about slavery and freedom? When a man has undertaken the administration of such a state, do you ask me if he shall engage in the administration of a state? ask me also if he shall govern (hold a magisterial office): again I will say to you, Fool, what greater government shall he exercise than that which he exercises now?

It is necessary also for such a man (the Cynic) to have a certain habit of body: for if he appears to be consumptive, thin and pale, his testimony has not then the same weight. For he must not only by showing the qualities of the soul prove to the vulgar that it is in his power independent of the things which they admire to be a good man, but he must also show by his body that his simple and frugal way of living in the open air does not injure even the body. See, he says, I am proof of this, and my own body also is. So

17

Diogenes used to do, for he used to go about fresh looking, and he attracted the notice of the many by his personal appearance. But if a Cynic is an object of compassion, he seems to be a beggar: all persons turn away from him, all are offended with him; for neither ought he to appear dirty so that he shall not also in this respect drive away men; but his very roughness ought to be clean and attractive.

There ought also to belong to the Cynic much natural grace and sharpness; and if this is not so, he is a stupid fellow, and nothing else: and he must have these qualities that he may be able readily and fitly to be a match for all circumstances that may happen. So Diogenes replied to one who said, "Are you the Diogenes who does not believe that there are gods?"[13] "And how," replied Diogenes, "can this be when I think that you are odious to the gods?" On another occasion in reply to Alexander, who stood by him when he was sleeping, and quoted Homer's line (Iliad, ii. 24).

" A' man a councillor should not sleep all night,"

he answered, when he was half asleep,

" The people's guardian and so full of cares."

But before all the Cynic's ruling faculty must be purer than the sun; and if it is not, he must necessarily be a cunning knave and a fellow of no principle, since while he himself is entangled in some vice he will reprove others.[14] For see how the matter stands: to these kings and tyrants their guards and arms give the power of reproving some persons, and of being able even to punish those who do wrong though they are themselves bad; but to a Cynic instead of arms and guards it is conscience (τὸ σuνειδός) which gives this power. When he knows that he has watched and laboured for mankind, and has slept pure, and sleep has left him still purer, and that he thought whatever he has thought as a friend of the gods, as a minister, as a participator of the power of Zeus, and that on all occasions he is ready to say

" Lead me, O Zeus, and thou, O Destiny ; "

and also, If so it pleases the gods, so let it be; why should

he not have confidence to speak freely to his own brothers,
to his children, in a word to his kinsmen? For this reason
he is neither over curious nor a busybody when he is in this
state of mind; for he is not a meddler with the affairs of
others when he is superintending human affairs, but he is
looking after his own affairs. If that is not so, you may also
say that the general is a busybody, when he inspects his soldiers, and examines them and watches them and punishes
the disorderly. But if while you have a cake under your
arm, you rebuke others, I will say to you, "Will you not
rather go away into a corner and eat that which you have
stolen; what have you to do with the affairs of others? For
who are you? are you the bull of the herd, or the queen of
the bees? Show me the tokens of your supremacy, such as
they have from nature. But if you are a drone claiming the
sovereignty over the bees, do you not suppose that your fellow citizens will put you down as the bees do the drones?"

The Cynic also ought to have such power of endurance as
to seem insensible to the common sort, and a stone: no man
reviles him, no man strikes him, no man insults him, but he
gives his body that any man who chooses may do with it
what he likes. For he bears in mind that the inferior must
be overpowered by the superior in that in which it is inferior;
and the body is inferior to the many, the weaker to the
stronger. He never then descends into such a contest in
which he can be overpowered; but he immediately withdraws
from things which belong to others, he claims not the things
which are servile. But where there is will and the use of
appearances, there you will see how many eyes he has so that
you may say, "Argus was blind compared with him." Is his
assent ever hasty, his movement (towards an object) rash,
does his desire ever fail in its object, does that which he
would avoid befall him, is his purpose unaccomplished, does
he ever find fault, is he ever humiliated, is he ever envious?
To these he directs all his attention and energy; but as to
every thing else he snores supine. All is peace; there is no
robber who takes away his will, [15] no tyrant. But what say
you as to his body? I say there is. And his possessions? I
say there is. And as to magistracies and honours?—What
does he care for them?—When then any person would

frighten him through them, he says to him, "Begone, look for children; masks are formidable to them; but I know that they are made of shell, and have nothing inside."

About such a matter as this you are deliberating. Therefore, if you please, I urge you in God's name, defer the matter, and first consider your preparation for it. For see what Hector says to Andromache, "Retire rather," he says, "into the house and weave: "

> " 'War is the work of men
> Of all indeed, but specially 'tis mine.' "
> Iliad, vi. 490

So he was conscious of his own qualification, and knew her weakness.

NOTES

[1] See the description of Thersites in the Iliad, ii. 212
[2] The office which in our times corresponds to this description of the Cynic, is the office of a teacher of religion

[3]
> "Quod petis hic est,
> Est Ulubris, animus si te non deficit æquus."
> Horace, Ep. i. 11, 30.

> " Willst du immer weiter schweifen?
> Sieh, das Gute liegt so nah.
> Lerne nur das Gluck ergreifen,
> Denn das Gluck ist immer da "
> Goethe.

[4] These men are supposed to have been strong gladiators. Crœsus the rich king of Lydia, who was taken prisoner by Cyrus the Persian.
[5] Man then is supposed to consist of a soul and of a body It may be useful to remember this when we are examining other passages in Epictetus.
[6] "It is observable that Epictetus seems to think it a necessary qualification in a teacher sent from God for the instruction of mankind to be destitute of all external advantages and a suffering character. Thus doth this excellent man, who had carried human reason to so great a height, bear testimony to the propriety of that method which the divine wisdom hath thought fit to follow in the scheme of the Gospel; whose great author had not *where to lay his head;* and which some in later ages have inconsiderately urged as an argument against the Christian religion. The infinite disparity between the proposal of the example of Diogenes in Epictetus and of our Redeemer in the New Testament is too obvious to need any enlargement." Mrs Carter.
[7] Some of the ancients, who called themselves philosophers, did blame God and his administration of the world; and there are men who do the same now. If a man is dissatisfied with the condition of the world, he has the power of going out of it, as Epictetus often says;

and if he knows, as he must know, that he can not alter the nature of man and the conditions of human life, he may think it wise to withdraw from a state of things with which he is not satisfied. If he believes that there is no God, he is at liberty to do what he thinks best for himself, and if he does believe that there is a God he may still think that his power of quitting the world is a power which he may exercise when he chooses. Many persons commit suicide, not because they are dissatisfied with the state of the world, but for other reasons. I have not yet heard of a modern philosopher who found fault with the condition of human things, and voluntarily retired from life. Our philosophers live as long as they can, and some of them take care of themselves and of all that they possess; they even provide well for the comfort of those whom they leave behind them. The conclusion seems to be that they prefer living in this world to leaving it, that their complaints are idle talk; and that being men of weak minds, and great vanity they assume the philosopher's name, and while they try to make others as dissatisfied as they profess themselves to be, they are really enjoying themselves after their fashion as much as they can. These men, though they may have the means of living with as much comfort as the conditions of human life permit, are dissatisfied, and they would, if they could, make as dissatisfied as themselves those who have less means of making life tolerable. These grumblers are not the men who give their money or their labour or their lives for increasing the happiness of mankind and diminishing the unavoidable sufferings of human life; but they find it easier to blame God, when they believe in him; or to find fault with things as they are, which is more absurd, when they do not believe in God, and when they ought to make the best that they can of the conditions under which we live.

⁷ "E cælo descendit γνῶθι σεαυτόν" Juvenal xi. 27. The expression, "Know thyself" is attributed to several persons, and to Socrates among them. Self-knowledge is one of the most difficult kinds of knowledge; and no man has it completely. Men either estimate their powers too highly, and this is named vanity, self conceit or arrogance; or they think too meanly of their powers and do not accomplish what they might accomplish, if they had reasonable self confidence.

⁸ Compare this with the Christian precepts of forbearance and love to enemies, Matthew v. 39-44. The reader will observe that Christ specifies higher injuries and provocations than Epictetus doth; and requires of *all* his followers, what Epictetus describes only as the duty of one or two *extraordinary* persons, as such."—Mrs. Carter.

⁹ The Stoics recommended marriage, the procreation of children, the discharge of magisterial offices, and the duties of social life generally

¹⁰ "It is remarkable that Epictetus here uses the same word (ἀπερισπάστως) with St Paul, 1 Cor vii. 35, and urges the same consideration, of applying wholly to the service of God, to dissuade from marriage. His observation too that the state of things was then (ὡς ἐν παρατάξει) like *that of an army prepared for battle*, nearly resembles the Apostle's (ἐνεστῶσα ὀνάγκη) *present necessity*. St. Paul says 2 Tim ii 4 (οὐδεὶς στρατευόμενος ἐμπλέκεται, etc.) "no man that warreth entangleth himself with the affairs of life." So Epictetus says here that a Cynic must not be (ἐμπεμλεγμένον) in relations, etc. From these and many other passages of Epictetus one would be inclined to think that he was not unacquainted with St. Paul's Epistles or that he had heard something of the Christian doctrine." Mrs Carter.

I do not find any evidence of Epictetus being acquainted with the

Epistles of Paul. It is possible that he had heard something of the Christian doctrine, but I have not observed any evidence of the fact. Epictetus and Paul have not the same opinion about marriage, for Paul says that " if they can not contain let them marry : for it is better to marry than to burn." Accordingly his doctrine is "to avoid fornication let every man have his own wife, and let every woman have her own husband " He does not directly say what a man should do when he is not able to maintain a wife; but the inference is plain what he will do (1 Cor vii. 2). Paul's view of marriage differs from that of Epictetus, who recommends marriage Paul does not : he writes, " I say therefore to the unmarried and widows, it is good for them if they abide even as I " He does not acknowledge marriage and the begetting of children as a duty ; which Epicetus did.

In the present condition of the world Epictetus says that the minister of God should not marry, because the cares of a family would distract him and make him unable to discharge his duties There is sound sense in this. A minister of God should not be distracted by the cares of a family, especially if he is poor.

· ¹² The wife of Crates was Hipparchia, who persisted against all advice in marrying Crates and lived with him exactly as he lived. Diogenes Laertius, vi. 96. Upton

¹³Diogenes Laertius, vi : 42

¹⁴ The Cynic is in Epictetus the minister of religion. He must be pure, for otherwise how can he reprove vice? This is a useful lesson to those whose business it is to correct the vices of mankind.

¹⁵This is quoted by M. Antoninus, xi. 36.

CHAPTER XXIII

FIRST say to yourself who you wish to be: then do accordingly what you are doing; for in nearly all other things we see this to be so. Those who follow athletic exercises first determine what they wish to be, then they do accordingly what follows. If a man is a runner in the long course, there is a certain kind of diet, of walking, rubbing, and exercise: if a man is a runner in the stadium, all these things are different; if he is a Pentathlete, they are still more different. So you will find it also in the arts. If you are a carpenter, you will have such, and such things; if a worker in metal, such things. For everything that we do, if we refer it to no end, we shall do it to no purpose; and if we refer it to the wrong end, we shall miss the mark. Further, there is a general end or purpose, and a particular purpose. First of all, we must act as a man. What is comprehended in this? We must not be like a sheep, though gentle; nor mischievous, like a wild beast. But the particular end has reference to each person's mode of life and his will. The lute-player acts as a lute-player, the carpenter as a carpenter, the philosopher as a philosopher, the rhetorician as a rhetorician. When then you say, Come and hear me read to you: take care first of all that you are not doing this without a purpose; then if you have discovered that you are doing this with reference to a purpose, consider if it is the right purpose. Do you wish to do good or to be praised? Immediately you hear him saying, To me what is the value of praise from the many? and he says well, for it is of no value to a musician, so far as he is a musician, nor to a geometrician. Do you then wish to be useful? in what? tell us that we may run to your audience room. Now can a man do anything useful to others, who has not received something useful himself? No, for neither can a man do any

263

thing useful in the carpenter's art, unless he is a carpenter; nor in the shoemaker's art, unless he is a shoemaker.

Do you wish to know then if you have received any advantage? Produce your opinions, philosopher What is the thing which desire promises? Not to fail in the object. What does aversion promise? Not to fall into that which you would avoid. Well; do we fulfill their promise? Tell me the truth; but if you lie, I will tell you. Lately when your hearers came together rather coldly, and did not give you applause, you went away humbled. Lately again when you had been praised, you went about and said to all, What did you think of me? Wonderful, master, I swear by all that is dear to me. But how did I treat of that particular matter? Which? The passage in which I described Pan and the nymphs?[2] Excellently. Then do you tell me that in desire and in aversion you are acting according to nature? Be gone; try to persuade somebody else. Did you not praise a certain person contrary to your opinion? and did you not flatter a certain person who was the son of a senator? Would you wish your own children to be such persons?—I hope not—Why then did you praise and flatter him? He is an ingenuous youth and listens well to discourses—How is this?—He admires me. You have stated your proof. Then what do you think? do not these very people secretly despise you? When then a man who is conscious that he has neither done any good nor ever thinks of it, finds a philosopher who says, You have a great natural talent, and you have a candid and good disposition, what else do you think that he says except this, This man has some need of me? Or tell me what act that indicates a great mind has he shown? Observe; he has been in your company a long time; he has listened to your discourses, he has heard you reading; has he become more modest? has he been turned to reflect on himself? has he perceived in what a bad state he is? has he cast away self-conceit? does he look for a person to teach him? He does. A man who will teach him to live? No, fool, but how to talk; for it is for this that he admires you also. Listen and hear what he says: This man writes with perfect art, much better than Dion.[3] This is altogether another thing. Does he say, This man is modest, faithful, free from perturbations? and even if he did say it, I should say to him, Since this man is faithful, tell me what this faithful man is. And if he could not tell me, I should add this. First understand what you say, and then speak.

You then, who are in a wretched plight and gaping after applause and counting your auditors, do you intend to be useful to others?—To-day many more attended my discourse. Yes, many; we suppose five hundred. That is nothing; suppose that there were a thousand—Dion never had so many hearers—How could he?—And they understand what is said beautifully. What is fine, master, can move even a stone—See, these are the words of a philosopher. This is the disposition of a man who will do good to others; here is a man who has listened to discourses, who has read what is written about Socrates as Socratic, not as the compositions of Lysias and Isocrates. "I have often wondered by what arguments."[4] Not so, but "by what argument": this is more exact than that—What, have you read the words at all in a different way from that in which you read little odes? For if you read them as you ought, you would not have been attending to such matters, but you would rather have been looking to these words: "Anytus and Melitus are able to kill me, but they cannot harm me:" "and I am always of such a disposition as to pay regard to nothing of my own except to the reason which on inquiry seems to me the best."[5] Hence who ever heard Socrates say, "I know something and I teach:" but he used to send different people to different teachers. Therefore they used to come to him and ask to be introduced to philosophers by him; and he would take them and recommend them —Not so; but as he accompanied them he would say, Hear me to-day discoursing in the house of Quadratus.[6] Why should I hear you? Do you wish to show me that you put words together cleverly? You put them together, man; and what good will it do you?—But only praise me —What do you mean by praising?—Say to me, admirable, wonderful.— Well, I say so. But if that is praise whatever it is which philosophers mean by the name ($\kappa \alpha \tau \eta \gamma o \rho \iota \alpha$)[7] of good, what have I to praise in you? If it is good to speak well, teach men, and I will praise you.—What then? ought a man to lis-

18

ten to such things without pleasure?—I hope not. For my
part I do not listen even to a lute-player without pleasure.
Must I then for this reason stand and play the lute?   Hear
what Socrates says, "Nor would it be seemly for a man of my
age, like a young man composing addresses, to appear before
you."[8] Like a young man, he says. For in truth this small
art is an elegant thing, to select words, and to put them together, and to come forward and gracefully to read them or
to speak, and while he is reading to say, "There are not many
who can do these things, I swear by all that you value."

Does a philosopher invite people to hear him?   As the
sun himself draws men to him, or as food does, does not
the philosopher also draw to him those who will receive benefit?   What physician invites a man to be treated by him?
Indeed I now hear that even the physicians in Rome do invite patients, but when I lived there, the physicians were invited.   "I invite you to come and hear that things are in a
bad way for you, and that you are taking care of every thing
except that of which you ought to take care, and that you are
ignorant of the good and the bad and are unfortunate and
unhappy." A fine kind of invitation: and yet if the words
of the philosopher do not produce this effect on you, he is
dead, and so is the speaker. Rufus was used to say: "If you
have leisure to praise me, I am speaking to no purpose."[9]
Accordingly he used to speak in such a way that every one of
us who were sitting there supposed that some one had accused him before Rufus: he so touched on what was doing,
he so placed before the eyes every man's faults.

The philosopher's school, ye men, is a surgery: you ought
not to go out of it with pleasure, but with pain For you
are not in sound health when you enter. one has dislocated
his shoulder, another has an abscess, a third a fistula, and a
fourth a headache. Then do I sit and utter to you little
thoughts and exclamations that you may praise me and go
away, one with his shoulder, in the same condition in which
he entered, another with his head still aching, and a third
with his fistula or his abscess just as they were?   Is it for
this then that young men shall quit home, and leave their
parents and their friends and kinsmen and property, that
they may say to you, Wonderful! when you are uttering

your exclamations. Did Socrates do this, or Zeno, or Cleanthes?

What then? is there not the hortatory style? Who denies it? as there is the style of refutation, and the didactic style. Who then ever reckoned a fourth style with these, the style of display? What is the hortatory style? To be able to show both to one person and to many the struggle in which they are engaged, and that they think more about any thing than about what they really wish. For they wish the things which lead to happiness, but they look for them in the wrong place. In order that this may be done, a thousand seats must be placed and men must be invited to listen, and you must ascend the pulpit in a fine robe or cloak and describe the death of Achilles. Cease, I intreat you by the gods, to spoil good words and good acts as much as you can. Nothing can have more power in exhortation than when the speaker shows to the hearers that he has need of them But tell me who when he hears you reading or discoursing is anxious about himself or turns to reflect on himself? or when he has gone out says, The philosopher hit me well: I must no longer do these things. But does he not, even if you have a great reputation, say to some person? He spoke finely about Xerxes;[10] and another says, No, but about the battle of Thermopylæ. Is this listening to a philosopher?

NOTES

[1] Epictetus in an amusing manner touches on the practice of Sophists, Rhetoricians, and others, who made addresses only to get praise This practice of reciting prose or verse compositions was common in the time of Epictetus, as we may learn from the letters of the younger Pliny, Juvenal, Martial, and the author of the treatise de Causis corruptæ eloquentiæ Upton.

[2] Such were the subjects which the literary men of the day delighted in.

[3] Dion of Prusa in Bithynia was named Chrysostomus (goldenmouthed) because of his eloquence. He was a rhetorician and sophist, as the term was then understood, and was living at the same time as Epictetus Eighty of his orations written in Greek are still extant, and some fragments of fifteen

[4] These words are the beginning of Xenophon's Memorabilia, i 1. The small critics disputed whether the text should read τίσι λόγοις, or τινι λόγω.

[5] From the Crito of Plato, c 6

[6] The rich, says Upton, used to lend their houses for recitations, as we learn from Pliny, Ep. viii 12 and Juvenal, vii. 40.

" Si dulcedine famæ
Succensus recites, maculosas commodat ædes."

Quadratus is a Roman name. There appears to be a confusion between Socrates and Quadratus The man says, No. Socrates would not do so; but he would do, as a man might do now. He would say on the road; I hope you will come to hear me I don't find anything in the notes on this passage; but it requires explanation

⁷ κατηγορία is one of Aristotle's common terms.

⁸ From Plato's Apology of Socrates.

⁹ Aulus Gellius, v. 1. Seneca, Ep. 52. Upton.

¹⁰ Cicero, de Officiis i 18 "Quæ magno animo et fortiter excellenterque gesta sunt, ea pescio quomodo pleniore ore laudamus Hinc Rhetorum campus de Marathone, Salamine, Platæis, Thermopylis, Leuctris."

CHAPTER XXIV

THAT WE OUGHT NOT TO BE MOVED BY A DESIRE FOR THOSE THINGS WHICH ARE NOT IN OUR POWER

LET not that which in another is contrary to nature be an evil to you: for you are not formed by nature to be depressed with others nor to be unhappy with others, but to be happy with them   If a man is unhappy, remember that his unhappiness is his own fault: for God has made all men to be happy, to be free from perturbations.   For this purpose he has given means to them, some things to each person as his own, and other things not as his own: some things subject to hindrance and compulsion and deprivation; and these things are not a man's own: but the things which are not subject to hindrances, are his own; and the nature of good and evil, as it was fit to be done by him who takes care of us and protects us like a father, he has made our own.—But you say, I have parted from a certain person, and he is grieved.—Why did he consider as his own that which belongs to another? why, when he looked on you and was rejoiced, did he not also reckon that you are mortal, that it is natural for you to part from him for a foreign country?   Therefore he suffers the consequences of his own folly.   But why do you or for what purpose bewail yourself?   Is it that you also have not thought of these things? but like poor women who are good for nothing, you have enjoyed all things in which you took pleasure, as if you would always enjoy them, both places and men and conversation; and now you sit and weep because you do not see the same persons and do not live in the same places — Indeed you deserve this, to be more wretched than crows and ravens who have the power of flying where they please and changing their nests for others, and crossing the seas without lamenting or regretting their former condition.—Yes, but this happens to them because they are irrational creatures.—Was reason then given to us by the gods for the purpose of unhappiness and misery, that we may pass our

lives in wretchedness and lamentation?   Must all persons
be immortal and must no man go abroad, and must we ourselves not go abroad, but remain rooted like plants; and if
any of our familiar friends goes abroad, must we sit and
weep; and on the contrary, when he returns, must we dance
and clap our hands like children?

Shall we not now wean ourselves and remember what we
have heard from the philosophers? if we did not listen to
them as if they were jugglers: they tell us that this world is
one city,[1] and the substance out of which it has been formed
is one, and that there must be a certain period, and that
some things must give way to others, that some must be dissolved, and others come in their place; some to remain in
the same place, and others to be moved: and that all things
are full of friendship, first of the gods,[2] and then of men
who by nature are made to be of one family; and some must
be with one another, and others must be separated, rejoicing
in those who are with them, and not grieving for those who
are removed from them, and man in addition to being by
nature of a noble temper and having a contempt of all things
which are not in the power of his will, also possesses this
property not to be rooted nor to be naturally fixed to the
earth, but to go at different times to different places, sometimes from the urgency of certain occasions, and at others
merely for the sake of seeing. So it was with Ulysses, who
saw

"Of many men the states, and learned their ways."[3]

And still earlier it was the fortune of Hercules to visit all
the inhabited world

"Seeing men's lawless deeds and their good rules of law:"[4]

casting out and clearing away their lawlessness and intro-
ducing in their place good rules of law.   And yet how many
friends do you think that he had in Thebes, how many in
Argos, how many in Athens? and how many do you think
that he gained by going about?   And he married also, when
it seemed to him a proper occasion, and begot children, and
left them without lamenting or regretting or leaving them
as orphans; for he knew that no man is an orphan; but it is

the father who takes care of all men always and continuously For it was not as mere report that he had heard that
Zeus is the father of men, for he thought that Zeus was his
own father, and he called him so, and to him he looked when
he was doing what he did.   Therefore he was enabled to
live happily in all places   And it is never possible for happiness and desire of what is not present to come together.
For that which is happy must have all[5] that it desires, must
resemble a person who is filled with food, and must have
neither thirst nor hunger.—But Ulysses felt a desire for
his wife and wept as he sat on a rock.—Do you attend to
Homer and his stories in every thing?   Or if Ulysses really
wept, what was he else than an unhappy man? and what
good man is unhappy?   In truth the whole is badly administered, if Zeus does not take care of his own citizens that
they may be happy like himself   But these things are not
lawful or right to think of: and if Ulysses did weep and lament, he was not a good man.   For who is good if he knows
not who he is? and who knows what he is, if he forgets
that things which have been made are perishable, and that
it is not possible for one human being to be with another
always?   To desire then things which are impossible is to
have a slavish character, and is foolish: it is the part of
a stranger, of a man who fights against God in the only way
that he can, by his opinions.

But my mother laments when she does not see me.—Why
has she not learned these principles? and I do not say this,
that we should not take care that she may not lament, but
I say that we ought not to desire in every way what is not
our own. And the sorrow of another is another's sorrow:
but my sorrow is my own.   I then will stop my own sorrow
by every means, for it is in my power: and the sorrow of
another I will endeavour to stop as far as I can; but I will
not attempt to do it by every means; for if I do, I shall be
fighting against God, I shall be opposing Zeus and shall be
placing myself against him in the administration of the universe; and the reward (the punishment) of this fighting
against God and of this disobedience not only will the children of my children pay, but I also shall myself, both by day
and by night, startled by dreams, perturbed, trembling at

every piece of news, and having my tranquillity depending on the letters of others.—Some person has arrived from Rome. I only hope that there is no harm. But what harm can happen to you, where you are not?—From Hellas (Greece) some one is come: I hope that there is no harm.—In this way every place may be the cause of misfortune to you. Is it not enough for you to be unfortunate there where you are, and must you be so even beyond sea, and by the report of letters? Is this the way in which your affairs are in a state of security?—Well then suppose that my friends have died in the places which are far from me.—What else have they suffered than that which is the condition of mortals? Or how are you desirous at the same time to live to old age, and at the same time not to see the death of any person whom you love? Know you not that in the course of a long time many and various kinds of things must happen; that a fever shall overpower one, a robber another, and a third a tyrant? Such is the condition around us, such are those who live with us in the world: cold and heat, and unsuitable ways of living, and journeys by land, and voyages by sea, and winds, and various circumstances which surround us, destroy one man, and banish another, and throw one upon an embassy and another into an army. Sit down then in a flutter at all these things, lamenting, unhappy, unfortunate, dependent on another, and dependent not on one or two, but on ten thousands upon ten thousands.

Did you hear this when you were with the philosophers? did you learn this? do you not know that human life is a warfare? that one man must keep watch, another must go out as a spy, and a third must fight? and it is not possible that all should be in one place, nor is it better that it should be so. But you neglecting to do the commands of the general complain when any thing more hard than usual is imposed on you, and you do not observe what you make the army become as far as it is in your power; that if all imitate you, no man will dig a trench, no man will put a rampart round, nor keep watch, nor expose himself to danger, but will appear to be useless for the purposes of an army. Again, in a vessel if you go as a sailor, keep to one place and stick to it. And if you are ordered to climb the mast, refuse; if

to run to the head of the ship, refuse; and what master of a
ship will endure you? and will he not pitch you overboard
as a useless thing, an impediment only and bad example to
the other sailors? And so it is here also: every man's life
is a kind of warfare, and it is long and diversified. You
must observe the duty of a soldier and do everything at the
nod of the general; if it is possible, divining what his wishes
are: for there is no resemblance between that general and
this, neither in strength nor in superiority of character. You
are placed in a great office of command and not in any mean
place; but you are always a senator. Do you not know that
such a man must give little time to the affairs of his household, but be often away from home, either as a governor
or one who is governed or discharging some office, or serving in war or acting as a judge? Then do you tell me that
you wish, as a plant, to be fixed to the same places and to
be rooted?—Yes, for it is pleasant.—Who says that it is
not? but a soup is pleasant, and a handsome woman is pleasant. What else do those say who make pleasure their end?
Do you not see of what men you have uttered the language?
that it is the language of Epicureans and catamites? Next
while you are doing what they do and holding their opinions,
do you speak to us the words of Zeno and of Socrates?
Will you not throw away as far as you can the things belonging to others with which you decorate yourself, though
they do not fit you at all? For what else do they desire than
to sleep without hindrance and free from compulsion, and
when they have risen to yawn at their leisure, and to wash
the face, then write and read what they choose, and then
talk about some trifling matter being praised by their friends
whatever they may say, then to go forth for a walk, and
having walked about a little to bathe, and then eat and sleep
such sleep as is the fashion of such men? why need we say
how? for one can easily conjecture. Come, do you also tell
your own way of passing the time which you desire, you
who are an admirer of truth and of Socrates and Diogenes. What do you wish to do in Athens? the same (that
others do), or something else? Why then do you call yourself a Stoic? Well, but they who falsely call themselves
Roman citizens,[6] are severely punished; and should those,

who falsely claim so great and reverend a thing and name, get off unpunished? or is this not possible, but the law divine and strong and inevitable is this, which exacts the severest punishments from those who commit the greatest crimes? For what does this law say? Let him who pretends to things which do not belong to him be a boaster, a vainglorious man;[7] let him who disobeys the divine administration be base, and a slave; let him suffer grief, let him be envious, let him pity;[8] and in a word let him be unhappy and lament.

Well then; do you wish me to pay court to a certain person? to go to his doors?[9]—If reason requires this to be done for the sake of country, for the sake of kinsmen, for the sake of mankind, why should you not go? You are not ashamed to go to the doors of a shoemaker, when you are in want of shoes, nor to the door of a gardener, when you want lettuces; and are you ashamed to go to the doors of the rich when you want any thing?—Yes, for I have no awe of a shoemaker—Don't feel any awe of the rich—Nor will I flatter the gardener—And do not flatter the rich—How then shall I get what I want?—Do I say to you, go as if you were certain to get what you want? And do not I only tell you, that you may do what is becoming to yourself? Why then should I still go? That you may have gone, that you may have discharged the duty of a citizen, of a brother, of a friend. And further remember that you have gone to the shoemaker, to the seller of vegetables, who have no power in any thing great or noble, though he may sell dear. You go to buy lettuces: they cost an obolus (penny), but not a talent. So it is here also. The matter is worth going for to the rich man's door—Well, I will go—It is worth talking about—Let it be so; I will talk with him—But you must also kiss his hand and flatter him with praise—Away with that, it is a talent's worth: it is not profitable to me, nor to the state nor to my friends, to have done that which spoils a good citizen and a friend.—But you will seem not to have been eager about the matter, if you do not succeed. Have you again forgotten why you went? Know you not that a good man does nothing for the sake of appearance, but for the sake of doing right?—What advantage is it then to him to have done right?—And what advantage is it to a man who writes the name of Dion to write it as he ought?—The advantage is to have written it.—Is there no reward then[10]?—Do you seek a reward for a good man greater than doing what is good and just? At Olympia you wish for nothing more, but it seems to you enough to be crowned at the games Does it seem to you so small and worthless a thing to be good and happy? For these purposes being introduced by the gods into this city (the world), and it being now your duty to undertake the work of a man, do you still want nurses also and a mamma, and do foolish women by their weeping move you and make you effeminate? Will you thus never cease to be a foolish child? know you not that he who does the acts of a child, the older he is, the more ridiculous he is?

In Athens did you see no one by going to his house?—I visited any man that I pleased—Here also be ready to see, and you will see whom you please: only let it be without meanness, neither with desire nor with aversion, and your affairs will be well managed. But this result does not depend on going nor on standing at the doors, but it depends on what is within, on your opinions. When you have learned not to value things which are external and not dependent on the will, and to consider that not one of them is your own, but that these things only are your own, to exercise the judgment well, to form opinions, to move towards an object, to desire, to turn from a thing, where is there any longer room for flattery, where for meanness? why do you still long for the quiet there (at Athens), and for the places to which you are accustomed? Wait a little and you will again find these places familiar: then, if you are of so ignoble a nature, again if you leave these also, weep and lament.

How then shall I become of an affectionate temper? By being of a noble disposition, and happy. For it is not reasonable to be mean-spirited nor to lament yourself, nor to depend on another, nor even to blame God or man. I entreat you, become an affectionate person in this way. by observing these rules. But if through this affection, as you name it, you are going to be a slave and wretched, there is no profit in being affectionate. And what prevents you from loving another as a person subject to mortality, as one who may go away from you. Did not Socrates love his own children? He did, but it was as a free man, as one who remembered that he must first be a friend to the gods. For this reason he violated nothing which was becoming to a good man, neither in making his defence nor by fixing a penalty on himself,[11] nor even in the former part of his life when he was a senator or when he was a soldier. But we are fully supplied with every pretext for being of ignoble temper, some for the sake of a child, some for a mother, and others for brethren's sake. But it is not fit for us to be unhappy on account of any person, but to be happy on account of all, but chiefly on account of God who has made us for this end. Well, did Diogenes[12] love nobody, who was so kind and so much a lover of all that for mankind in general he willingly undertook so much labour and bodily sufferings? He did love mankind, but how? As became a minister of God, at the same time caring for men, and being also subject to God. For this reason all the earth was his country, and no particular place; and when he was taken prisoner he did not regret Athens nor his associates and friends there, but even he became familiar with the pirates and tried to improve them; and being sold afterwards he lived in Corinth as before at Athens; and he would have behaved the same, if he had gone to the country of the Perrhæbi.[13] Thus is freedom acquired For this reason he used to say, "Ever since Antisthenes made me free, I have not been a slave." How did Antisthenes make him free? Hear what he says: Antisthenes taught me what is my own, and what is not my own; possessions are not my own, nor kinsmen, domestics, friends, nor reputation, nor places familiar, nor mode of life; all these belong to others. What then is your own? The use of appearances. This he showed to me, that I possess it free from hindrance, and from compulsion, no person can put an obstacle in my way, no person can force me to use appearances otherwise than I wish Who then has any power over me? Philip or Alexander, or Perdiccas or the great king? How have they this power? For if a man is going to be overpowered by a man, he must long before be overpowered by things. If then pleasure is not able to subdue a man, nor pain, nor fame, nor wealth, but he is able, when he chooses, to spit out all his poor body in a man's face and depart from life, whose slave can he still be? But if he dwelt with pleasure in Athens, and was overpowered by this manner of life, his affairs would have been at every man's command; the stronger would have the power of grieving him. How do you think that Diogenes would have flattered the pirates that they might sell him to some Athenian, that sometime he might see that beautiful Piræus, and the Long Walls and the Acropolis? In what condition would you see them? As a captive, a slave and mean: and what would be the use of it for you?—Not so: but I should see them as a free man— Show me, how you would be free. Observe, some person has caught you, who leads you away from your accustomed place of abode and says, "You are my slave, for it is in my power to hinder you from living as you please, it is in my power to treat you gently, and to humble you: when I choose, on the contrary you are cheerful and go elated to Athens." What do you say to him who treats you as a slave? What means have you of finding one who will rescue you from slavery? Or can not you even look him in the face, but without saying more do you intreat to be set free? Man, you ought to go gladly to prison, hastening, going before those who lead you there. Then, I ask you, are you unwilling to live in Rome and desire to live in Hellas (Greece)? And when you must die, will you then also fill us with your lamentations, because you will not see Athens nor walk about in the Lyceion? Have you gone abroad for this? was it for this reason you have sought to find some person from whom you might receive benefit? What benefit? That you may solve syllogisms more readily, or handle hypothetical arguments? and for this reason did you leave brother, country, friends, your family, that you might return when you had learned these things? So you did not go abroad to obtain constancy of mind, nor freedom from perturbation, nor in order that being secure from harm you may never complain of any person, accuse no person, and no man may wrong you, and thus you may maintain your relative position without impediment? This is a fine traffic that you have gone abroad for in syllogisms and sophistical arguments and hypothetical: if you like, take your place in the agora (market or public place) and proclaim them for sale like dealers in physic.[14] Will you not deny even all that you have learned that you may not bring a bad name on your theorems as useless? What harm has philosophy done you? Wherein has Chrysippus injured you that you should prove by your acts that his labours are useless? Were the evils that you had there (at home) not enough, those which were the cause of your pain and lamentation, even if you had not gone abroad? Have you added more to the list? And if you again have other acquaintances and friends, you will have more causes for lamentation; and the same also if you take an affection for another country. Why then do you live to surround yourself with other sorrows upon sorrows through which you are unhappy? Then, I ask you, do you call this affection? What affection, man! If it is a good thing, it is the cause of no evil: if it is bad, I have nothing to do with it. I am formed by nature for my own good: I am not formed for my own evil.

What then is the discipline for this purpose? · First of all the highest and the principal, and that which stands as it were at the entrance, is this: when you are delighted with anything, be delighted as with a thing which is not one of those which can not be taken away, but as with something of such a kind, as an earthen pot is, or a glass cup, that when it has been broken, you may remember what it was, and may not be troubled. So in this matter also: if you kiss your own child, or your brother or friend, never give full license to the appearance (φαντασίαν), and allow not your pleasure to go as far as it chooses; but check it, and curb it as those who stand behind men in their triumphs and remind them that they are mortal.[15] Do you also remind yourself in like manner, that he whom you love is mortal, and that what you love is nothing of your own: it has been given to you for the present, not that it should not be taken from you, nor has it been given to you for all time, but as a fig is given to you or a bunch of grapes at the appointed season of the year. But if you wish for these things in winter, you are a fool. So if you wish for your son or friend when it is not allowed to you, you must know that you are wishing for a fig in winter. For such as winter is to a fig, such is every event which happens from the universe to the things which are taken away according to its nature. And further, at the times when you are delighted with a thing, place before yourself the contrary appearances. What harm is it while you are kissing your child to say with a lisping voice, "To-morrow you will die;" and to a friend also, "To-morrow you will go away or I shall, and never shall we see one another again?"—But these are words of bad omen.—And some incantations also are of bad omen; but because they are useful, I don't care for this; only let them be useful. But do you call things to be of bad omen except those which are significant of some evil? Cowardice is a word of bad omen, and meanness of spirit, and sorrow, and grief and shamelessness. These words are of bad omen. and yet we ought not to hesitate to utter them in order to protect ourselves against the things. Do you tell me that a name which is significant of any natural thing is of bad omen? say that even for the ears of corn to be reaped is of bad omen, for it signifies the destruction of the ears, but not of the world. Say that the falling of the leaves also is of bad omen, and for the dried fig to take the place of the green fig, and for raisins to be made from the grapes. For all these things are changes from a former state into other states; not a destruction, but a certain fixed economy and administration. Such is going away from home and a small change: such is death, a greater change, not from the state which now is to that which is not, but to that which is not now.—Shall I then no longer exist? —You will not exist, but you will be something else, of which the world now has need: for you also came into existence not when you chose, but when the world had need of you.[16]

Wherefore the wise and good man, remembering who he is and whence he came, and by whom he was produced, is attentive only to this, how he may fill his place with due regularity, and obediently to God. Dost thou still wish me to exist (live)? I will continue to exist as free, as noble in nature, as thou hast wished me to exist: for thou hast made me free from hindrance in that which is my own. But hast thou no further need of me? I thank thee; and so far I have remained for thy sake, and for the sake of no other person, and now in obedience to thee I depart. How dost thou depart? Again, I say, as thou hast pleased, as free, as thy servant, as one who hast known thy commands and thy prohibitions. And so long as I shall stay in thy service, whom dost thou will me to be? A prince or a private man, a senator or a common person, a soldier or a general, a teacher or a master of a family? whatever place and position thou mayest assign to me, as Socrates says, I will die ten thousand times rather than desert them And where dost thou will me to be? in Rome or Athens, or Thebes or Gyara. Only remember me there where I am. If thou sendest me to a place where there are no means for men living according to nature, I shall not depart (from life) in disobedience to thee, but as if thou wast giving me the signal to retreat: I do not leave thee, let this be far from my intention, but I perceive that thou hast no need of me. If means of living according to nature be allowed to me, I will seek no other place than that in which I am, or other men than those among whom I am.

Let these thoughts be ready to hand by night and by day: these you should write, these you should read: about these you should talk to yourself, and to others. Ask a man, Can you help me at all for this purpose? and further, go to another and to another. Then if any thing that is said be contrary to your wish, this reflection first will immediately relieve you, that it is not unexpected. For it is a great thing in all cases to say, I knew that I begot a son who is mortal.[17] For so you also will say, I knew that I am mortal, I knew that I may leave my home, I knew that I may be ejected from it, I knew that I may be led to prison. Then if you turn round and look to yourself, and seek the place from which comes that which has happened, you will forthwith recollect that it comes from the place of things which are out of the power of the will, and of things which are not my own. What then is it to me? Then, you will ask, and this is the chief thing: And who is it that sent it? The leader, or the general, the state, the law of the state. Give it me then, for I must always obey the law in every thing. Then, when the

appearance (of things) pains you, for it is not in your power
to prevent this, contend against it by the aid of reason, conquer it: do not allow it to gain strength nor to lead you to
the consequences by raising images such as it pleases and as
it pleases. If you be in Gyara, do not imagine the mode of
living at Rome, and how many pleasures there were for him
who lived there and how many there would be for him who
returned to Rome: but fix your mind on this matter, how a
man who lives in Gyara ought to live in Gyara like a man of
courage. And if you be in Rome, do not imagine what the
life in Athens is, but think only of the life in Rome.

Then in the place of all other delights substitute this, that
of being conscious that you are obeying God, than not in
word, but in deed you are performing the acts of a wise and
good man. For what a thing it is for a man to be able to say
to himself, Now whatever the rest may say in solemn manner in the schools and may be judged to be saying in a way
contrary to common opinion (or in a strange way) this I am
doing; and they are sitting and discoursing of my virtues and inquiring about me and praising me; and of this
Zeus has willed that I shall receive from myself a demonstration, and shall myself know if he has a soldier such as he
ought to have, a citizen such as he ought to have, and if he
has chosen to produce me to the rest of mankind as a witness
of the things which are independent of the will: See that
you fear without reason, that you foolishly desire what you
do desire: seek not the good in things external; seek it in
yourselves: if you do not, you will not find it. For this purpose he leads me at one time hither, at another time sends
me thither, shows me to men as poor, without authority, and
sick; sends me to Gyara, leads me into prison, not because
he hates me, far from him be such a meaning, for who hates
the best of his servants? nor yet because he cares not for me,
for he does not neglect any even of the smallest things;[18]
but he does this for the purpose of exercising me and making
use of me as a witness to others. Being appointed to such a
service, do I still care about the place in which I am, or with
whom I am, or what men say about me? and do I not entirely direct my thoughts to God and to his instructions and
commands?

Having these things (or thoughts) always in hand, and exercising them by yourself, and keeping them in readiness, you will never be in want of one to comfort you and strengthen you. For it is not shameful to be without something to eat, but not to have reason sufficient for keeping away fear and sorrow. But if once you have gained exemption from sorrow and fear, will there any longer be a tyrant for you, or a tyrant's guard, or attendants on Cæsar? Or shall any appointment to offices at court cause you pain, or shall those who sacrifice in the Capitol on the occasion of being named to certain functions, cause pain to you who have received so great authority from Zeus? Only do not make a proud display of it, nor boast of it; but shew it by your acts; and if no man perceives it, be satisfied that you are yourself in a healthy state and happy.

NOTES

[1] See ii. 5, 26.

[2] See iii. 13, 15.

[3] Homer, Odyssey i. 3.

[4] Odyssey, xvii. 487.

[5] ἀπέχειν. See iii. 2, 13 Paul to the Philippians, iv. 18

[6] Suetonius (Claudius, 25) says: "Peregrinæ conditionis homines vetuit usurpare Romana nomina, duntaxat gentilia. Civitatem Romanam usurpantes in campo, Esquilino securi percussit"

[7] This is a denunciation of the hypocrite

[8] "Pity" perhaps means that he will suffer the perturbation of pity, when he ought not to feel it. I am not sure about the exact meaning.

[9] "What follows hath no connection with what immediately preceded; but belongs to the general subject of the chapter" Mrs Carter
"The person with whom Epictetus chiefly held this discourse, seems to have been instructed by his friends to pay his respects to some great man at Nicopolis (perhaps the procurator, iii. 4. 1) and to visit his house." Schweighäuser.

[10] The reward of virtue is in the acts of virtue. The Stoics taught that virtue is its own reward. When I was a boy I have written this in copies, but I did not know what it meant. I know now that few people believe it; and like the man here, they inquire what reward they shall have for doing as they ought to do. A man of common sense would give no other answer than what Epictetus gives. But that will not satisfy all The heathens must give the answer: "For what more dost thou want when thou hast done a man a service? Art thou not content that thou hast done something conformable to thy nature, and dost thou seek to be paid for it? just as if the eye demanded a recompense for seeing or the feet for walking" M Antoninus, ix. 42 Compare Seneca, de Vita Beata, c. 9.

[11] It was the custom at Athens when the court (the dicasts) had determined to convict an accused person, in some cases at least, to ask

him what penalty he proposed to be inflicted on himself, but Socrates refused to do this or to allow his friends to do it, for he said that to name the penalty was the same as admitting his guilt (Xenophon, Apologia, 23). Socrates said that if he did name a proper penalty for himself, it would be that he should daily be allowed to dine in the Prytaneium (Plato, Apology, c. 26, Cicero, De Oratore, i. 54).

[12] The character of Diogenes is described very differently by Epictetus from that which we read in common books.

[13] A people in Thessaly between the river Peneius and Mount Olympus. It is the same as if Epictetus had said to any remote country.

[14] This is an old practice, to go about and sell physic to people. Cicero (Pro Cluentio, c 14) speaks of such a quack (pharmacopola), who would do a poisoning job for a proper sum of money. I have seen a travelling doctor in France who went about in a cart, and rang a bell, at the sound of which people came round him. Some who were deaf had stuff poured into their ears, paid their money, and made way for others who had other complaints

[15] It was the custom in Roman triumphs for a slave to stand behind the triumphant general in his chariot and to remind him that he was still mortal. Juvenal, x 41

[16] I am not sure if Epictetus ever uses κόσμος in the sense of Universe, the "universum" of philosophers. I think he sometimes uses it in the common sense of the world, the earth and all that is on it Epictetus appears to teach that when a man dies, his existence is terminated. The body is resolved into the elements of which it is formed, and these elements are employed for other purposes. Consistently with this doctrine he may have supposed that the powers, which we call rational and intellectual, exist in man by virtue only of the organisation of his brain which is superior to that of all other animals; and that what we name the soul has no existence independent of the body It was an old Greek hypothesis that at death the body returned to earth from which it came, and the soul ($\pi\nu\epsilon\tilde{\upsilon}\mu\alpha$) returned to the regions above, from which it came. I can not discover any passage in Epictetus in which the doctrine is taught that the soul has an existence independent of the body. The opinions of Marcus Antoninus on this matter are contained in his book, iv. 14, 21, and perhaps elsewhere: but they are rather obscure. A recent writer has attempted to settle the question of the existence of departed souls by affirming that we can find no place for them either in heaven or in hell; for the modern scientific notion, as I suppose that it must be named, does not admit the conception of a place heaven or a place hell (Strauss, Der Alte und der Neue Glaube, p. 129)

We may name Paul a contemporary of Epictetus, for though Epictetus may have been the younger, he was living at Rome during Nero's reign (A. D. 54-68); and it is affirmed, whether correctly or not, I do not undertake to say, that Paul wrote from Ephesus his first epistle to the Corinthians (Cor. 1. 16, 8) in the beginning of A D 56 Epictetus it is said, lived in Rome, till the time of the expulsion of the philosophers by Domitian, when he retired to Nicopolis an old man, and taught there. Paul's first epistle to the Corinthians (c. 15) contains his doctrine of the resurrection, which is accepted, I believe, by all, or nearly all, if there are any exceptions, who profess the Christian faith · but it is not understood by all in the same way

Paul teaches that Christ died for our sins, that he was buried and rose again on the third day; and that after his resurrection he was seen by many persons. Then he asks, if Christ rose from the dead, how can some say that there is no resurrection of the dead? "But if there be no resurrection of the dead, then is Christ not risen" (v. 13); and (v. 19), "if in this life only we have hope in Christ, we are of all men most miserable." But he affirms again (v. 20) that "Christ is risen and become the first fruits of them that slept." In v. 32, he asks what advantages he has from his struggles in Ephesus, "if the dead rise not : let us eat and drink, for to-morrow we die" He seems not to admit the value of life, if there is no resurrection of the dead; and he seems to say that we shall seek or ought to seek only the pleasures of sense, because life is short, if we do not believe in a resurrection of the dead. It may be added that there is not any direct assertion in this chapter that Christ ascended to heaven in a bodily form, or that he ascended to heaven in any way. He then says (v. 35), "But some man will say, How are the dead raised up? and with what body do they come?" He answers his question (v. 36), "Thou fool, that which thou sowest is not quickened except it die;" and he adds that "God giveth it (the seed) a body as it hath pleased him, and to every seed his own body." We all know that the body which is produced from the seed, is not the body "that shall be;" and we also know that the seed which is sown does not die, and that if the seed died, no body would be produced from such seed. His conclusion is that the dead "is sown a natural body; it is raised a spiritual body" (σῶμα πνευματικόν). I believe that the commentators do not agree about this "spiritual body," but it seems plain that Paul did not teach that the body which will rise will be the same as the body which is buried. He says (v. 50) that "flesh and blood can not inherit the kingdom of God." Yet in the Apostles' Creed we pronounce our belief in the "resurrection of the body"; but in the Nicene Creed it is said we look " for the resurrection of the dead," which is a different thing or may have a different meaning from " the resurrection of the body " In the ministration of baptism to such as are of riper years, the person to be baptized is asked " Dost thou believe in God the Father Almighty," etc in the terms of the Church Creeds, but in place of the resurrection of the body or of the dead, he is asked if he believes " in the resurrection of the flesh."

The various opinions of divines of the English church on the resurrection of the body are stated by A. Clissold in the Practical Nature of the Theological Writings of E Swedenborg in a letter to Whately, Archbishop of Dublin, 1859, 2nd ed

[17] Seneca de Consol. ad Pol. c. 30; Cicero, Tuscul. Disp iii. 13.

[18] Compare i, 12. 2, ii. 14. 11, iii. 26. 28. "Compare this with the description of the universal care of Providence, Matthew, x. 29, 30, and the occasion on which it was produced." Mrs. Carter.

CHAPTER XXV.

TO THOSE WHO FALL OFF (DESIST) FROM THEIR PURPOSE

CONSIDER as to the things which you proposed to yourself at first, which you have secured, and which you have not; and how you are pleased when you recall to memory the one, and are pained about the other; and if it is possible, recover the things wherein you failed. For we must not shrink when we are engaged in the greatest combat, but we must even take blows. For the combat before us is not in wrestling and the Pancration, in which both the successful and the unsuccessful may have the greatest merit, or may have little, and in truth may be very fortunate or very unfortunate; but the combat is for good fortune and happiness themselves. Well then, even if we have renounced the contest in this matter (for good fortune and happiness), no man hinders us from renewing the combat again, and we are not compelled to wait for another four years that the games at Olympia may come again;[1] but as soon as you have recovered and restored yourself, and employ the same zeal, you may renew the combat again; and if again you renounce it, you may again renew it; and if you once gain the victory, you are like him who has never renounced the combat. Only do not through a habit of doing the same thing (renouncing the combat) begin to do it with pleasure, and then like a bad athlete go about after being conquered in all the circuit of the games like quails who have run away.[2]

The sight of a beautiful young girl overpowers me. Well, have I not been overpowered before? An inclination arises in me to find fault with a person; for have I not found fault with him before? You speak to us as if you had come off (from these things) free from harm, just as if a man should say to his physician who forbids him to bathe, "Have I not bathed before?" If then the physician can say to him, "Well, and what then happened to you after the bath? Had you not a fever, had you not a headache?" And when you found fault with a person lately, did you not do the act of a malignant person, of a trifling babbler; did you not cherish this habit in you by adding to it the corresponding acts? And when you were overpowered by the young girl, did you come off unharmed? Why then do you talk of what you did before? You ought, I think, remembering what you did, as slaves remember the blows which they have received, to abstain from the same faults. But the one case is not like the other; for in the case of slaves the pain causes the remembrance: but in the case of your faults, what is the pain, what is the punishment; for when have you been accustomed to fly from evil acts?[3] Sufferings then of the trying character are useful to us, whether we choose or not.

NOTES

[1] These games were celebrated once in four years.

[2] "All the circuit of the games" means the circuit of the Pythian, Isthmian, Nemean, and Olympic games. A man who had contended in these four games victoriously was named Periodonices, or Periodeutes. Upton

The Greeks used to put quails in a cockpit, as those who are old enough may remember that we used to put game cocks to fight with one another. Schweighauser describes a way of trying the courage of these quails from Pollux (ix 109), but I suppose that the birds fought also with one another.

Upton supposed that the words Ἀλλ' οὐχ ὅμοιον . . . to κακῶς ἐνεργῆσαι, in the translation, "But the one case is not" . . to "fly from evil acts," are said by the adversary of Epictetus, and Mrs Carter has followed Upton in the translation. But then there is no sense in the last sentence Οἱ πόνοι ἄρα, etc., in the translation, "Sufferings then," etc The reader may consult Schweighäuser's note. I suppose that Epictetus is speaking the words "But the one case," etc. to the end of the chapter. The adversary, who is not punished like a slave, and has no pains to remind him of his faults, is supposed so far not to have felt the consequences of his bad acts, but Epictetus concludes that sufferings of a painful character would be useful to him, as they are to all persons who do what they ought not to do. There is perhaps some difficulty in the word πειρατηρίων. But I think that Schweig. has correctly explained the passage.

CHAPTER XXVI

TO THOSE WHO FEAR WANT[1]

ARE you not ashamed at being more cowardly and more mean than fugitive slaves? How do they when they run away leave their masters? on what estates do they depend, and what domestics do they rely on? Do they not after stealing a little which is enough for the first days, then afterwards move on through land or through sea, contriving one method after another for maintaining their lives? And what fugitive slave ever died of hunger?[2] But you are afraid lest necessary things should fail you, and are sleepless by night. Wretch, are you so blind, and don't you see the road to which the want of necessaries leads?—Well, where does it lead?—To the same place to which a fever leads, or a stone that falls on you, to death. Have you not often said this yourself to your companions? have you not read much of this kind, and written much? and how often have you boasted that you were easy as to death?

Yes: but my wife and children also suffer hunger.[3]—Well then, does their hunger lead to any other place? Is there not the same descent to some place for them also? Is not there the same state below for them? Do you not choose then to look to that place full of boldness against every want and deficiency, to that place to which both the richest and those who have held the highest offices, and kings themselves and tyrants must descend? or to which you will descend hungry, if it should so happen, but they burst by indigestion and drunkenness. What beggar did you hardly ever see who was not an old man, and even of extreme old age? But chilled with cold day and night, and lying on the ground, and eating only what is absolutely necessary they approach near to the impossibility of dying.[4] Can not you write? Can not you teach (take care of) children? Can not you be a watchman at another person's door?—But it is shameful to come to such a necessity.—Learn then first what are the things which are shameful, and then tell us that you are a philoso-

287

pher: but at present do not, even if any other man call you so, allow it.

Is that shameful to you which is not your own act, that of which you are not the cause, that which has come to you by accident, as a headache, as a fever? If your parents were poor, and left their property to others, and if while they live, they do not help you at all, is this shameful to you? Is this what you learned with the philosophers? Did you never hear that the thing which is shameful ought to be blamed, and that which is blameable is worthy of blame? Whom do you blame for an act which is not his own, which he did not do himself? Did you then make your father such as he is, or is it in your power to improve him? Is this power given to you? Well then, ought you to wish the things which are not given to you, or to be ashamed if you do not obtain them? And have you also been accustomed while you were studying philosophy to look to others and to hope for nothing from yourself? Lament then and groan and eat with fear that you may not have food to-morrow. Tremble about your poor slaves lest they steal, lest they run away, lest they die. So live, and continue to live, you who in name only have approached philosophy, and have disgraced its theorems as far as you can by showing them to be useless and unprofitable to those who take them up; you who have never sought constancy, freedom from perturbation. and from passions: you who have not sought any person for the sake of this object. but many for the sake of syllogisms; you who have never thoroughly examined any of these appearances by yourself, Am I able to bear, or am I not able to bear? What remains for me to do? But as if all your affairs were well and secure, you have been resting on the third topic,[5] that of things being unchanged, in order that you may possess unchanged —what? cowardice, mean spirit, the admiration of the rich, desire without attaining any end, and avoidance (ἔκκλισιν) which fails in the attempt? About security in these things you have been anxious.

Ought you not to have gained something in addition from reason, and then to have protected this with security? And whom did you ever see building a battlement all round and not encircling it with a wall?[6] And what door-keeper is

placed with no door to watch? But you practise in order
to be able to prove—what? You practise that you may not
be tossed as on the sea through sophisms, and tossed about
from what? Shew me first what you hold, what you measure, or what you weigh; and shew me the scales or the me-
dimnus (the measure); or how long will you go on measuring the dust?⁷ Ought you not to demonstrate those things
which make men happy, which make things go on for them
in the way as they wish, and why we ought to blame no man,
accuse no man, and acquiesce in the administration of the
universe? Shew me these. "See, I shew them: I will resolve syllogisms for you."—This is the measure, slave; but
it is not the thing measured. Therefore you are now paying
the penalty for what you neglected, philosophy: you tremble,
you lie awake, you advise with all persons; and if your
deliberations are not likely to please all, you think that you
have deliberated ill. Then you fear hunger, as you suppose ·
but it is not hunger that you fear, but you are afraid that you
will not have a cook, that you will not have another to purchase provisions for the table, a third to take off your shoes, ·
a fourth to dress you, others to rub you, and to follow you,
in order that in the bath, when you have taken off your
clothes and stretched yourself out like those who are crucified
you may be rubbed on this side and on that, and then the
aliptes (rubber) may say (to the slave), "Change his position,
present the side, take hold of his head, shew the shoulder;"
And then when you have left the bath and gone home, you
may call out, "Does no one bring me something to eat?" And
then, "Take away the tables, sponge them:" You are afraid
of this, that you may not be able to lead the life of a sick man.
But learn the life of those who are in health, how slaves live,
how labourers, how those live who are genuine philosophers;
how Socrates lived, who had a wife and children; how Diogenes lived, and how Cleanthes⁸ who attended to the school
and drew water. If you choose to have these things, you
will have them every where, and you will live in full confidence. Confiding in what? In that alone in which a man
can confide, in that which is secure, in that which is not subject to hindrance, in that which can not be taken away, that
is in your own will. And why have you made yourself so use-

19

less and good for nothing that no man will choose to receive
you into his house, no man to take care of you? but if a utensil
entire and useful were cast abroad, every man who found it,
would take it up and think it a gain; but no man will take
you up, and every man will consider you a loss. So can not
you discharge the office even of a dog, or of a cock? Why
then do you choose to live any longer, when you are what
you are?

Does any good man fear that he shall fail to have food?
To the blind it does not fail, to the lame it does not: shall
it fail to a good man? And to a good soldier there does not
fail to be one who gives him pay, nor to a labourer, nor to
a shoemaker: and to the good man shall there be wanting
such a person?[9] Does God thus neglect the things that he
has established, his ministers, his witnesses, whom alone he
employs as examples to the uninstructed, both that he exists,
and administers well the whole, and does not neglect human
affairs, and that to a good man there is no evil either when he
is living or when he is dead? What then when he does not
supply him with food? What else does he do than like a
good general he has given me the signal to retreat? I obey,
I follow, assenting to the words of the commander, praising
his acts· for I came when it pleased him, and I will also go
away when it pleases him; and while I lived, it was my
duty to praise God both by myself, and to each person severally and to many. He does not supply me with many things,
nor with abundance, he does not will me to live luxuriously;
for neither did he supply Hercules who was his own son; but
another (Eurystheus) was king of Argos and Mycenæ, and
Hercules obeyed orders, and laboured, and was exercised.
And Eurystheus was what he was, neither king of Argos nor
of Mycenæ, for he was not even king of himself; but Hercules was ruler and leader of the whole earth and sea, who
purged away lawlessness, and introduced justice and holiness;[10] and he did these things both naked and alone. And
when Ulysses was cast out shipwrecked, did want humiliate
him, did it break his spirit? but how did he go off to the vir-
gins to ask for necessaries, to beg which is considered most
shameful?[11]

"As a lion bred in the mountains trusting in his strength."[12]

Relying on what? Not on reputation nor on wealth nor on the power of a magistrate, but on his own strength, that is, on his opinions about the things which are in our power and those which are not. For these are the only things which make men free, which make them escape from hindrance, which raise the head (neck) of those who are depressed, which make them look with steady eyes on the rich and on tyrants. And this was (is) the gift given to the philosopher. But you will not come forth bold, but trembling about your trifling garments and silver vessels. Unhappy man, have you thus wasted your time till now?

What then, if I shall be sick? You will be sick in such a way as you ought to be.—Who will take care of me?—God; your friends.—I shall lie down on a hard bed.—But you will lie down like a man.—I shall not have a convenient chamber.—You will be sick in an inconvenient chamber.—Who will provide for me the necessary food?—Those who provide for others also. You will be sick like Manes.[13]—And what also will be the end of the sickness? Any other than death?—Do you then consider that this the chief of all evils to man and the chief mark of mean spirit and of cowardice is not death, but rather the fear of death? Against this fear then I advise you to exercise yourself: to this let all your reasoning tend, your exercises, and reading; and you will know that thus only are men made free.

NOTES

[1] " Compare this chapter with the beautiful and affecting discourses of our Saviour on the same subject, Matthew vi. 25-34, Luke xii 22-30." Mrs. Carter. The first verse of Matthew begins, "Take no thought for your life, what ye shall eat or what ye shall drink," etc No Christian literally follows the advice of this and the following verses, and he would be condemned by the judgment of all men if he did.

[2] It is very absurd to suppose that no fugitive slave ever died of hunger. How could Epictetus know that?

[3] He supposes that the man who is dying of hunger has also wife and children, who will suffer the same dreadful end. The consolation, if it is any, is that the rich and luxurious and kings will also die. The fact is true Death is the lot of all But a painful death by hunger can not be alleviated by a man knowing that all must die in some way. It seems as if the philosopher expected that even women and children should be philosophers, and that the husband in his philosophy should calmly contemplate the death of wife and children by starvation This is an example of the absurdity to which even a wise man carried his philosophy, and it is unworthy of the teacher's general good sense.

[4] We see many old beggars who endure what others could not endure; but they all die at last, and would have died earlier if their beggar life had begun sooner. The living in the open air and wandering about help them to last longer, but the exposure to cold and wet and to the want of food hastens their end The life of a poor old beggar is neither so long nor so comfortable as that of a man, who has a good home and sufficient food, and lives with moderation.

[5] See iii c 2

[6] "Plato using the same simile teaches that last of all disciplines dialectic ought to be learned." Schweighauser

[7] This is good advice. When you propose to measure, to estimate things, you should first tell us what the things are before you attempt to fix their value; and what is the measure or scales that you use.

[8] Cleanthes, the successor of Zeno in his school, was a great example of the pursuit of knowledge under difficulties: during the night he used to draw water from the wells for the use of the gardens: during the day he employed himself in his studies. He was the author of a noble hymn to Zeus, which is extant.

[9] It seems strange that Epictetus should make such assertions when we know that they are not true Shortly afterward he himself speaks even of the good man not being supplied with food by God

[10] Compare Hebrews xi and xii, in which the Apostle and Philosopher reason in nearly the same manner and even use the same terms; but how superior is the example urged by the Apostle to Hercules and Ulysses!" Mrs. Carter

[11] The story of Ulysses asking Nausicaa and her maids for help when he was cast naked on the land is in the Odyssey vi 127.

[12] Odyssey, vi 130.

[13] Manes is a slave's name Diogenes had a slave named Manes, his only slave, who ran away, and though Diogenes was informed where the slave was, he did not think it worth while to have him brought back. He said, it would be a shame if Manes could live without Diogenes, and Diogenes could not live without Manes.

BOOK IV

CHAPTER I

ABOUT FREEDOM

H E is free who lives as he wishes to live;[1] who is neither
subject to compulsion nor to hindrance, nor to force;
whose movements to action (ὁρμαί) are not impeded,
whose desires attain their purpose, and who does not
fall into that which he would avoid (ἐκκλίσεις ἀπερίπτωτοι).
Who then chooses to live in error? No man. Who chooses to
live deceived, liable to mistake, unjust, unrestrained, discontented, mean? No man. Not one then of the bad lives as
he wishes; nor is he then free. And who chooses to live in
sorrow, fear, envy, pity, desiring and failing in his desires,
attempting to avoid something and falling into it? Not one.
Do we then find any of the bad free from sorrow, free from
fear, who does not fall into that which he would avoid, and
does not obtain that which he wishes? Not one; nor then
do we find any bad man free.[2]

If then a man who has been twice consul should hear this,
if you add, "But you are a wise man; this is nothing to
you;" he will pardon you. But if you tell him the truth, and
say, "You differ not at all from those who have been thrice
sold as to being yourself not a slave," what else ought you to
expect than blows? For he says, "What, I a slave, I whose
father was free, whose mother was free, I whom no man can
purchase: I am also of senatorial rank, and a friend of
Cæsar, and I have been a consul, and I own many slaves"
In the first place, most excellent senatorial man, perhaps your
father also was a slave in the same kind of servitude, and
your mother, and your grandfather and all your ancestors in
an ascending series. But even if they were as free as it is

293

possible, what is this to you? What if they were of a noble nature, and you of a mean nature; if they were fearless, and you a coward; if they had the power of self-restraint, and you are not able to exercise it.

And what, you may say, has this to do with being a slave? Does it seem to you to be nothing to do a thing unwillingly, with compulsion, with groans, has this nothing to do with being a slave? It is something, you say: but who is able to compel me, except the lord of all, Cæsar? Then even you yourself have admitted that you have one master. But that he is the common master of all, as you say, let not this console you at all: but know that you are a slave in a great family. So also the people of Nicopolis are used to exclaim, "By the fortune of Cæsar,³ we are free."

However, if you please, let us not speak of Cæsar at present. But tell me this· did you never love any person, a young girl, or slave, or free? What then is this with respect to being a slave or free? Were you never commanded by the person beloved to do something which you did not wish to do? have you never flattered your little slave? have you never kissed her feet? And yet if any man compelled you to kiss Cæsar's feet, you would think it an insult and excessive tyranny. What else then is slavery? Did you never go out by night to some place whither you did not wish to go, did you not expend what you did not wish to expend, did you not utter words with sighs and groans, did you not submit to abuse and to be excluded?⁴ But if you are ashamed to confess your own acts, see what Thrasonides⁵ says and does, who having seen so much military service as perhaps not even you have, first of all went out by night, when Geta (a slave) does not venture out, but if he were compelled by his master, would have cried out much and would have gone out lamenting his bitter slavery. Next, what does Thrasonides say? "A worthless girl has enslaved me, me whom no enemy ever did Unhappy man, who are the slave even of a girl, and a worthless girl. Why then do you still call yourself free? and why do you talk of your service in the army?" Then he calls for a sword and is angry with him who out of kindness refuses it; and he sends presents to her who hates him, and intreats and weeps, and on the other hand having had a little success

he is elated. But even then how? was he free enough
neither to desire nor to fear?

Now consider in the case of animals, how we employ the
notion of liberty. Men keep tame lions shut up, and feed
them, and some take them about; and who will say that this
lion is free?[6] Is it not the fact that the more he lives at his
ease, so much the more he is in a slavish condition? and who
if he had perception and reason would wish to be one of these
lions? Well, these birds when they are caught and are kept
shut up, how much do they suffer in their attempts to escape?[7] and some of them die of hunger rather than submit to
such a kind of life And as many of them as live, hardly
live and with suffering pine away; and if they ever find any
opening, they make their escape. So much do they desire
their natural liberty, and to be independent and free from
hindrance. And what harm is there to you in this? What
do you say? I am formed by nature to fly where I choose,
to live in the open air, to sing when I choose: you deprive me
of all this, and say, what harm is it to you? For this reason
we shall say that those animals only are free, which can not
endure capture, but as soon as they are caught, escape from
captivity by death. So Diogenes also somewhere says that
there is only one way to freedom, and that is to die content:
and he writes to the Persian king, "You can not enslave
the Athenian state any more than you can enslave fishes."
How is that? can not I catch them? If you catch them, says
Diogenes, they will immediately leave you, as fishes do; for
if you catch a fish, it dies; and if these men that are caught
shall die, of what use to you is the preparation for war?
These are the words of a free man who had carefully examined the thing, and, as was natural, had discovered it.
But if you look for it in a different place from where it is,
what wonder if you never find it?

The slave wishes to be set free immediately. Why? Do
you think that he wishes to pay money to the collectors of
twentieths?[8] No; but because he imagines that hitherto
through not having obtained this, he is hindered and unfortunate. If I shall be set free, immediately it is all happiness,
I care for no man, I speak to all as an equal and like to them,
I go where I choose, I come from any place I choose, and go

,where I choose. Then he is set free; and forthwith having no place where he can eat, he looks for some man to flatter, some one with whom he shall sup. then he either works with his body or endures the most dreadful things;[9] and if he can obtain a manger, he falls into a slavery much worse than his former slavery; or even if he is become rich, being a man without any knowledge of what is good, he loves some little girl, and in his unhappiness laments and desires to be a slave again. He says, what evil did I suffer in my state of slavery? Another clothed me, another supplied me with shoes, another fed me, another looked after me in sickness; and I did only a few services for him. But now a wretched man, what things I suffer, being a slave to many instead of to one. But however, he says, if I shall acquire rings,[10] then I shall live most prosperously and happily. First, in order to acquire these rings, he submits to that which he is worthy of: then when he has acquired them, it is again all the same. Then he says, If I shall be engaged in military service, I am free from all evils. He obtains military service. He suffers as much as a flogged slave, and nevertheless he asks for a second service and a third. After this, when he has put the finishing stroke (the colophon)[11] to his career, and is become a senator, then he becomes a slave by entering into the assembly, then he serves the finer and most splendid slavery— not to be a fool, but to learn what Socrates taught, what is the nature of each thing that exists, and that a man should not rashly adapt preconceptions ($\pi\rho o\lambda\acute{\eta}\psi\epsilon\iota\varsigma$) to the several things which are. For this is the cause to men of all their evils, they not being able to adapt the general preconceptions to the several things. But we have different opinions (about the cause of our evils). One man thinks that he is sick: not so however, but the fact is that he does not adapt his preconceptions right. Another thinks that he is poor; another that he has a severe father or mother; and another again that Cæsar is not favourable to him. But all this is one and only one thing, the not knowing how to adapt the preconceptions. For who has not a preconception of that which is bad, that it is hurtful, that it ought to be avoided, that it ought in every way to be guarded against? One preconception is not repugnant to another, only where it comes to the matter of ad-

aptation.   What then is this evil, which is both hurtful, and
a thing to be avoided? He answers not to be Cæsar's friend,
—He is gone far from the mark, he has missed the adaptation, he is embarrassed, he seeks the things which are not at
all pertinent to the matter; for when he has succeeded in
being Cæsar's friend, nevertheless he has failed in finding
what he sought.   For what is that which every man seeks?
To live secure, to be happy, to do every thing as he wishes,
not to be hindered, nor compelled.   When then he is become
the friend of Cæsar, is he free from hindrance? free from
compulsion, is he tranquil, is he happy?   Of whom shall we
inquire?   What more trustworthy witness have we than this
very man who is become Cæsar's friend?   Come forward
and tell us when did you sleep more quietly, now or before
you became Cæsar's friend?   Immediately you hear the answer, "Stop, I entreat you, and do not mock me: you know
not what miseries I suffer, and sleep does not come to me;
but one comes and says, 'Cæsar is already awake, he is now
going forth;' then come troubles and cares."—Well, when
did you sup with more pleasure, now or before? Hear what
he says about this also. He says that if he is not invited, he is
pained: and if he is invited, he sups like a slave with his master, all the while being anxious that he does not say or do any
thing foolish.   And what do you suppose that he is afraid
of; lest he should be lashed like a slave?   How can he expect
any thing so good?   No, but as befits so great a man,
Cæsar's friend, he is afraid that he may lose his head.   And
when did you bathe more free from trouble, and take your
gymnastic exercise more quietly?   In fine, which kind of
life did you prefer? your present or your former life?   I
can swear that no man is so stupid or so ignorant of truth as
not to bewail his own misfortunes the nearer he is in friendship to Cæsar.

Since then neither those who are called kings live as they
choose, nor the friends of kings, who finally are those who
are free?   Seek, and you will find; for you have aids from
nature for the discovery of truth.   But if you are not able
yourself by going along these ways only to discover that
which follows, listen to those who have made the inquiry.
What do they say? Does freedom seem to you a good thing?.

20

The greatest good.   Is it possible then that he who obtains
the greatest good can be unhappy or fare badly?   No.
Whomsoever then you shall see unhappy, unfortunate, lamenting, confidently declare that they are not free.   I do
declare it.   We have now then got away from buying and
selling and from such arrangements about matters of property : for if you have rightly assented to these matters, if the
great king (the Persian king) is unhappy, he can not be free,
nor can a little king, nor a man of consular rank, nor one who
has been twice consul.—Be it so.

Further then answer me this question also, does freedom
seem to you to be something great and noble and valuable?
—How should it not seem so?   Is it possible then when a
man obtains anything so great and valuable and noble to be
mean?—It is not possible.—When then you see any man subject to another or flattering him contrary to his own opinion,
confidently affirm that this man also is not free; and not only
if he do this for a bit of supper, but also if he does it for a
government (province) or a consulship : and call these men
little slaves who for the sake of little matters do these things,
and those who do so for the sake of great things call great
slaves, as they deserve to be.—This is admitted also.—Do you
think that freedom is a thing independent and self governing?—Certainly.—Whomsoever then it is in the power of
another to hinder and compel, declare that he is not free.
And do not look, I entreat you, after his grandfathers and
great grandfathers, or inquire about his being bought or
sold; but if you hear him saying from his heart and with feeling, "Master," even if the twelve fasces precede him (as consul), call him a slave.   And if you hear him say, "Wretch
that I am, how much I suffer," call him a slave.   If finally
you see him lamenting, complaining, unhappy, call him a
slave though he wears a prætexta.   If then he is doing
nothing of this kind, do not yet say that he is free, but learn
his opinions, whether they are subject to compulsion, or may
produce hindrance, or to bad fortune; and if you find him
such, call him a slave who has a holiday in the Saturnalia :[12]
say that his master is from home: he will return soon, and
you will know what he suffers.   Who will return?   Whoever
has in himself the power over anything which is desired by

the man, either to give it to him or to take it away? Thus then have we many masters? We have: for we have circumstances as masters prior to our present masters; and these circumstances are many. Therefore it must of necessity be that those who have the power over any of these circumstances must be our masters. For no man fears Cæsar himself, but he fears death, banishment, deprivation of his property, prison, and disgrace. Nor does any man love Cæsar, unless Cæsar is a person of great merit, but he loves wealth, the office of tribune, prætor or consul. When we love, and hate and fear these things, it must be that those who have the power over them must be our masters. Therefore we adore them even as gods; for we think that what possesses the power of conferring the greatest advantage on us is divine. Then we wrongly assume ($\dot{v}\pi o\tau\acute{a}\delta\delta o\mu\epsilon v$) that a certain person has the power of conferring the greatest advantages; therefore he is something divine. For if we wrongly assume that a certain person has the power of conferring the greatest advantages, it is a necessary consequence that the conclusion from these premises must be false.

What then is that which makes a man free from hindrance and makes him his own master? For wealth does not do it, nor consulship, nor provincial government, nor royal power; but something else must be discovered. What then is that which when we write makes us free from hindrance and unimpeded? The knowledge of the art of writing. What then is it in playing the lute? The science of playing the lute. Therefore in life also it is the science of life. You have then heard in a general way: but examine the thing also in the several parts. Is it possible that he who desires any of the things which depend on others can be free from hindrance? No—Is it possible for him to be unimpeded? No —Therefore he can not be free. Consider then; whether we have nothing which is in our own power only, or whether we have all things, or whether some things are in our own power, and others in the power of others.—What do you mean?—When you wish the body to be entire (sound), is it in your power or not?—It is not in my power—When you wish it to be healthy?—Neither is this in my power.—When you wish it to be handsome?—Nor is this—Life or death?—

Neither is this in my power.[18]—Your body then is another's, subject to every man who is stronger than yourself?—It is. —But your estate, is it in your power to have it when you please, and as long as you please, and such as you please?— No.—And your slaves?—No.—And your clothes?—No.— And your house?—No.—And your horses?—Not one of these things.—And if you wish by all means your children to live, or your wife, or your brother, or your friends, is it in your power?—This also is not in my power.

Whether then have you nothing which is in your own power, which depends on yourself only and can not be taken from you, or have you any thing of the kind?—I know not. —Look at the thing then thus, and examine it. Is any man able to make you assent to that which is false?[14]—No man.— In the matter of assent then you are free from hindrance and obstruction?—Granted.—Well; and can a man force you to desire to move towards that to which you do not choose?— He can, for when he threatens me with death or bonds, he compels me to desire to move towards it If then, you despise death and bonds, do you still pay any regard to him?— No.—Is then the despising of death an act of your own or is it not yours?—It is my act.—Is it your own act then also to desire to move towards a thing: or is it not so?—It is my own act.—But to desire to move away from a thing, whose act is that? This also is your act.—What then if I have attempted to walk, suppose another should hinder me?—What part of you does he hinder? does he hinder the faculty of assent?—No: but my poor body.—Yes, as he would do with a stone.—Granted; but I no longer walk.—And who told you that walking is your own act free from hindrance? for I said that this only was free from hindrance, to desire to move: but where there is need of body and its co-operation, you have heard long ago that nothing is your own.—Granted this also —And who can compel you to desire what you do not wish?—No man.—And to propose or intend, or in short to make use of the appearances which present themselves, can any man compel you?—He can not do this: but he will hinder me when I desire from obtaining what I desire.—If you desire any thing which is your own, and one of these things which can not be hindered, how will he hinder you?—

He can not in any way.—Who then tells you that he who desires the things that belong to another is free from hindrance?

Must I then not desire health? By no means, nor any thing else that belongs to another: for what is not in your power to acquire or to keep when you please, this belongs to another. Keep then far from it not only your hands, but more than that, even your desires. If you do not, you have surrendered yourself as a slave; you have subjected your neck, if you admire[15] any thing not your own, to every thing that is dependent on the power of others and perishable, to which you have conceived a liking —Is not my hand my own? —It is a part of your own body; but it is by nature earth, subject to hindrance, compulsion, and the slave of every thing which is stronger. And why do I say your hand? You ought to possess your whole body as a poor ass loaded, as long as it is possible, as long as you are allowed. But if there be a press,[16] and a soldier should lay hold of it, let it go, do not resist, nor murmur; if you do, you will receive blows, and never the less you will lose the ass. But when you ought to feel thus with respect to the body, consider what remains to be done about all the rest, which is provided for the sake of the body. When the body is an ass, all the other things are bits belonging to the ass, pack-saddles, shoes,[17] barley, fodder. Let these also go: get rid of them quicker and more readily than of the ass.

When you have made this preparation, and have practised this discipline, to distinguish that which belongs to another from that which is your own, the things which are subject to hindrance from those which are not, to consider the things free from hindrance to concern yourself, and those which are not free not to concern yourself, to keep your desire steadily fixed to the things which do concern yourself, and turned from the things which do not concern yourself, do you still fear any man? No one. For about what will you be afraid? about the things which are your own, in which consists the nature of good and evil? and who has power over these things? who can take them away? who can impede them? No man can, no more that he can impede God. But will you be afraid about your body and your possessions, about things which are not yours, about things which in no way concern you? and what else have you been studying from the beginning than to distinguish between your own and not your own, the things which are in your power and not in your power, the things subject to hindrance and not subject? and why have you come to the philosophers? was it that you may never the less be unfortunate and unhappy? You will then in this way, as I have supposed you to have done, be without fear and disturbance. And what is grief to you? for fear comes from what you expect, but grief from that which is present. But what further will you desire? For of the things which are within the power of the will, as being good and present, you have a proper and regulated desire: but of the things which are not in the power of the will you do not desire any one, and so you do not allow any place to that which is irrational, and impatient, and above measure hasty.

When then you are thus affected towards things, what man can any longer be formidable to you? For what has a man which is formidable to another, either when you see him or speak to him or finally are conversant with him? Not more than one horse has with respect to another, or one dog to another, or one bee to another bee. Things indeed are formidable to every man; and when any man is able to confer these things on another or to take them away, then he too becomes formidable. How then is an acropolis (a stronghold or fortress, the seat of tyranny) demolished? Not by the sword, not by fire, but by opinion. For if we abolish the acropolis which is in the city, can we abolish also that of fever, and that of beautiful women? Can we in a word abolish the acropolis which is in us and cast out the tyrants within us, whom we have daily over us, sometimes the same tyrants, at other times different tyrants? But with this we must begin, and with this we must demolish the acropolis and eject the tyrants, by giving up the body, the parts of it, the faculties of it, the possessions, the reputation, magisterial offices, honours, children, brothers, friends, by considering all these things as belonging to others. And if tyrants have been ejected from us, why do I still shut in the acropolis by a wall of circumvallation,[18] at least on my account; for if it still stands, what does it do to me? why do I still eject (the ty-

rant's) guards? For where do I perceive them? against others they have their fasces, and their spears and their swords.
But I have never been hindered in my will, nor compelled
when I did not will And how is this possible? I have placed
my movements towards action (ὁρμήν) in obedience to
God.[19] Is it his will that I shall have fever? It is my will
also Is it his will that I should move towards any thing?
It is my will also. Is it his will that I should obtain any
thing? It is my wish also.[20] Does he not will? I do not
wish. Is it his will that I die, is it his will that I be put to the
rack? It is my will then to die : it is my will then to be put to
the rack. Who then is still able to hinder me contrary to my
own judgment, or to compel me? No more than he can hinder or compel Zeus.

Thus the more cautious of travellers also act. A traveller
has heard that the road is infested by robbers; he does not
venture to enter on it alone, but he waits for the companion-
ship on the road either of an ambassador, or of a quæstor,
or of a proconsul, and when he has attached himself to such
persons he goes along the road safely. So in the world[21] the
wise man acts. There are many companies of robbers, tyrants, storms, difficulties, losses of that which is dearest.
Where is there any place of refuge? how shall he pass along
without being attacked by robbers? what company shall he
wait for that he may pass along in safety? to whom shall he
attach himself? To what person generally? to the rich man,
to the man of consular rank? and what is the use of that to
me? Such a man is stripped himself, groans and laments.
But what if the fellow companion himself turns against me
and becomes my robber, what shall I do? I will be a friend of
Cæsar : when I am Cæsar's companion no man will wrong
me. In the first place, that I may become illustrious, what
things must I endure and suffer? how often and by how
many must I be robbed? Then, if I become Cæsar's friend,
he also is mortal. And if Cæsar from any circumstance becomes my enemy, where is it best for me to retire? Into a
desert? Well, does fever not come there? What shall be done
then? Is it not possible to find a safe fellow traveller, a faithful one, strong, secure against all surprises? Thus he consid-

ers and perceives that if he attaches himself to God, he will make his journey in safety.

How do you understand, "attaching yourself to God?" In this sense, that whatever God wills, a man also shall will; and what God does not will, a man also shall not will. How then shall this be done? In what other way than by examining the movements ($\acute{o}\rho\mu\grave{a}s$, the acts) of God[22] and his administration? What has he given to me as my own and in my own power? what has he reserved to himself? He has given to me the things which are in the power of the will ($\tau\grave{a}$ $\pi\rho o\alpha\iota\rho\epsilon\tau\iota\kappa\grave{a}$:) he has put them in my power free from impediment and hindrance. How was he able to make the earthly body free from hindrance? [He could not], and accordingly he has subjected to the revolution of the whole ($\tau\widetilde{\eta}$ $\tau\widetilde{\omega}\nu$ $\acute{o}\lambda\omega\nu$ $\pi\epsilon\rho\text{-}\varphi\iota\acute{o}\delta$)[23] possessions, household things, house, children, wife. Why then do I fight against God? why do I will what does not depend on the will? why do I will to have absolutely what is not granted to me? But how ought I to will to have things? In the way in which they are given and as long as they are given. But he who has given takes away.[24] Why then do I resist? I do not say that I shall be a fool if I use force to one who is stronger, but I shall first be unjust. For whence had I things when I came into the world?—My father gave them to me.—And who gave them to him? and who made the sun? and who made the fruits of the earth? and who the seasons? and who made the connection of men with one another and their fellowship?

Then after receiving everything from another and even yourself, are you angry and do you blame the giver if he takes any thing from you? Who are you, and for what purpose did you come into the world? Did not he (God) introduce you here, did he not show you the light, did he not give you fellow workers, and perceptions and reason? and as whom did he introduce you here? did he not introduce you as subject to death, and as one to live on earth with a little flesh, and to observe his administration, and to join with him in the spectacle and the festival for a short time? Will you not then, as long as you have been permitted, after seeing the spectacle and the solemnity, when he leads you out, go with adoration of him and thanks for what you have heard and seen?—No; but I would still enjoy the feast.—The initiated too would wish to be longer in the initiation: [25] and perhaps also those at Olympia to see other athletes; but the solemnity is ended: go away like a grateful and modest man; make room for others. others also must be born, as you were, and being born they must have a place, and houses and necessary things. And if the first do not retire, what remains? Why are you insatiable? Why are you not content? why do you contract the world?—Yes, but I would have my little children with me and my wife.—What, are they yours? do they not belong to the giver, and to him who made you? then will you not give up what belongs to others? will you not give way to him who is superior?—Why then did he introduce me into the world on these conditions?—And if the conditions do not suit you, depart.[26] He has no need of a spectator who is not satisfied. He wants those who join in the festival, those who take part in the chorus, that they may rather applaud, admire, and celebrate with hymns the solemnity. But those who can bear no trouble, and the cowardly he will not unwillingly see absent from the great assembly ($\pi\alpha\nu\acute{\eta}\gamma\nu\rho\iota\varsigma$); for they did not when they were present behave as they ought to do at a festival nor fill up their place properly, but they lamented, found fault with the deity, fortune, their companions; not seeing both what they had, and their own powers, which they received for contrary purposes, the powers of magnanimity, of a generous mind, manly spirit, and what we are now inquiring about, freedom.—For what purpose then have I received these things?—To use them —How long?—So long as he who has lent them chooses.—What if they are necessary to me?—Do not attach yourself to them and they will not be necessary: do not say to yourself that they are necessary, and then they are not necessary.

This study you ought to practise from morning to evening, beginning with the smallest things and those most liable to damage, with an earthen pot, with a cup. Then proceed in this way to a tunic, to a little dog, to a horse, to a small estate in land: then to yourself, to your body, to the parts of your body, to your children, to your wife, to your brothers. Look all round and throw these things from you (which are

not yours). Purge your opinions, so that nothing cleave to
you of the things which are not your own, that nothing grow
to you, that nothing give you pain when it is torn from you;
and say, while you are daily exercising yourself as you do
there (in the school), not that you are philosophizing, for
this is an arrogant (offensive) expression, but that you are
presenting an asserter of freedom: for this is really freedom.
To this freedom Diogenes was called by Antisthenes, and he
said that he could no longer be enslaved by any man. For
this reason when he was taken prisoner, how did he behave
to the pirates? Did he call any of them master? and I do not
speak of the name, for I am not afraid of the word, but of
the state of mind, by which the word is produced. How did
he reprove them for feeding badly their captives? How was
he sold? Did he seek a master? no; but a slave. And when
he was sold how did he behave to his master?[27] Immediately
he disputed with him and said to his master that he ought
not to be dressed as he was, nor shaved in such a manner; and
about the children he told them how he ought to bring them
up And what was strange in this? for if his master had
bought an exercise master, would he have employed him in
the exercises of the palæstra as a servant or as a master? and
so if he had bought a physician or an architect. And so in every matter, it is absolutely necessary that he who has skill
must be the superior of him who has not. Whoever then generally possesses the science of life, what else must he be than
master? For who is master in a ship? The man who governs
the helm? Why? Because he who will not obey him suffers
for it. But a master can give me stripes. Can he do it then
without suffering for it? So I also used to think. But because
he can not do it without suffering for it, for this reason it is
not in his power: and no man can do what is unjust without
suffering for it. And what is the penalty for him who puts his
own slave in chains? what do you think that is? The fact
of putting the slave in chains:—and you also will admit this,
if you choose to maintain the truth, that man is not a wild
beast, but a tame animal. For when is a vine doing badly?
When it is in a condition contrary to its nature. When is a
cock? Just the same. Therefore a man also is so. What then
is a man's nature? To bite, to kick, and to throw into prison

and to behead? No; but to do good, to co-operate with others, to wish them well. At that time then he is in a bad condition, whether you choose to admit it or not, when he is acting foolishly.

Socrates then did not fare badly?—No; but his judges and his accusers did.—Nor did Helvidius at Rome fare badly?— No; but his murderer did. How do you mean?—The same as you do when you say that a cock has not fared badly when he has gained the victory and been severely wounded; but that the cock has fared badly when he has been defeated and is unhurt: nor do you call a dog fortunate, who neither pursues game nor labours, but when you see him sweating,[28] when you see him in pain and panting violently after running. What paradox (unusual thing) do we utter if we say that the evil in every thing is that which is contrary to the nature of the thing? Is this a paradox? for do you not say this in the case of all other things? Why then in the case of man only do you think differently? But because we say that the nature of man is tame (gentle) and social and faithful, you will not say that this is a paradox? It is not.—What then, is it a paradox to say that a man is not hurt when he is whipped, or put in chains, or beheaded? does he not, if he suffers nobly, come off even with increased advantage and profit? But is he not hurt who suffers in a most pitiful and disgraceful way, who in place of a man becomes a wolf, or viper, or wasp?

Well then, let us recapitulate the things which have been agreed on. The man who is not under restraint is free, to whom things are exactly in that state in which he wishes them to be; but he who can be restrained or compelled or hindered, or thrown into any circumstances against his will, is a slave. But who is free from restraint? He who desires nothing that belongs to (is in the power of) others. And what are the things which belong to others? Those which are not in our power either to have or not to have, or to have of a certain kind or in a certain manner.[29] Therefore the body belongs to another, the parts of the body belong to another, possession (property) belongs to another. If then you are attached to any of these things as your own, you will pay the penalty which it is proper for him to pay who desires what belongs to another. This road leads to freedom, this is the only way of escaping from slavery, to be able to say at last with all your soul

> "Lead me, O Zeus, and thou O destiny,
> The way that I am bid by you to go "

But what do you say, philosopher? The tyrant summons you to say something which does not become you. Do you say it or do you not? Answer me.—Let me consider.—Will you consider now? But when you were in the school, what was it which you used to consider? Did you not study what are the things that are good and what are bad, and what things are neither one nor the other?—I did.—What then was our opinion?—That just and honourable acts were good; and that unjust and disgraceful (foul) acts were bad.—Is life a good thing?—No.—Is death a bad thing?—No.—Is prison?—No.—But what did we think about mean and faithless words and betrayal of a friend and flattery of a tyrant? —That they are bad.—Well then, you are not considering, nor have you considered nor deliberated. For what is the matter for consideration; is it whether it is becoming for me, when I have it in my power, to secure for myself the greatest of good things, and not to secure for myself (that is, not to avoid) the greatest evils? A fine inquiry indeed, and necessary, and one that demands much deliberation. Man, why do you mock us? Such an inquiry is never made. If you really imagined that base things were bad and honourable things were good, and that all other things were neither good nor bad, you would not even have approached this inquiry nor have come near it; but immediately you would have been able to distinguish them by the understanding as you would do (in other cases) by the vision. For when do you inquire if black things are white, if heavy things are light, and do not comprehend the manifest evidence of the senses? How then do you now say that you are considering whether things which are neither good nor bad ought to be avoided more than things which are bad? But you do not possess these opinions; and neither do these things seem to you to be neither good nor bad, but you think that they are the greatest evils; nor do you think those other things (mean and faithless words, etc.) to be evils, but matters which do not concern us at all. For thus from the beginning you have accustomed yourself. Where am I? In the schools: and are any listening to me? I am discoursing among philosophers. But I have gone out of the school. Away with this talk of scholars and fools   Thus a friend is overpowered by the testimony of a philosopher:[30] thus a philosopher becomes a parasite; thus he lets himself for hire for money: thus in the senate a man does not say what he thinks; in private (in the school) he proclaims his opinions.[31] You are a cold and miserable little opinion, suspended from idle words as from a hair. But keep yourself strong and fit for the uses of life and initiated by being exercised in action. How do you hear (the report)?—I do not say, that your child is dead—for how could you bear that?—but that your oil is spilled, your wine drunk up. Do you act in such a way that one standing by you while you are making a great noise, may say this only, "Philosopher, you say something different in the school. Why do you deceive us?   Why, when you are only a worm, do you say that you are a man?   I should like to be present when one of the philosophers is with a woman, that I might see how he is exerting himself, and what words he is uttering, and whether he remembers his title of philosopher, and the words which he hears or says or reads."

And what is this to liberty? Nothing else than this, whether you who are rich choose or not.—And who is your evidence for this?—who else than yourselves? who have a powerful master (Cæsar), and who live in obedience to his nod and motion, and who faint if he only looks at you with a scowling countenance; you who court old women[32] and old men, and say, "I can not do this: it is not in my power." Why is it not in your power?   Did you not lately contend with me and say that you are free? But Aprulla[33] has hindered me?   Tell the truth then, slave, and do not run away from your masters, nor deny, nor venture to produce any one to assert your freedom (καρπιστήν), when you have so many evidences of your slavery.   And indeed when a man is compelled by love to do something contrary to his opinion (judgment), and at the same time sees the better, but has not the strength to follow it, one might consider him still more

worthy of excuse as being held by a certain violent and in a
manner a divine power.[34] But who could endure you who
are in love with old women and old men, and wipe the old
women's noses, and wash them and give them presents, and
also wait on them like a slave when they are sick, and at the
same time wish them dead, and question the physicians
whether they are sick unto death? And again, when in order
to obtain these great and much-admired magistracies and
honours, you kiss the hands of these slaves of others, and so
you are not the slave even of free men. Then you walk about
before me in stately fashion a prætor or a consul.   Do I not
know how you became a prætor, by what means you got your
consulship, who gave it to you? I would not even choose to
live, if I must live by help of Felicion,[35] and endure his arrogance and servile insolence: for I know what a slave is, who
is fortunate, as he thinks, and puffed up by pride.

You then, a man may say, are you free? I wish, by the
Gods, and pray to be free; but I am not yet able to face my
masters, I still value my poor body, I value greatly the preservation of it entire, though I do not possess it entire.[36] But I
can point out to you a free man, that you may no longer seek
an example. Diogenes was free. How was he free?—not because he was born of free parents, but because he was himself
free, because he had cast off all the handles of slavery, and it
was not possible for any man to approach him, nor had any
man the means of laying hold of him to enslave him. He had
everything easily loosed, everything only hanging to him.
If you laid hold of his property, he would have rather let it
go and be yours, than he would have followed you for it: if
you had laid hold of his leg, he would have let go his leg; if
of all his body, all his poor body; his intimates, friends,
country, just the same. For he knew from whence he had
them, and from whom, and on what conditions. His true
parents indeed, the Gods, and his real country he would never
have deserted, nor would he have yielded to any man in obedience to them and to their orders, nor would any man have
died for his country more readily For he was not used to inquire when he should be considered to have done anything
on behalf of the whole of things (the universe, or all the
world), but he remembered that every thing which is done

comes from thence and is done on behalf of that country and is commanded by him who administers it. Therefore see what Diogenes himself says and writes :—"For this reason," he says, "Diogenes, it is in your power to speak both with the King of the Persians and with Archidamus the king of the Lacedæmonians, as you please." Was it because he was born of free parents? I suppose all the Athenians and all the Lacedæmonians because they were born of slaves, could not talk with them (these kings) as they wished, but feared and paid court to them. Why then does he say that it is in his power? Because I do not consider the poor body to be my own, because I want nothing, because law[37] is every thing to me, and nothing else is. These were the things which permitted him to be free.

And that you may not think that I show you the example of a man who is a solitary person, who has neither wife nor children, nor country, nor friends, nor kinsmen, by whom he could be bent and drawn in various directions, take Socrates and observe that he had a wife and children, but he did not consider them as his own; that he had a country, so long as it was fit to have one, and in such a manner as was fit; friends and kinsmen also, but he held all in subjection to law and to the obedience due to it. For this reason he was the first to go out as a soldier, when it was necessary, and in war he exposed himself to danger most unsparingly;[38] and when he was sent by the tyrants to seize Leon, he did not even deliberate about the matter, because he thought that it was a base action, and he knew that he must die (for his refusal), if it so happened.[39] And what difference did that make to him? for he intended to preserve something else, not his poor flesh, but his fidelity, his honourable character. These are things which could not be assailed nor brought into subjection. Then when he was obliged to speak in defence of his life, did he behave like a man who had children, who had a wife? No, but he behaved like a man who has neither. And what did he do when he was (ordered) to drink the poison,[40] and when he had the power of escaping from prison, and when Crito said to him, Escape for the sake of your children, what did Socrates say?[41] did he consider the power of escape as an unexpected gain? By no means: he considered what was fit and proper; but the rest he did not even look at or take into the reckoning. For he did not choose, he said, to save his poor body, but to save that which is increased and saved by doing what is just, and is impaired and destroyed by doing what is unjust. Socrates will not save his life by a base act; he who would not put the Athenians to the vote when they clamoured that he should do so,[42] he who refused to obey the tyrants, he who discoursed in such a manner about virtue and right behaviour It is not possible to save such a man's life by base acts, but he is saved by dying, not by running away. For the good actor also preserves his character by stopping when he ought to stop, better than when he goes on acting beyond the proper time. What then shall the children of Socrates do? "If," said Socrates, "I had gone off to Thessaly, would you have taken care of them; and if I depart to the world below, will there be no man to take care of them?" See how he gives to death a gentle name and mocks it. But if you and I had been in his place, we should have immediately answered as philosophers that those who act unjustly must be repaid in the same way, and we should have added, "I shall be useful to many, if my life is saved, and if I die, I shall be useful to no man." For, if it had been necessary, we should have made our escape by slipping through a small hole. And how in that case should we have been useful to any man? for where would they have been then staying?[43] or if we were useful to men while we were alive, should we not have been much more useful to them by dying when we ought to die, and as we ought? And now Socrates being dead, no less useful to men, and even more useful, is the remembrance of that which he did or said when he was alive.[44]

Think of these things, these opinions, these words: look to these examples, if you would be free, if you desire the thing according to its worth. And what is the wonder if you buy so great a thing at the price of things so many and so great? For the sake of this which is called liberty, some hang themselves, others throw themselves down precipices, and sometimes even whole cities have perished: and will you not for the sake of the true and unassailable and secure liberty give back to God when he demands them the things which he has given? Will you not, as Plato says, study not to die only, but also to endure torture, and exile, and scourging and in a word to give up all which is not your own? If you will not, you will be a slave among slaves, even if you be ten thousand times a consul, and if you make your way up to the Palace (Cæsar's residence), you will no less be a slave; and you will feel, that perhaps philosophers utter words which are contrary to common opinion (paradoxes), as Cleanthes also said, but not words contrary to reason. For you will know by experience that the words are true, and that there is no profit from the things which are valued and eagerly sought to those who have obtained them; and to those who have not yet obtained them there is an imagination ($\phi a \nu \tau a \sigma i a$), that when these things are come, all that is good will come with them; then, when they are come, the feverish feeling is the same, the tossing to and fro is the same, the satiety, the desire of things which are not present; for freedom is acquired not by the full possession of the things which are desired, but by removing the desire. And that you may know that this is true, as you have laboured for those things, so transfer your labour to these; be vigilant for the purpose of acquiring an opinion which will make you free; pay court to a philosopher instead of to a rich old man: be seen about a philosopher's doors: you will not disgrace yourself by being seen; you will not go away empty nor without profit, if you go to the philosopher as you ought, and if not (if you do not succeed), try at least: the trial (attempt) is not disgraceful.

NOTES

[1] Cicero, Paradox. v. "Quid enim libertas? Potestas vivendi ut velis. Quis igitur vivit ut vult, nisi qui recta sequitur," etc
[2] "Whoever committeth sin, is the servant of sin," John viii. 34. Mrs. Carter.
[3] A usual form of oath. See ii 20, 29 Upton compares the Roman expression "Per Genium," as in Horace, Epp. i. 7, 94—

"Quod te per Genium, dextramque, Deosque Penates
Obsecro et obtestor."

[4] A lover's exclusion by his mistress was a common topic, and a serious cause of complaint (Lucretius, iv. 1172):

"At lacrimans exclusus amator limina sæpe
Floribus et sertis operit."

See also Horace, Odes, i. 25.

⁵ Thrasonides was a character in one of Menander's plays, entitled Μισούμενος or the Hated.

⁶ It must have been rather difficult to manage a tame lion; but we read of such things among the Romans. Seneca, Epp. 41.

⁷ The keeping of birds in cages, parrots and others, was also common among the Romans. Ovid (Amor. ii. 6) has written a beautiful elegy on the death of a favourite parrot.

⁸ See ii. 1, 26. The εικοστώναι were the Publicani, men who farmed this and other taxes. A tax of a twentieth of the value of a slave when manumitted was established at an early time (Livy vii. 16). It appears from this passage that the manumitted slave paid the tax out of his savings (peculium). See ii. 1, note 7.

⁹ The reader may guess the meaning.

¹⁰ A gold ring was worn by the Equites; and accordingly to desire the gold ring is the same as to desire to be raised to the Equestrian class.

¹¹ The colophon. See ii. 14, note 5. After the words "most splendid slavery" it is probable that some words have accidentally been omitted in the manuscript.

¹² Saturnalia. See i 25, note 3.
At this season the slaves had liberty to enjoy themselves and to talk freely with their masters. Hence Horace says Sat ii. 74—

"Age, libertate Decembri,
Quando ita majores voluerunt utere."

¹³ Schweighäuser observes that death is in our power, as the Stoics taught; and Epictetus often tells us that the door is open. He suggests that the true reading may be και ούκ αποθανείν. I think that the text is right. Epictetus asks is "Life or Death" in our power. He means no more than if he had said Life only.

¹⁴ He means that which seems to you to be false. See iii. 22, 42.

"In the matter of assent then": this is the third τόπος or "locus" or division in philosophy (iii. 2, 1-5). As to the will, compare i. 17, note 10. Epictetus affirms that a man can not be compelled to assent, that is to admit, to allow, or, to use another word, to believe in that which seems to him to be false, or, to use the same word again, to believe in that in which he does not believe. When the Christian uses the two creeds, which begin with the words, "I believe, etc.," he knows or he ought to know, that he can not compel an unbeliever to accept the same belief. He may by pains and penalties of various kinds compel some persons to profess or to express the same belief; but as no pains or penalties could compel some Christians to deny their belief, so I suppose that perhaps there are men who could not be compelled to express this belief when they have it not. The case of the believer and the unbeliever however are not the same. The believer may be strengthened in his belief by the belief that he will in some way be punished by God, if he denies that which he believes. The unbeliever will not have the same motive or reason for not expressing his assent to that which he does not believe. He believes that it is and will be all the same to him with respect to God, whether he gives his assent to that which he does not believe or refuses his assent. There remains nothing then to trouble him if he expresses his assent to that which he does not believe, except the opinion of those who know that he does not believe, or his own reflections on expressing his assent to that which he does not believe; or in other words his publication of a lie, which may probably do no harm to any man or in any way. I believe that some men are strong enough, under some circumstances at least, to refuse their assent to any thing which they do not believe; but I do not affirm that they would do this under all circumstances

To return to the matter under consideration, a man can not be compelled by any power to accept voluntarily a thing as true, when he believes that it is not true; and this act of his is quite independent of the matter whether his unbelief is well founded or not He does not believe because he can not believe. Yet it is said (Mark xvi 16) in the received text, as it now stands, "He that believeth and is baptized shall be saved; but he that believeth not, shall be damned" (condemned) The cause, as it is called, of this unbelief is explained by some theologians; but all men do not admit the explanation to be sufficient; and it does not concern the present subject.

¹⁴ The word "admire" is θαυμάσης in the original The word is often used by Epictetus, and Horace uses "admirari" in this Stoical sense See i. 29 2, note.

¹⁵ The word is ἀγγαρεία, a word of Persian origin (Herodotus, viii. 98). It means here the seizure of animals for military purposes when it is necessary. Upton refers to Matthew 5, v. 41, Mark 15, c. 21 for similar uses of the verb ἀγγαρεύω.

¹⁷ Here he speaks of asses being shod. The Latin translation of the word (ὑποζημάτια) in Epictetus is "ferreæ calces." I suppose they could use nothing but iron

¹⁸ The word is ἀποτειχίζω, which means what I have translated. The purpose of circumvallation was to take and sometimes also to destroy a fortress. Schweig. translates the word by "destruam," and that is perhaps not contrary to the meaning of the text; but it is not the exact meaning of the word.

¹⁹ In this passage and in what follows we find the emphatic affirmation of the duty of conformity and of the subjection of man's will to the will of God. The words are conclusive evidence of the doctrine of Epictetus that a man ought to subject himself in all things to the will of God or to that which he believes to be the will of God. No Christian martyr ever proclaimed a more solemn obedience to God's will. The Christian martyr indeed has given perfect proof of his sincerity by enduring torments and death: the heathen philosopher was not put to the same test, and we can not therefore say that he would have been able to bear it.

²⁰ In this passage the distinction must be observed between θέλω and βούλομαι which the Latin translators have not observed, nor Mrs. Carter See Schweig.'s note on s. 90.

²¹ ἐν τῷ κόσμῳ : he means "on earth."

²² Schweig. expresses his surprise that Epictetus has applied this word (ὁρμάς) to God. He says that Wolf has translated it "Dei appetitionem," and Upton "impetum." He says that he has translated it "consilium."

It is not unusual for men to speak of God in the same words in which they speak of man

²³ See ii 1, 18. Schweig. expected that Epictetus would have said "body and possessions, etc." I assume that Epictetus did say "body and possessions, etc.," and that his pupil or some copyist of manuscripts has omitted the word "body."

²⁴ "The Lord gave and the Lord hath taken away. Job i. 21" Mrs. Carter.

²⁵ The initiated (μύσται) are those who were introduced with solemn ceremonies into some great religious body. These ceremonies are described by Dion Prus. Orat. xii., quoted by Upton.

[26] "And this is all the comfort, every serious reader will be apt to say, which one of the best philosophers, in one of his noblest discourses, can give to the good man under severe distress? 'Either tell yourself that present suffering void of future hope, is no evil, or give up your existence and mingle with the elements of the Universe'! Unspeakably more rational and more worthy of infinite goodness is our blessed Master's exhortation to the persecuted Christian: 'Rejoice and be exceedingly glad, for great is your reward in heaven.'" Mrs Carter.

I do not think that Mrs. Carter has represented correctly the teaching of Epictetus He is addressing men who were not Christians, but were, as he assumes, believers in God or in the gods, and his argument is that a man ought to be contented with things as they are, because they are from God If he can not be contented with things as they are, and make the best of them, the philosopher can say no more to the man. He tells him to depart. What else could he say to a grumbler, who is also a believer in God? If he is not a believer, Epictetus might say the same to him also The case is past help or advice.

The Christian doctrine, of which probably Epictetus knew nothing, is very different It promises future happiness on certain conditions to Christians, but to Christians only, if I understand it right.

[27] See the same story in Aulus Gellius (ii. c. 18), who says that Xeniades, a Corinthian, bought Diogenes, manumitted him and made him the master of his children

[28] I do not know if dogs sweat: at least in a state of health I have never seen it. But this is a question for the learned in dog science.

[29] As Upton remarks, Epictetus is referring to the four categories of the Stoics

[30] "Stoicus occidit Bareum, delator amicum,
        Discipulumque senex."

                                              Juvenal, iii 116.

Epictetus is supposed to allude to the crime of Egnatius Celer who accused Barea Soranus at Rome in the reign of Nero (Tacit. Ann. xvi. 32).

[31] Mrs Carter says that "there is much obscurity and some variety of reading in the lines of the original" But see Schweig's notes Epictetus is showing that talk about philosophy is useless: philosophy should be practical.

[32] Horace Sat ii. 5

[33] Aprulla is a Roman woman's name. It means some old woman who is courted for her money.

[34] Compare Plato (Symposium, p. 206): "All men conceive both as to the body and as to the soul, and when they have arrived at a certain age, our nature desires to procreate But it can not procreate in that which is ugly, but in that which is beautiful For the conjunction of man and woman is generation, but this act is divine, and this in the animal which is mortal is divine, conceiving and begetting." See what is said in ii. 23, note 5 on marrying In a certain sense the procreation of children is a duty, and consequently the providing for them is also a duty. It is the fulfilling of the will and purpose of the Deity to people the earth; and therefore the act of procreation is divine So a man's duty is to labour in some way, and if necessary, to earn his living and sustain the life which he has received; and this is also a divine act Paul's opinion of marriage is contained in Cor. i 7. Some of his teaching on this matter has been justly condemned. He has no conception of the true nature of marriage;

at least he does not show that he has in this chapter. His teaching is impracticable, contrary to that of Epictetus, and to the nature and constitution of man, and it is rejected by the good sense of Christians who affect to receive his teaching; except, I suppose, by the superstitious body of Christians, who recommend and commend the so-called religious, and unmarried life.

[35] Felicion   See i. 19.

[36] Epictetus alludes to his lameness: compare i. 8. 14, i. 16. 20, and other passages. Upton.

[37] The sense of "law" (ὀνόμος), can be collected from what follows Compare the discourse of Socrates on obedience to the law. (Criton, c. 11, etc)

[38] Socrates fought at Potidæa, Amphipolis and Delium.   He is said to have gained the prize for courage at Delium.   He was a brave soldier as well as a philosopher, a union of qualities not common.   (Plato's Apology.)

[39] Socrates with others was ordered by the Thirty tyrants, who at that time governed Athens, to arrest Leon in the island of Salamis and to bring him to be put to death. But Socrates refused to obey the order. Few men would have done what he did under the circumstances. (Plato's Apology; M Antoninus, vii 66.)

[40] Cicero, Tuscul. Disp. i. 29.

[41] The Dialogue of Plato, named Criton, contains the arguments which were used by his friends to persuade Socrates to escape from prison, and the reply of Socrates.

[42] This alludes to the behaviour of Socrates when he refused to put to the vote the matter of the Athenian generals and their behaviour after the naval battle of Arginusæ   The violence of the weather prevented the commanders from collecting and honourably burying those who fell in the battle; and the Athenians after their hasty fashion, wished all the commanders to be put to death.   But Socrates, who was in office at this time resisted the unjust clamour of the people   Xenophon Hellenica, i c 7, 15; Plato, Apologia; Xenophon, Memorab. i 1, 18.

[43] The original is ποῦ γὰρ ἂν ἔτι ἔμενον ἐκεῖνοι; this seems to mean, if we had escaped and left the country, where would those have been to whom we might have been useful? They would have been left behind, and we could have done nothing for them

[44] This is the conclusion about Socrates, whom Epictetus highly valued: the remembrance of what Socrates did and said is even more useful than his life "The life of the dead," says Cicero of Servius Sulpicius, the great Roman jurist and Cicero's friend, "rests in the remembrance of the living." Epictetus has told us of some of the acts of Socrates, which prove him to have been a brave and honest man He does not tell us here what Socrates said, which means what he taught; but he knew what it was Modern writers have expounded the matter at length, and in a form which Epictetus would not or could not have used — Socrates left to others the questions which relate to the material world, and he first taught, as we are told, the things which concern man's daily life and his intercourse with other men: in other words he taught Ethic (the principles of morality). Fields and trees, he said, will teach me nothing, but man in his social state will: and man then is the proper subject of the philosophy of Socrates.   The beginning of this knowledge was, as he said, to know himself according to the precept of the Delphic oracle "Know thyself" (γνῶθι σεαυτόν): and the object of his philosophy was to comprehend the nature of man as a moral being in all relations; and among these the

relation of man to God as the father of all, creator and ruler of all, as Plato expresses it. Socrates taught that what we call death is not the end of man; death is only the road to another life. "The death of Socrates was conformable to his life and teaching. Socrates died not only with the noblest courage and tranquillity, but he also refused, as we are told, to escape from death, which the laws of the state permitted, by going into exile or paying a fine, because as he said, if he had himself consented to a fine or allowed others to propose it, (Xenophon, Apol § 22), such an act would have been an admission of his guilt Both (Socrates and Jesus) offered themselves with the firmest resolution for a holy cause, which was so far from being lost through their death that it only served rather to make it the general cause of mankind." (Das Christliche des Platonismus oder Socrates and Christus, by F. C. Baur.)

This essay by Baur is very ingenious. Perhaps there are some readers who will disagree with him on many points in the comparison of Socrates and Christ. However the essay is well worth the trouble of reading.

The opinion of Rousseau in his comparison of Jesus and Socrates is in some respects more just than that of Baur, though the learning of the Frenchman is very small when compared with that of the German. "What prejudices, what blindness must a man have," says Rousseau, "when he dares to compare the son of Sophronicus with the son of Mary!—the death of Socrates philosophising tranquil with his friends is the most gentle that a man could desire: that of Jesus expiring in torments, insulted, jeered, cursed by a whole people, is the most horrible that a man could dread Socrates taking the poisoned cup blesses him who presents it and weeps, Jesus in his horrible punishment prays for his savage executioners. Yes, if the life and the death of Socrates are those of a sage, the life and the death of Jesus are those of a God." (Rousseau, Emile, vol. iii. p. 166. Amsterdam, 1765.)

CHAPTER II

ON FAMILIAR INTIMACY

TO this matter before all you must attend, that you be never so closely connected with any of your former intimates or friends as to come down to the same acts as he does.[1] If you do not observe this rule, you will ruin yourself. But if the thought arises in your mind, "I shall seem disobliging to him and he will not have the same feeling towards me," remember that nothing is done without cost, nor is it possible for a man if he does not do the same things to be the same man that he was. Choose then which of the two you will have, to be equally loved by those by whom you were formerly loved, being the same with your former self; or, being superior, not to obtain from your friends the same that you did before For if this is better, immediately turn away to it, and let no other considerations draw you in a different direction. For no man is able to make progress (improvement), when he is wavering between opposite things; but if you have preferred this (one thing) to all things, if you choose to attend to this only, to work out this only, give up every thing else. But if you will not do this, your wavering will produce both these results: you will neither improve as you ought, nor will you obtain what you formerly obtained. For before by plainly desiring the things which were worth nothing, you pleased your associates. But you can not excel in both kinds, and it is necessary that so far as you share in the one, you must fall short in the other. You can not, when you do not drink with those with whom you used to drink, be agreeable to them as you were before. Choose then whether you will be a hard drinker and pleasant to your former associates or a sober man and disagreeable to them. You can not, when you do not sing with those with whom you used to sing, be equally loved by them. Choose then in this matter also which of the two you will have. For if it is better to be modest and orderly than for a man to say he is a jolly fellow, give up the rest, renounce it, turn away from it, have nothing to do with such men. But if this behaviour shall not please you, turn altogether to the opposite: become a catamite, an adulterer, and act accordingly, and you will get what you wish. And jump up in the theatre and bawl out in praise of the dancer. But characters so different can not be mingled: you can not act both Thersites and Agamemnon. If you intend to be Thersites,[2] you must be hump-backed and bald: if Agamemnon, you must be tall and handsome, and love those who are placed in obedience to you.

NOTES

[1] He means that you must not do as he does, because he does this or that act The advice is in substance, Do not do as your friend does simply because he is your friend.

[2] See Iliad, ii. 216; and for the description of Agamemnon, Iliad, iii. 167.

CHAPTER III

WHAT THINGS WE SHOULD EXCHANGE FOR OTHER THINGS

KEEP this thought in readiness, when you lose any thing external, what you acquire in place of it; and if it be worth more, never say, I have had a loss; neither if you have got a horse in place of an ass, or an ox in place of a sheep, nor a good action in place of a bit of money, nor in place of idle talk such tranquillity as befits a man, nor in place of lewd talk if you have acquired modesty If you remember this, you will always maintain your character such as it ought to be. But if you do not, consider that the times of opportunity are perishing, and that whatever pains you take about yourself, you are going to waste them all and overturn them. And it needs only a few things for the loss and overturning of all, namely a small deviation from reason. For the steerer of a ship to upset it, he has no need of the same means as he has need of for saving it: but if he turns it a little to the wind, it is lost; and if he does not do this purposely, but has been neglecting his duty a little, the ship is lost. Something of the kind happens in this case also: if you only fall a nodding a little, all that you have up to this time collected is gone. Attend therefore to the appearances of things, and watch over them; for that which you have to preserve is no small matter, but it is modesty and fidelity and constancy, freedom from the affects, a state of mind undisturbed, freedom from fear, tranquillity, in a word liberty For what will you sell these things? See what is the value of the things which you will obtain in exchange for these.—But shall I not obtain any such thing for it?—See, and if you do in return get that, see what you receive in place of it. I possess decency, he possesses a tribuneship: he possesses a prætorship, I possess modesty. But I do not make acclamations where it is not becoming: I will not stand up where I ought not;[1] for I am free, and a friend of God, and so I obey him willingly. But I must not claim (seek) any thing else, neither body nor possession, nor magistracy, nor good report, nor in fact any thing. For he (God) does not allow me to claim (seek) them : for if he had chosen, he would have made them good for me;' but he has not done so, and for this reason I can not transgress his commands. Preserve that which is your own good in every thing; and as to every other thing, as it is permitted, and so far as to behave consistently with reason in respect to them, content with this only. If you do not, you will be unfortunate, you will fail in all things, you will be hindered, you will be impeded. These are the laws which have been sent from thence (from God) ; these are the orders. Of these laws a man ought to be an expositor, to these he ought to submit, not to those of Masurius and Cassius.[2]

NOTES

[1] He alludes to the factions in the theatres, iii 4, 4; iv. 2-9. Upton
[2] Masurius Sabinus was a great Roman jurisconsult in the times of Augustus and Tiberius. He is sometimes named Masurius only (Persius, v. 90)   C Cassius Longinus was also a jurist, and, it is said, a descendant of the Cassius, who was one of the murderers of the dictator Caius Cæsar. He lived from the time of Tiberius to that of Vespasian.

CHAPTER IV

TO THOSE WHO ARE DESIROUS OF PASSING LIFE IN TRANQUILLITY

REMEMBER that not only the desire of power and of riches makes us mean and subject to others, but even the desire of tranquillity, and of leisure, and of travelling abroad, and of learning. For to speak plainly, whatever the external thing may be, the value which we set upon it places us in subjection to others. What then is the difference between desiring to be a senator or not desiring to be one; what is the difference between desiring power or being content with a private station; what is the difference between saying, I am unhappy, I have nothing to do, but I am bound to my books as a corpse; or saying, I am unhappy, I have no leisure for reading? For as salutations and power are things external and independent of the will, so is a book. For what purpose do you choose to read? Tell me For if you only direct your purpose to being amused or learning something, you are a silly fellow and incapable of enduring labour.[1] But if you refer reading to the proper end, what else is this than a tranquil and happy life ($\varepsilon \dot{v} \delta o \iota a$)? But if reading does not secure for you a happy and tranquil life, what is the use of it? But it does secure this, the man replies, and for this reason I am vexed that I am deprived of it. —And what is this tranquil and happy life, which any man can impede, I do not say Cæsar or Cæsar's friend, but a crow, a piper, a fever, and thirty thousand other things? But a tranquil and happy life contains nothing so sure as continuity and freedom from obstacle Now I am called to do something: I will go then with the purpose of observing the measures (rules) which I must keep,[2] of acting with modesty, steadiness, without desire and aversion to things external,[3] and then that I may attend to men, what they say, how they are moved;[4] and this not with any bad disposition, or that I may have something to blame or to ridicule; but I turn to myself, and ask if I also commit the same faults.

How then shall I cease to commit them? Formerly I also acted wrong, but now I do not; thanks to God.

Come, when you have done these things and have attended to them, have you done a worse act than when you have read a thousand verses or written as many? For when you eat, are you grieved because you are not reading? are you not satisfied with eating according to what you have learned by reading, and so with bathing and with exercise? Why then do you not act consistently in all things, both when you approach Cæsar, and when you approach any person? If you maintain yourself free from perturbation, free from alarm, and steady; if you look rather at the things which are done and happen than are looked at yourself; if you do not envy those who are preferred before you; if surrounding circumstances (ὕλαι) do not strike you with fear or admiration, what do you want? Books? How or for what purpose? for is not this (the reading of books) a preparation for life? and is not life itself (living) made up of certain other things than this? This is just as if an athlete should weep when he enters the stadium, because he is not being exercised outside of it. It was for this purpose that you used to practise exercise; for this purpose were used the haltéres (weights),[5] the dust, the young men as antagonists; and do you seek for those things now when it is the time of action? This is just as if in the topic (matter) of assent when appearances present themselves, some of which can be comprehended, and some can not be comprehended, we should not choose to distinguish them but should choose to read what has been written about comprehension (κατάληψις).

What then is the reason of this? The reason is that we have never read for this purpose, we have never written for this purpose, so that we may in our actions use in a way conformable to nature the appearances presented to us; but we terminate in this, in learning what is said, and in being able to expound it to another, in resolving a syllogism,[6] and in handling the hypothetical syllogism. For this reason where our study (purpose) is, there alone is the impediment. Would you have by all means the things which are not in your power? Be prevented then, be hindered, fail in your purpose. But if we read what is written about action (efforts,)ὁρμή, not that we may see what is said about action, but that we may act well: if we read what is said about desire and aversion (avoiding things), in order that we may neither fail in our desires, nor fall into that which we try to avoid; if we read what is said about duty (officium), in order that remembering the relations (of things to one another) we may do nothing irrationally nor contrary to these relations; we should not be vexed in being hindered as to our readings, but we should be satisfied with doing the acts which are conformable (to the relations), and we should be reckoning not what so far we have been accustomed to reckon: To-day I have read so many verses, I have written so many; but (we should say), To-day I have employed my action as it is taught by the philosophers; I have not employed my desire; I have used avoidance (ἐκκλίσει) only with respect to things which are within the power of my will; I have not been afraid of such a person, I have not been prevailed upon by the entreaties of another; I have exercised my patience,[7] my abstinence, my co-operation with others; and so we should thank God for what we ought to thank him.

But now we do not know that we also in another way are like the many. Another man is afraid that he shall not have power: you are afraid that you will. Do not do so, my man; but as you ridicule him who is afraid that he shall not have power, so ridicule yourself also. For it makes no difference whether you are thirsty like a man who has a fever, or have a dread of water like a man who is mad. Or how will you still be able to say as Socrates did, "If so it pleases God, so let it be?" Do you think that Socrates if he had been eager to pass his leisure in the Lyceum or in the Academy and to discourse daily with the young men, would have readily served in military expeditions so often as he did, and would he not have lamented and groaned, "Wretch that I am; I must now be miserable here, when I might be sunning myself in the Lyceum?" Why, was this your business, to sun yourself? And is it not your business to be happy, to be free from hindrance, free from impediment? And could he still have been Socrates, if he had lamented in this way: how would he still have been able to write Pæans in his prison?[8]

In short remember this, that what you shall prize which is

beyond your will, so far you have destroyed your will. But these things are out of the power of the will, not only power (authority), but also a private condition: not only occupation (business), but also leisure.—Now then must I live in this tumult?—Why do you say tumult?—I mean among many men.—Well what is the hardship? Suppose that you are at Olympia · imagine it to be a panegyris (public assembly), where one is calling out one thing, another is doing another thing, and a third is pushing another person: in the baths there is a crowd: and who of us is not pleased with this assembly, and leaves it unwillingly? Be not difficult to please nor fastidious about what happens.—Vinegar is disagreeable, for it is sharp; honey is disagreeable, for it disturbs my habit of body. I do not like vegetables. So also I do not like leisure; it is a desert : I do not like a crowd; it is confusion.— But if circumstances make it necessary for you to live alone or with a few, call it quiet, and use the thing as you ought: 'talk with yourself, exercise the appearances (presented to you), work up your preconceptions. If you fall into a crowd, call it a celebration of games, a panegyris, a festival: try to enjoy the festival with other men. For what is a more pleasant sight to him who loves mankind than a number of men? We see with pleasure herds of horses or oxen: we are delighted when we see many ships: who is pained when he sees many men?—But they deafen me with their cries.—Then your hearing is impeded. What then is this to you? Is then the power of making use of appearances hindered? And who prevents you from using according to nature inclination to a thing and aversion from it; and movement towards a thing and movement from it? What tumult (confusion) is able to do this?

Do you only bear in mind the general rules: what is mine, what is not mine; what is given (permitted) to me; what does God will that I should do now? what does he not will? A little before he willed you to be at leisure, to talk with yourself, to write about these things, to read, to hear, to prepare yourself. You had sufficient time for this. Now he says to you: "Come now to the contest, show us what you have learned, how you have practised the athletic art. How long

will you be exercised alone? Now is the opportunity for you
to learn whether you are an athlete worthy of victory, or one
of those who go about the world and are defeated." Why
then are you vexed? No contest is without confusion. There
must be many who exercise themselves for the contest, many
who call out to those who exercise themselves, many masters,
many spectators.—But my wish is to live quietly.—Lament
then and groan as you deserve to do. For what other is a
greater punishment than this to the untaught man and to him
who disobeys the divine commands, to be grieved, to lament,
to envy, in a word to be disappointed and to be unhappy?
Would you not release yourself from these things?—And
how shall I release myself?—Have you not often heard, that
you ought to remove entirely desire, apply aversion (turning away) to those things only which are within your power,
that you ought to give up every thing, body, property, fame,
books, tumult, power, private station? for whatever way you
turn, you are a slave, you are subjected, you are hindered, you
are compelled, you are entirely in the power of others. But
keep the words of Cleanthes in readiness.

"Lead me, O Zeus, and thou necessity." *

Is it your will that I should go to Rome? I will go to
Rome. To Gyara? I will go to Gyara. To Athens? I will go
to Athens. To prison? I will go to prison. If you should
once say, "When shall a man go to Athens?" you are undone. It is a necessary consequence that this desire, if it is
not accomplished, must make you unhappy; and if it is accomplished, it must make you vain, since you are elated at
things at which you ought not to be elated; and on the other
hand, if you are impeded, it must make you wretched because you fall into that which you would not fall into. Give
up then all these things.—Athens is a good place.—But happiness is much better; and to be free from passions, free from
disturbance, for your affairs not to depend on any man. There
is tumult at Rome and visits of salutation.[10] But happiness
is an equivalent for all troublesome things. If then the time
comes for these things, why do you not take away the wish
to avoid them? what necessity is there to carry a burden like

an ass, and to be beaten with a stick? But if you do not so, consider that you must always be a slave to him who has it in his power to effect your release, and also to impede you, and you must serve him as an evil genius.

There is only one way to happiness, and let this rule be ready both in the morning and during the day and by night: the rule is not to look towards things which are out of the power of our will, to think that nothing is our own, to give up all things to the Divinity, to Fortune; to make them the superintendents of these things, whom Zeus also has made so; for a man to observe that only which is his own, that which can not be hindered; and when we read, to refer our reading to this only, and our writing and our listening. For this reason I can not call the man industrious, if I hear this only, that he reads and writes; and even if a man adds that he reads all night, I can not say so, if he knows not to what he should refer his reading. For neither do you say that a man is industrious if he keeps awake for a girl; nor do I. But if he does it (reads and writes) for reputation, I say that he is a lover of reputation. And if he does it for money, I say that he is a lover of money, not a lover of labour, and if he does it through love of learning, I say that he is a lover of learning. But if he refers his labour to his own ruling power (ἡγεμονικόν), that he may keep it in a state conformable to nature and pass his life in that state, then only do I say that he is industrious. For never commend a man on account of these things which are common to all, but on account of his opinions (principles); for these are the things which belong to each man, which make his actions bad or good. Remembering these rules, rejoice in that which is present, and be content with the things which come in season.[11] If you see any thing which you have learned and inquired about occurring to you in your course of life (or opportunely applied by you to the acts of life), be delighted at it. If you have laid aside or have lessened bad disposition and a habit of reviling; if you have done so with rash temper, obscene words, hastiness, sluggishness; if you are not moved by what you formerly were, and not in the same way as you once were, you can celebrate a festival daily, to-day because you have behaved well in one act, and to-morrow because you have behaved well in another. How much greater is this a reason for making sacrifices than a consulship or the government of a province? These things come to you from yourself and from the gods. Remember this, who gives these things and to whom, and for what purpose. If you cherish yourself in these thoughts, do you still think that it makes any difference where you shall be happy, where you shall please God? Are not the gods equally distant from all places? Do they not see from all places alike that which is going on?

NOTES

[1] See Bishop Butler's remarks in the Preface to his Sermons vol. ii. He speaks of the "idle way of reading and considering things, by this means, time even in solitude is happily got rid of without the pain of attention neither is any part of it more put to the account of idleness, one can scarce forbear saying, is spent with less thought than great part of that which is spent in reading"

[2] "Sed veræ numerosque modosque ediscere vitæ." Hor. Epp ii 2, 144   M Antoninus, iii. 1

[3] "The readers perhaps may grow tired with being so often told what they will find it very difficult to believe, That because externals are not in our power, they are nothing to us   But in excuse for this frequent repetition, it must be considered that the Stoics had reduced themselves to a necessity of dwelling on this consequence, extravagant as it is, by rejecting stronger aids.   One can not indeed avoid highly admiring the very few, who attempted to amend and exalt themselves on this foundation   No one perhaps ever carried the attempt so far in practice, and no one ever spoke so well in support of the argument as Epictetus   Yet, notwithstanding his great abilities and the force of his example, one finds him strongly complaining of the want of success, and one sees from this circumstance as well as from others in the Stoic writings, That virtue can not be maintained in the world without the hope of a future reward." Mrs Carter.

[4] Compare Horace, Sat 1. 4, 133; "Noque enim cum lectulus," etc.

[5] See 1. 4, note 5, iii. 15, 4; and i 24, 1, 1. 29, 34.   The athletes were oiled, but they used to rub themselves with dust to be enabled to lay hold of one another.

[6] M. Antoninus, i. 17, thanks the Gods that he did not waste his time in the resolution of syllogisms.

[7] See Aulus Gellius xvii. 19, where he quotes Epictetus on what Gellius expresses by "intolerantia" and "incontinentia"   Compare M. Antoninus (v. 33) on the precept Ἀνέχου and Ἀπέχου.

[8] Plato in the Phædon (c. 4) says that Socrates in his prison wrote a hymn to Apollo.

[9] Cleanthes was a Stoic philosopher, who also wrote some poetry.

[10] He alludes to the practice of dependents paying formal visits in the morning at the houses of the great and powerful at Rome   Upton refers to Virgil, Georgics, ii. 461

[11] See Antoninus, vi 2; and ix. 6 "Thy present opinion founded on understanding, and thy present conduct directed to social good, and thy present disposition of contentment with everything which happens—that is enough."

CHAPTER V

THE wise and good man neither himself fights with any person, nor does he allow another, so far as he can prevent it. And an example of this as well as of all other things is proposed to us in the life of Socrates, who not only himself on all occasions avoided fights (quarrels), but would not allow even others to quarrel. See in Xenophon's "Symposium" how many quarrels he settled, how further he endured Thrasymachus and Polus and Callicles; how he tolerated his wife, and how he tolerated his son who attempted to confute him and to cavil with him. For he remembered well that no man has in his power another man's ruling principle. He wished therefore for nothing else than that which was his own. And what is this? Not that this or that man may act according to nature, for that is a thing which belongs to another; but that while others are doing their own acts, as they choose, he may nevertheless be in a condition conformable to nature and live in it, only doing what is his own to the end that others also may be in a state conformable to nature. For this is the object always set before him by the wise and good man. Is it to be commander (a prætor) of an army? No; but if it is permitted him, his object is in this matter to maintain his own ruling principle. Is it to marry? No; but if marriage is allowed to him, in this matter his object is to maintain himself in a condition conformable to nature. But if he would have his son not to do wrong or his wife, he would have what belongs to another not to belong to another: and to be instructed is this, to learn what things are a man's own and what belongs to another.

How then is there left any place for fighting (quarrelling) to a man who has this opinion (which he ought to have)? Is he surprised at any thing which happens, and does it appear new to him? Does he not expect that which comes from the bad to be worse and more grievous than what actually befalls him? And does he not reckon as pure gain whatever they '(the bad) may do which falls short of extreme wickedness? Such a person has reviled you. Great thanks to him for not having struck you. But he has struck me also. Great thanks that he did not wound you. But he wounded me also. Great thanks that he did not kill you. For when did he learn or in what school that man is a tame[1] animal, that men love one another, that an act of injustice is a great harm to him who does it. Since then he has not learned this and is not convinced of it, why shall he not follow that which seems to be for his own interest? Your neighbour has thrown stones. Have you then done any thing wrong? But the things in the house have been broken. Are you then a utensil? No; but a free power of will.[2] What then is given to you (to do) in answer to this? If you are like a wolf, you must bite in return, and throw more stones. But if you consider what is proper for a man, examine your storehouse, see with what faculties you came into the world. Have you the disposition of a wild beast, have you the disposition of revenge for an injury? When is a horse wretched? When he is deprived of his natural faculties, not when he can not crow like a cock, but when he can not run. When is a dog wretched? Not when he can not fly, but when he can not track his game. Is then a man also unhappy in this way, not because he can not strangle lions or embrace statues,[3] for he did not come into the world in the possession of certain powers from nature for this purpose, but because he has lost his probity and his fidelity? People ought to meet and lament such a man for the misfortunes into which he has fallen; not indeed to lament because a man has been born or has died,[4] but because it has happened to him in his life time to have lost the things which are his own, not that which he received from his father, not his land and house, and his inn, and his slaves; for not one of these things is a man's own, but all belong to others, are service, and subject to account (ὑπεύθυνα). at different times given to different persons by those who have them in their power: but I mean the things which belong to him as a man, the marks (stamps) in his mind with which he came into the world, such as we seek also on coins, and if we find them, we approve of the coins, and if we do not find the marks, we reject them. What is the stamp on this sestertius?

The stamp of Trajan. Present it. It is the stamp of Nero. Throw it away: it can not be accepted, it is counterfeit.[5] So also in this case: What is the stamp of his opinions? It is gentleness, a sociable disposition, a tolerant temper, a disposition to mutual affection. Produce these qualities. I accept them: I consider this man a citizen, I accept him as a neighbour, a companion in my voyages. Only see that he has not Nero's stamp. Is he passionate, is he full of resentment, is he fault-finding? If the whim seizes him, does he break the heads of those who come in his way? (If so), why then did you say that he is a man? Is every thing judged (determined) by the bare form? If that is so, say that the form in wax[6] is an apple and has the smell and taste of an apple. But the external figure is not enough. neither then is the nose enough and the eyes to make the man, but he must have the opinions of a man. Here is a man who does not listen to reason, who does not know when he is refuted: he is an ass: in another man the sense of shame is become dead: he is good for nothing, he is any thing rather than a man. This man seeks whom he may meet and kick or bite, so that he is not even a sheep or an ass, but a kind of wild beast.

What then? would you have me to be despised?—By whom? by those who know you? and how shall those who know you despise a man who is gentle and modest? Perhaps you mean by those who do not know you? What is that to you? For no other artisan cares for the opinion of those who know not his art.—But they will be more hostile to me for this reason.—Why do you say "me"? Can any man injure your will, or prevent you from using in a natural way the appearances which are presented to you? In no way can he. Why then are you still disturbed and why do you choose to show yourself afraid? And why do you not come forth and proclaim that you are at peace with all men whatever they may do, and laugh at those chiefly who think that they can harm you? These slaves, you can say, know not either who I am, nor where lies my good or my evil, because they have no access to the things which are mine.

In this way also those who occupy a strong city mock the besiegers, (and say): "What trouble these men are now taking for nothing: our wall is secure, we have food for a very

long time, and all other resources." These are the things
which make a city strong and impregnable: but nothing else
than his opinions makes a man's soul impregnable. For what
wall is so strong, or what body is so hard, or what possession
is so safe, or what honour (rank, character) so free from assault (as a man's opinions)? All (other) things every where
are perishable, easily taken by assault, and if any man in any
way is attached to them, he must be disturbed, expect what is
bad, he must fear, lament, find his desires disappointed, and
fall into things which he would avoid. Then do we not
choose to make secure the only means of safety which are
offered to us, and do we not choose to withdraw ourselves
from that which is perishable and servile, and to labour at
the things which are imperishable and by nature free; and
do we not remember that no man either hurts another or
does good to another, but that a man's opinion about each
thing, is that which hurts him, is that which overturns him;
this is fighting, this is civil discord, this is war? That which
made Eteocles and Polynices[7] enemies was nothing else than
this opinion which they had about royal power, their opinion
about exile, that the one is the extreme of evils, the other the
greatest good. Now this is the nature of every man to seek
the good, to avoid the bad;[8] to consider him who deprives
us of the one and involves us in the other an enemy and
treacherous, even if he be a brother, or a son, or a father.
For nothing is more akin to us than the good: therefore if
these things (externals) are good and evil, neither is a
father a friend to sons, nor a brother to a brother, but
all the world is every where full of enemies, treacherous
men, and sycophants. But if the will ($\pi\rho\sigma\alpha\acute{\iota}\rho\epsilon\acute{o}\iota\varsigma$, the purpose, the intention) being what it ought to be, is the only
good; and if the will being such as it ought not to be, is the
only evil, where is there any strife, where is there reviling?
about what? about the things which do not concern us? and
strife with whom? with the ignorant, the unhappy, with those
who are deceived about the chief things?

Remembering this Socrates managed his own house and
endured a very ill-tempered wife and a foolish (ungrateful?)
son.[9] For in what did she show her bad temper? In pouring
water on his head as much as she liked, and in trampling on

the cake (sent to Socrates). And what is this to me, if I think that these things are nothing to me? But this is my business; and neither tyrant shall check my will nor a master; nor shall the many check me who am only one, nor shall the stronger check me who am the weaker; for this power of being free from check (hindrance) is given by God to every man. For these opinions make love in a house (family), concord in a state, among nations peace, and gratitude to God; they make a man in all things cheerful (confident) in externals as about things which belong to others, as about things which are of no value.[10] We indeed are able to write and to read these things, and to praise them when they are read, but we do not even come near to being convinced of them. Therefore what is said of the Lacedæmonians, "Lions at home, but in Ephesus foxes," will fit in our case also, "Lions in the school, but out of it foxes."[11]

NOTES

[1] See ii 10, 14, iv. 1. So Plato says (Legg vi), that a man who has had right education is wont to be the most divine and the tamest of animals. Upton.

On the doing wrong to another, see Plato's Crito and Epictetus iv. 1.

[2] See iii 1

[3] Like Hercules and Diogenes. See iii 12 2.

[4] The allusion is to a passage (a fragment) in the Cresphontes of Euripides translated by Cicero into Latin Iambics (Tusc. Disp i 48)—

> ἔδει γὰρ ἡμᾶς σύλλογον ποιουμένους
> τὸν φύντα θρηνεῖν εἰς ὅσ' ἔρχεται κάκα.
> τὸν δ' αὖ θανόντα καὶ πόνων πεπαυμένον
> χαίροντας, εὐφημοῦντας ἐκπέμπειν δόμων.

Herodotus (v. 4) says of the Trausi, a Thracian tribe: "when a child is born, the relatives sit round it and lament over all the evils which it must suffer on coming into the world and enumerate all the calamities of mankind: but when one dies, they hide him in the earth with rejoicing and pleasure, reckoning all the evils from which he is now released and in possession of all happiness"

[5] This does not mean, it is said, that Nero issued counterfeit coins, for there are extant many coins of Nero which both in form and in the purity of the metal are complete' A learned numismatist, Francis Wise, fellow of Trinity College, Oxford, in a letter to Upton, says that he can discover no reason for Nero's coins being rejected in commercial dealings after his death except the fact of the tyrant having been declared by the Senate to be an enemy to the Commonwealth (Suetonius, Nero, c 49) When Domitian was murdered, the Senate ordered his busts to be taken down, as the French now do after a revolution and all memorials of him to be destroyed (Suetonius, Domitian, c. 23) Dion also reports

(LX) that when Caligula was murdered, it was ordered that all the brass coin which bore his image should be melted, and, I suppose, coined again. There is more on this subject in Wise's letter

I do not believe that genuine coins would be refused in commercial dealings for the reasons which Wise gives, at least not refused in parts distant from Rome. Perhaps Epictetus means that some people would not touch the coins of the detestable Nero.

⁶ He says τὸ κήρινον, which Mrs. Carter translates "a piece of wax." Perhaps it means "a piece of wax in the form of an apple."

⁷ Eteocles and Polynices were the sons of the unfortunate Œdipus, who quarrelled about the kingship of Thebes and killed one another. This quarrel is the subject of the Seven against Thebes of Æschylus and the Phœnissæ of Euripides See II. 22, note 3

⁸ "Every man in everything he does naturally acts upon the forethought and apprehension of avoiding evil or obtaining good." Bp. Butler, Analogy, Chap. 2. The bishop's "naturally" is the φύσις of Epictetus.

⁹ Socrates' wife Xanthippe is charged by her eldest son Lamprocles with being so ill-tempered as to be past all endurance (Xenophon, Memorab. II. 2, 7). Xenophon in this chapter has reported the conversation of Socrates with his son on this matter

Diogenes Laertius (II.) tells the story of Xanthippe pouring water on the head of Socrates, and dirty water, as Seneca says (De Constantia, c. 18). Ælian (XI 12) reports that Alcibiades sent Socrates a large and good cake, which Xanthippe trampled under her feet. Socrates only laughed and said, "Well then, you will not have your share of it." The philosopher showed that his philosophy was practical by enduring the torment of a very ill-tempered wife, one of the greatest calamities that can happen to a man, and the trouble of an undutiful son

¹⁰ This is one of the wisest and noblest expressions of Epictetus.

¹¹ See Aristophanes, the "Peace," v 1188:

πολλὰ γὰρ δή μ' ἠδίκησαν,
ὄντες οἴκοι μὲν λέοντες,
ἐν μάχῃ δ' ἀλώπεκες.

CHAPTER VI

I AM grieved, a man says, at being pitied. Whether then is the fact of your being pitied a thing which concerns you, or those who pity you? Well, is it in your power to stop this pity?—It is in my power, if I show them that I do not require pity.—And whether then are you in the condition of not deserving (requiring) pity, or are you not in that condition?—I think that I am not: but these persons do not pity me, for the things for which, if they ought to pity me, it would be proper, I mean, for my faults; but they pity me for my poverty, for not possessing honourable offices, for diseases and deaths and other such things.—Whether then are you prepared to convince the many, that not one of these things is an evil, but that it is possible for a man who is poor and has no office ($\dot{\alpha}\nu\dot{\alpha}\rho\chi o\nu\tau\iota$) and enjoys no honour to be happy; or to shew yourself to them as rich and in power? For the second of these things belongs to a man who is boastful, silly and good for nothing. And consider by what means the pretence must be supported. It will be necessary for you to hire slaves and to possess a few silver vessels, and to exhibit them in public, if it is possible, though they are often the same, and to attempt to conceal the fact that they are the same, and to have splendid garments, and all other things for display, and to show that you are a man honoured by the great, and to try to sup at their houses, or to be supposed to sup there, and as to your person to employ some mean arts, that you may appear to be more handsome and nobler than you are. These things you must contrive, if you choose to go by the second path in order not to be pitied. But the first way is both impracticable and long, to attempt the very thing which Zeus has not been able to do, to convince all men what things are good and bad.[1] Is this power given to you? This only is given to you, to convince yourself; and you have not convinced yourself. Then I ask you, do you attempt to persuade other men? and who has lived so long with you as

you with yourself? and who has so much power of convincing you as you have of convincing yourself; and who is better disposed and nearer to you than you are to yourself?
How then have you not yet convinced yourself in order to
learn? At present are not things upside down? Is this
what you have been earnest about doing,[2] to learn to be free
from grief and free from disturbance, and not to be humbled
(abject), and to be free? Have you not heard then that
there is only one way which leads to this end, to give up
(dismiss) the things which do not depend on the will, to
withdraw from them, and to admit that they belong to
others? For another man then to have an opinion about
you, of what kind is it?—It is a thing independent of the
will.—Then is it nothing to you?—It is nothing.—When
then you are still vexed at this and disturbed, do you think
that you are convinced about good and evil?

Will you not then, letting others alone, be to yourself both
scholar and teacher?—The rest of mankind will look after
this, whether it is to their interest to be and to pass their lives
in a state contrary to nature: but to me no man is nearer than
myself. What then is the meaning of this, that I have listened to the words of the philosophers and I assent to them,
but in fact I am no way made easier (more content)? Am I
so stupid? And yet in all other things such as I have chosen,
I have not been found very stupid; but I learned letters
quickly, and to wrestle, and geometry, and to resolve syllogisms. Has not then reason convinced me? and indeed no
other things have I found from the beginning so approved
and chosen (as the things which are rational): and now I
read about these things, hear about them, write about them;
I have so far discovered no reason stronger than this (living
according to nature). In what then am I deficient? Have
the contrary opinions not been eradicated from me? Have
the notions (opinions) themselves not been exercised nor
used to be applied to action, but as armour are laid aside and
rusted and can not fit me? And yet neither in the exercises
of the palæstra, nor in writing or reading am I satisfied with
learning, but I turn up and down the syllogisms which are
proposed, and I make others, and sophistical syllogisms also.
But the necessary theorems by proceeding from which a man

22

can become free from grief, fear, passions (affects), hindrance, and a free man, these I do not exercise myself in nor do I practise in these the proper practice (study). Then I care about what others will say of me, whether I shall appear to them worth notice, whether I shall appear happy.—

Wretched man, will you not see what you are saying about yourself? What do you appear to yourself to be? in your opinions, in your desires, in your aversions from things (ἐν τῷ ἐκκλίνειν), in your movements (purposes, ἐν ὁρμῇ) in your preparation (for anything), in your designs (plans), and in other acts suitable to a man? But do you trouble yourself about this, whether others pity you?—Yes, but I am pitied not as I ought to be.—Are you then pained at this? and is he who is pained, an object of pity?—Yes.—How then are you pitied not as you ought to be? For by the very act that you feel (suffer) about being pitied, you make yourself deserving of pity. What then says Antisthenes? Have you not heard? "It is a royal thing, O Cyrus, to do right (well) and to be ill spoken of." My head is sound, and all think that I have the headache. What do I care for that? I am free from fever, and people sympathize with me as if I had a fever, (and say), "Poor man, for so long a time you have not ceased to have fever." I also say with a sorrowful countenance, "In truth it is now a long time that I have been ill." What will happen then? As God may please: and at the same time I secretly laugh at those who are pitying me. What then hinders the same thing being done in this case also? I am poor, but I have a right opinion about poverty. Why then do I care if they pity me for my poverty? I am not in power (not a magistrate): but others are: and I have the opinion which I ought to have about having and not having power. Let them look to it who pity me: but I am neither hungry nor thirsty nor do I suffer cold; but because they are hungry or thirsty they think that I too am. What then shall I do for them? Shall I go about and proclaim and say, "Be not mistaken, men, I am very well, I do not trouble myself about poverty, nor want of power, nor in a word about anything else than right opinions. These I have free from restraint I care for nothing at all."—What foolish talk is this? How

do I possess right opinions when I am not content with being
what I am, but am uneasy about what I am supposed to be?

But you say, others will get more and be preferred to me.—
What then is more reasonable than for those who have laboured about any thing to have more in that thing in which
they have laboured? They have laboured for power, you
have laboured about opinions; and they have laboured for
wealth, you for the proper use of appearances. See if they
have more than you in this about which you have laboured,
and which they neglect; if they assent better than you with
respect to the natural rules (measures) of things; if they are
less disappointed than you in their desires; if they fall less
into things which they would avoid than you do; if in their
intentions, if in the things which they propose to themselves,
if in their purposes, if in their motions towards an object they
take a better aim; if they better observe a proper behaviour,
as men, as sons, as parents, and so on as to the other names
by which we express the relations of life. But if they exercise power, and you do not, will you not choose to tell yourself the truth, that you do nothing for the sake of this
(power), and they do all? And it is most unreasonable that
he who looks after anything should obtain less than he who
does not look after it.

Not so: but since I care about right opinions, it is more
reasonable for me to have power.—Yes in the matter about
which you do care, in opinions. But in a matter in which
they have cared more than you, give way to them. The case
is just the same as if because you have right opinions, you
thought that in using the bow you should hit the mark better
than an archer, and in working in metal you should succeed
better than a smith. Give up then your earnestness about
opinions and employ yourself about the things which you
wish to acquire; and then lament, if you do not succeed; for
you deserve to lament. But now you say that you are occupied with other things, that you are looking after other
things; but the many say this truly, that one act has no community with another.[3] He who has risen in the morning
seeks whom (of the house of Cæsar) he shall salute, to
whom he shall say something agreeable, to whom he shall
send a present, how he shall please the dancing man, how by

· bad behaviour to one he may please another. When he prays, he prays about these things; when he sacrifices, he sacrifices for these things: the saying of Pythagoras

"Let sleep not come upon thy languid eyes"*

he transfers to these things. Where have I failed in the matters pertaining to flattery? What have I done? Any thing like a free man, any thing like a noble minded man? And if he finds any thing of the kind, he blames and accuses himself: "Why did you say this? Was it not in your power to lie? Even the philosophers say that nothing hinders us from telling a lie." But do you, if indeed you have cared about nothing else except the proper use of appearances, as soon as you have risen in the morning reflect, "What do I want in order to be free from passion (affects), and free from per- ·turbation? What am I? Am I a poor body, a piece of property, a thing of which something is said? I am none of these. But what am I? I am a rational animal. What then is required of me?" Reflect on your acts. Where have I omitted the things which conduce to happiness (εὔροιαν)? What have I done which is either unfriendly or unsocial? what have I not done as to these things which I ought to have done?

So great then being the difference in desires, actions, wishes, would you still have the same share with others in those things about which you have not laboured, and they have laboured? Then are you surprised if they pity you, and are you vexed? But they are not vexed if you pity them. Why? Because they are convinced that they have that which is good, and you are not convinced. For this reason you are not satisfied with your own, but you desire that which they have: but they are satisfied with their own, and do not desire what you have: since if you were really convinced, that with respect to what is good, it is you who are the possessor of it and that they have missed it, you would not even have thought of what they say about you.

¹ Here it is implied that there are things which God can not do   Perhaps he means that as God has given man certain powers of will and

therefore of action, he can not at the same time exercise the contradictory powers of forcing man's will and action; for this would be at the same time to give power and to take it away. Butler remarks (Analogy, chap. 5) "the present is so far from proving in event a discipline of virtue to the generality of men that on the contrary they seem to make it a discipline of vice." In fact all men are not convinced and can not be convinced in the present constitution of things "what things are good and bad."

[3] Something is perhaps wrong in the text here.

[3] Schweig. says that he has not observed that this proverb is mentioned by any other writer, and that he does not quite see the meaning of it, unless it be what he expresses in the Latin version (iv. 10, 24), "alterum opus cum altero nihil commune habet" I think that the context explains it: if you wish to obtain a particular end, employ the proper means, and not the means which do not make for that end

[4] Epictetus is making a parody of the verses of Pythagoras. See Schweig 's remarks on the words "He who has risen, etc." I have of necessity translated κακοηθισάμενος in an active sense; but if this is right, I do not understand how the word is used so.

CHAPTER VII

WHAT makes the tyrant formidable? The guards, you say, and their swords, and the men of the bed-chamber, and those who exclude them who would enter. Why then if you bring a boy (child) to the tyrant when he is with his guards, is he not afraid; or is it because the child does not understand these things? If then any man does understand what guards are and that they have swords, and comes to the tyrant for this very purpose because he wishes to die on account of some circumstance and seeks to die easily by the hand of another, is he afraid of the guards? No, for he wishes for the thing which makes the guards formidable. If then any man neither wishing to die nor to live by all means, but only as it may be permitted, approaches the tyrant, what hinders him from approaching the tyrant without fear? Nothing. If then a man has the same opinion about his property as the man whom I have instanced has about his body; and also about his children and his wife, and in a word is so affected by some madness or despair that he cares not whether he possesses them or not, but like children who are playing with shells care (quarrel) about the play, but do not trouble themselves about the shells, so he too has set no value on the materials (things), but values the pleasure that he has with them and the occupation, what tyrant is then formidable to him, or what guards, or what swords?

Then through madness is it possible for a man to be so disposed towards these things, and the Galilæans through habit,[1] and is it possible that no man can learn from reason and from demonstration that God has made all the things in the universe and the universe itself completely free from hindrance and perfect, and the parts of it for the use of the whole? All other animals indeed are incapable of comprehending the administration of it; but the rational animal man has faculties for the consideration of all these things, and for understanding that it is a part, and what kind of a part it is, and that it is right for the parts to be subordinate to the whole. And besides this being naturally noble, magnanimous and free, man sees that of the things which surround him some are free from hindrance and in his power, and the other things are subject to hindrance and in the power of others; that the things which are free from hindrance are in the power of the will; and those which are subject to hindrance are the things which are not in the power of the will. And for this reason if he thinks that his good and his interest be in these things only which are free from hindrance and in his own power, he will be free, prosperous, happy, free from harm, magnanimous, pious, thankful to God[2] for all things; in no matter finding fault with any of the things which have not been put in his power, nor blaming any of them. But if he thinks that his good and his interest are in externals and in things which are not in the power of his will, he must of necessity be hindered, be impeded, be a slave to those who have the power over the things which he admires (desires) and fears; and he must of necessity be impious because he thinks that he is harmed by God, and he must be unjust because he always claims more than belongs to him; and he must of necessity be abject and mean.

What hinders a man, who has clearly separated (comprehended), these things, from living with a light heart and bearing easily the reins, quietly expecting every thing which can happen, and enduring that which has already happened? Would you have me to bear poverty? Come and you will know what poverty is when it has found one who can act well the part of a poor man Would you have me to possess power? Let me have power, and also the trouble of it. Well, banishment? Wherever I shall go, there it will be well with me; for here also where I am, it was not because of the place that it was well with me, but because of my opinions which I shall carry off with me: for neither can any man deprive me of them; but my opinions alone are mine and they can not be taken from me, and I am satisfied while I have them, wherever I may be and whatever I am doing. But now it is time to die. Why do you say, to die? Make no tragedy show of the thing, but speak of it as it is: it is now time for the matter '(of the body)' to be resolved into the things out of which it was composed. And what is the formidable thing here? what is going to perish of the things which are in the universe?[3] what new thing or wondrous is going to happen? Is it for this reason that a tyrant is formidable? Is it for this reason that the guards appear to have swords which are large and sharp? Say this to others: but I have considered about all these things; no man has power over me. I have been made free; I know his commands, no man can now lead me as a slave. I have a proper person to assert my freedom; I have proper judges. (I say) are you not the master of my body? What then is that to me? Are you not the master of my property? What then is that to me? Are you not the master of my exile or of my chains? Well, from all these things and all the poor body itself I depart at your bidding, when you please. Make trial of your power, and you will know how far it reaches.

· Whom then can I still fear? Those who are over the bed-chamber? Lest they should do, what? Shut me out? If they find that I wish to enter, let them shut me out. Why then do you go to the doors? Because I think it befits me, while the play (sport) lasts, to join in it. How then are you not shut out? Because unless some one allows me to go in, I do not choose to go in, but am always content with that which happens; for I think that what God chooses is better than what I choose.[4] I will attach myself as a minister and follower to him; I have the same movements (pursuits) as he has, I have the same desires; in a word, I have the same will (συνθέλω). There is no shutting out for me, but for those who would force their way in. Why then do not I force my way in? Because I know that nothing good is distributed within to those who enter. But when I hear any man called fortunate because he is honoured by Cæsar, I say, what does he happen to get? A province (the government of a province). Does he also obtain an opinion such as he ought? The office of a Prefect. Does he also obtain the power of using his office well? Why do I still strive to enter (Cæsar's chamber)? A man scatters dried figs and nuts: the children seize them, and fight with one another; men do not, for they think them to be a small matter. But if a man should throw about shells, even

the children do not seize them. Provinces are distributed: let
children look to that. Money is distributed: let children look
to that. Prætorships, consulships are distributed: let children scramble for them, let them be shut out, beaten, kiss the
hands of the giver, of the slaves: but to me these are only
dried figs and nuts. What then? If you fail to get them,
while Cæsar is scattering them about, do not be troubled: if
a dried fig come into your lap, take it and eat it; for so far
you may value even a fig. But if I shall stoop down and turn
another over, or be turned over by another, and shall flatter
those who have got into (Cæsar's) chamber, neither is a
dried fig worth the trouble, nor any thing else of the things
which are not good, which the philosophers have persuaded
me not to think good.

Show me the swords of the guards. See how big they are,
and how sharp. What then do these big and sharp swords
do? They kill And what does a fever do? Nothing else.
And what else a (falling) tile? Nothing else. Would you
then have me to wonder at these things and worship them,
and go about as the slave of all of them? I hope that this
will not happen: but when I have once learned that every
thing which has come into existence must also go out of
it, that the universe may not stand still nor be impeded, I no
longer consider it any difference whether a fever shall do it
or a tile, or a soldier. But if a man must make a comparison
between these things, I know that the soldier will do it with
less trouble (to me), and quicker. When then I neither fear
any thing which a tyrant can do to me, nor desire any thing
which he can give, why do I still look on with wonder (admiration)? Why am I still confounded? Why do I fear the
guards? Why am I pleased if he speaks to me in a friendly
way, and receives me, and why do I tell others how he spoke
to me? Is he a Socrates, is he a Diogenes that his praise
should be a proof of what I am? Have I been eager to imitate his morals? But I keep up the play and go to him, and
serve him so long as he does not bid me to do any thing
foolish or unreasonable. But if he says to me, "Go and bring
Leon of Salamis," I say to him, "Seek another, for I am no
longer playing." (The tyrant says): "Lead him away (to
prison)." I follow; that is part of the play. But your

head will be taken off —Does the tyrant's head always remain where it is, and the heads of you who obey him?—But
you will be cast out unburied.—If the corpse is I, I shall be
cast out; but if I am different from the corpse, speak more
properly according as the fact is, and do not think of frightening me.   These things are formidable to children and
fools.   But if any man has once entered a philosopher's
school and knows not what he is, he deserves to be full of
fear and to flatter those whom afterwards he used to flatter;
(and) if he has not yet learned that he is not flesh nor bones
nor sinews ($\nu\epsilon\tilde{\nu}\rho\alpha$), but he is that which makes use of these
parts of the body and governs them and follows (under-
stands) the appearances of things.[5]

Yes, but this talk makes us despise the laws.—And what
kind of talk makes men more obedient to the laws that employ such talk? And the things which are in the power of a
fool are not law.[6] And yet see how this talk makes us disposed as we ought to be even to these men (fools); since it
teaches us to claim in opposition to them none of the things
in which they are able to surpass us. This talk teaches us as
to the body to give it up, as to property to give that up also,
as to children, parents, brothers, to retire from these, to give
up all; it only makes an exception of the opinions, which even
Zeus has willed to be the select property of every man. What
transgression of the laws is there here, what folly? Where
you are superior and stronger, there I gave way to you: on
the other hand, where I am superior, do you yield to me; for
I have studied (cared for) this, and you have not. It is your
study to live in houses with floors formed of various stones,[7]
how your slaves and dependents shall serve you, how you
shall wear fine clothing, have many hunting men, lute players, and tragic actors.   Do I claim any of these? have you
made any study of opinions, and of your own rational faculty? Do you know of what parts it is composed, how they
are brought together, how they are connected, what powers
it has, and of what kind? Why then are you vexed, if another
who has made it his study, has the advantage over you in
these things?. But these things are the greatest. And who
hinders you from being employed about these things and
looking after them? And who has a better stock of books, of

leisure, of persons to aid you? Only turn your mind at last to these things, attend, if it be only a short time, to your own ruling faculty[8] (ἡγεμονικόν): consider what this is that you possess, and whence it came, this which uses all other (faculties), and tries them, and selects and rejects. But so long as you employ yourself about externals you will possess them (externals) as no man else does; but you will have this (the ruling faculty) such as you choose to have it, sordid and neglected.

NOTES

[1] See Schweig.'s note on the text By the Galilæans it is probable that Epictetus means the Christians, whose obstinacy Antoninus also mentions (xi 3). Epictetus, a contemporary of St Paul, knew little about the Christians, and only knew some examples of their obstinate adherence to the new faith and the fanatical behaviour of some of the converts That there were wild fanatics among the early Christians is proved on undoubted authority; and also that there always have been such, and now are such. The abuse of any doctrines or religious opinions is indeed no argument against such doctrines or religious opinions, and it is a fact quite consistent with experience that the best things are liable to be perverted, misunderstood, and misused.

[2] "This agrees with Eph. v. 20: 'Give thanks always for all things to God.'" Mrs. Carter. The words are the same in both except that the Apostle has εὐχαριστοῦντες and Epictetus has χάριν ἔχον.

[3] He says that the body will be resolved into the things of which it is composed: none of them will perish. The soul, as he has said elsewhere, will go to him who gave it (iii 13) But I do not suppose that he means that the soul will exist as having a separate consciousness

[4] "Nevertheless not as I will, but as thou wilt" Matthew xxvi 39 Mrs. Carter "Our resignation to the will of God may be said to be perfect, when our will is lost and resolved up into his; when we rest in his will as our end, as being itself most just and right and good" Bp Butler, Sermon on the Love of God.

[5] Here Epictetus admits that there is some power in man which uses the body, directs and governs it. He does not say what the power is nor what he supposes it to be "Upon the whole then our organs of sense and our limbs are certainly instruments, which the living persons, ourselves, make use of to perceive and move with" Butler's Analogy, chap. i.

[6] The will of a fool does not make law, he says. Unfortunately it does, if we use the word law in the strict sense of law: for law is a general command from a person, an absolute king, for example, who has power to enforce it on those to whom the command is addressed, or if not to enforce it, to punish for disobedience to it. This strict use of the word "law" is independent of the quality of the command, which may be wise or foolish, good or bad But Epictetus does not use the word "law" in the strict sense.

[7] The word is λιθοστρώτοις which means what we name Mosaic floors or pavements. The word λιθόστρωτον is used by John xix. 13, and rendered in our version by "pavement."

* This term ($\tau\grave{o}\ \dot{\eta}\gamma\varepsilon\mu o\nu\iota\kappa\acute{o}\nu$) has been often used by Epictetus (i. 26. 15, etc), and by Antoninus   Here Epictetus gives a definition or description of it: it is the faculty by which we reflect and judge and determine, a faculty which no other animal has, a faculty which in many men is neglected, and weak because it is neglected; but still it ought to be what its constitution forms it to be, a faculty which "plainly bears upon it marks of authority over all the rest, and claims the absolute direction of them all, to allow or forbid their gratification" (Bp. Butler, Preface to his Sermons).

CHAPTER VIII

AGAINST THOSE WHO HASTILY RUSH INTO THE USE OF THE PHILOSOPHIC DRESS

NEVER praise nor blame a man because of the things which are common (to all, or to most), and do not ascribe to him any skill or want of skill; and thus you will be free from rashness and from malevolence. This man bathes very quickly. Does he then do wrong? Certainly not. But what does he do? He bathes very quickly. Are all things then done well? By no means: but the acts which proceed from right opinions are done well; and those which proceed from bad opinions are done ill. But do you, until you know the opinion from which a man does each thing, neither praise nor blame the act. But the opinion is not easily discovered from the external things (acts). This man is a carpenter. Why? Because he uses an axe. What then is this to the matter? This man is a musician because he sings. And what does that signify? This man is a philosopher. Because he wears a cloak and long hair. And what does a juggler wear? For this reason if a man sees any philosopher acting indecently, immediately he says, "See what the philosopher is doing." But he ought because of the man's indecent behaviour rather to say that he is not a philosopher. For if this is the preconceived notion (πρόληψις) of a philosopher and what he professes, to wear a cloak and long hair, men would say well; but if what he professes is this rather, to keep himself free from faults, why do we not rather, because he does not make good his professions, take from him the name of philosopher? For so we do in the case of all other arts. When a man sees another handling an axe badly, he does not say, "What is the use of the carpenter's art? See how badly carpenters do their work." But he says just the contrary, " This man is not a carpenter, for he uses an axe badly." In the same way if a man hears another singing badly, he does not say, "See how musicians sing." But rather, "this man is not a musician." But it is in the matter of philosophy only that people do this. When they see a man acting contrary to the profession of a philosopher, they do not take away his title, but they assume him to be a philosopher, and from his acts deriving the fact that he is behaving indecently they conclude that there is no use in philosophy.

What then is the reason of this? Because we attach value to the notion (πρόληψιν) of a carpenter, and to that of a musician, and to the notion of other artisans in like manner, but not to that of a philosopher, and we judge from externals only that it is a thing confused and ill defined. And what other kind of art has a name from the dress and the hair; and has not both theorems and a material and an end? What then is the material (matter) of the philosopher? Is it a cloak? No, but reason. What is his end? Is it to wear a cloak? No, but to possess the reason in a right state. Of what kind are his theorems? Are they those about the way in which the beard becomes great or the hair long? No, but rather what Zeno says, to know the elements of reason, what kind of a thing each of them is, and how they are fitted to one another, and what things are consequent upon them? Will you not then see first if he does what he professes when he acts in an unbecoming manner, and then blame his study (pursuit)? But now when you yourself are acting in a sober way, you say in consequence of what he seems to you to be doing wrong, "Look at the philosopher," as if it were proper to call by the name of philosopher one who does these things; and further, "This is the conduct of a philosopher." But you do not say, "Look at the carpenter," when you know that a carpenter is an adulterer or you see him to be a glutton; nor do you say, "See the musician." Thus to a certain degree even you perceive (understand) the profession of a philosopher, but you fall away from the notion, and you are confused through want of care.

But even the philosophers themselves as they are called pursue the thing (philosophy), by beginning with things which are common to them and others: as soon as they have assumed a cloak and grown a beard, they say, "I am a philosopher."[1] But no man will say, "I am a musician," if he has bought a plectrum (fiddlestick) and a lute: nor will he say, "I am a smith," if he has put on a cap and apron. But the dress is fitted to the art; and they take their name from the art, and not from the dress. For this reason Euphrates used to say well, "A long time I strove to be a philosopher without people knowing it; and this," he said, "was useful to me: for first I knew that when I did any thing well, I did not do it for the sake of the spectators, but for the sake of myself: I ate well for the sake of myself: I had my countenance well composed and my walk: all for myself and for God. Then, as I struggled alone, so I alone also was in danger: in no respect through me, if I did anything base or unbecoming, was philosophy endangered: nor did I injure the many by doing any thing wrong as a philosopher. For this reason those who did not know my purpose used to wonder how it was that while I conversed and lived altogether with all philosophers, I was not a philosopher myself. And what was the harm for me to be known to be a philosopher by my acts and not by outward marks?[2] See how I eat, how I drink, how I sleep, how I bear and forbear, how I co-operate, how I employ desire, how I employ aversion (turning from things), how I maintain the relations (to things) those which are natural or those which are acquired, how free from confusion, how free from hindrance. Judge of me from this, if you can. But if you are so deaf and blind that you can not conceive even Hephæstus to be a good smith, unless you see the cap on his head, what is the harm in not being recognized by so foolish a judge?"

So Socrates was not known to be a philosopher by most persons: and they used to come to him and ask to be introduced to philosophers. Was he vexed then as we are, and did he say, "And do you not think that I am a philosopher?" No, but he would take them and introduce them, being satisfied with one thing, with being a philosopher, and being pleased also with not being thought to be a philosopher, he was not annoyed: for he thought of his own occupation. What is the work of an honourable and good man? To have many pupils? By no means. They will look to this matter who are earnest about it. But was it his business to examine carefully difficult theorems? Others will look after these matters also. In what then was he,[8] and who was he and whom did he wish to be? He was in that (employed in that) wherein there was hurt (damage) and advantage. "If any man can damage me," he says, "I am doing nothing · if I am waiting for another man to do me good, I am nothing. If I wish for any thing, and it does not happen, I am unfortunate." To such a contest he invited every man, and I do not think that he would have declined the contest with any one What do you suppose? was it by proclaiming and saying, " I am such a man?" Far from it, but by being such a man. For further, this is the character of a fool and a boaster to say, "I am free from passions and disturbance · do not be ignorant, my friends, that while you are uneasy and disturbed about things of no value, I alone am free from all perturbation." So is it not enough for you to feel no pain, unless you make this proclamation: "Come together all who are suffering gout, pains in the head, fever, ye who are lame, blind, and observe that I am sound (free) from every ailment." This is empty and disagreeable to hear, unless like Æsculapius you are able to show immediately by what kind of treatment they also shall be immediately free from disease, and unless you show your own health as an example.

For such is the Cynic who is honoured with the sceptre and the diadem by Zeus, and says, "That you may see, O men, that you seek happiness and tranquillity not where it is, but where it is not, behold I am sent to you by God as an example, I who have neither property nor house, nor wife nor children, not even a bed, nor coat nor household utensil; and see how healthy I am: try me, and if you see that I am free from perturbations, hear the remedies and how I have been cured (treated)." This is both philanthropic and noble. But see whose work it is, the work of Zeus, or of him whom he may judge worthy of this service, that he may never exhibit any thing to the many, by which he shall make of no effect his own testimony, whereby he gives testimony to virtue, and bears evidence against external things:

"His beauteous face pales not, nor from his cheeks
He wipes a tear."[4]

And not this only, but he neither desires nor seeks any

thing, nor man, nor place, nor amusement, as children seek
the vintage or holidays; always fortified by modesty as
others are fortified by walls and doors and doorkeepers.

But now (these men) being only moved to philosophy,
as those who have a bad stomach are moved to some kinds
of food which they soon loathe, straightway (rush) towards
the sceptre and to the royal power. They let the hair grow,
they assume the cloak, they show the shoulder bare, they
quarrel with those whom they meet, and if they see a man in
a thick winter coat, they quarrel with him. Man, first exercise yourself in winter weather · see your movements (inclinations) that they are not those of a man with a bad
stomach or those of a longing woman. First strive that it be
not known what you are: be a philosopher to yourself (or,
philosophize to yourself) a short time. Fruit grows thus:
the seed must be buried for some time, hid, grow slowly in
order that it may come to perfection. But if it produces the
ear before the jointed stem, it is imperfect, a produce of the
garden of Adonis.[5] Such a poor plant are you also: you
have blossomed too soon; the cold weather will scorch you
up. See what the husbandmen say about seeds when there
is warm weather too early. They are afraid lest the seeds
should be too luxuriant, and then a single frost should lay
hold of them and show that they are too forward. Do you
also consider, my man: you have shot out too soon, you
have hurried towards a little fame before the proper season:
you think that you are something, a fool among fools: you
will be caught by the frost, and rather you have been frost-
bitten in the root below, but your upper parts still blossom
a little, and for this reason you think that you are still alive
and flourishing. Allow us to ripen in the natural way:
why do you bare (expose) us? why do you force us? we
are not yet able to bear the air. Let the root grow, then
acquire the first joint, then the second, and then the third;
in this way then the fruit will naturally force itself out, even
if I do not choose. For who that is pregnant and filled with
such great principles does not also perceive his own powers
and move towards the corresponding acts? A bull is not
ignorant of his own nature and his powers, when a wild
beast shows itself, nor does he wait for one to urge him on;
nor a dog when he sees a wild animal. · But if I have the

23

powers of a good man, shall I wait for you to prepare me for my own (proper) acts? At present I have them not, believe me. Why then do you wish me to be withered up before the time, as you have been withered up?

NOTES

[1] Compare Horace, Ep. i. 19, 12, etc.

> "Quid, si quis vultu torvo ferus et pede nudo
> Exiguæque togæ simulet textore Catonem,
> Virtutemne repræsentet moresque Catonis?"

[2] "Yea a man may say, Thou hast faith, and I have works: shew me thy faith without thy works, and I will shew thee my faith by my works." Epistle of James, ii. 18 So a moral philosopher may say, I show my principles, not by what I profess, but by that which I do.

[3] "In what then was he" seems to mean in what did he employ himself'?

[4] Odyssey, xi. 528.

[5] "The gardens of Adonis" are things growing in earthen vessels, carried about for show only, not for use 'The gardens of Adonis" is a proverbial expression applied to things of no value, to plants, for instance, which last only a short time, have no roots, and soon wither Such things, we may suppose, were exhibited at the festivals of Adonis. Schweighauser's note.

CHAPTER IX

WHEN you see another man in the possession of
power (magistracy), set against this the fact that
you have not the want (desire) of power; when
you see another rich, see what you possess in place
of riches: for if you possess nothing in place of them, you
are miserable; but if you have not the want of riches, know
that you possess more than this man possesses and what is
worth much more. Another man possesses a handsome
woman (wife): you have the satisfaction of not desiring a
handsome wife. Do these things appear to you to be small?
And how much would these persons give, these very men
who are rich, and in possession of power, and live with handsome women, to be able to despise riches, and power and
these very women whom they love and enjoy? Do you not
know then what is the thirst of a man who has a fever? He
possesses that which is in no degree like the thirst of a man
who is in health · for the man who is in health ceases to be
thirsty after he has drunk; but the sick man being pleased for
a short time has a nausea, he converts the drink into bile,
vomits, is griped, and more thirsty. It is such a thing to have
desire of riches and to possess riches, desire of power and to
possess power, desire of a beautiful woman and to sleep with
her: to this is added jealousy, fear of being deprived of the
thing which you love, indecent words, indecent thoughts,
unseemly acts.

And what do I lose? you will say. My man, you were
modest, and you are so no longer. Have you lost nothing?
In place of Chrysippus and Zeno you read Aristides and
Evenus;[2] have you lost nothing? In place of Socrates and
Diogenes, you admire him who is able to corrupt and seduce
most women. You wish to appear handsome and try to make
yourself so, though you are not. You like to display splendid
clothes that you may attract women; and if you find any fine

355

oil (for the hair), you imagine that you are happy. But formerly you did not think of any such thing, but only where there should be decent talk, a worthy man, and a generous conception. Therefore you slept like a man, walked forth like a man, wore a manly dress, and used to talk in a way becoming a good man; then do you say to me, I have lost nothing? So do men lose nothing more than coin? Is not modesty lost? Is not decent behaviour lost? is it that he who has lost these things has sustained no loss? Perhaps you think that not one of these things is a loss.   But there was a time when you reckoned this the only loss and damage, and you were anxious that no man should disturb you from these (good) words and actions.

Observe, you are disturbed from these good words and actions by nobody, but by yourself.   Fight with yourself, restore yourself to decency, to modesty, to liberty.   If any man ever told you this about me, that a person forces me to be an adulterer, to wear such a dress as yours, to perfume myself with oils, would you not have gone and with your own hand have killed the man who thus calumniated me?   Now will you not help yourself? and how much easier is this help?   There is no need to kill any man, nor to put him in chains, nor to treat him with contumely, nor to enter the Forum (go to the courts of law), but it is only necessary for you to speak to yourself who will be most easily persuaded, with whom no man has more power of persuasion than yourself. First of all, condemn what you are doing, and then when you have condemned it, do not despair of yourself, and be not in the condition of those men of mean spirit, who, when they have once given in, surrender themselves completely and are carried away as if by a torrent. But see what the trainers of boys do. Has the boy fallen? Rise, they say, wrestle again till you are made strong.   Do you also do something of the same kind: for be well assured that nothing is more tractable than the human soul. You must exercise the will,[3] and the thing is done, it is set right: as on the other hand. only fall a nodding (be careless), and the thing is lost. for from within comes ruin and from within comes help. Then (you say) what good do I gain? And what greater good do you seek than this?[4] From a shameless man

you will become a modest man, from a disorderly you will
become an orderly man, from a faithless you will become a
faithful man, from a man of unbridled habits a sober man.
If you seek any thing more than this, go on doing what you
are doing : not even a God can now help you.

NOTES

[1] "They, who are desirous of taking refuge in Heathenism from the
strictness of the Christian morality, will find no great consolation in reading this chapter of Epictetus." Mrs Carter.

[2] Aristides was a Greek, but his period is not known He was the author of a work, named Milesiaca or Milesian stories. All that we know
of the work is that it was of a loose description, amatory and licentious
It was translated into Latin by L Cornelius Sisenna, a contemporary of
the Dictator Sulla; and it is mentioned by Plutarch (Life of Crassus, c.
32), and several times by Ovid (Tristia II 413 etc). Evenus was perhaps a poet We know nothing of this Evenus, but we may conjecture
from being here associated with Aristides what his character was.

[3] The power of the will is a fundamental principle with Epictetus. The
will is strong in some, but very feeble in others; and sometimes, as experience seems to show, it is incapable of resisting the power of old habits

[4] Virtue is its own reward, said the Stoics. This is the meaning of
Epictetus, and it is consistent with his principles that a man should live
conformably to his nature, and so he will have all the happiness of which
human nature is capable. Mrs. Carter has a note here, which I do not
copy, and I hardly understand It seems to refer to the Christian doctrine of a man being rewarded in a future life according to his works:
but we have no evidence that Epictetus believed in a future life, and he
therefore could not go further than to maintain that virtuous behaviour
is the best thing in this short life, and will give a man the happiness
which he can obtain in no other way.

CHAPTER X

THE difficulties of all men are about external things, their helplessness is about externals. What shall I do, how will it be, how will it turn out, will this happen, will that? All these are the words of those who are turning themselves to things which are not within the power of the will. For who says, "How shall I not assent to that which is false? how shall I not turn away from the truth?" If a man be of such a good disposition as to be anxious about these things, I will remind him of this, Why are you anxious? The thing is in your own power: be assured: do not be precipitate in assenting before you apply the natural rule On the other side, if a man is anxious (uneasy) about desire, lest it fail in its purpose and miss its end, and with respect to the avoidance of things, lest he should fall into that which he would avoid, I will first kiss (love) him, because he throws away the things about which others are in a flutter (others desire) and their fears, and employs his thoughts about his own affairs and his own condition. Then I shall say to him, if you do not choose to desire that which you will fail to obtain nor to attempt to avoid that into which you will fall, desire nothing which belongs to (which is in the power of) others, nor try to avoid any of the things which are not in your power. If you do not observe this rule, you must of necessity fail in your desires and fall into that which you would avoid. What is the difficulty here? where is there room for the words, How will it be? and How will it turn out? and will this happen or that?

Now is not that which will happen independent of the will? Yes. And the nature of good and of evil is it not in the things which are within the power of the will? Yes. Is it in your power then to treat according to nature every thing which happens? Can any person hinder you? No man. No longer then say to me, How will it be? For however it may be, you will dispose of it well,[1] and the result to you will be a fortunate one. What would Hercules have been if he said, "How shall a great lion not appear to me, or a great boar, or savage men?" And what do you care for that? If a great boar appear, you will fight a greater fight: if bad men appear, you will relieve the earth of the bad. Suppose then that I lose my life in this way. You will die a good man, doing a noble act. For since we must certainly die, of necessity a man must be found doing something either following the employment of a husbandman, or digging, or trading, or serving in a consulship, or suffering from indigestion or from diarrhœa. What then do you wish to be doing when you are found by death? I for my part would wish to be found doing something which belongs to a man, beneficent, suitable to the general interest, noble. But if I can not be found doing things so great, I would be found doing at least that which I can not be hindered from doing, that which is permitted me to do, correcting myself, cultivating the faculty which makes use of appearances, labouring at freedom from the affects (labouring at tranquillity of mind), rendering to the relations of life their due; if I succeed so far, also (I would be found) touching on (advancing to) the third topic (or head), safety in the forming judgments about things.[2] If death surprises me when I am busy about these things, it is enough for me if I can stretch out my hands to God and say: "The means which I have received from thee for seeing thy administration (of the world) and following it, I have not neglected. I have not dishonoured thee by my acts: see how I have used my perceptions, see how I have used my preconceptions: have I ever blamed thee? have I been discontented with any thing that happens, or wished it to be otherwise? have I wished to transgress the (established) relations (of things)? That thou hast given me life, I thank thee for what thou hast given: so long as I have used the things which are thine I am content; take them back and place them wherever thou mayest choose; for thine were all things, thou gavest them to me."[3] Is it not enough to depart in this state of mind, and what life is better and more becoming than that of a man who is in this state of mind? and what end is more happy?[4]

But that this may be done (that such a declaration may be

made), a man must receive (bear) no small things, nor are
the things small which he must lose (go without)   You can
not both wish to be a consul and to have these things (the
power of making such a dying speech), and to be eager to
have lands, and these things also; and to be solicitous about
slaves and about yourself. But if you wish for any thing
which belongs to another, that which is your own is lost.
This is the nature of the thing: nothing is given or had for
nothing [5] And where is the wonder? If you wish to be a
consul, you must keep awake, run about, kiss hands, waste
yourself with exhaustion at other men's doors, say and do
many things unworthy of a free man, send gifts to many,
daily presents to some And what is the thing that is got?
Twelve bundles of rods (the consular fasces), to sit three or
four times on the tribunal, to exhibit the games in the Circus
and to give suppers in small baskets.[6]   Or, if you do not
agree about this, let some one show me what there is besides
these things.   In order then to secure freedom from pas-
sions ($\dot{a}\pi a\theta\epsilon\dot{\iota}a\varsigma$), tranquillity, to sleep well when you do sleep,
to be really awake when you are awake, to fear nothing, to
be anxious about nothing, will you spend nothing and give
no labour? But if any thing belonging to you be lost while
you are thus busied, or be wasted badly, or another obtains
what you ought to have obtained, will you immediately be
vexed at what has happened? Will you not take into the account on the other side what you receive and for what, how
much for how much? Do you expect to have for nothing
things so great? And how can you? One work (thing) has
no community with another. You can not have both external things after bestowing care on them and your own ruling
faculty:[7] but if you would have those, give up this. If you
do not, you will have neither this nor that, while you are
drawn in different ways to both. [8]   The oil will be spilled, the
household vessels will perish: (that may be), but I shall be
free from passions (tranquil).—There will be a fire when I
am not present, and the books will be destroyed: but I shall
treat appearances according to nature.—Well; but I shall
have nothing to eat. If I am so unlucky, death is a harbour;
and death is the harbour for all; this is the place of refuge;
and for this reason not one of the things in life is difficult; as

soon as you choose, you are out of the house, and are smoked
no more.[9] Why then are you anxious, why do you lose your
sleep, why do you not straightway, after considering wherein
your good is and your evil, say, "Both of them are in my
power? Neither can any man deprive me of the good, nor
involve me in the bad against my will. Why do I not throw
myself down and snore? for all that I have is safe. As to the
things which belong to others, he will look to them who gets
them, as they may be given by him who has the power. Who
am I who wish to have them in this way or in that? is a
power of selecting them given to me? has any person made
me the dispenser of them? Those things are enough for me
over which I have power: I ought to manage them as well
as I can: and all the rest, as the master of them (God) may
choose."

When a man has these things before his eyes, does he keep
awake and turn hither and thither? What would he have, or
what does he regret, Patroclus or Antilochus or Menelaus?[10]
For when did he suppose that any of his friends was immortal, and when had he not before his eyes that on the morrow or the day after he or his friend must die? Yes, he says,
but I thought that he would survive me and bring up my son.
—You were a fool for that reason, and you were thinking of
what was uncertain. Why then do you not blame yourself,
and sit crying like girls?—But he used to set my food before
me.—Because he was alive, you fool, but now he can not;
but Automedon[11] will set it before you, and if Automedon
also dies, you will find another. But if the pot, in which
your meat was cooked, should be broken, must you die of
hunger, because you have not the pot which you are accustomed to? Do you not send and buy a new pot? He says:

"No greater ill than this could fall on me."[12]

Why is this your ill? Do you then instead of removing it
blame your mother (Thetis) for not foretelling it to you that
you might continue grieving from that time? What do you
think? do you not suppose that Homer wrote this that we
may learn that those of noblest birth, the strongest and the
richest, the most handsome, when they have not the opinions

which they ought to have, are not prevented from being most wretched and unfortunate?

[1] See a passage in Plutarch on Tranquillity from Euripides, the great storehouse of noble thoughts, from which ancient writers drew much good matter; and perhaps it was one of the reasons why so many of his plays and fragments have been preserved.

> " We must not quarrel with the things that are,
> For they care not for us: but he who feels them
> If he disposes well of things, fares well "

[2] See iii c. 2.
[3] "Thine they were, and thou gavest them to me." John xvii. 6.— Mrs. Carter
[4] "I wish it were possible to palliate the ostentation of this passage, by applying it to the ideal perfect character; but it is in a general way that Epictetus hath proposed such a dying speech, as can not without shocking arrogance be uttered by any one born to die. Unmixed as it is with any acknowledgment of faults or imperfections, at present, or with any sense of guilt on account of the past, it must give every sober reader a very disadvantageous opinion of some principles of the philosophy on which it is founded, as contradictory to the voice of conscience, and formed on absolute ignorance or neglect of the condition and circumstances of such a creature as man."—Mrs. Carter.

I am inclined to think that Epictetus does refer to the "ideal perfect character"· but others may not understand him in this way. When Mrs Carter says "but it is in a general . dying speech," she can hardly suppose, as her words seem to mean, that Epictetus proposed such a dying speech, for every man or even for many men, for he knew and has told us how bad many men are, and how few are good according to his measure and rule: in fact his meaning is plainly expressed The dying speech may even be stronger in the sense in which Mrs Carter understands it, in my translation, where I have rendered one passage in the text by the words "I have not dishonoured thee by my acts," which she translates, "as far as in me lay, I have not dishonoured thee;" which apparently means, "as far as I could, I have not dishonoured thee " The Latin translation "quantum in me fuit," seems rather ambiguous to me.

There is a general confession of sins in the prayer book of the Church of England, part of which Epictetus would not have rejected, I think Of course the words which form the peculiar Christian character of the confession would have been unintelligible to him. It is a confession which all persons of all conditions are supposed to make. If all persons made the confession with sincerity, it ought to produce a corresponding behaviour and make men more ready to be kind to one another, for all who use it confess that they fail in their duty, and it ought to lower pride and banish arrogance from the behaviour of those in wealth and condition are elevated above the multitude. But I have seen it somewhere said, I can not remember where, but said in no friendly spirit to Christian prayer, that some men both priests and laymen prostrate themselves in humility before God and indemnify themselves by arrogance to man
[5] See iv. 2, 2.

⁸ These were what the Romans named "sportulæ," in which the rich used to give some eatables to poor dependents who called to pay their respects to the great at an early hour.

"Nunc sportula primo
Limine parva sedet turbæ rapienda togatæ "
.Juvenal, Sat. i. 95.

⁷ "You can not serve God and Mammon." Matthew vi. 24. Mrs. Carter.
⁸ See iv. 2, 5.
⁹ Compare i. 25, 18, and i 9, 20.
¹⁰ Epictetus refers to the passage in the Iliad xxiv. 5, where Achilles is lamenting the death of Patroclus and can not sleep
¹¹ "This is a wretched idea of friendship ; but a necessary consequence of the Stoic system. What a fine contrast to this gloomy consolation are the noble sentiments of an Apostle? Value your deceased friend, says Epictetus, as a broken pipkin ; forget him, as a thing worthless, lost and destroyed   St. Paul, on the contrary, comforts the mourning survivors ; bidding them not sorrow, as those who have no hope . but remember that the death of good persons is only a sleep ; from which they will soon arise to a happy immortality." Mrs. Carter.
Epictetus does not say, "value your deceased friend as a broken pipkin." Achilles laments that he has lost the services of his friend at table, a vulgar kind of complaint, he is thinking of his own loss, instead of his friend. The answer is such a loss as he laments is easily repaired ; the loss of such a friend is as easily repaired as the loss of a cooking vessel. Mrs. Carter in her zeal to contrast the teaching of the Apostle with that of Epictetus seems to forget for the time that Epictetus, so far as we know, did not accept or did not teach the doctrine of a future life As to what he thought of friendship, if it was a real friendship, such as we can conceive, I am sure that he did not think of it, as Mrs. Carter says that he did ; for true friendship implies many of the virtues which Epictetus taught and practised He has a chapter on Friendship, ii 22, which I suppose that Mrs. Carter did not think of, when she wrote this note.
¹² Iliad xix. 321.

CHAPTER XI

ABOUT PURITY (CLEANLINESS)

SOME persons raise a question whether the social feeling is contained in the nature of man; and yet I think that these same persons would have no doubt that love of purity is certainly contained in it, and that if man is distinguished from other animals by any thing, he is distinguished by this. When then we see any other animal cleaning itself, we are accustomed to speak of the act with surprise, and to add that the animal is acting like a man: and on the other hand, if a man blames an animal for being dirty, straightway as if we were making an excuse for it, we say that of course the animal is not a human creature. So we suppose that there is something superior in man, and that we first receive it from the gods. For since the gods by their nature are pure and free from corruption, so far as men approach them by reason, so far do they cling to purity and to a love (habit) of purity. But since it is impossible that man's nature (οὐσία) can be altogether pure being mixed (composed) of such materials, reason is applied, as far as it is possible, and reason endeavours to make human nature love purity

The first then and highest purity is that which is in the soul; and we say the same of impurity. Now you could not discover the impurity of the soul as you could discover that of the body: but as to the soul, what else could you find in it than that which makes it filthy in respect to the acts which are her own? Now the acts of the soul are movement towards an object or movement from it, desire, aversion, preparation, design (purpose), assent. What then is it which in these acts makes the soul filthy and impure? Nothing else than her own bad judgments (κρίματα). Consequently the impurity of the soul is the soul's bad opinions; and the purification of the soul is the planting in it of proper opinions; and the soul is pure which has proper opinions, for the soul alone in her own acts is free from perturbation and pollution.

Now we ought to work at something like this in the body also, as far as we can. It was impossible for the defluxions of the nose not to run when man has such a mixture in his body. For this reason nature has made hands and the nostrils themselves as channels for carrying off the humours. If then a man sucks up the defluxions, I say that he is not doing the act of a man. It was impossible for a man's feet not to be made muddy and not be soiled at all when he passes through dirty places. For this reason nature (God) has made water and hands. It was impossible that some impurity should not remain in the teeth from eating: for this reason, she says, wash the teeth. Why? In order that you may be a man and not a wild beast or a hog. It was impossible that from the sweat and the pressing of the clothes there should not remain some impurity about the body which requires to be cleaned away. For this reason water, oil, hands, towels, scrapers (strigils),[1] nitre, sometimes all other kinds of means are necessary for cleaning the body. You do not act so: but the smith will take off the rust from the iron (instruments), and he will have tools prepared for this purpose, and you yourself wash the platter when you are going to eat, if you are not completely impure and dirty: but will you not wash the body nor make it clean? Why? he replies. I will tell you again; in the first place, that you may do the acts of a man; then, that you may not be disagreeable to those with whom you associate. You do something of this kind even in this matter, and you do not perceive it. you think that you deserve to stink. Let it be so: deserve to stink. Do you think that also those who sit by you, those who recline at table with you, that those who kiss you deserve the same? Either go into a desert, where you deserve to go, or live by yourself, and smell yourself. For it is just that you alone should enjoy your own impurity. But when you are in a city, to behave so inconsiderately and foolishly, to what character do you think that it belongs? If nature had entrusted to you a horse, would you have overlooked and neglected him? And now think that you have been entrusted with your own body as with a horse; wash it, wipe it, take care that no man turns away from it, that no one gets out of the way for it. But who does not get out of the way of a dirty man, of a stinking man, of a man whose skin is foul, more than he does out of the way of a man who is daubed with muck? That smell is from without, it is put upon him; but the other smell is from want of care, from within, and in a manner from a body in putrefaction.

But Socrates washed himself seldom.—Yes, but his body was clean and fair: and it was so agreeable and sweet that the most beautiful and the most noble loved him, and desired to sit by him rather than by the side of those who had the handsomest forms. It was in his power neither to use the bath nor to wash himself, if he chose; and yet the rare use of water had an effect. [If you do not choose to wash with warm water, wash with cold.[2]]   But Aristophanes says

"Those who are pale, unshod, 'tis those I mean."[3]

For Aristophanes says of Socrates that he also walked the air and stole clothes from the palæstra.[4]   But all who have written about Socrates bear exactly the contrary evidence in his favour; they say that he was pleasant not only to hear, but also to see.[5] On the other hand they write the same about Diogenes.[6] For we ought not even by the appearance of the body to deter the multitude from philosophy; but as in other things a philosopher should show himself cheerful and tranquil, so also he should in the things that relate to the body; "See, ye men, that I have nothing, that I want nothing: see how I am without a house, and without a city, and an exile, if it happens to be so,[7] and without a hearth I live more free from trouble and more happily than all of noble birth and than the rich.   But look at my poor body also and observe that it is not injured by my hard way of living." But if a man says this to me, who has the appearance (dress) and face of a condemned man, what God shall persuade me to approach philosophy, if it makes men such persons? Far from it; I would not choose to do so, even if I were going to become a wise man.   I indeed would rather that a young man, who is making his first movements towards philosophy, should come to me with his hair carefully trimmed than

with it dirty and rough, for there is seen in him a certain
notion (appearance) of beauty and a desire of (attempt
at) that which is becoming; and where he supposes it
to be, there also he strives that it shall be. It is only necessary to show him (what it is) and to say: "Young man,
you seek beauty, and you do well; you must know then
that it (is produced) grows in that part of you where
you have the rational faculty; seek it there where you
have the movements towards and the movements from
things, where you have the desires towards, and the
aversion from things; for this is what you have in yourself
of a superior kind; but the poor body is naturally only earth:
why do you labour about it to no purpose? if you shall learn
nothing else, you will learn from time that the body is nothing." But if a man comes to me daubed with filth, dirty, with
a moustache down to his knees, what can I say to him, by
what kind of resemblance can I lead him on? For about
what has he busied himself which resembles beauty, that I
may be able to change him and say, Beauty is not in this,
but in that? Would you have me to tell him, that beauty
consists not in being daubed with muck, but that it lies in the
rational part? Has he any desire of beauty? has he any
form of it in his mind? Go and talk to a hog, and tell him
not to roll in the mud.

For this reason the words of Xenocrates touched Polemon
also, since he was a lover of beauty, for he entered (the
room) having in him certain incitements (ἐναύσματα) to love
of beauty, but he looked for it in the wrong place.[8] For
nature has not made even the animals dirty which live with
man. Does a horse ever wallow in the mud, or a well bred
dog? But the hog, the dirty geese, and worms and spiders do, which are banished furthest from human intercourse. Do you then being a man choose to be not as one of
the animals which live with man, but rather a worm, or a
spider? Will you not wash yourself somewhere some time
in such manner as you choose?[9] Will you not wash off the
dirt from your body? Will you not come clean that those
with whom you keep company may have pleasure in being
with you? But do you go with us even into the temples in

such a state, where it is not permitted to spit or blow the
nose, being a heap of spittle and of snot?

What then? does any man (that is, do I) require you to
ornament yourself? Far from it; except to ornament that
which we really are by nature, the rational faculty, the opinions, the actions; but as to the body only so far as purity,
only so far as not to give offence. But if you are told that
you ought not to wear garments dyed with purple, go and
daub your cloak with muck or tear it.[10] But how shall I
have a neat cloak? Man, you have water; wash it. Here is
a youth worthy of being loved,[11] here is an old man worthy
of loving and being loved in return, a fit person for a man to
intrust to him a son's instruction, to whom daughters and
young men shall come, if opportunity shall so happen, that
the teacher shall deliver his lessons to them on a dunghill
Let this not be so: every deviation comes from something
which is in man's nature; but this (deviation) is near being ·
something not in man's nature.

NOTES

[1] The ζύστρα, as Epictetus names it, was the Roman "strigilis,"
which was used for the scraping and cleaning of the body in bathing.
Persius (v. 126) writes—

"I, puer, et strigiles Crispini ad balnea defer."

The strigiles "were of bronze or iron of various forms. They were
applied to the body much in the same way as we see a piece of hoop
applied to a sweating horse." Pompeii, edited by Dr. Dyer.
[2] See what is said of this passage in the latter part of this chapter.
[3] Nubes, v. 102
[4] Aristophanes, Nubes, v 225, and v. 179
[5] Zenophon, Memorab. iii. 12.
[6] See iii 22.
[7] Diogenes, it is said, was driven from his native town Sinope in Asia
on a charge of having debased or counterfeited the coinage. Upton.
It is probable that this is false.
[8] As to Polemon see iii 1, 14
[9] It has been suggested that the words "if you do not choose to wash
with warm water, wash with cold," p. 366, belong to this place.
[10] This is the literal translation: but it means "will you go, etc., tear
it?"
[11] "The youth, probably, means the scholar, who neglects neatness;
and the old man, the tutor, that gives him no precept or example of it."
Mrs. Carter.

CHAPTER XII

ON ATTENTION

WHEN you have remitted your attention for a short time, do not imagine this, that you will recover it when you choose; but let this thought be present to you, that in consequence of the fault committed to-day your affairs must be in a worse condition for all that follows. For first, and what causes most trouble, a habit of not attending is formed in you; then a habit of deferring your attention. And continually from time to time you drive away by deferring it the happiness of life, proper behaviour, the being and living conformably to nature. If then the procrastination of attention is profitable, the complete omission of attention is more profitable; but if it is not profitable, why do you not maintain your attention constant? —To-day I choose to play.—Well then, ought you not to play with attention?—I choose to sing.—What then hinders you from doing so with attention? Is there any part of life excepted, to which attention does not extend? For will you do it (any thing in life) worse by using attention, and better by not attending at all? And what else of the things in life is done better by those who do not use attention? Does he who works in wood work better by not attending to it? Does the captain of a ship manage it better by not attending? and is any of the smaller acts done better by inattention? Do you not see that when you have let your mind loose, it is no longer in your power to recall it, either to propriety, or to modesty, or to moderation: but you do every thing that comes into your mind in obedience to your inclinations.

To what things then ought I to attend? First to those general (principles) and to have them in readiness, and without them not to sleep, not to rise, not to drink, not to eat, not to converse (associate) with men; that no man is master of another man's will, but that in the will alone is the good and the bad. No man then has the power either to procure for me good or to involve me in any evil, but I alone myself over myself have power in these things. When then these things are secured to me, why need I be disturbed about external things? What tyrant is formidable, what disease, what poverty, what offence (from any man)? Well, I have not pleased a certain person. Is he then (the pleasing of him) my work, my judgment? No. Why then should I trouble myself about him?—But he is supposed to be some one (of importance).—He will look to that himself; and those who think so will also. But I have one whom I ought to please, to whom I ought to subject myself, whom I ought to obey, God and those who are next to him. He has placed me with myself, and has put my will in obedience to myself alone, and has given me rules for the right use of it; and when I follow these rules in syllogisms, I do not care for any man who says any thing else (different): in sophistical argument, I care for no man. Why then in greater matters do those annoy me who blame me? What is the cause of this perturbation? Nothing else than because in this matter (topic) I am not disciplined. For all knowledge (science) despises ignorance and the ignorant; and not only the sciences, but even the arts. Produce any shoemaker that you please, and he ridicules the many in respect to his own work (business). Produce any carpenter.

First then we ought to have these (rules) in readiness, and to do nothing without them, and we ought to keep the soul directed to this mark, to pursue nothing external, and nothing which belongs to others (or is in the power of others), but to do as he has appointed who has the power; we ought to pursue altogether the things which are in the power of the will, and all other things as it is permitted. Next to this we ought to remember who we are, and what is our name, and to endeavour to direct our duties towards the character (nature) of our several relations (in life) in this manner: what is the season for singing, what is the season for play, and in whose presence; what will be the consequence of the act; whether our associates will despise us, whether we shall despise them; when to jeer (σκῶψαι), and whom to ridicule; and on what occasion to comply and with whom; and finally, in complying how to maintain our own character. But wherever you have deviated from any of these rules, there is damage immediately, not from any thing external, but from the action itself.

What then? is it possible to be free from faults (if you do all this)? It is not possible; but this is possible, to direct your efforts incessantly to being faultless. For we must be content if by never remitting this attention we shall escape at least a few errors. But now when you have said, "To-morrow I will begin to attend," you must be told that you are saying this, "To-day I will be shameless, disregardful of time and place, mean; it will be in the power of others to give me pain; to-day I will be passionate, and envious." See how many evil things you are permitting yourself to do. If it is good to use attention to-morrow, how much better is it to do so to-day? if to-morrow it is in your interest to attend, much more is it to-day, that you may be able to do so to-morrow also, and may not defer it again to the third day.

CHAPTER XIII

WHEN a man has seemed to us to have talked with simplicity (candour) about his own affairs, how is it that at last we are ourselves also induced to discover to him our own secrets and we think this to be candid behaviour? In the first place because it seems unfair for a man to have listened to the affairs of his neighbour, and not to communicate to him also in turn our own affairs; next, because we think that we shall not present to them the appearance of candid men when we are silent about our own affairs. Indeed men are often accustomed to say, I have told you all my affairs, will you tell me nothing of your own? where is this done?—Besides, we have also this opinion that we can safely trust him who has already told us his own affairs; for the notion rises in our mind that this man could never divulge our affairs because he would be cautious that we also should not divulge his. In this way also the incautious are caught by the soldiers at Rome. A soldier sits by you in a common dress and begins to speak ill of Cæsar; then you, as if you had received a pledge of his fidelity by his having begun the abuse, utter yourself also what you think, and then you are carried off in chains.[1]

Something of this kind happens to us also generally. Now as this man has confidently intrusted his affairs to me, shall I also do so to any man whom I meet? (No), for when I have heard, I keep silence, if I am of such a disposition; but he goes forth and tells all men what he has heard. Then if I hear what has been done, if I be a man like him, I resolve to be revenged, I divulge what he has told me; I both disturb others and am disturbed myself. But if I remember that one man does not injure another, and that every man's acts injure and profit him, I secure this, that I do not any thing like him, but still I suffer what I do suffer through my own silly talk.

True: but it is unfair when you have heard the secrets of

372

your neighbour for you in your turn to communicate nothing
to him.—Did I ask you for your secrets, my man? did you
communicate your affairs on certain terms, that you should
in return hear mine also? If you are a babbler and think
that all who meet you are friends, do you wish me also to be
like you? But why, if you did well in intrusting your affairs
to me, and it is not well for me to intrust mine to you, do you
wish me to be so rash? It is just the same as if I had a cask
which is water-tight, and you one with a hole in it, and you
should come and deposit with me your wine that I might put
it into my cask, and then should complain that I also did not
intrust my wine to you, for you have a cask with a hole in it.
How then is there any equality here? You intrusted your
affairs to a man who is faithful, and modest, to a man who
thinks that his own actions alone are injurious and (or) useful, and that nothing external is. Would you have me intrust mine to you, a man who has dishonoured his own faculty of will, and who wishes to gain some small bit of money
or some office or promotion in the court (emperor's palace),
even if you should be going to murder your own children,
like Medea? Where (in what) is this equality (fairness)?
But show yourself to me to be faithful, modest, and steady:
show me that you have friendly opinions; show that your
cask has no hole in it; and you will see how I shall not wait
for you to trust me with your affairs, but I myself shall come
to you and ask you to hear mine. For who does not choose
to make use of a good vessel? Who does not value a benevolent and faithful adviser? who will not willingly receive a
man who is ready to bear a share, as we may say, of the difficulty of his circumstances, and by this very act to ease the
burden, by taking a part of it.

True: but I trust you; you do not trust me.—In the first
place, not even do you trust me, but you are a babbler, and
for this reason you can not hold anything; for indeed, if it
is true that you trust me, trust your affairs to me only; but
now whenever you see a man at leisure, you seat yourself by
him and say: "Brother, I have no friend more benevolent
than you nor dearer; I request you to listen to my affairs."
And you do this even to those who are not known to you at

all. But if you really trust me, it is plain that you trust me because I am faithful and modest, not because I have told my affairs to you. Allow me then to have the same opinion about you. Show me that if one man tells his affairs to another, he who tells them is faithful and modest. For if this were so, I would go about and tell my affairs to every man, if that would make me faithful and modest. But the thing is not so, and it requires no common opinions (principles). If then you see a man who is busy about things not dependent on his will and subjecting his will to them, you must know that this man has ten thousand persons to compel and hinder him. He has no need of pitch or the wheel to compel him to declare what he knows :[2] but a little girl's nod, if it should so happen, will move him, the blandishment of one who belongs to Cæsar's court, desire of a magistracy or of an inheritance, and things without end of that sort. You must remember then among general principles that secret discourses (discourses about secret matters) require fidelity and corresponding opinions. But where can we now find these easily? Or if you can not answer that question, let some one point out to me a man who can say: I care only about the things which are my own, the things which are not subject to hindrance, the things which are by nature free. This I hold to be the nature of the good: but let all other things be as they are allowed; I do not concern myself.

NOTES

[1] The man, whether a soldier or not, was an informer, one of those vile men who carried on this shameful business under the empire. He was what Juvenal names a "delator." Upton, who refers to the life of Hadrian by Ælius Spartianus, speaks even of this emperor employing soldiers named Frumentarii for the purpose of discovering what was said and done in private houses John the Baptist (Luke iii 14) in answer to the question of the soldiers, "And what shall we do?" said unto them "Do violence to no man, neither accuse any falsely; and be content with your wages." Upton.

[2] The wheel and pitch were instruments of torture to extract confessions. See ii. 6, 18, and Schweighäuser's note there.

END OF THE DISCOURSES OF EPICTETUS

MEDITATIONS OF
MARCUS AURELIUS ANTONINUS

Meditations of Aurelius
George Long

Landmarks of Civilization

MARCUS AURELIUS

From a bust in Rome

Meditations of
[arcus Aurelius Antonin

Translated by
George Long

With a Critical and Biographical Introduction
by John Lancaster Spalding

Illustrated

New York
D. Appleton and Company
1904

MARCUS AURELIUS

———◆◆———

THE intimate thoughts of a wise and noble man concerning whatever touches the human heart most
nearly are necessarily interesting, and when he who
utters them has stood for years at the head of a vast and
powerful empire his words receive a new significance,
which is still further heightened by the fact that he writes
not for the public, but simply to render to himself an account of himself. This is what we have in the " Meditations " of Marcus Aurelius, the Roman emperor, a man
so modest, so sincere, so kindly, so magnanimous, that to
know him is to conceive a higher opinion of the race which
in him attains to such dignity and virtue. He was born
at Rome in the year 121 of the Christian era, and died in
180, a few weeks before his fifty-ninth birthday. He was
the nephew and adopted son of Antoninus Pius, whom from
early manhood he assisted in administering public affairs.
He became emperor at the age of forty, and reigned nine-
teen years, twelve of which he passed in Asia Minor, Syria,
Greece, Egypt, and the countries on the Danube, putting
down rebellion or defending the empire against the at-
tacks of the barbarians, having at the same time to face
various public misfortunes—inundations, famines, earthquakes, fires, and pestilence—which caused widespread
misery and dismay. But though constantly surrounded by
grave difficulties and dangers, and compelled to travel to

almost every part of the empire, he not only found time to devote himself, as a wise and careful ruler, to even the minor interests and details of government, but also to occupy himself with the study of philosophy and his own improvement. It is the history of his inner life, as recorded in his journal, which has made him immortal, and placed him in the company of the few in whom the lovers of wisdom and perfection find it possible to take genuine delight. The book has small literary merit. The language is without elegance or distinction. He tells us that he had learned to abstain from rhetoric and poetry and fine writing. He studied simplicity and plainness in all things. He jots down detached thoughts, often merely gives us notes or indications, and his views are seldom profound or original. He is a Stoic, but does not develop or follow consistently any system of philosophy. He wavers and is uncertain precisely in those things in which a firm-rooted faith is most inspiring and invigorating. Running all through his " Meditations " there is an undercurrent of sadness and despondency. Is it because he is compelled to labour in a vocation for which Nature did not intend him, or is it due to the sight of the corruption and worthlessness of those by whom he was surrounded, indicating plainly to him that the fabric of Roman civilization was falling to ruin, or is it to be attributed to the fatalism which determines and controls his world-view? There was little either in the condition of society or in his own religious faith to cheer and strengthen; and yet it is impossible to live with him in his book without feeling that we are in the company of one of the best, wisest, and bravest of men, of one who, placed on the summit of power and splendour, was never for a moment blinded by the glitter and the show, but, looking steadfastly at the heart of things, remained simple, sincere, modest, self-controlled, and loving. We forget that he was an emperor; we care not in what style he utters himself; we are not curious about his metaphysical theories, or disposed to argue and dispute; it is enough that we are in his presence, that we hear his words of wisdom and Stoic piety, with the reverence, candour, and devoutness with which he speaks them.

He is a born teacher of morals, a born preacher of the surpassing worth of the inner life; and this natural bent was confirmed by his education, of which he has given an account in the first book of the " Meditations," where he mentions with gratitude that he was not sent to a public school, and that his tutors were men of character and learn-, ing. " To the gods," he says, " I am indebted for having good grandfathers, good parents, a good sister, good teachers, good associates, good kinsmen and friends— nearly everything good." He began his studies, as was the custom of the time, with rhetoric and poetry, but at the age of twelve he became a pupil of the Stoics, and adopted their austere practices as well as their dress, lead- ing a life so abstemious and laborious as to injure his health, which remained delicate. Much of his youth was passed in the country, at the villa of Lorium, where, while con- tinuing to read, he engaged in the pleasures of the chase, mingled with the vintagers, and occupied himself with ath- letic sports. Here, too, he enjoyed more exclusively the society and conversation of his mother, from whom, he tells us, he learned piety and beneficence, and abstinence not only from evil deeds, but even from evil thoughts, and simplicity in his way of living far removed from the habits of the rich. By her influence also he was strengthened to preserve intact the virginal flower of his youth. Nor does he forget to mention the admirable precepts given by his tutors, who taught him to love work, to deny himself, to endure misfortunes without complaint, not to deviate from his purpose, to be considerate of others, not to listen to evil speech, to be grave without affectation, and not

to seek excuses for neglecting duty. Rusticus, whom he
thanks for having made him acquainted with the "Discourses of Epictetus," warned him against the study of
what is merely speculative or ornamental. The example
of his masters made a greater impression even than their
words; and what touched him most was their patience,
firmness, equanimity, mildness, beneficence, uprightness,
and sincerity. In these " Meditations " there is not the
faintest trace of vanity. He is lowly minded and the most
modest of men. His candour and truthfulness are perfect. A lie seems to him to be an outrage upon his nature,
upon the divinity that dwells in him. He strives not only
to think and feel, but to love what he speaks. He is present
in these thoughts, and we almost seem to have bodily sight
of him as he lived and bore himself nearly eighteen hundred years ago.

The habit of recollection, of self-examination was recommended and practised by the Stoics before the time of
Marcus Aurelius. " Each day," says Seneca, " we should
call our soul to account. This was the custom of Sextius,
who, before taking his nightly rest, invariably passed his
conduct in review: Of what fault hast thou cured thyself
to-day? What passion hast thou combated? In what hast
thou become better? " And the philosopher goes on to
tell us how each evening, when the light was taken from
his room, and his wife, from respect for his pious practice,
became silent, he also was accustomed to recall whatever
he had done or spoken during the day, without dissimulat-
ing or omitting anything whatever; and that when he found
aught blameworthy, he pardoned himself only on condition that the fault should not again be committed. All
that concerns a good life was brought into this inquiry—
the right use of time, the avoidance of the occasions of
wrongdoing, human respect, the keeping guard over one's
thoughts and words, mindfulness of the presence of God,

of the certainty of death, and of the necessity of being prepared to meet it with courage and dignity. We do not
know that Marcus Aurelius practised this daily and methodical examination of conscience, but he certainly habit-
ually meditated the great moral truths, living in ideas,
not in material interests; in principles, not in passions. In
his youth even, as we learn from one of his letters to
Fronto, he was accustomed to make extracts from the
books he read, and to these little volumes, into which he
had gathered the fine essence of the best writers, he doubtless often recurred. In this way he cultivated a taste for
the brief and pregnant sayings of the Stoic and other philosophers, and found in them new incentives to lead a
worthy life. A great thought, a winged word may have
power not only to rouse the conscience and the will, but
it may remain with us as a permanent stimulus to virtuous
conduct. A phrase may fasten itself in the mind as though
rivetted with bolts of steel, or it may insinuate itself into
the current of our opinions and beliefs, and, blending with
it, make the waters of life purer and sweeter. He loved
thoughts of this kind, and he has written many which will
continue to be a source of joy and strength as long as generous minds and hearts shall be found on earth. What he
says has additional charm and power because he says it,
because it is the utterance of a genuine man, the purity
and nobleness of whose character can not be called in question, the testimony which his contemporaries bore to his
wisdom, magnanimity, and goodness being confirmed by
the consenting voice of succeeding generations. How
pleasant and invigorating it is to read considerations like
these: " Such as thy habitual thoughts, such also will be
the character of thy mind, for the soul is dyed by the
thoughts. Dye it then with a continuous series of such
thoughts as these; for instance, that where a man can live,
there he can also live well. Live with the gods. Hold

good to consist in the disposition to justice and the practice of it, and in this let thy desire terminate. The greatest part of what we say or do being unnecessary, if a man takes this away, he will have more leisure and less uneasiness. We ought to check in the series of our thoughts everything that is without a purpose and useless. What more dost thou want when thou hast done a man a service? Art thou not content that thou hast done something conformable to thy nature, and dost thou seek to be paid for it, just as if the eye demanded a recompense for seeing or the feet for walking? Have I done something for the general good? Well, then, I have had my reward. Let it not be in any man's power to say truly of thee that thou art not simple or that thou art not good, but let him be a liar whoever shall think anything of this kind about thee. Let men see, let them know a real man who lives according to Nature. If they can not endure him, let them kill him. Look within. Within is the fountain of good, and it will ever bubble up if thou wilt ever dig."

Epictetus and Seneca had taught much of what is best in the "Thoughts" of Marcus Aurelius, but in his company we seem to breathe the air of a higher and serener world. He is meek and patient, affectionate and helpful. In his words there is nothing to recall the hard and haughty spirit of stoicism. He lives with his soul, but he finds the good of life in doing good. He is a worker, not a dreamer. He strives always to behave like a Roman, like a man; he never thinks of himself apart from his fellowmen. What is not useful for the swarm is not useful for the bee. His purpose is to keep himself holy, and to labour for the salvation of men, for the welfare of society. He seeks inner perfection in the midst of courts and camps, but neglects no duty which his high office imposes. In his tent, surrounded by barbarous hordes, he directs his armies, and still has time to write his tender and lofty thoughts.

In these he finds the strength to bear the awful burden 'which is laid upon him. Each morning he reminds himself that he awakens to do a man's work. Philosophy is his mother, while the court is but a stepmother. " Return to philosophy frequently, and repose in her, through whom what thou meetest with in the court appears to thee tolerable, and thou appearest tolerable in the court." He is conscious of the temptations and dangers of his exalted position, and frequently makes them the subject of his " Meditations." " Take care that thou art not made into a Cæsar, that thou art not dyed with this dye, for such things happen. Keep thyself then simple, good, pure, serious, free from affectation, a friend of justice, a worshipper of the gods, kind, affectionate, strenuous in all proper acts. Strive to continue to be such as philosophy wished to make thee. Reverence the gods, and help men." He encourages himself in this noble purpose by recalling the example of Antoninus, his adoptive father—his constancy, his evenness in all things, his piety, the serenity of his countenance, his sweetness, his disregard of empty fame, and his efforts to understand things. He remembers how he bore with those who blamed him unjustly; how he did nothing in a hurry; how he refused to listen to calumnies; how he was content with little; how laborious, patient, and firm he was; how tolerant of those who opposed his opinions; how eager to learn.

Men must have a chief, as the world a ruler, the herd a leader; but this chief is not above the laws. His ideal is that " of a polity in which there is the same law for all, a polity administered with regard to equal rights and equal freedom of speech, and the idea of a kingly government which respects most of all the freedom of the governed." He abhors whatever is arbitrary or unjust, and finds nothing so odious as the character of a tyrant, which he couples with such epithets as black, bestial, animal, stupid, counterfeit, scurrilous, and fraudulent. He admires the martyrs of patriotism who have been the victims of tyrannical emperors. His knowledge of the incredible cruelties of some of his predecessors on the imperial throne seemed to drive him almost to excessive leniency. When he heard of the assassination of Avidius Cassius, who at the head of the armies of Asia had revolted, and against whom he was marching, he said he was sorry to be deprived of the pleasure of pardoning him. He does not think with the elder Stoics that to be virtuous one must be harsh and unbending. "In mildness and goodness," he says, "there is a higher quality of manliness." His constant aim is to unite benignity with firmness. He does not wish to be too severe even with himself. "It is not right that I should afflict myself, I who have never willingly given pain to any one." He has the tenderness and delicacy of soul of a noble woman. There is a large benevolence and sympathy in his judgment of men, even when they are perverse ' He is ever ready to be of help; he is full of affection and clemency. The temple he built he dedicated to Goodness, a divinity hitherto unknown in Rome. "Love men," he says, "but with a genuine love." "Thou dost not yet love men with all thy heart." "It is not enough to forgive; thou must love those who do thee wrong." The only revenge he permits is to make one's self unlike the evildoer. Correct, if thou canst, the wicked; if not, suffer them: for this good-will has been given thee Be like the vine, which bears its fruit and asks no reward. For the rest, to be a blessing to others is to be a friend to one's self. When there is question of doing good, one should be of those who know not what they do—a benefactor without thinking that any one is his debtor. What may be called his great precept is: Love mankind; follow God. He has no weak thoughts about his own happiness. It is well enough with him when he lives in accord with uni-

versal law, when he fulfils his duties as a child of God and
a member of the whole human family. Besides, has he not
a sure refuge within his own heart, where at every moment he may live with the thoughts which give peace to
the soul? It is not necessary for him to seek the seashore
or the mountains to avoid distractions, for it is always in
his power to retire into himself, and to find there the things
which induce the tranquil mind—those brief and fundamental principles which, whenever he recurs to them, make
him calm and strong, and send him back free from all discontent to his appointed work. Thus he lives in intimate
communion with the divinity present within him, and
seeks in the contemplation of the laws of reason protection from temptation, discouragement, and weakness His
favourite virtues are justice and truth; but he is in tune
with whatever makes for magnanimity, freedom, strength,
and holiness of life. He cares not for fame, or wealth, or
power, or pleasure Things are largely what we think
they are, and if we but understand that virtue is the only
essential good, we shall not deem poverty, or ill health, or
pain, or death an evil. One may be a divine man and be
unknown, while they who are praised are praised, for the
most part, ignorantly or by the false and the fickle. What,
after all, is man? The earth is but a point, and the present
in which alone we can live but a moment lost between
two infinities. Fame is good when it increases the will
and the power to do good, else it is naught, mere sound,
and emptiness. The clapping of hands and the clapping
of tongues are vanities in which none but the childish take
delight. The emotion with which he touches on the favourite theme of dull and gloomy declaimers—the hollowness
and evanescence of human life and grandeur—imparts a
certain charm and freshness to his words: " Consider the
times of Vespasian! Thou wilt see all these things—people marrying, bringing up children, sick, dying, warring,

feasting, trafficking, cultivating the ground, flattering, obstinately arrogant, suspecting, plotting, wishing for somebody to die, grumbling about the present, loving, heaping
up treasure, desiring to be consuls or kings. We see, then,
that life of these people no longer exists at all. Again,
go to the times of Trajan. All is again the same. Their
life, too, is gone." He is full of commonplaces on this and
kindred subjects. He does not weary of them, but hunts
for arguments and comparisons to express his sense of the
worthlessness of fame, of the shortness of life, and the vanity of all things, especially of those which attract with the
bait of pleasure or terrify by pain, or are noised abroad by
the voices of men. What belongs to the body is a stream,
and what belongs to the soul is a dream and a vapour. All
pass quickly and are buried in oblivion, both they who
remember and they who are remembered. As he grows
older his sense of the hopeless sadness of life grows keener.
He is still resigned, still obedient to the eternal laws, but
he advances into ever-deepening gloom, where no ray of
light falls. His health was broken, and the evils which
he had worn himself out in trying to overcome were breaking forth again on every side. In the midst of his own
family he was unhappy. His wife, though she has doubtless been the victim of calumny, had ceased to sympathize
with him, and hated his friends. She had grown weary
of his philosophy and of the society of philosophers. His
austerity, his melancholy, his aversion to gaiety and splendour, his grave maxims, were offensive to her pleasure-
craving nature. Though he gave no heed to the malicious
rumours about her, though he continued to love her as
" his good and faithful spouse," he was depressed by the
knowledge of her lack of heart for him. Commodus, his
son and successor, was a cause of still more poignant sorrow than Faustina. He was a mere animal, without intelligence or feeling, and though but seventeen years old at

the time of his father's death, he had already manifested something of the dispositions which made him later one of the most brutal tyrants by whom the world has been cursed.

The emperor has been blamed for not disinheriting him and adopting some one worthy to rule; but he had been proclaimed Cæsar while yet a boy, and by the time his evil nature had revealed itself Marcus was too infirm to take so decisive a step. In fact, it would have been necessary to murder him, for had he been left alive the military party, already disgusted with the rule of the philosophers, as shown in the revolt of Avidius, would have placed him at the head of the army, and plunged the empire into the horrors of civil war. And then what is more natural than that a father should believe that time and responsibility would correct the faults of his youthful son? Nevertheless, Commodus filled him with forebodings and increased his weight of care and pain, which already was too heavy for his declining strength. His friends are dead, the barbarians are in arms, the corruption of morals is spreading, faith in the gods has degenerated into gross superstition, the reforms which he had laboured to bring about are superficial and ineffectual, the laws had been made better, but the life of the people continued to become more false and brutal, the army was losing its old-time loyalty and discipline—on all sides the signs of decadence were manifest.

In the midst of a falling world, in the presence of the northern hordes, menacing destruction and ruin, the emperor still meditates, still studies how he may fortify his soul. He does not despise death, but waits for it, content to see it come. It will deliver him from the sight of the corruption by which he is surrounded. His departure will not be from men who have the same principles as himself. "Come quick, O Death! lest perchance I, too, should for-

get myself." There will not be lacking those who are
glad to see him go, whose lives his very presence condemns: " Let us at last breathe freely, being relieved from
this schoolmaster." In dying he will go away from those
for whom he strove, prayed, and cared so much, but who
nevertheless wish to see him depart, hoping thereby to get
some little advantage. " Why, then, should he desire to
stay longer? " It is better to be dead than to live as they.
Thou art in the grasp of fatal laws; be not like a pig that
squeals and struggles when it is sacrificed, but accept with
resignation what destiny decrees. Men are but leaves
which the wind seizes and scatters on the ground. Thus
weariness of life grows upon him, until he seems to be
without God and without hope in the world. In fact, he
had neither a philosophy nor a religion which can satisfy
the human heart. He was never able to settle for himself
the ultimate problems, the foundations of all ethical principles—God, immortality, and the freedom of the will.
He speaks as a polytheist, or a deist, or a pantheist, according to his mood. At Athens he founded chairs of philosophy for the Platonic, Stoic, Peripatetic, and Epicurean
schools, giving the same honour to the atheist as to the
believer in the gods. At times he seems to doubt even
that to which he holds most firmly. His grasp of speculative truth is feeble; he is strong and helpful only as a
teacher of the conduct of life. Outside of this we find in
him little but uncertainty and confusion. His moral principles even rest on no foundation of dogma, or, if on any,
it is that of cosmic pantheism. His theology is as vague
and variable as his philosophy. He has no settled con-
victions concerning the soul and its immortality. When
our little boat comes to shore and we get out, he leaves it
undecided whether it is to enter on another life or simply
to lose all sensation, to cease to be. His thought moves
between alternatives. " To go from among men, if there

are gods, is not a thing to be afraid of, for the gods will
not involve thee in evil; but if, indeed, they do not exist,
or if they have no concern about human affairs, what is it
to me to live in a universe devoid of gods or devoid of
providence? " Then he reassures himself and declares that
the gods do exist, and that they do care for human things;
at least they place the avoidance of real evils in a man's
power. But death and life, honour and dishonour, pain
and pleasure, are neither good nor evil, and therefore they
happen alike to all. God is for him the universal reason,
the immutable law which governs all things. He is the
whole, he is nature itself; the indwelling force which
gives order and beauty to the universe. How this divinity, this inexorable fate, is to be reconciled with Providence
and with the freedom of the will, or be made an object of
prayer and adoration, he does not attempt to explain.
" Out of the universe from the beginning everything which
happens has been apportioned and spun out to thee."
" Accept everything which happens, even if it seem disagreeable, because it leads to this, to the health of the
universe and to the prosperity and felicity of Zeus." Here
he joins theism and pantheism, but by Zeus he really means
the universe, the universal substance of which the individual has but a very small portion. As this universal substance exists necessarily, from it by fatal laws the thread
of each one's destiny is spun. " Whatever may happen
to thee was prepared for thee from all eternity, and the
implication of causes was from eternity spinning the thread
of thy being." At times he seems to regard the universe
as an immense animal, " one living being, having one substance and one soul." But it is perhaps wrong to insist
on the theoretical views of a man who had little intellectual
curiosity, and cared hardly at all for what is speculative.
Still it is impossible not to recognise that he himself felt
that the help which pantheism can offer the soul is inef-
25

fectual. Even a philosopher can derive small comfort from
the thought that his absorption into the mass of matter is
for the interest of the All, which contains nothing that is
not for its advantage. For the multitude such a belief is
without worth or meaning. Stoic morality is interesting
chiefly on account of its influence upon men like Epictetus
and Marcus Aurelius, who found in it a source of strength
in the midst of the universal corruption in which Greco-
Roman civilization was disappearing. It could never have
become a principle of social regeneration. The fatalism
on which it rests makes enthusiasm impossible. Its resignation is despondency; its indifference, hopelessness. It
lacks vitality and joyousness. There is in it no love of
life, no belief in progress. The Stoic sage stands alone,
conscious of his own virtue, in the midst of a world of liars
and hypocrites. He is not angry with men; he is kind
even, and glad to be of help; but, in truth, he has little
sympathy with them. They are blind and perverse, an
infinite number of fools, who are deprived of that which
alone can make life bearable. Hence stoicism necessarily
fails. It can neither interest nor influence the mass of mankind. It is dry and hard. It inspires no glad emotion,
no immortal hope. It does not thrill the soul with the consciousness that Life is lord of Death, that truth and love lie
at the heart of being, that whether we live or whether we die
we are borne in the arms of the eternal Father, who knows
and cares for each, even the least of his children. It can
not make us feel that the loving spirit of God leads us
forth into the land of righteousness, that we are reborn
into a kingdom of peace and joy and blessedness. It can
not give the faith which overcomes all things, and guides
us through the portals of death into everlasting life. It
has no words of pardon and comfort for sinners who repent. The power that was to regenerate the world, was
already active under the eyes of Marcus Aurelius, but was

wholly misunderstood by him. He alludes to the Christian religion once only. "What a soul," he writes, "that is which is ready, if at any moment it must be separated from the body, and ready either to be extinguished, or dispersed, or to continue to exist; but so that this readiness comes from a man's own judgment, not from mere obstinacy, as with the Christians!" From his point of view the martyrs were obdurate fanatics and enemies of the empire. Of his humanity and tolerance there can be no doubt, but, unfortunately, there can be just as little doubt that he persecuted the Christians, or at the least permitted them to be persecuted. Intensely moral natures are apt to be narrow and rigid, and though several apologies for the new faith were addressed to him, he either never read them or was incapable of taking a world-view so utterly opposed to that of the Stoic philosophy. They who are placed in high stations are often the last to see the real trend of things, for the possession of power, like the possession of wealth or the indulgence of appetite, seems to impede insight; and this kind-hearted and spiritual-minded man had not a suspicion of the true nature of the teaching of Christ. It did not appeal to him as a philosophy, and as a religion it seemed to him atheistic, for it denied the existence of the gods whom he revered and whose worship he thought inseparable from loyalty to the empire. He felt, as all the thoughtful minds of the time felt, that here was a new spirit, which, if it should prevail, would lead to the overthrow of the old civilization. He may not have held with Tacitus that the Christians were convicted of hatred of the human race, but he believed that they were the enemies of the Roman state. The ancients looked upon religion as essentially a national affair. They had no conception of what we mean by liberty of conscience. The appeal from Cæsar to God was for them meaningless, if not impious. When the Christians declared that they were ready to obey all civil and military laws, but reserved to themselves freedom to worship God according to the principles of their faith, which forbade them to offer sacrifice to idols, they uttered words which their enemies could not understand, words which Christians themselves in later ages have often been unable or unwilling to understand.

It was but two or three years before the death of Marcus Aurelius that the persecution broke forth at Lyons. The emperor, who became prematurely old, was in feeble health and surrounded by dangers and difficulties. The populace, eager to believe the Christians guilty of the most atrocious crimes, attributed whatever evils befell the state to the anger of the gods against their contemners, and clamoured for their punishment. The emperor yielded to the popular fury, and the church of Lyons gave to the world an example of heroism which, if ever equalled, has never been surpassed. It is the very irony of fate that Marcus Aurelius should be counted among the persecutors of the Christians, that his name should be coupled with those of Nero and Domitian. It is doubtful whether he himself issued a new edict or simply permitted those of his predecessors to be enforced. Melito, Bishop of Sardis, who addressed a letter to the emperor, leads us to suppose that he had sent forth decrees which resulted in the martyrdom of St. Polycarp, Bishop of Smyrna, ten years before the persecution at Lyons.

On the other hand, Tertullian, writing twenty years after the death of Marcus Aurelius, affirms in the most positive manner that he protected the Christians; that if he did not expressly revoke the edicts of former emperors against them, he at least rendered them ineffective by establishing penalties against their accusers. It seems probable that he was not an active persecutor; but he certainly lived and died with an utter misconception of the religion which even then was the only vital force left to a perishing world.

He was, nevertheless, one of the most just and clement of men. There is little genuine wisdom and goodness anywhere, and what there is is rarely found in the palaces of kings and emperors. Let us try to imagine a European ruler or an American President of our day who should be busy with the thoughts and aspirations of Marcus Aurelius. The mere idea seems to be grotesque. He is one in whom the wise have recognised the genuine goodness which has the mark of universality, which, like the best culture, lifts its possessor above party and country, and makes him a blessing for mankind and for all time.

In reading his "Meditations" we are always in the presence of a magnanimous man, of a great soul whose kindliness and good faith we can not doubt unless we ourselves lack love and truth. He will remain in literature as one of its great spiritual forces. He has the vital touch which gives immortality, because it reveals a noble and interesting personality. There is in him the indefinable something which makes writing literature. It is doubtless largely sincerity, the perfect truthfulness which makes the word the mirror of the man. Much of what he says is said by Seneca and Epictetus, but in it there is an accent of his own which gives it a fresh meaning, a new quality. In these disconnected "Thoughts," in spite of repetitions, of incorrectness, and obscurity, there breathes a soul that can not die, there stands forth a character which all men must deem it a privilege to know. The book is alive with the high and rare qualities which go to the making of a true and noble man. In the little casket found in the tent on the Danube where he died there was stored a life which death could not extinguish. The "Meditations" with which he fortified his own spirit in the struggle for better and higher life have consoled and will continue to console kindred spirits in every age; for whatever his doubts and misgivings, his faith in duty and affection, in the supreme

worth of righteousness, was never shaken.   His victories
are forgotten; his efforts to improve the laws, to spread
enlightenment, to help the orphans, are hardly remembered;
but fame, for which he cared not at all, is his forever, and
of our many vanities perhaps the least vain is the fame
which rests on words that never lose their power to inspire,
to illumine, and to strengthen.   The whole earth is the
sepulchre of illustrious men, but it is so only when the
greatness of soul which shone forth in their lives is kept in
imperishable vigour in some immortal book.   ·

                    JOHN LANCASTER SPALDING.

CONTENTS

xxi

LIST OF ILLUSTRATIONS

MEDITATIONS

BOOK I

FROM my grandfather Verus[1] [I learned] good morals and the government of my temper.

From the reputation and remembrance of my father,[2] modesty and manly character.

From my mother,[3] piety and beneficence, and abstinence, not only from evil deeds, but even from evil thoughts; and further, simplicity in my way of living, far removed from the habits of the rich.

From my great-grandfather,[4] not to have frequented public schools, and to have had good teachers at home, and to know that on such things a man should spend liberally.

From my governor, to be neither of the green nor of the blue party at the games in the Circus, nor a partizan either of the Parmularius or the Scutarius at the gladiators' fights; from him too I learned endurance of labour, and to want little, and to work with my own hands, and not to meddle with other people's affairs, and not to be ready to listen to slander.

From Diognetus,[5] not to busy myself about trifling things, and not to give credit to what was said by miracle-workers and jugglers about incantations and the driving away of dæmons and such things; and not to breed quails [for fighting], nor to give myself up passionately to such things; and to endure freedom of speech; and to have become intimate with philosophy; and to have been a hearer, first of Bacchius,

then of Tandasis and Marcianus; and to have written dialogues in my youth; and to have desired a plank bed and
a skin, and whatever else of the kind belongs to the Grecian
discipline.

From Rusticus[6] I received the impression that my character required improvement and discipline; and from him I
learned not to be led astray to sophistic emulation, nor to
writing on speculative matters, nor to delivering little hortatory orations, nor to showing myself off as a man who practises much discipline, or does benevolent acts in order to
make a display; and to abstain from rhetoric, and poetry, and
fine writing; and not to walk about in the house in my out-
door dress, nor to do other things of the kind; and to
write my letters with simplicity, like the letter which Rusticus wrote from Sinuessa to my mother; and with respect
to those who have offended me by words, or done me wrong,
to be easily disposed to be pacified and reconciled, as soon as
they have shown a readiness to be reconciled; and to read
carefully, and not to be satisfied with a superficial understanding of a book; nor hastily to give my assent to those
who talk overmuch; and I am indebted to him for being acquainted with the discourses of Epictetus,[7] which he communicated to me out of his own collection.

From Apollonius[8] I learned freedom of will and undeviating steadiness of purpose; and to look to nothing else, not
even for a moment, except to reason; and to be always the
same, in sharp pains, on the occasion of the loss of a child,
and in long illness; and to see clearly in a living example that
the same man can be both most resolute and yielding, and
not peevish in giving his instruction; and to have had before my eyes a man who clearly considered his experience
and his skill in expounding philosophical principles as the
smallest of his merits; and from him I learned how to receive
from friends what are esteemed favours, without being either
humbled by them or letting them pass unnoticed.

From Sextus,[9] a benevolent disposition, and the example
of a family governed in a fatherly manner, and the idea of
living conformably to nature; and gravity without affectation, and to look carefully after the interests of friends, and
to tolerate ignorant persons, and those who form opinions

without consideration :*¹⁰ he had the power of readily accom-
modating himself to all, so that intercourse with him was
more agreeable than any flattery; and at the same time he was
most highly venerated by those who associated with him:
and he had the faculty both of discovering and ordering, in
an intelligent and methodical way, the principles necessary
for life; and he never showed anger or any other passion, but
was entirely free from passion, and also most affectionate;
and he could express approbation without noisy display, and
he possessed much knowledge without ostentation.

From Alexander¹¹ the grammarian, to refrain from fault-
finding, and not in a reproachful way to chide those who
uttered any barbarous or solecistic or strange-sounding expression; but dexterously to introduce the very expression
which ought to have been used, and in the way of answer or
giving confirmation, or joining in an inquiry about the thing
itself, not about the word, or by some other fit suggestion.

From Fronto¹² I learned to observe what envy, and
duplicity, and hypocrisy are in a tyrant, and that generally
those among us who are called Patricians are rather deficient
in paternal affection.

From Alexander the Platonic, not frequently nor without
necessity to say to any one, or to write in a letter, that I have
no leisure; nor continually to excuse the neglect of duties
required by our relation to those with whom we live, by
alleging urgent occupations.

From Catulus,¹³ not to be indifferent when a friend finds
fault, even if he should find fault without reason, but to try
to restore him to his usual disposition; and to be ready to
speak well of teachers, as it is reported of Domitius and
Athenodotus; and to love my children truly.

From my brother¹⁴ Severus, to love my kin, and to
love truth, and to love justice; and through him I learned to
know Thrasea, Helvidius, Cato, Dion, Brutus;¹⁵ and from
him I received the idea of a polity in which there is the same
law for all, a polity administered with regard to equal rights
and equal freedom of speech, and the idea of a kingly government which respects most of all the freedom of the governed;
I learned from him also * consistency and undeviating steadiness in my regard for philosophy; and a disposition to do

good, and to give to others readily, and to cherish good
hopes, and to believe that I am loved by my friends; and in
him I observed no concealment of his opinions with respect
to those whom he condemned, and that his friends had no
need to conjecture what he wished or did not wish, but it was
quite plain.

From Maximus[16] I learned self-government, and not to
be led aside by anything; and cheerfulness in all circumstances, as well as in illness; and a just admixture in the
moral character of sweetness and dignity, and to do what
was set before me without complaining. ' I observed that
everybody believed that he thought as he spoke, and that in
all that he did he never had any bad intention; and he never
showed amazement and surprise, and was never in a hurry,
and never put off doing a thing, nor was perplexed nor de-
jected, nor did he ever laugh to disguise his vexation, nor, on
the other hand, was he ever passionate or suspicious. He
was accustomed to do acts of beneficence, and was ready to
forgive, and was free from all falsehood; and he presented
the appearance of a man who could not be diverted from
right rather than of a man who had been improved. I observed, too, that no man could ever think that he was despised by Maximus, or ever venture to think himself a better
man. He had also the art of being humorous in an agreeable way.*

In my father[17] I observed mildness of temper, and unchangeable resolution in the things which he had determined
after due deliberation; and no vain glory in those things
which men call honours; and a love of labour and perseverance;
and a readiness to listen to those who had anything to propose for the common weal; and undeviating firmness in giving to every man according to his deserts; and a knowledge
derived from experience of the occasions for vigorous action
and for remission. And I observed that he had overcome all
passion for boys; and he considered himself no more than
any other citizen; and he released his friends from all obligation to sup with him or to attend him of necessity when he
went abroad, and those who had failed to accompany him, by
reason of any urgent circumstances, always found him the
same. I observed too his habit of careful inquiry in all mat-

ters of deliberation, and his persistency, and that he never
stopped his investigation through being satisfied with appearances which first present themselves; and that his disposition was to keep his friends, and not to be soon tired of
them, nor yet to be extravagant in his affection; and to be
satisfied on all occasions, and cheerful; and to foresee things
a long way off, and to provide for the smallest without display; and to check immediately popular applause and all flattery; and to be ever watchful over the things which were
necessary for the administration of the empire, and to be a
good manager of the expenditure, and patiently to endure
the blame which he got for such conduct; and he was neither
superstitious with respect to the gods, nor did he court men
by gifts or by trying to please them, or by flattering the populace; but he showed sobriety and firmness in all things and
never any mean thoughts or action, nor love of novelty.
And the things which conduce in any way to the commodity
of life, and of which fortune gives an abundant supply, he
used without arrogance and without excusing himself; so
that when he had them, he enjoyed them without affectation,
and when he had them not, he did not want them. No one
could ever say of him that he was either a sophist or a
[home-bred] flippant slave or a pedant; but every one ac-
knowledged him to be a man ripe, perfect, above flattery, able
to manage his own and other men's affairs. Besides this, he
honoured those who were true philosophers, and he did not
reproach those who pretended to be philosophers, nor yet
was he easily led by them. He was also easy in conversation, and he made himself agreeable without any offensive
affectation. He took a reasonable care of his body's health,
not as one who was greatly attached to life, nor out of regard to personal appearance, nor yet in a careless way, but
so that, through his own attention, he very seldom stood in
need of the physician's art, or of medicine or external appli-
cations. He was most ready to give way without envy to
those who possessed any particular faculty, such as that of
eloquence, or knowledge of the law or of morals, or of anything else; and he gave them his help, that each might enjoy
reputation according to his deserts; and he always acted conformably to the institutions of his country, without showing

any affectation of doing so.   Further, he was not fond of
change nor unsteady, but he loved to stay in the same places,
and to employ himself about the same things; and after his
paroxysms of headache he came immediately fresh and
vigorous to his usual occupations.   His secrets were not
many, but very few and very rare, and these only about public matters; and he showed prudence and economy in the
exhibition of the public spectacles and the construction of
public buildings, his donations to the people, and in such
things, for he was a man who looked to what ought to be
done, not to the reputation which is got by a man's acts.   He
did not take the bath at unseasonable hours; he was not fond
of building houses, nor curious about what he ate, nor about
the texture and colour of his clothes, nor about the beauty
of his slaves.[18]   His dress came from Lorium, his villa on
the coast, and from Lanuvium generally.[19]   We know how
he behaved to the toll-collector at Tusculum who asked his
pardon; and such was all his behaviour.   There was in him
nothing harsh, nor implacable, nor violent, nor, as one may
say, anything carried to the sweating point; but he examined
all things severally, as if he had abundance of time, and without confusion, in an orderly way, vigorously and consistently.   And that might be applied to him which is recorded
of Socrates,[20] that he was able both to abstain from, and to
enjoy, those things which many are too weak to abstain from,
and can not enjoy without excess.   But to be strong enough
both to bear the one and to be sober in the other is the mark
of a man who has a perfect and invincible soul, such as he
showed in the illness of Maximus.

To the gods I am indebted for having good grandfathers,
good parents, a good sister, good teachers, good associates,
good kinsmen and friends, nearly everything good.   Further,
I owe it to the gods that I was not hurried into any offence
against any of them, though I had a disposition which, if
opportunity had offered, might have led me to do something
of this kind; but, through their favour, there never was such
a concurrence of circumstances as put me to the trial. Further,
I am thankful to the gods that I was not longer brought up
with my grandfather's concubine, and that I preserved the
flower of my youth, and that I did not make proof of my

virility before the proper season, but even deferred the time; that I was subjected to a ruler and a father who was able to take away all pride from me, and to bring me to the knowledge that it is possible for a man to live in a palace without wanting either guards or embroidered dresses, or torches and statues, and similar show; but that it is in such a man's power to bring himself very near to the fashion of a private person, without being for this reason either meaner, in thought, or more remiss in action, with respect to the things which must be done for the public interest in a manner that befits a ruler. I thank the gods for giving me such a brother,[21] who was able by his moral character to rouse me to vigilance over myself, and who, at the same time, pleased me by his respect and affection; that my children have not been stupid nor deformed in body; that I did not make more proficiency in rhetoric, poetry, and the other studies, in which I should perhaps have been completely engaged, if I had seen that I was making progress in them; that I made haste to place those who brought me up in the station of honour, which they seemed to desire, without putting them off with hope of my doing it some time afterward, because they were then still young; that I knew Apollonius, Rusticus, Maximus; that I received clear and frequent impressions about living according to nature, and what kind of a life that is, so that, so far as depended on the gods, and their gifts, and help, and inspirations, nothing hindered me from forthwith living according to nature, though I still fall short of it through my own fault, and through not observing the admonitions of the gods, and, I may almost say, their direct instructions; that my body has held out so long in such a kind of life; that I never touched either Benedicta or Theodotus, and that, after having fallen into amatory passions, I was cured; and, though I was often out of humour with Rusticus, I never did anything of which I had occasion to repent; that, though it was my mother's fate to die young, she spent the last years of her life with me; that, whenever I wished to help any man in his need, or on any other occasion, I was never told that I had not the means of doing it; and that to myself the same necessity never happened, to receive anything from another;

that I have such a wife, so obedient; and so affectionate, and so simple; that I had abundance of good
masters for my children; and that remedies have been shown
to me by dreams, both others, and against bloodspitting and
giddiness[22] * * * * * * ; and that, when I had an inclination to philosophy, I did not fall into the hands of any
sophist, and that I did not waste my time on writers [of his-
tories], or in the resolution of syllogisms, or occupy myself
about the investigation of appearances in the heavens; for all
these things require the help of the gods and fortune.

Among the Quadi at the Granua.[23]

NOTES

[1]Annius Verus was his grandfather's name.   There is no verb in this
section connected with the word "from," nor in the following sections
of this book; and it is not quite certain what verb should be supplied.
What I have added may express the meaning here, though there are
sections which it will not fit. If he does not mean to say that he learned
all these good things from the several persons whom he mentions, he
means that he observed certain good qualities in them, or received
certain benefits from them, and it is implied that he was the better for
it, or at least might have been; for it would be a mistake to understand
Marcus as saying that he possessed all the virtues which he observed in
his kinsmen and teachers.

[2] His father's name was Annius Verus.

[3] His mother was Domitia Calvilla, named also Lucilla.

[4] Perhaps his mother's grandfather, Catilius Severus.

[5] In the works of Justinus there is printed a letter to one Diognetus,
whom the writer names "most excellent."   He was a Gentile, but he
wished very much to know what the religion of the Christians was,
what God they worshipped, and how this worship made them despise
the world and death, and neither believe in the gods of the Greeks nor
observe the superstition of the Jews; and what was this love to one
another which they had, and why this new kind of religion was introduced now and not before.   My friend Mr. Jenkins, rector of Lyminge
in Kent, has suggested to me that this Diognetus may have been the
tutor of M Antoninus.

[6] Q Junius Rusticus was a Stoic philosopher, whom Antoninus valued
highly, and often took his advice.

[7]Antoninus says, τοῖς Ἐπικτητείοις ὑπομνήμασιν, which must not
be translated, "the writings of Epictetus," for Epictetus wrote nothing.
His pupil Arrian has preserved for us all that we know of Epictetus

[8] Apollonius of Chalcis came to Rome in the time of Pius to be Marcus's preceptor   He was a rigid Stoic.

[9] Sextus of Chæronea, a grandson of Plutarch, or nephew, as some
say; but more probably a grandson

[10] "I have placed in some passages an *, which indicates corruption in
the text or great uncertainty in the meaning "—Long's Preface.

[11] Alexander was a Grammaticus, a native of Phrygia. He wrote a commentary on Homer, and the rhetorician Aristides wrote a panegyric on Alexander in a funeral oration.

[12] M Cornelius Fronto was a rhetorician, and in great favour with Marcus There are extant various letters between Marcus and Fronto

[13] Cinna Catulus, a Stoic philosopher.

[14] The word brother may not be genuine Antoninus had no brother. It has been supposed that he may mean some cousin. Schultz in his translation omits "brother," and says that this Severus is probably Claudius Severus, a peripatetic.

[15] We know from Tacitus (Annal. XIII, XVI, 21; and other passages), who Thrasea and Helvidius were Plutarch has written the lives of the two Catos, and of Dion and Brutus. Antoninus probably alludes to Cato of Utica, who was a Stoic.

[16] Claudius Maximus was a Stoic philosopher, who was highly esteemed also by Antoninus Pius, Marcus' predecessor. The character of Maximus is that of a perfect man.

[17] He means his adoptive father, his predecessor, the Emperor Antoninus Pius.

[18] This passage is corrupt, and the exact meaning is uncertain.

[19] Lorium was a villa on the coast north of Rome, and there Antoninus was brought up, and he died there. This also is corrupt.

[20] Xenophon, Memorab. 1, 3, 15.

[21] The emperor had no brother, except L. Verus, his brother by adoption.

[22] This is corrupt.

[23] The Quadi lived in the southern part of Bohemia and Moravia; and Antoninus made a campaign against them. Granua is probably the river Graan, which flows into the Danube.

If these words are genuine, Antoninus may have written this first book during the war with the Quadi. In the first edition of Antoninus, and in the older editions, the first three sections of the second book make the conclusion of the first book. Gataker placed them at the beginning of the second book.

BOOK II,

B EGIN the morning by saying to thyself, I shall meet
with the busybody, the ungrateful, arrogant, deceitful,
envious, unsocial. All these things happen to them by
reason of their ignorance of what is good and evil.
But I who have seen the nature of the good that it is beautiful,
and of the bad that it is ugly, and the nature of him who does
wrong, that it is akin to me, not [only] of the same blood or ·
seed, but that it participates in [the same] intelligence and
[the same] portion of the divinity, I can neither be injured
by any of them, for no one can fix on me what is ugly, nor
can I be angry with my kinsman, nor hate him. For we are
made for co-operation, like feet, like hands, like eyelids, like
the rows of the upper and lower teeth.[1]   To act against one
another then is contrary to nature; and it is acting against
one another to be vexed and to turn away.

· Whatever this is that I am, it is a little flesh and breath,
and the ruling part. Throw away thy books; no longer distract thyself: it is not allowed; but as if thou wast now
dying, despise the flesh; it is blood and bones and a network,
a contexture of nerves, veins, and arteries. See the breath
also, what kind of a thing it is, air, and not always the same,
but every moment sent out and again sucked in. The third
then is the ruling part. consider thus: Thou art an old man;
no longer let this be a slave, no longer be pulled by the strings
like a puppet to unsocial movements, no longer be either dissatisfied with thy present lot, or shrink from the future.

All that is from the gods is full of providence. That
which is from fortune is not separated from nature or without an interweaving and involution with the things which
are ordered by providence. From thence all things flow; and
there is besides necessity, and that which is for the advantage
of the whole universe, of which thou art a part. But that is

good for every part of nature which the nature of the whole
brings, and what serves to maintain this nature. Now the
universe is preserved, as by the changes of the elements so
by the changes of things compounded of the elements. Let
these principles be enough for thee, let them always be fixed
opinions. But cast away the thirst after books, that thou
mayest not die murmuring, but cheerfully, truly, and from
thy heart thankful to the gods.

Remember how long thou hast been putting off these
things, and how often thou hast received an opportunity
from the gods, and yet dost not use it. Thou must now at
last perceive of what universe thou art a part, and of what
administrator of the universe thy existence is an efflux, and
that a limit of time is fixed for thee, which if thou dost not
use for clearing away the clouds from thy mind, it will go
and thou wilt go, and it will never return.

Every moment think steadily as a Roman and a man to
do what thou hast in hand with perfect and simple dignity,
and feeling of affection, and freedom, and justice; and to
give thyself relief from all other thoughts. And thou wilt
give thyself relief, if thou doest every act of thy life as if it
were the last, laying aside all carelessness and passionate aversion from the commands of reason, and all hypocrisy, and
self-love, and discontent with the portion which has been
given to thee. Thou seest how few the things are, the which
if a man lays hold of, he is able to live a life which flows in
quiet, and is like the existence of the gods; for the gods on
their part will require nothing more from him who observes
these things.

Do wrong[2] to thyself, do wrong to thyself, my soul; but
thou wilt no longer have the opportunity of honouring thyself. Every man's life is sufficient.* But thine is nearly
finished, though thy soul reverences not itself, but places thy
felicity in the souls of others.

Do the things external which fall upon thee, distract thee?
Give thyself time to learn something new and good, and
cease to be whirled around. But then thou must also avoid
being carried about the other way. For those too are triflers
who have wearied themselves in life by their activity, and

yet have no object to which to direct every movement, and, in a word, all their thoughts.

Through not observing what is in the mind of another a man has seldom been seen to be unhappy; but those who do not observe the movements of their own minds must of necessity be unhappy.

This thou must always bear in mind, what is the nature of the whole, and what is my nature, and how this is related to that, and what kind of a part it is of what kind of a whole; and that there is no one who hinders thee from always doing and saying the things which are according to the nature of which thou art a part.

Theophrastus, in his comparison of bad acts—such a comparison as one would make in accordance with the common notions of mankind—says, like a true philosopher, that the offences which are committed through desire are more blameable than those which are committed through anger. For he who is excited by anger seems to turn away from reason with a certain pain and unconscious contraction; but he who offends through desire, being overpowered by pleasure, seems to be in a manner more intemperate and more womanish in his offences. Rightly then, and in a way worthy of philosophy, he said that the offence which is committed with pleasure is more blameable than that which is committed with pain; and on the whole the one is more like a person who has been first wronged and through pain is compelled to be angry; but the other is moved by his own impulse to do wrong, being carried towards doing something by desire.

Since it is possible[3] that thou mayest depart from life this very moment, regulate every act and thought accordingly. But to go away from among men, if there are gods, is not a thing to be afraid of, for the gods will not involve thee in evil; but if indeed they do not exist, or if they have no concern about human affairs, what is it to me to live in a universe devoid of gods or devoid of providence? But in truth they do exist, and they do care for human things, and they have put all the means in man's power to enable him not to fall into real evils. And as to the rest, if there was anything evil, they would have provided for this also, that it should be

altogether in a man's power not to fall into it. Now that
which does not make a man worse, how can it make a man's
life worse? But neither through ignorance, nor having the
knowledge but not the power to guard against or correct
these things, is it possible that the nature of the universe has
overlooked them; nor is it possible that it has made so great
a mistake, either through want of power or want of skill, that
good and evil should happen indiscriminately to the good
and the bad. But death certainly, and life, honour and dishonour, pain and pleasure, all these things equally happen to
good men and bad, being things which make us neither better
nor worse. Therefore they are neither good nor evil.

How quickly all things disappear, in the universe the bodies
themselves, and in time the remembrance of them; what is
the nature of all sensible things, and particularly those which
attract with the bait of pleasure or terrify by pain, or are
noised abroad by vapoury fame; how worthless, and con-
temptible, and sordid, and perishable, and dead they are—all
this it is the part of the intellectual faculty to observe. To
observe too who these are whose opinions and voices give
reputation; what death is, and the fact that, if a man looks
at it in itself, and by the abstractive power of reflection re-
solves into their parts all the things which present themselves
to the imagination in it, he will then consider it to be nothing
else than an operation of nature; and if any one is afraid of
an operation of nature, he is a child. This, however, is not
only an operation of nature, but it is also a thing which conduces to the purposes of nature. To observe too how man
comes near to the deity, and by what part of him, and when
this part of man is so disposed.*

Nothing is more wretched than a man who traverses
everything in a round, and pries into the things beneath the
earth, as the poet[4] says, and seeks by conjecture what is in
the minds of his neighbours, without perceiving that it is
sufficient to attend to the dæmon within him, and to reverence it sincerely. And reverence of the dæmon consists in
keeping it pure from passion and thoughtlessness, and dis-
satisfaction with what comes from gods and men. For the
things from the gods merit veneration for their excellence;
and the things from men should be dear to us by reason of

kinship; and sometimes even, in a manner, they move our
pity by reason of men's ignorance of good and bad; this
defect being not less than that which deprives us of the
power of distinguishing things that are white and black.

Though thou shouldest be going to live three thousand
years, and as many times ten thousand years, still remember
that no man loses any other life than this which he now lives,
nor lives any other than this which he now loses. The
longest and shortest are thus brought to the same. For the
present is the same to all, though that which perishes is not
the same;* and so that which is lost appears to be a mere moment. For a man can not lose either the past or the future:
for what a man has not, how can any one take this from
him? These two things then thou must bear in mind; the
one, that all things from eternity are of like forms and come
round in a circle, and that it makes no difference whether
a man shall see the same things during a hundred years or
two hundred, or an infinite time; and the second, that the
longest liver and he who will die soonest lose just the same.
For the present is the only thing of which a man can be deprived, if it is true that this is the only thing which he has,
and that a man can not lose a thing if he has it not.

Remember that all is opinion. For what was said by the
Cynic Monimus is manifest: and manifest too is the use of
what was said, if a man receives what may be got out of it
as far as it is true.

The soul of man does violence to itself, first of all, when
it becomes an abscess and, as it were, a tumour on the universe, so far as it can. For to be vexed at anything which
happens is a separation of ourselves from nature, in some
part of which the natures of all other things are contained.
In the next place, the soul does violence to itself when it
turns away from any man, or even moves towards him with
the intention of injuring, such as are the souls of those who
are angry. In the third place, the soul does violence to itself
when it is overpowered by pleasure or by pain. Fourthly,
when it plays a part, and does or says anything insincerely and
untruly. Fifthly, when it allows any act of its own and any
movement to be without an aim and does anything thought-
lessly and without considering what it is, it being right that

even the smallest things be done with reference to an end; and the end of rational animals is to follow the reason and the law of the most ancient city and polity.

Of human life the time is a point, and the substance is in a flux, and the perception dull, and the composition of the whole body subject to putrefaction, and the soul a whirl, and fortune hard to divine, and fame a thing devoid of judgment. And, to say all in a word, everything which belongs to the body is a stream, and what belongs to the soul is a dream and vapour, and life is a warfare and a stranger's sojourn, and after-fame is oblivion. What then is that which is able to conduct a man? One thing and only one, philosophy. But this consists in keeping the dæmon within a man free from violence and unharmed, superior to pains and pleasures, doing nothing without a purpose, nor yet falsely and with hypocrisy, not feeling the need of another man's doing or not doing anything; and besides, accepting all that happens, and all that is allotted, as coming from thence, wherever it is, from whence he himself came; and, finally, waiting for death with a cheerful mind, as being nothing else than a dissolution of the elements of which every living being is compounded. But if there is no harm to the elements themselves in each continually changing into another, why should a man have any apprehension about the change and dissolution of all the elements? For it is according to nature and nothing is evil which is according to nature.

This in Carnuntum.[5]

NOTES

[1] Xenophon, Mem. II, 3, 18.

[2] Perhaps it should be "thou art doing violence to thyself," ὑβρίζεις, not ὑβρίζε.

[3] Or it may mean "since it is in thy power to depart;" which gives a meaning somewhat different.

[4] Pindar in the "Theætetus" of Plato.

[5] Carnuntum was a town of Pannonia, on the south side of the Danube, about thirty miles east of Vindobona (Vienna). Orosius (VII, 15) and Eutropius (VIII, 13) say that Antoninus remained three years at Carnuntum during his war with the Marcomanni.

BOOK III

WE ought to consider not only that our life is daily wasting away and a smaller part of it is left, but another thing also should be taken into account, that if a man should live longer, it is quite uncertain whether the understanding will still continue sufficient for the comprehension of things, and retain the power of contemplation which strives to acquire the knowledge of the divine and the human. For if he shall begin to fall into dotage, perspiration, and nutrition, and imagination, and appetite, and whatever else there is of the kind, will not fail; but the power of making use of ourselves, and filling up the measure of our duty, and clearly separating all appearances, and considering whether a man should now depart from life, and whatever else of the kind absolutely requires a disciplined reason, all this is already extinguished. We must make haste then, not only because we are daily nearer to death, but also because the conception of things and the understanding of them cease first.

We ought to observe also that even the things which follow after the things which are produced according to nature contain something pleasing and attractive. For instance, when bread is baked some parts are split at the surface, and these parts which thus open, and have a certain fashion contrary to the purpose of the baker's art, are beautiful in a manner, and in a peculiar way excite a desire for eating. And again, figs, when they are quite ripe, gape open, and in the ripe olives the very circumstance of their being near to rottenness adds a peculiar beauty to the fruit. And the ears of corn bending down, and the lion's eyebrows, and the foam which flows from the mouth of wild boars, and many other things—though they are far from being beautiful, if a man should examine them severally—still, because

16

they are consequent upon the things which are formed by nature, help to adorn them, and they please the mind; so that if a man should have a feeling and deeper insight with respect to the things which are produced in the universe, there is hardly one of those which follow by way of consequence which will not seem to him to be in a manner disposed so as to give pleasure. And so he will see even the real gaping jaws of wild beasts with no less pleasure than those which painters and sculptors show by imitation; and in an old woman and an old man he will be able to see a certain maturity and comeliness; and the attractive loveliness of young persons he will be able to look on with chaste eyes; and many such things will present themselves, not pleasing to every man, but to him only who has become truly familiar with nature and her works.

Hippocrates, after curing many diseases himself, fell sick and died. The Chaldæi foretold the deaths of many, and then fate caught them too. Alexander, and Pompeius, and Caius Cæsar, after so often completely destroying whole cities, and in battle cutting to pieces many ten thousands of cavalry and infantry, themselves too at last departed from life Heraclitus, after so many speculations on the conflagration of the universe, was filled with water internally and died smeared all over with mud. And lice destroyed Democritus; and other lice killed Socrates. What means all this? Thou hast embarked, thou hast made the voyage, thou art come to shore; get out. If indeed to another life, there is no want of gods, not even there. But if to a state without sensation, thou wilt cease to be held by pains and pleasures, and to be a slave to the vessel, which is as much inferior as that which serves it is superior:* for the one is intelligence and deity; the other is earth and corruption.

Do not waste the remainder of thy life in thoughts about others, when thou dost not refer thy thoughts to some object of common utility. For thou losest the opportunity of doing something else, when thou hast such thoughts as these, What is such a person doing, and why, and what is he saying, and what is he thinking of, and what is he contriving. and whatever else of the kind makes us wander away from the observation of our own ruling power. We ought then

to check in the series of our thoughts everything that is
without a purpose and useless, but most of all the over curious feeling and the malignant; and a man should use himself to think of those things only about which if one should
suddenly ask, What hast thou now in thy thoughts? with
perfect openness thou mightest immediately answer, This or
That; so that from thy words it should be plain that everything in thee is simple and benevolent, and such as befits a
social animal, and one that cares not for thoughts about
pleasure or sensual enjoyments at all, nor has any rivalry, or
envy and suspicion, or anything else for which thou wouldst
blush if thou shouldst say that thou hadst it in thy mind. For
the man who is such and no longer delays being among the
number of the best, is like a priest and minister of the
gods, using too the [deity] which is planted within him,
which makes the man uncontaminated by pleasure, unharmed by any pain, untouched by any insult, feeling no wrong, a fighter in the noblest fight, one
who can not be overpowered by any passion, dyed
deep with justice, accepting with all his soul everything
which happens and is assigned to him as his portion; and
not often, nor yet without great necessity and for the general
interest, imagining what another says, or does, or thinks.
For it is only what belongs to himself that he makes the matter for his activity; and he constantly thinks of that which
is allotted to himself out of the sum total of things, and he
makes his own acts fair, and he is persuaded that his own
portion is good.   For the lot which is assigned to each man
is carried along with him and carries him along with it.*
And he remembers also that every rational animal is his kinsman, and that to care for all men is according to man's nature; and a man should hold on to the opinion not of all, but
of those only who confessedly live according to nature.   But
as to those who live not so, he always bears in mind what kind
of men they are both at home and from home, both by night
and by day, and what they are, and with what men they live
an impure life. Accordingly, he does not value at all the
praise which comes from such men, since they are not even
satisfied with themselves   .
Labour not unwillingly, nor without regard to the com-

mon interest, nor without due consideration, nor with distraction; nor let studied ornament set off thy thoughts, and be not either a man of many words, or busy about too many things.   And further, let the deity which is in thee be the guardian of a living being, manly and of ripe age, and engaged in matter political, and a Roman, and a ruler, who has taken his post like a man waiting for the signal which summons him from life, and ready to go, having need neither of oath nor of any man's testimony.   Be cheerful also, and·seek not external help nor the tranquillity which others give. A man then must stand erect, not be kept erect by others.

If thou findest in human life anything better than justice, truth, temperance, fortitude, and, in a word, anything better than thy own mind's self-satisfaction in the things which it enables thee to do according to right reason, and in the condition that is assigned to thee without thy own choice; if, I say, thou seest anything better than this, turn to it with all thy soul, and enjoy that which thou hast found to be the best. But if nothing appears to be better than the deity which is planted in thee, which has subjected to itself all thy appetites, and carefully examines all the impressions, and, as Socrates said, has detached itself from the persuasions of sense, and has submitted itself to the gods, and cares for mankind; if thou findest everything else smaller and of less value than this, give place to nothing else, for if thou dost once diverge and incline to it, thou wilt no longer without distraction be able to give the preference to that good thing which is thy proper possession and thy own for it is not right that anything of any other kind, such as praise from the many, or power, or enjoyment of pleasure, should come into competition with that which is rationally and politically [or, practically] good.   All these things, even though they may seem to adapt themselves [to the better things] in a small degree, obtain the superiority all at once, and carry us away.   But do thou, I say, simply and freely choose the better, and hold to it —But that which is useful is the better.—Well then, if it is useful to thee as a rational being, keep to it; but if it is only useful to thee as an animal, say so, and maintain thy judgment without arrogance: only take care that thou makest the inquiry by a sure method.

Never value anything as profitable to thyself which shall compel thee to break thy promise, to lose thy self-respect, to hate any man; to suspect, to curse, to act the hypocrite, to desire anything which needs walls and curtains: for he who has preferred to everything else his own intelligence, and dæmon, and the worship of its excellence, acts no tragic part, does not groan, will not need either solitude or much company; and, what is chief of all, he will live without either pursuing or flying from [death]; but whether for a longer or a shorter time he shall have the soul inclosed in the body, he cares not at all: for even if he must depart immediately, he will go as readily as if he were going to do anything else which can be done with decency and order; taking care of this only all through life, that his thoughts turn not away from anything which belongs to an intelligent animal and a member of a civil community

In the mind of one who is chastened and purified thou wilt find no corrupt matter, nor impurity, nor any sore skinned over. Nor is his life incomplete when fate overtakes him, as one may say of an actor who leaves the stage before ending and finishing the play. Besides, there is in him nothing servile, nor affected, nor too closely bound [to other things], nor yet detached [from other things], nothing worthy of blame, nothing which seeks a hiding-place.

Reverence the faculty which produces opinion. On this faculty it entirely depends whether there shall exist in thy ruling part any opinion inconsistent with nature and the constitution of the rational animal. And this faculty promises freedom from hasty judgment, and friendship towards men, and obedience to the gods.

Throwing away then all things, hold to these only which are few; and besides bear in mind that every man lives only this present time, which is an indivisible point, and that all the rest of his life is either past or it is uncertain. Short then is the time which every man lives, and small the nook of the earth where he lives; and short too the longest posthumous fame, and even this only continued by a succession of poor human beings, who will very soon die, and who know not even themselves, much less him who died long ago

To the aids which have been mentioned let this one still

be added:—Make for thyself a definition or description of
the thing which is presented to thee, so as to see distinctly
what kind of a thing it is in its substance, in its nudity, in its
complete entirety, and tell thyself its proper name, and the
names of the things of which it has been compounded, and
into which it will be resolved. For nothing is so productive
of elevation of mind as to be able to examine methodically
and truly every object which is presented to thee in life, and
always to look at things so as to see at the same time what
kind of universe this is, and what kind of use everything
performs in it, and what value everything has with reference
to the whole, and what with reference to man, who is a citizen of the highest city, of which all other cities are like families; what each thing is, and of what it is composed, and
how long it is the nature of this thing to endure which now
makes an impression on me, and what virtue I have need of
with respect to it, such as gentleness, manliness, truth, fidelity, simplicity, contentment, and the rest. Wherefore, on
every occasion a man should say: this comes from god; and
this is according to the apportionment* and spinning of the
thread of destiny, or similar coincidence and chance; and
this is from one of the same stock, and a kinsman and partner,
one who knows not however what is according to his nature.
But I know; for this reason I behave towards him, according to the natural law of fellowship, with benevolence and
justice. At the same time however in things indifferent[1] I
attempt to ascertain the value of each.

If thou workest at that which is before thee, following
right reason seriously, vigorously, calmly, without allowing
anything else to distract thee, but keeping thy divine part
pure, as if thou shouldst be bound to give it back immediately; if thou holdest to this, expecting nothing, fearing
nothing, but satisfied with thy present activity according to
nature, and with heroic truth in every word and sound which
thou utterest, thou wilt live happy. And there is no man
who is able to prevent this.

As physicians have always their instruments and knives
ready for cases which suddenly require their skill, so do thou
have principles ready for the understanding of things divine
and human, and for doing everything, even the smallest, with

a recollection of the bond which unites the divine and human
to one another.   For neither wilt thou do anything well
which pertains to man without at the same time having a reference to things divine; nor the contrary.

No longer wander at hazard; for neither wilt thou read
thy own memoirs,[2] nor the acts of the ancient Romans and
Hellenes, and the selections from books which thou wast re-
serving for thy old age.[3]   Hasten then to the end which
thou hast before thee, and, throwing away idle hopes, come
to thy own aid, if thou carest at all for thyself, while it is in
thy power.

They know not how many things are signified by the
words stealing, sowing, buying, keeping quiet, seeing what
ought to be done; for this is not effected by the eyes, but by
another kind of vision.

Body, soul, intelligence: to the body belongs sensations,
to the soul appetites, to the intelligence principles.   To receive the impressions of forms by means of appearances belongs even to animals; to be pulled by the strings of desire
belongs both to wild beasts and to men who have made
themselves into women, and to a Phalaris and a Nero: and to
have the intelligence that guides to the things which appear
suitable belongs also to those who do not believe in the gods,
and who betray their country, and do their impure deeds
when they have shut the doors.   If then everything else is
common to all that I have mentioned, there remains that
which is peculiar to the good man, to be pleased and content
with what happens, and with the thread which is spun for
him; and not to defile the divinity which is planted in his
breast, nor disturb it by a crowd of images, but to preserve it
tranquil, following it obediently as a god, neither saying anything contrary to the truth, nor doing anything contrary to
justice.   And if all men refuse to believe that he lives a simple, modest, and contented life, he is neither angry with any
of them, nor does he deviate from the way which leads to the
end of life, to which a man ought to come pure, tranquil,
ready to depart, and without any compulsion, perfectly reconciled to his lot.

NOTES

[1] "Est et horum quæ media appellamus grande discrimen."—Seneca Ep. 82

[2] Ὑπομνήματα: or memoranda, notes and the like.

[3] Compare Fronto, II, 9; a letter of Marcus to Fronto, who was then consul "Feci tamen mihi per hos dies excerpta ex libris sexaginta in quinque tomis." But he says some of them were small books.

BOOK IV

THAT which rules within, when it is according to nature, is so affected with respect to the events which happen, that it always easily adapts itself to that which is possible and is presented to it. For it requires no definite material, but it moves toward its purpose, under certain conditions however; and it makes a material for itself out of that which opposes it, as fire lays hold of what falls into it, by which a small light would have been extinguished: but when the fire is strong, it soon appropriates to itself the matter which is heaped upon it, and consumes it, and rises higher by means of this very material.

Let no act be done without a purpose, nor otherwise than according to the perfect principles of art.

Men seek retreats for themselves, houses in the country, sea-shores, and mountains; and thou too art wont to desire such things very much. But this is altogether a mark of the most common sort of men, for it is in thy power, whenever thou shalt choose, to retire into thyself. For nowhere either with more quiet or more freedom from trouble does a man retire than into his own soul, particularly when he has within him such thoughts that by looking into them he is immediately in perfect tranquillity; and I affirm that tranquillity is nothing else than the good ordering of the mind. Constantly then give to thyself this retreat, and renew thyself; and let thy principles be brief and fundamental, which, as soon as thou shalt recur to them, will be sufficient to cleanse the soul completely, and to send thee back free from all discontent with the things to which thou returnest. For with what art thou discontented? With the badness of men? Recall to thy mind this conclusion, that rational animals exist for one another, and that to endure is a part of justice, and that men do wrong involuntarily; and consider how many already, after mutual enmity, suspicion, hatred, and fighting, have been stretched dead, reduced to ashes; and be quiet at last.——But perhaps thou art dissatisfied with that which is assigned to thee out of the universe.——Recall to thy recollection this alternative; either there is providence or atoms [fortuitous concurrence of things]; or remember the arguments by which it has been proved that the world is a kind of political community [and be quiet at last].——But perhaps corporeal things will still fasten upon thee.——Consider then further that the mind mingles not with the breath, whether moving gently or violently, when it has once drawn itself apart and discovered its own power, and think also of all that thou hast heard and assented to about pain and pleasure [and be quiet at last].——But perhaps the desire of the thing called fame will torment thee.——See how soon everything is forgotten, and look at the chaos of infinite time on each side of [the present], and the emptiness of applause, and the changeableness and want of judgment in those who pretend to give praise, and the narrowness of the space within which it is circumscribed [and be quiet at last].   For the whole earth is a point, and how small a nook in it is this thy dwelling, and how few are there in it, and what kind of people are they who will praise thee.

This then remains: Remember to retire into this little territory of thy own,[1] and above all do not distract or strain thyself, but be free, and look at things as a man, as a human being, as a citizen, as a mortal.   But among the things readiest to thy hand to which thou shalt turn, let there be these, which are two.   One is that things do not touch the soul, for they are external and remain immovable; but our perturbations come only from the opinion which is within. The other is that all these things, which thou seest, change immediately and will no longer be; and constantly bear in mind how many of these changes thou hast already witnessed   The universe is transformation: life is opinion.

If our intellectual part is common, the reason also, in respect of which we are rational beings, is common: if this is so, common also is the reason which commands us what to do, and what not to do; if this is so, there is a common law also; if this is so, we are fellow-citizens; if this is so, we

are members of some political community; if this is so, the
world is in a manner a state.[2]   For of what other common
political community will any one say that the whole human
race are members?   And from thence, from this common
political community comes also our very intellectual faculty
and reasoning faculty, and our capacity for law; or whence
do they come?   For as my earthly part is a portion given to
me from certain earth, and that which is watery from another element, and that which is hot and fiery from some
peculiar source (for nothing comes out of that which is nothing, as nothing also returns to non-existence), so also the
intellectual part comes from some source.

Death is such as generation is, a mystery of nature; a
composition out of the same elements, and a decomposition
into the same; and altogether not a thing of which any man
should be ashamed, for it is not contrary to [the nature of]
a reasonable animal, and not contrary to the reason of our
constitution.

It is natural that these things should be done by such
persons, it is a matter of necessity; and if a man will not
have it so, he will not allow the fig-tree to have juice.   But
by all means bear this in mind, that within a very short time
both thou and he will be dead; and soon not even your names
will be left behind.

Take away thy opinion, and then there is taken away the
complaint, "I have been harmed." Take away the complaint, "I have been harmed," and the harm is taken away.

That which does not make a man worse than he was,
also does not make his life worse, nor does it harm him
either from without or from within.

The nature of that which is [universally] useful has been
compelled to do this.

Consider that everything which happens, happens justly,
and if thou observest carefully, thou wilt find it to be so.
I do not say only with respect to the continuity of the series
of things, but with respect to what is just, and as if it were
done by one who assigns to each thing its value. Observe
then as thou hast begun; and whatever thou doest, do it in
conjunction with this, the being good, and in the sense in

which a man is properly understood to be good. Keep to this in every action.

Do not have such an opinion of things as he has who does thee wrong, or such as he wishes thee to have, but look at them as they are in truth.

A man should always have these two rules in readiness; the one, to do only whatever the reason of the ruling and legislating faculty may suggest for the use of men; the other, to change thy opinion, if there is any one at hand who sets thee right and moves thee from any opinion. But this change of opinion must proceed only from a certain persuasion, as of what is just or of common advantage, and the like, not because it appears pleasant or brings reputation.

Hast thou reason? I have.—Why then dost not thou use it? For if this does its own work, what else dost thou wish?

Thou hast existed as a part. Thou shalt disappear in that which produced thee; but rather thou shalt be received back into its seminal principle by transmutation.

Many grains of frankincense on the same altar: one falls before, another falls after; but it makes no difference.

Within ten days thou wilt seem a god to those to whom thou art now a beast and an ape, if thou wilt return to thy principles and the worship of reason.

Do not act as if thou wert going to live ten thousand years. Death hangs over thee. While thou livest, while it is in thy power, be good.

How much trouble he avoids who does not look to see what his neighbour says or does or thinks, but only to what he does himself, that it may be just and pure; or as Agathon* says, look not round at the depraved morals of others, but run straight along the line without deviating from it.

He who has a vehement desire for posthumous fame does not consider that every one of those who remember him will himself die very soon; then again also they who have succeeded them, until the whole remembrance shall have been extinguished as it is transmitted through men who foolishly admire and perish. But even suppose that those who will remember are immortal, and that the remembrance will be immortal, what then is this to thee? And I say not what is it to the dead, but what is it to the living. · What is praise, except* indeed so far as it has* a certain utility? For thou now rejectest unseasonably the gift of nature, clinging to something else . . . ⌈ *.

Everything which is in any way beautiful is beautiful in itself, and terminates in itself, not having praise as part of itself. Neither worse then nor better is a thing made by being praised. I affirm this also of the things which are called beautiful by the vulgar, for example, material things and works of art. That which is really beautiful has no need of anything; not more than law, not more than truth, not more than benevolence or modesty. Which of these things is beautiful because it is praised, or spoiled by being blamed? Is such a thing as an emerald made worse than it was, if it is not praised? or gold, ivory, purple, a lyre, a little knife, a flower, a shrub?

If souls continue to exist, how does the air contain them from eternity?—But how does the earth contain the bodies of those who have been buried from time so remote? For as here the mutation of these bodies after a certain continuance, whatever it may be, and their dissolution make room for other dead bodies; so the souls which are removed into the air after subsisting for some time are transmuted and diffused, and assume a fiery nature by being received into the seminal intelligence of the universe, and in this way make room for the fresh souls which come to dwell there. And this is the answer which a man might give on the hypothesis of souls continuing to exist. But we must not only think of the number of bodies which are thus buried, but also of the number of animals which are daily eaten by us and the other animals. For what a number is consumed, and thus in a manner buried in the bodies of those who feed on them? And nevertheless this earth receives them by reason of the changes [of these bodies] into blood, and the transformations into the aerial or of the fiery element.

What is the investigation into the truth in this matter? The division into that which is material and that which is the cause of form [the formal].

Do not be whirled about, but in every movement have respect to justice, and on the occasion of every impression maintain the faculty of comprehension [or understanding].

Everything harmonizes with me, which is harmonious to thee, O Universe. Nothing for me is too early nor too late, which is in due time for thee. Everything is fruit to me which thy seasons bring, O Nature: from thee are all things, in thee are all things, to thee all things return. The poet says, Dear city of Cecrops; and wilt not thou say, Dear city of Zeus?

Occupy thyself with few things, says the philosopher, if thou wouldst be tranquil.—But consider if it would not be better to say, Do what is necessary, and whatever the reason of the animal which is naturally social requires, and as it requires. For this brings not only the tranquillity which comes from doing well, but also that which comes from doing few things. For the greatest part of what we say and do being unnecessary, if a man takes this away, he will have more leisure and less uneasiness. Accordingly on every occasion a man should ask himself, Is this one of the unnecessary things? Now a man should take away not only unnecessary acts, but also unnecessary thoughts, for thus superfluous acts will not follow after.

Try how the life of the good man suits thee, the life of him who is satisfied with his portion out of the whole, and satisfied with his own just acts and benevolent disposition.

Hast thou seen those things? Look also at these. Do not disturb thyself. Make thyself all simplicity. Does any one do wrong? Is it to himself that he does the wrong. Has anything happened to thee? Well; out of the universe from the beginning everything which happens has been apportioned and spun out of thee. In a word, thy life is short Thou must turn to profit the present by the aid of reason and justice. Be sober in thy relaxation.

Either it is a well arranged universe[3] or a chaos huddled together, but still a universe. But can a certain order subsist in thee, and disorder in the All? And this too when all things are so separated and diffused and sympathethic.

A black character, a womanish character, a stubborn character, bestial, childish, animal, stupid, counterfeit, scurrilous, fraudulent, tyrannical!

If he is a stranger to the universe who does not know

what is in it, no less is he a stranger who does not know what is going on in it. He is a runaway, who flies from social reason; he is blind, who shuts the eyes of the understanding; he is poor, who has need of another, and has not from himself all things which are useful for life. He is an abscess on the universe who withdraws and separates himself from the reason of our common nature through being displeased with the things which happen, for the same nature produces this, and has produced thee too: he is a piece rent asunder from the state, who tears his own soul from that of reasonable animals.

The one is a philosopher without a tunic, and the other without a book: here is another half naked· Bread I have not, he says, and I abide by reason—And I do not get the means of living out of my learning,* and I abide [by my reason].

Love the art, poor as it may be, which thou hast learned, and be content with it; and pass through the rest of life like one who has intrusted to the gods with his whole soul all that he has, making thyself neither the tyrant nor the slave of any man.

Consider, for example, the times of Vespasian. Thou wilt see all these things, people marrying, bringing up children, sick, dying, warring, feasting, trafficking, cultivating the ground, flattering, obstinately arrogant, suspecting, plotting, wishing for some to die, grumbling about the present, loving, heaping up treasure, desiring consulship, kingly power. Well then that life of these people no longer exists at all. Again, remove to the times of Trajan. Again, all is the same. Their life too is gone. In like manner view also the other epochs of time and of whole nations, and see how many after great efforts soon fell and were resolved into the elements. But chiefly thou shouldst think of those whom thou hast thyself known distracting themselves about idle things, neglecting to do what was in accordance with their proper constitution, and to hold firmly to this and to be content with it. And herein it is necessary to remember that the attention given to everything has its proper value and proportion. For thus thou wilt not be dissatisfied, if thou appliest thyself to smaller matters no further than is fit.

The words which were formerly familiar are now antiquated: so also the names of those who were famed of old, are now in a manner antiquated, Camillus, Cæso, Volesus, Leonnatus, and a little afterward, also Scipio and Cato, then Augustus, then also Hadrianus and Antoninus. For all things soon pass away and become a mere tale, and complete oblivion soon buries them. And I say this of those who have shone in a wondrous way. For the rest, as soon as they have breathed out their breath, they are gone, and no man speaks of them. And, to conclude the matter, what is even an eternal remembrance? A mere nothing. What then is that about which we ought to employ our serious pains? This one thing, thoughts just, and acts social, and words which never lie, and a disposition which gladly accepts all that happens, as necessary, as usual, as flowing from a principle and source of the same kind.

Willingly give thyself up to Clotho, allowing her to spin thy thread* into whatever things she pleases.

Everything is only for a day, both that which remembers and that which is remembered

Observe constantly that all things take place by change, and accustom thyself to consider that the nature of the Universe loves nothing so much as to change the things which are and to make new things like them. For everything that exists is in a manner the seed of that which will be. But thou art thinking only of seeds which are cast into the earth or into a womb: but this is a very vulgar notion.

Thou wilt soon die, and thou art not yet simple, nor free from perturbations, nor without suspicion of being hurt by external things, nor kindly disposed towards all; nor dost 'thou yet place wisdom only in acting justly.

Examine men's ruling principles, even those of the wise, what kind of things they avoid, and what kind they pursue.

What is evil to thee does not subsist in the ruling principle of another; nor yet in any turning and mutation of thy corporeal covering. Where is it then? It is in that part of thee in which subsists the power of forming opinions about evils. Let this power then not form [such] opinions, and all is well. And if that which is nearest to it, the poor body, is cut, burnt, filled with matter and rottenness, neverthe-

28

less let the part which forms opinions about these things be quiet, that is, let it judge that nothing is either bad or good which can happen equally to the bad man and the good. For that which happens equally to him who lives contrary to nature and to him who lives according to nature, is neither according to nature nor contrary to nature.

Constantly regard the universe as one living being, having one substance and one soul; and observe how all things have reference to one perception, the perception of this one living being; and how all things act with one movement; and how all things are the co-operating causes of all things which exist; observe too the continuous spinning of the thread and the contexture of the web.

Thou art a little soul bearing about a corpse, as Epictetus used to say.

It is no evil for things to undergo change, and no good for things to subsist in consequence of change.

Time is like a river made up of the events which happen, and a violent stream: for as soon as a thing has been seen, it is carried away, and another comes in its place, and this will be carried away too.

Everything which happens is as familiar and well known as the rose in spring and the fruit in summer; for such is disease, and death, and calumny, and treachery, and whatever else delights fools or vexes them.

In the series of things those which follow are always aptly fitted to those which have gone before; for this series is not like a mere enumeration of disjointed things, which has only a necessary sequence, but it is a rational connection: and as all existing things are arranged together harmoniously, so the things which come into existence exhibit no mere succession, but a wonderful relationship.

Always remember the saying of Heraclitus, that the death of earth is to become water, and the death of water is to become air, and the death of air is to become fire, and reversely. And think too of him who forgets whither the way leads, and that men quarrel with that with which they are most constantly in communion, the reason which governs the universe; and the things which they daily meet with seem to them strange· and consider that we ought not to act and speak as if we were asleep, for even in sleep we seem to act and speak; and that* we ought not, like children who learn from their parents, simply to act and speak as we have been taught.*

If any god told thee that thou shalt die to-morrow, or certainly on the day after to-morrow, thou wouldst not care much whether, it was on the third day or on the morrow, unless thou wast in the highest degree mean-spirited,—for how small is the difference?—so think it no great thing to die after as many years as thou canst name rather than to-morrow.

Think continually how many physicians are dead after often contracting their eyebrows over the sick; and how many astrologers after predicting with great pretensions the deaths of others; and how many philosophers after endless discourses on death or immortality; how many heroes after killing thousands; and how many tyrants who have used their power over men's lives with terrible insolence as if they were immortal; and how many cities are entirely dead, so to speak, Helice[4] and Pompeii and Herclanum, and others innumerable. Add to the reckoning all whom thou hast known, one after another. One man after burying another has been laid out dead, and another buries him; and all this in a short time. To conclude, always observe how ephemeral and worthless human things are, and what was yesterday a little mucus, to-morrow will be a mummy or ashes. Pass then through this little space of time conformably to nature, and end thy journey in content, just as an olive falls off when it is ripe, blessing nature who produced it, and thanking the tree on which it grew.

Be like the promontory against which the waves continually break, but it stands firm and tames the fury of the water around it.

Unhappy am I, because this has happened to me—Not so, but happy am I, though this has happened to me, because I continue free from pain, neither crushed by the present nor fearing the future. For such a thing as this might have happened to every man; but every man would not have continued free from pain on such an occasion. Why then is that rather a misfortune than this a good fortune? And dost thou in all cases call that a man's misfortune, which is not a deviation from man's nature? And does a thing seem to thee to be a deviation from man's nature, when it is not contrary to the will of man's nature. Well, thou knowest the will of nature. Will then this which has happened prevent thee from being just, magnanimous, temperate, prudent, secure against inconsiderate opinions and falsehood; will it prevent thee from having modesty, freedom, and everything else by the presence of which man's nature obtains all that is its own? Remember too on every occasion which leads thee to vexation to apply this principle: not that this is a misfortune, but that to bear it nobly is good fortune.

It is a vulgar, but still a useful help towards contempt of death, to pass in review those who have tenaciously stuck to life. What more then have they gained than those who have died early? Certainly they lie in their tombs somewhere at last, Cadicianus, Fabius, Julianus, Lepidus, or any one else like them, who have carried out many to be buried, and then were carried out themselves. Altogether the interval is small [between birth and death]; and consider with how much trouble, and in company with what sort of people and in what a feeble body this interval is laboriously passed. Do not then consider life a thing of any value.* For look to the immensity of time behind thee, and to the time which is before thee, another boundless space. In this infinity then what is the difference between him who lives three days and him who lives three generations?[5]

Always run to the short way; and the short way is the natural: accordingly say and do everything in conformity with the soundest reason. For such a purpose frees a man from trouble,* and warfare, and all artifice and ostentatious display.

NOTES

[1] Tecum habita, noris quam sit tibi curta supellex —Persius, IV, 52.
[2] Compare Cicero, De Legibus, I. 7.
[3] Antoninus here uses the word κόσμος both in the sense of the Universe and of Order; and it is difficult to express his meaning.
[4] Ovid, Met xv, 293:
    Si quæras Helicen et Burin Achaidas urbes,
    Invenies sub aquis
[5] An allusion to Homer's Nestor who was living at the war of Troy among the third generation, like old Parr with his hundred and fifty-

two years, and some others in modern times who have beaten Parr by twenty or thirty years, if it is true, and yet they died at last. The word is τριγερηνίου in Antoninus. Nestor is named τριγέρων by some writers; but here perhaps there is an allusion to Homer's Γερήνιος ἰππότα Νέϭτωρ.

BOOK V

IN the morning when thou risest unwillingly, let this thought be present—I am rising to the work of a human being. Why then am I dissatisfied if I am going to do the things for which I exist and for which I was brought into the world? Or have I been made for this, to lie in the bedclothes and keep myself warm?—But this is more pleasant—Dost thou exist then to take thy pleasure, and not at all for action or exertion? Dost thou not see the little plants, the little birds, the ants, the spiders, the bees working together to put in order their several parts of the universe? And art thou unwilling to do the work of a human being, and dost thou not make haste to do that which is according to thy nature?—But it is necessary to take rest also—It is necessary: however nature has fixed bounds to this too: she has fixed bounds both to eating and drinking, and yet thou goest beyond these bounds, beyond what is sufficient; yet in thy acts it is not so, but thou stoppest short of what thou canst do. So thou lovest not thyself, for if thou didst, thou wouldst love thy nature and her will. But those who love their several arts exhaust themselves in working at them unwashed and without food; but thou valuest thy own nature less than the turner values the turning art, or the dancer the dancing art, or the lover of money values his money, or the vainglorious man his little glory. And such men, when they have a violent affection to a thing, choose neither to eat nor to sleep rather than to perfect the things which they care for. But are the acts which concern society more vile in thy eyes and less worthy of thy labour?

How easy it is to repel and to wipe away every impression which is troublesome or unsuitable, and immediately to be in all tranquillity.

Judge every word and deed which are according to na-

ture to be fit for thee; and be not diverted by the blame
which follows from any people nor by their words, but if a
thing is good to be done or said, do not consider it unworthy
of thee. For those persons have their peculiar leading principle and follow their peculiar movement; which things do
not thou regard, but go straight on, following thy own nature and the common nature; and the way of both is one.

I go through the things which happen according to nature
until I shall fall and rest, breathing out my breath into that
element out of which I daily draw it in, and falling upon
that earth out of which my father collected the seed, and
my mother the blood, and my nurse the milk; out of which
during so many years I have been supplied with food and
drink: which bears me when I tread on it and abuse it for
so many purposes.

Thou sayest, Men can admire the sharpness of thy wits—
Be it so: but there are many other things of which thou
canst not say, I am not formed for them by nature. Show
those qualities then which are altogether in thy power: sincerity, gravity, endurance of labour, aversion to pleasure,
contentment with thy portion and with few things, benevolence, frankness, no love of superfluity, freedom from trifling, magnanimity. Dost thou not see how many qualities
thou art immediately able to exhibit, in which there is no
excuse of natural incapacity and unfitness, and yet thou still
remainest voluntarily below the mark? or art thou compelled through being defectively furnished by nature to murmur, and to be stingy, and to flatter, and to find fault with
thy poor body, and to try to please men, and to make great
display, and to be so restless in thy mind? No by the gods:
but thou mightest have been delivered from these things long
ago. Only if in truth thou canst be charged with being
rather slow and dull of comprehension, thou must exert thyself about this also, not neglecting it nor yet taking pleasure
in thy dulness.

One man, when he has done a service to another, is ready
to set it down to his account as a favour conferred. Another
is not ready to do this, but still in his own mind he thinks
of the man as his debtor, and he knows what he has done.
A third in a manner does not even know what he has done,

but he is like a vine which has produced grapes, and seeks for nothing more after it has once produced its proper fruit. As a horse when he has run, a dog when he has tracked the game, a bee when it has made the honey, so a man when he has done a good act, does not call out for others to come and see, but he goes on to another act, as a vine goes on to produce again the grapes in season—Must a man then be one of these, who in a manner act thus without observing it?—Yes—But this very thing is necessary, the observation of what a man is doing: for, it may be said, it is characteristic of the social animal to perceive that he is working in a social manner, and indeed to wish that his social partner also should perceive it—It is true what thou sayest, but thou dost not rightly understand what is now said: and for this reason thou wilt become one of those of whom I spoke before, for even they are misled by a certain show of reason. But if thou wilt choose to understand the meaning of what is said, do not fear that for this reason thou wilt omit any social act.

A prayer of the Athenians: "Rain, rain, O dear Zeus, down on the ploughed fields of the Athenians and on the plains." In truth we ought not to pray at all, or we ought to pray in this simple and noble fashion.

Just as we must understand when it is said, That Æsculapius prescribed to this man horse-exercise, or bathing in cold water or going without shoes; so we must understand it when it is said, That the nature of the universe prescribed to this man disease or mutilation or loss or anything else of the kind. For in the first case Prescribed means something like this: he prescribed this for this man as a thing adapted to procure health; and in the second case it means, That which happens[1] to [or, suits] every man is fixed in a manner for him suitably to his destiny. For this is what we mean when we say that things are suitable to us, as the workmen say of squared stones in walls or the pyramids, that they are suitable, when they fit them to one another in some kind of connection. For there is altogether one fitness [harmony]. And as the universe is made up out of all bodies to be such a body as it is, so out of all existing causes necessity [destiny] is made up to be such a cause as it is. And even those who are completely ignorant understand what I mean, for they

say, It [necessity, destiny] brought this to such a person.—
This then was brought and this was prescribed to him. Let
us then receive these things, as well as those which Æsculapius prescribes. Many as a matter of course even among
his prescriptions are disagreeable, but we accept them in the
hope of health. Let the perfecting and accomplishment of
the things, which the common nature judges to be good, be
judged by thee to be of the same kind as thy health. And so
accept everything which happens, even if it seem disagreeable, because it leads to this, to the health of the universe and
to the prosperity and felicity of Zeus [the universe]. For
he would not have brought on any man what he has brought,
if it were not useful for the whole. Neither does the nature
of anything, whatever it may be, cause anything which is
not suitable to that which is directed by it. For two reasons
then it is right to be content with that which happens to
thee; the one, because it was done for thee and prescribed for
thee, and in a manner had reference to thee, originally from
the most ancient causes spun with thy destiny; and the other,
because even that which comes severally to every man is to
the power which administers the universe a cause of felicity
and perfection, nay even of its very continuance. For the
integrity of the whole is mutilated, if thou cuttest off anything whatever from the conjunction and the continuity
either of the parts or of the causes. And thou dost cut off,
as far as it is in thy power, when thou art dissatisfied, and in
a manner triest to put anything out of the way

Be not disgusted, nor discouraged, nor dissatisfied, if thou
dost not succeed in doing everything according to right principles but when thou hast failed, return back again, and be
content if the greater part of what thou doest is consistent
with man's nature, and love this to which thou returnest; and
do not return to philosophy as if she were a master, but act like
those who have sore eyes and apply a bit of sponge and egg,
or as another applies a plaster, or drenching with water.
For thus thou wilt not fail to* obey reason, and thou wilt
repose in it. And remember that philosophy requires only
the things which thy nature requires; but thou wouldst have
something else which is not according to nature—It may
be objected, Why what is more agreeable than this [which I

am doing] ?—But is not this the very reason why pleasure deceives us? And consider if magnanimity, freedom, simplicity, equanimity, piety, are not more agreeable. For what is more agreeable than wisdom itself, when thou thinkest of the security and the happy course of all things which depend on the faculty of understanding and knowledge?

Things are in such a kind of envelopment that they have seemed to philosophers, not a few nor those common philosophers, altogether unintelligible; nay even to the Stoics themselves they seem difficult to understand. And all our assent is changeable; for where is the man who never changes? Carry thy thoughts then to the objects themselves, and consider how short-lived they are and worthless, and that they may be in the possession of a filthy wretch or a whore or a robber. Then turn to the morals of those who live with thee, and it is hardly possible to endure even the most agreeable of them, to say nothing of a man being hardly able to endure himself. In such darkness then and dirt and in so constant a flux both of substance and of time, and of motion and of things moved, what there is worth being highly prized or even an object of serious pursuit, I can not imagine. But on the contrary it is a man's duty to comfort himself, and to wait for the natural dissolution and not to be vexed at the delay, but to rest in these principles only: the one, that nothing will happen to me which is not conformable to the nature of the universe; and the other, that it is in my power never to act contrary to my god and dæmon: for there is no man who will compel me to this.

About what am I now employing my own soul? On every occasion I must ask myself this question, and inquire, what have I now in this part of me which they call the ruling principle? and whose soul have I now? that of a child, or of a young man, or of a feeble woman, or of a tyrant, or of a domestic animal, or of a wild beast?

What kind of things those are which appear good to the many we may learn even from this. For if any man should conceive certain things as being really good, such as prudence, temperance, justice, fortitude, he would not after having first conceived these endure to listen to anything* which should not be in harmony with what is really good.*

But if a man has first conceived as good the things which appear to the many to be good, he will listen and readily receive as very applicable that which was said by the comic writer.* Thus even the many perceive the difference.* For were it not so, this saying would not offend and would not be rejected [in the first case], while we receive it when it is said of wealth, and of the means which further luxury and fame, as said fitly and wittily. Go on then and ask if we should value and think those things to be good, to which after their first conception in the mind the words of the comic writer might be aptly applied—that he who has them, through pure abundance has not a place to ease himself in.

I am composed of the formal and the material; and neither of them will perish into non-existence, as neither of them came into existence out of non-existence. Every part of me then will be reduced by change into some part of the universe, and that again will change into another part of the universe, and so on forever. And by consequence of such a change I too exist, and those who begot me, and so on for ever in the other direction For nothing hinders us from saying so, even if the universe is administered according to definite periods [of revolution].

Reason and the reasoning art [philosophy] are powers which are sufficient for themselves and for their own works. They move then from a first principle which is their own, and they make their way to the end which is proposed to them; and this is the reason why such acts are named Catorthóseis or right acts, which word signifies that they proceed by the right road.

None of these things ought to be called a man's, which do not belong to a man, as man. They are not required of a man, nor does man's nature promise them, nor are they the means of man's nature attaining its end. Neither then does the end of man lie in these things, nor yet that which aids to the accomplishment of this end, and that which aids towards this end is that which is good. Besides, if any of these things did belong to man, it would not be right for a man to despise them and to set himself against them; nor would a man be worthy of praise who showed that he did not want these things, nor would he who stinted himself in any of

them be good, if indeed these things were good.   But now
the more of these things a man deprives himself of, or of
other things like them, or even when he is deprived of any
of them, the more patiently he endures the loss, just in the
same degree he is a better man.

Such as are thy habitual thoughts, such also will be the
character of thy mind; for the soul is dyed by the thoughts.
Dye it then with a continuous series of such thoughts as
these: for instance, that where a man can live, there he
can also live well.   But he must live in a palace;—well then,
he can also live well in a palace.   And again, consider that
for whatever purpose each thing has been constituted, for
this it has been constituted, and towards this it is carried;
and its end is in that towards which it is carried; and where
the end is, there also is the advantage and the good of each
thing.   Now the good for the reasonable animal is society;
for that we are made for society has been shown above.   Is
it not plain that the inferior exist for the sake of the superior? but the things which have life are superior to those
which have not life, and of those which have life the superior are those which have reason.

To seek what is impossible is madness: and it is impossible that the bad should not do something of this kind.

Nothing happens to any man which he is not formed by
nature to bear.   The same things happen to another, and
either because he does not see that they have happened or because he would show a great spirit, he is firm and remains
unharmed.   It is a shame then that ignorance and conceit
should be stronger than wisdom.

Things themselves touch not the soul, not in the least
degree; nor have they admission to the soul, nor can they
turn or move the soul: but the soul turns and moves itself
alone, and whatever judgments it may think proper to make,
such it makes for itself the things which present themselves
to it.

In one respect man is the nearest thing to me, so far
as I must do good to men and endure them.   But so far as
some men make themselves obstacles to my proper acts, man
becomes to me one of the things which are indifferent, no
less than the sun or wind or a wild beast.   Now it is true

that these may impede my action, but they are no impediments to my affects and disposition, which have the power of acting conditionally and changing: for the mind converts and changes every hindrance to its activity into an aid; and so that which is a hindrance is made a furtherance to an act; and that which is an obstacle on the road helps us on this road.

Reverence that which is best in the universe; and this is that which makes use of all things and directs all things. And in like manner also reverence that which is best in thyself; and this is of the same kind as that. For in thyself also, that which makes use of everything else, is this, and thy life is directed by this.

That which does no harm to the state, does no harm to the citizen. In the case of every appearance of harm apply this rule: if the state is not harmed by this, neither am I harmed. But if the state is harmed, thou must not be angry with him who does harm to the state. Show him where his error is.

Often think of the rapidity with which things pass by and disappear, both the things which are and the things which are produced. For substance is like a river in a continual flow, and the activities of things are in constant change, and the causes work in infinite varieties; and there is hardly anything which stands still. And consider this which is near to thee, this boundless abyss of the past and of the future in which all things disappear. How then is he not a fool who is puffed up with such things or plagued about them and makes himself miserable? for they vex him only for a time, and a short time.

Think of the universal substance, of which thou hast a very small portion; and of universal time, of which a short and indivisible interval has been assigned to thee; and of that which is fixed by destiny, and how small a part of it thou art.

Does another do me wrong? Let him look to it. He has his own disposition, his own activity. I now have what the universal nature wills me to have; and I do what my nature now wills me to do.

Let the part of thy soul which leads and governs be undisturbed by the movements in the flesh, whether of pleasure or of pain; and let it not unite with them, but let it circumscribe itself and limit those affects to their parts. But when these affects rise up to the mind by virtue of that other sympathy that naturally exists in a body which is all one, then thou must not strive to resist the sensation, for it is natural: but let not the ruling part of itself add to the sensation the opinion that it is either good or bad.

Live with the gods. And he does live with the gods who constantly shows to them that his own soul is satisfied with that which is assigned to him, and that it does all that the dæmon wishes, which Zeus hath given to every man for his guardian and guide, a portion of himself. And this is every man's understanding and reason.

Art thou angry with him whose arm-pits stink? art thou angry with him whose mouth smells foul? What good will this anger do thee? He has such a mouth, he has such arm-pits: it is necessary that such an emanation must come from such things—but the man has reason, it will be said, and he is able, if he takes pains, to discover wherein he offends—I wish thee well of thy discovery. Well then, and thou hast reason: by thy rational faculty stir up his rational faculty; show him his error, admonish him. For if he listens, thou wilt cure him, and there is no need of anger.

As thou intendest to live when thou art gone out....so it is in thy power to live here. But if men do not permit thee, then get away out of life, yet so as if thou wert suffering no harm. The house is smoky, and I quit it. Why dost thou think that this is any trouble? But so long as nothing of the kind drives me out, I remain, am free, and no man shall hinder me from doing what I choose; and I choose to do what is according to the nature of the rational and social animal.

The intelligence of the universe is social. Accordingly it has made the inferior things for the sake of the superior, and it has fitted the superior to one another. Thou seest how it has subordinated, co-ordinated and assigned to everything its proper portion, and has brought together into concord with one another the things which are the best.

How hast thou behaved hitherto to the gods, thy parents,

brethren, children, teachers, to those who looked after thy infancy, to thy friends, kinsfolk, to thy slaves? Consider if thou hast hitherto behaved to all in such a way that this may be said of thee:

"Never has wronged a man in deed or word."

And call to recollection both how many things thou hast passed through, and how many things thou hast been able to endure: and that the history of thy life is now complete and thy service is ended: and how many beautiful things thou hast seen: and how many pleasures and pains thou hast despised; and how many things called honourable thou hast spurned; and to how many ill-minded folks thou hast shown a kind disposition.

Why do unskilled and ignorant souls disturb him who has skill and knowledge? What soul then has skill and knowledge? That which knows beginning and end, and knows the reason which pervades all substance and through all time by fixed periods [revolutions] administers the universe.

Soon, very soon, thou wilt be ashes, or a skeleton, and either a name or not even a name; but name is sound and echo. And the things which are much valued in life are empty and rotten and trifling, and [like] little dogs biting one another, and little children quarrelling, laughing, and then straightway weeping. But fidelity and modesty and justice and truth are fled

"Up to Olympus from the wide-spread earth."

What then is there which still detains thee here? if the objects of sense are easily changed and never stand still, and the organs of perception are dull and easily receive false impressions; and the poor soul itself is an exhalation from blood. But to have good repute amidst such a world as this is an empty thing. Why then dost thou not wait in tranquillity for thy end, whether it is extinction or removal to another state? And until that time comes, what is sufficient? Why, what else than to venerate the gods and bless them, and to do good to men, and to practise tolerance and self-restraint;[2] but as to everything which is beyond the limits of the poor flesh and breath, to remember that this is neither thine nor in thy power.

Thou canst pass thy life in an equable flow of happiness, if thou canst go by the right way, and think and act in the right way. These two things are common both to the soul of god and to the soul of man, and to the soul of every rational being, not to be hindered by another; and to hold good to consist in the disposition to justice and the practice of it, and in this to let thy desire find its termination.

If this is neither my own badness, nor an effect of my own badness, and the common weal is not injured, why am I troubled about it? and what is the harm to the common weal?

Do not be carried along inconsiderately by the appearance of things, but give help [to all] according to thy ability and their fitness; and if they should have sustained loss in matters which are indifferent, do not imagine this to be a damage. For it is a bad habit. But as the old man, when he went away, asked back his foster-child's top, remembering that it was a top, so do thou in this case also

When thou art calling out on the Rostra, hast thou forgotten, man, what these things are?—Yes; but they are objects of great concern to these people—wilt thou too then be made a fool for these things?—I was once a fortunate man, but I lost it, I know not how.—But fortunate means that a man has assigned to himself a good fortune: and a good fortune is good disposition of the soul, good emotions, good actions.[3]

NOTES

[1] In this section there is a play on the meaning of συμβαίνειν

[2] This is the Stoic precept ἀνέχου καὶ ἀπέχου. The first part teaches us to be content with men and things as they are. The second part teaches us the virtue of self-restraint, or the government of our passions

[3] This section is unintelligible Many of the words may be corrupt, and the general purport of the section can not be discovered. Perhaps several things have been improperly joined in one section I have translated it nearly literally. Different translators give the section a different turn, and the critics have tried to mend what they can not understand.

BOOK VI

THE substance of the universe is obedient and compliant; and the reason which governs it has in itself no cause for doing evil, for it has no malice, nor does it do evil to anything, nor is anything harmed by it. But all things are made and perfected according to this reason.

Let it make no difference to thee whether thou art cold or warm, if thou art doing thy duty; and whether thou art drowsy or satisfied with sleep; and whether ill-spoken of or praised; and whether dying or doing something else. For it is one of the acts of life, this act by which we die: it is sufficient then in this act also to do well what we have in hand.

Look within. Let neither the peculiar quality of anything nor its value escape thee.

All existing things soon change, and they will either be reduced to vapour, if indeed all substance is one, or they will be dispersed.

The reason which governs knows what its own disposition is, and what it does, and on what material it works.

The best way of avenging thyself is not to become like [the wrong doer].

Take pleasure in one thing and rest in it, in passing from one social act to another social act, thinking of God.

The ruling principle is that which rouses and turns itself, and while it makes itself such as it is and such as it wills to be, it also makes everything which happens appear to itself to be such as it wills.

In conformity to the nature of the universe every single thing is accomplished, for certainly it is not in conformity to any other nature that each thing is accomplished, either a nature which externally comprehends this, or a nature which

47

is comprehended within this nature, or a nature external and independent of this.

The universe is either a confusion, and a mutual involution of things, and a dispersion; or it is unity, and order, and providence. If then it is the former, why do I desire to tarry in a fortuitous combination of things and such a disorder? and why do I care about anything else than how I shall at last become earth? and why am I disturbed, for the dispersion of my elements will happen whatever I do. But if the other supposition is true, I venerate, and I am firm, and I trust in him who governs.

When thou hast been compelled by circumstances to be disturbed in a manner, quickly return to thyself and do not continue out of tune longer than the compulsion lasts; for thou wilt have more mastery over the harmony by continually recurring to it.

If thou hadst a step-mother and a mother at the same time, thou wouldst be dutiful to thy step-mother, but still thou wouldst constantly return to thy mother. Let the court and philosophy now be to thee step-mother and mother: return to philosophy frequently and repose in her, through whom what thou meetest with in the court appears to thee tolerable, and thou appearest tolerable in the court.

When we have meat before us and such eatables, we receive the impression, that this is the dead body of a fish, and this is the dead body of a bird or of a pig; and again, that this Falernian is only a little grape juice, and this purple robe some sheep's wool dyed with the blood of a shell-fish: such then are these impressions, and they reach the things themselves and penetrate them, and so we see what kind of things they are. Just in the same way ought we to act all through life, and where there are things which appear most worthy of our approbation, we ought to lay them bare and look at their worthlessness and strip them of all the words by which they are exalted. For outward show is a wonderful perverter of the reason, and when thou art most sure that thou art employed about things worth thy pains, it is then that it cheats thee most. Consider then what Crates says of Xenocrates himself.

Most of the things which the multitude admire are referred to objects of the most general kind, those which are held together by cohesion or natural organization, such as stones, wood, fig-trees, vines, olives. But those which are admired by men, who are a little more reasonable, are referred to the things which are held together by a living principle, as flocks, herds. Those which are admired by men who are still more instructed are the things which are held together by a rational soul, not however a universal soul, but rational so far as it is a soul skilled in some art, or expert in some other way, or simply rational so far as it possesses a number of slaves. But he who values a rational soul, a soul universal and fitted for political life, regards nothing else except this; and above all things he keeps his soul in a condition and in an activity conformable to reason and social life, and he co-operates to this end with those who are of the same kind as himself.

Some things are hurrying into existence, and others are hurrying out of it; and of that which is coming into existence part is already extinguished. Motions and changes are continually renewing the world, just as the uninterrupted course of time is always renewing the infinite duration of ages. In this flowing stream then, on which there is no abiding, what is there of the things which hurry by on which a man would set a high price? It would be just as if a man should fall in love with one of the sparrows which fly by, but it has already past out of sight. Something of this kind is the very life of every man, like the exhalation of the blood and the respiration of the air. For such as it is to have once drawn in the air and to have given it back, which we do every moment, just the same is it with the whole respiratory power which thou didst receive at thy birth yesterday and the day before, to give it back to the element from which thou didst first draw it.

Neither is transpiration, as in plants, a thing to be valued, nor respiration, as in domesticated animals and wild beasts, nor the receiving of impressions by the appearances of things, nor being moved by desires as puppets by strings, nor assembling in herds, nor being nourished by food; for this is just like the act of separating and parting with the useless part of our food. What then is worth being valued? To be received with clapping of hands? No. Neither must we value the clapping of tongues, for the praise which comes from the many is a clapping of tongues. Suppose then that thou hast given up this worthless thing called fame, what remains that is worth valuing? This in my opinion, to move thyself and to restrain thyself in conformity to thy proper constitution, to which end both all employments and arts lead. For every art aims at this, that the thing which has been made should be adapted to the work for which it has been made; and both the vine-planter who looks after the vine, and the horse-breaker, and he who trains the dog, seek this end But the education and the teaching of youth aim at something. In this then is the value of the education and the teaching. And if this is well, thou wilt not seek any-thing else. Wilt thou not cease to value many other things too? Then thou wilt be neither free, nor sufficient for thy own happiness, nor without passion. For of necessity thou must be envious, jealous, and suspicious of those who can take away those things, and plot against those who have that which is valued by thee. Of necessity a man must be alto-gether in a state of perturbation who wants any of these things; and besides, he must often find fault with the gods. But to reverence and honour thy own mind will make thee content with thyself, and in harmony with society, and in agreement with the gods, that is, praising all that they give and have ordered.

Above, below, all around are the movements of the elements. But the motion of virtue is in none of these: it is something more divine, and advancing by a way hardly ob-served it goes happily on its road.

How strangely men act. They will not praise those who are living at the same time and living with themselves; but to be themselves praised by posterity, by those whom they have never seen or ever will see, this they set much value on. But this is very much the same as if thou shouldst be grieved because those who have lived before thee did not praise thee.

If a thing is difficult to be accomplished by thyself, do not think that it is impossible for man : but if anything is possible for man and conformable to his nature, think that this can be attained by thyself too.

In the gymnastic exercises suppose that a man has torn thee with his nails, and by dashing against thy head has inflicted a wound. Well, we neither show any signs of vexation, nor are we offended, nor do we suspect him afterwards as a treacherous fellow; and yet we are on our guard against him, not however as an enemy, nor yet with suspicion, but we quietly get out of his way. Something like this let thy behaviour be in all the other parts of life; let us overlook many things in those who are like antagonists in the gymnasium. For it is in our power, as I said, to get out of the way, and to have no suspicion nor hatred.

If any man is able to convince me and show me that I do not think or act rightly, I will gladly change; for I seek the truth by which no man was ever injured. But he is injured who abides in his error and ignorance.

I do my duty: other things trouble me not; for they are either things without life, or things without reason, or things that have rambled and know not the way.

As to the animals which have no reason and generally all things and objects, do thou, since thou hast reason and they have none, make use of them with a generous and liberal spirit. But towards human beings, as they have reason, behave in a social spirit. And on all occasions call on the gods, and do not perplex thyself about the length of time in which thou shalt do this; for even three hours so spent are sufficient.

Alexander the Macedonian and his groom by death were brought to the same state; for either they were received among the same seminal principles of the universe, or they were alike dispersed among the atoms.

Consider how many things in the same indivisible time take place in each of us, things which concern the body and things which concern the soul: and so thou wilt not wonder if many more things, or rather all things which come into existence in that which is the one and all, which we call Cosmos, exist in it at the same time.

If any man should propose to thee the question, how the name Antoninus is written, wouldst thou with a straining of the voice utter each letter? What then if they grow angry, wilt thou be angry too? Wilt thou not go on with

composure and number every letter? Just so then in this
life also remember that every duty is made up of certain
parts. These it is thy duty to observe and without being
disturbed or showing anger towards those who are angry
with thee to go on thy way and finish that which is set before thee.

How cruel it is not to allow men to strive after the things
which appear to them to be suitable to their nature and profitable! And yet in a manner thou dost not allow them to do
this, when thou art vexed because they do wrong. For they
are certainly moved towards things because they suppose
them to be suitable to their nature and profitable to them—
But it is not so—Teach them then, and show them without
being angry.

Death is a cessation of the impressions through the senses,
and of the pulling of the strings which move the appetites,
and of the discursive movements of the thoughts, and of the
service to the flesh.

It is a shame for the soul to be first to give way in this
life, when thy body does not give way.

Take care that thou art not made into a Cæsar, that thou
art not dyed with this dye; for such things happen. Keep
thyself then simple, good, pure, serious, free from affectation, a friend of justice, a worshipper of the gods, kind, affectionate, strenuous in all proper acts. Strive to continue to
be such as philosophy wished to make thee. Reverence the
gods, and help men. Short is life. There is only one fruit
of this earthly life, a pious disposition and social acts. Do
everything as a disciple of Antoninus. Remember his constancy in every act which was conformable to reason, and his
evenness in all things, and his piety, and the serenity of his
countenance, and his sweetness, and his disregard of empty
fame, and his efforts to understand things; and how he
would never let anything pass without having first most
carefully examined it and clearly understood it; and how he
bore with those who blamed him unjustly without blaming
them in return; how he did nothing in a hurry; and how he
listened not to calumnies, and how exact an examiner of
manners and actions he was; and not given to reproach people, nor timid, nor suspicious, nor a sophist; and with how

little he was satisfied, such as lodging, bed, dress, food, servants; and how laborious and patient; and how he was able on account of his sparing diet to hold out to the evening, not even requiring to relieve himself by any evacuations except at the usual hour; and his firmness and uniformity in his friendships, and how he tolerated freedom of speech in those who opposed his opinions; and the pleasure that he had when any man showed him anything better; and how religious he was without superstition. Imitate all this that thou mayest have as good a conscience, as he had, when thy last hour comes.

Return to thy sober senses and call thyself back; and when thou hast roused thyself from sleep and hast perceived that they were only dreams which troubled thee, now in thy waking hours look at these [the things about thee] as thou didst look at those [the dreams].

I consist of a little body and a soul. Now to this little body all things are indifferent, for it is not able to perceive differences. But to the understanding those things only are indifferent, which are not the works of its own activity. But whatever things are the works of its own activity, all these are in its power. And of these however only those which are done with reference to the present; for as to the future and the past activities of the mind, even these are for the present indifferent.

Neither the labour which the hand does nor that of the foot is contrary to nature, so long as the foot does the foot's work and the hand the hand's. So then neither to a man as a man is his labour contrary to nature, so long as it does the things of a man. But if the labour is not contrary to his nature, neither is it an evil to him.

How many pleasures have been enjoyed by robbers, patricides, tyrants.

Dost thou not see how the handicraftsmen accommodate themselves up to a certain point to those who are not skilled in their craft,—nevertheless they cling to the reason [the principles] of their art and do not endure to depart from it? Is it not strange if the architect and the physician shall have more respect to the reason [the principles] of their own arts than man to his own reason, which is common to him and the gods?

Asia, Europe are corners of the universe: all the sea a drop in the universe; Athos a little clod of the universe: all the present time is a point in eternity. All things are little, changeable, perishable. All things come from thence, from that universal ruling power either directly proceeding or by way of sequence. And accordingly the lion's gaping jaws, and that which is poisonous, and every harmful thing, as a thorn, as mud, are after-products of the grand and the beautiful. Do not then imagine that they are of another kind from that which thou dost venerate, but form a just opinion of the source of all.

He who has seen present things has seen all, both everything which has taken place from all eternity and everything which will be for time without end; for all things are of one kin and of one form.

Frequently consider the connection of all things in the universe and their relation to one another. For in a manner all things are implicated with one another, and all in this way are friendly to one another; for one thing comes in order after another, and this is by virtue of the* active movement and mutual conspiration and the unity of the substance.

Adapt thyself to the things with which thy lot has been cast: and the men among whom thou hast received thy portion, love them, and do it truly [sincerely].

Every instrument, tool, vessel, if it does that for which it has been made, is well, and yet he who made it is not there. But in the things which are held together by nature there is within and there abides in them the power which made them; wherefore the more is it fit to reverence this power, and to think, that, if thou dost live and act according to its will, everything in thee is in conformity to intelligence. And thus also in the universe the things which belong to it are in conformity to intelligence.

'Whatever of the things which are not within thy power thou shalt suppose to be good for thee or evil, it must of necessity be that, if such a bad thing befall thee or the loss of such a good thing, thou wilt blame the gods, and hate men too, those who are the cause of the misfortune or the loss, or those who are suspected of being likely to be the cause; and indeed we do much injustice, because we make a difference between these things [because we do not regard these things as indifferent*]. But if we judge only those things which are in our power to be good or bad, there remains no reason either for finding fault with god or standing in a hostile attitude to man.[1]

We are all working together to one end, some with knowledge and design, and others without knowing what they do; as men also when they are asleep, of whom it is Heraclitus, I think, who says that they are labourers and co-operators in the things which take place in the universe. But men co-operate after different fashions; and even those co-operate abundantly, who find fault with what happens and those who try to oppose it and to hinder it; for the universe has need even of such men as these. It remains then for thee to understand among what kind of workmen thou placest thyself; for he who rules all things will certainly make a right use of thee, and he will receive thee among some part of the co-operators and of those whose labours conduce to one end. But be not thou such a part as the mean and ridiculous verse in the play, which Chrysippus speaks of.[2]

Does the sun undertake to do the work of the rain, or Æsculapius the work of the Fruit-bearer [the earth]? And how is it with respect to each of the stars, are they not different and yet they work together to the same end?

If the gods have determined about me and about the things which must happen to me, they have determined well, for it is not easy even to imagine a deity without forethought; and as to doing me harm, why should they have any desire towards that? for what advantage would result to them from this or to the whole, which is the special object of their providence? But if they have not determined about me individually, they have certainly determined about the whole at least, and the things which happen by way of sequence in this general arrangement I ought to accept with pleasure and to be content with them. But if they determine about nothing —which it is wicked to believe, or if we do believe it, let us neither sacrifice, nor pray, nor swear by them, nor do anything else which we do as if the gods were present and

29

lived with us—but if however the gods determine about none of the things which concern us, I am able to determine about myself, and I can inquire about that which is useful: and that is useful to every man which is conformable to his own constitution and nature. But my nature is rational and social; and my city and country, so far as I am Antoninus, is Rome, but so far as I am a man, it is the world. The things then which are useful to these cities are alone useful to me.

Whatever happens to every man, this is for the interest of the universal. this might be sufficient. But further thou wilt observe this also as a general truth, if thou dost observe, that whatever is profitable to any man is profitable also to other men. But let the word profitable be taken here in the common sense as said of things of the middle kind [neither good nor bad].

As it happens to thee in the amphitheatre and such places, that the continual sight of the same things and the uniformity make the spectacle wearisome, so it is in the whole of life; for all things above, below, are the same and from the same. How long then?

Think continually that all kinds of men and of all kinds of pursuits and of all nations are dead, so that thy thoughts come down even to Philistion and Phœbus and Origanion. Now turn thy thoughts to the other kinds [of men]. To that place then we must remove, where there are so many great orators, and so many noble philosophers, Heraclitus, Pythagoras, Socrates; so many heroes of former days, and so many generals after them, and tyrants; besides these, Eudoxus, Hipparchus, Archimedes, and other men of acute natural talents, great minds, lovers of labour, versatile, confident, mockers even of the perishable and ephemeral life of man, as Menippus and such as are like him. As to all these consider that they have long been in the dust. What harm then is this to them; and what to those whose names are altogether unknown? One thing here is worth a great deal, to pass thy life in truth and justice, with a benevolent disposition even to liars and unjust men.

When thou wishest to delight thyself, think of the virtues of those who live with thee; for instance, the activity of one, and the modesty of another, and the liberality of a third, and some other good quality of a fourth. For nothing delights so much as the examples of the virtues, when they are exhibited in the morals of those who live with us and present themselves in abundance, as far as is possible. Wherefore we must keep them before us.

Thou art not dissatisfied, I suppose, because thou weighest only so many litrae and not three hundred. Be not dissatisfied then that thou must live only so many years and not more; for as thou are satisfied with the amount of substance which has been assigned to thee, so be content with the time.

Let us try to persuade them [men], but act even against their will, when the principles of justice lead that way If however any man by using force stands in thy way, betake thyself to contentment and tranquillity, and at the same time employ the hindrance towards the exercise of some other virtue; and remember that thy attempt was with a reservation [conditionally], that thou didst not desire to do impossibilities. What then didst thou desire?—Some such effort as this—But thou attainest thy object, if the things to which thou wast moved are [not] accomplished.*

He who loves fame considers another man's activity to be his own good; and he who loves pleasure, his own sensations; but he who has understanding, considers his own acts to be his own good.

It is in our power to have no opinion about a thing, and not to be disturbed in our soul; for things themselves have no natural power to form our judgments.

Accustom thyself to attend carefully to what is said by another, and as much as it is possible, be in the speaker's mind.

That which is not good for the swarm, neither is it good for the bee.

If sailors abused the helmsman or the sick the doctor, would they listen to anybody else; or how could the helmsman secure the safety of those in the ship or the doctor the health of those whom he attends?

How many together with whom I came into the world are already gone out of it.

To the jaundiced honey tastes bitter, and to those bitten by mad dogs water causes fear; and to little children the ball is a fine thing. Why then am I angry? Dost thou think that a false opinion has less power than the bile in the jaundiced or the poison in him who is bitten by a mad dog?

No man will hinder thee from living according to the reason of thy own nature: nothing will happen to thee contrary to the reason of the universal nature.

What kind of people are those whom men wish to please, and for what objects, and by what kind of acts? How soon will time cover all things, and how many it has covered already.

NOTES

[1] Cicero, De Natura Deorum, III, 32.
[2] Plutarch, adversus Stoicos, c. 14.

BOOK VII

WHAT is badness? It is that which thou hast often seen. And on the occasion of everything which happens, keep this in mind, that it is that which thou hast often seen. Everywhere up and down thou wilt find the same things, with which the old histories are filled, those of the middle ages and those of our own day; with which cities and houses are filled now. There is nothing new. all things are both familiar and short-lived.

How can our principles become dead, unless the impressions [thoughts] which correspond to them are extinguished? But it is in thy power continuously to fan these thoughts into a flame. I can have that opinion about anything, which I ought to have. If I can, why am I disturbed? The things which are external to my mind have no relation at all to my mind.—Let this be the state of thy affects, and thou standest erect. To recover thy life is in thy power. Look at things again as thou didst use to look at them; for in this consists the recovery of thy life.

The idle business of show, plays on the stage, flocks of sheep, herds, exercises with spears, a bone cast to little dogs, a bit of bread into fish-ponds, labourings of ants and burden-carrying, runnings about of frightened little mice, puppets pulled by strings—[all alike]. It is thy duty then in the midst of such things to show good humour and not a proud air; to understand however that every man is worth just so much as the things are worth about which he busies himself.

In discourse thou must attend to what is said, and in every movement thou must observe what is doing. And in the one thou shouldst see immediately to what end it refers, but in the other watch carefully what is the thing signified.

Is my understanding sufficient for this or not? If it is

59

sufficient, I use it for the work as an instrument given by the universal nature. But if it is not sufficient, then either I retire from the work and give way to him who is able to do it better, unless there be some reason why I ought not to do so; or I do it as well as I can, taking to help me the man who with the aid of my ruling principle can do what is now fit and useful for the general good. For whatsoever either by myself or with another I can do, ought to be directed to this only, to that which is useful and well suited to society.

How many after being celebrated by fame have been given up to oblivion; and how many who have celebrated the fame of others have long been dead.

Be not ashamed to be helped; for it is thy business to do thy duty like a soldier in the assault on a town. How then, if being lame thou canst not mount up on the battlements alone, but with the help of another it is possible?

Let not future things disturb thee, for thou wilt come to them, if it shall be necessary, having with thee the same reason which now thou usest for present things.

All things are implicated with one another, and the bond is holy; and there is hardly anything unconnected with any other thing. For things have been co-ordinated, and they combine to form the same universe [order]. For there is one universe made up of all things, and one god who pervades all things, and one substance, and one law, [one] common reason in all intelligent animals, and one truth; if indeed there is also one perfection for all animals which are of the same stock and participate in the same reason.

Everything material soon disappears in the substance of the whole; and everything formal [causal] is very soon taken back into the universal reason; and the memory of everything is very soon overwhelmed in time.

To the rational animal the same act is according to nature and according to reason.

Be thou erect, or be made erect.

Just as it is with the members in those bodies which are united in one, so it is with rational beings which exist separately, for they have been constituted for one co-operation. And the perception of this will be more apparent to thee, if thou often sayest to thyself that I am a member [μέλος] of

the system of rational beings. But if [using the letter *r*]
thou sayest that thou art a part [μέρος], thou dost not yet love
men from thy heart; beneficence does not yet delight thee for
its own sake; thou still doest it barely as a thing of propriety; and not yet as doing good to thyself.

Let there fall externally what will on the parts which can
feel the effects of this fall. For those parts which have felt
will complain, if they choose. But I, unless I think that
what has happened is an evil, am not injured. And it is in
my power not to think so.

Whatever any one does or says, I must be good, just
as if the gold, or the emerald, or the purple were always saying this, Whatever any one does or says, I must be emerald
and keep my colour.

The ruling faculty does not disturb itself; I mean, does
not frighten itself or cause itself pain.* But if any one else
can frighten or pain it, let him do so. For the faculty itself
will not by its own opinion turn itself into such ways. Let
the body itself take care, if it can, that it suffer nothing, and
let it speak, if it suffers. But the soul itself, that which is
subject to fear, to pain, which has completely the power of
forming an opinion about these things, will suffer nothing,
for it will never deviate* into such a judgment. The leading principle in itself wants nothing, unless it makes a want
for itself; and therefore it is both free from perturbation
and unimpeded, if it does not disturb and impede itself.

Eudæmonia [happiness] is a good dæmon, or a good
thing. What then art thou doing here, O imagination? go
away, I entreat thee by the gods, as thou didst come, for I
want thee not. But thou art come according to thy old
fashion. I am not angry with thee: only go away.

Is any man afraid of change? Why what can take place
without change? What then is more pleasing or more suitable to the universal nature? And canst thou take a bath
unless the wood undergoes a change? and canst thou be nourished, unless the food undergoes a change? And can anything else that is useful be accomplished without change?
Dost thou not see then that for thyself also to change is just
the same, and equally necessary for the universal nature? ˙

Through the universal substance as through a furious

torrent all bodies are carried, being by their nature united
with and co-operating with the whole, as the parts of our
body with one another.   How many a Chrysippus, how
many a Socrates, how many an Epictetus has time already
swallowed up?   And let the same thought occur to thee with
reference to every man and thing.

One thing only troubles me, lest I should do something
which the constitution of man does not allow, or in the way
which it does not allow, or what it does not allow now.

Near is thy forgetfulness of all things; and near the forgetfulness of thee by all.

It is peculiar to man to love even those who do wrong.
And this happens, if when they do wrong it occurs to thee
that they are kinsmen, and that they do wrong through
ignorance and unintentionally, and that soon both of you will
die; and above all, that the wrong-doer has done thee no
harm, for he has not made thy ruling faculty worse than it
was before.

The universal nature out of the universal substance, as
if it were wax, now moulds a horse, and when it has broken
this up, it uses the material for a tree, then for a man, then
for something else; and each of these things subsists for a
very short time.   But it is no hardship for the vessel to be
broken up, just as there was none in its being fastened together.

A scowling look is altogether unnatural; when it is often
assumed,[1] the result is that all comeliness dies away. and at
last is so completely extinguished that it can not be again
lighted up at all.   Try to conclude from this very fact that
it is contrary to reason.   For if even the perception of doing
wrong shall depart, what reason is there for living any
longer?

Nature which governs the whole will soon change all
things which thou seest, and out of their substance will make
other things, and again other things from the substance of
them, in order that the world may be ever new.

When a man has done thee any wrong, immediately consider with what opinion about good or evil he has done
wrong.   For when thou hast seen this, thou wilt pity him,
and wilt neither wonder nor be angry.   For either thou thy-

self thinkest the same thing to be good that he does or another thing of the same kind. It is thy duty then to pardon him. But if thou dost not think such things to be good or evil, thou wilt more readily be well disposed to him who is in error.

Think not so much of what thou hast not as of what thou hast: but of the things which thou hast select the best, and then reflect how eagerly they would have been sought, if thou hadst them not. At the same time however take care that thou dost not through being so pleased with them accustom thyself to overvalue them, so as to be disturbed if ever thou shouldst not have them.

Retire into thyself. The rational principle which rules has this nature, that it is content with itself when it does what is just, and so secures tranquillity.

Wipe out the imagination. Stop the pulling of the strings Confine thyself to the present. Understand well what happens either to thee or to another. Divide and distribute every object into the causal [formal] and the material. Think of thy last hour. Let the wrong which is done by a man stay there where the wrong was done.

Direct thy attention to what is said. Let thy understanding enter into the things that are doing and the things which do them.

Adorn thyself with simplicity and modesty and with indifference towards the things which lie between virtue and vice. Love mankind. Follow God. The poet says that Law rules all—* And it is enough to remember that law rules all.²—*

About death: whether it is a dispersion, or a resolution into atoms, or annihilation, it is either extinction or change.

About pain: the pain which is intolerable carries us off; but that which lasts a long time is tolerable; and the mind maintains its own tranquillity by retiring into itself,* and the ruling faculty is not made worse. But the parts which are harmed by pain, let them, if they can, give their opinion about it.

About fame: look at the minds [of those who seek fame], observe what they are, and what kind of things they avoid, and what kind of things they pursue. And consider that as
30

the heaps of sand piled on one another hide the former sands, so in life the events which go before are soon covered by those which come after.

From Plato :[3] the man who has an elevated mind and takes a view of all time and of all substance, dost thou suppose it possible for him to think that human life is anything great? it is not possible, he said.—Such a man then will think that death also is no evil—Certainly not.

From Antisthenes: It is royal to do good and to be abused.

It is a base thing for the countenance to be obedient and to regulate and compose itself as the mind commands, and for the mind not to be regulated and composed by itself.

It is not right to vex ourselves at things,

For they care nought about it.[4]

To the immortal gods and us give joy.

Life must be reaped like the ripe ears of corn:

One man is born; another dies.[5]

If gods care not for me and for my children,

There is a reason for it.

For the good is with me, and the just.[6]

No joining others in their wailing, no violent emotion.

From Plato :[7]　But I would make this man a sufficient answer, which is this:　Thou sayest not well, if thou thinkest that a man who is good for anything at all ought to compute the hazard of life or death, and should not rather look to this only in all that he does, whether he is doing what is just or unjust, and the works of a good or a bad man.

For thus it is, men of Athens,[7] in truth: wherever a man has placed himself thinking it the best place for him, or has been placed by a commander, there in my opinion he ought to stay and to abide the hazard, taking nothing into the reckoning, either death or anything else, before the baseness [of deserting his post].

But, my good friend, reflect whether that which is noble and good is not something different from saving and being saved; for* as to a man living such or such a time, at least one who is really a man, consider if this is not a thing to be dismissed from the thoughts :* and there must be no love of life: but as to these matters a man must intrust them to the deity and believe what the women say, that no man can escape his destiny, the next inquiry being how he may best live the time that he has to live.[8]

Look round at the courses of the stars, as if thou wert going along with them; and constantly consider the changes of the elements into one another; for such thoughts purge away the filth of the earthly life.

This is a fine saying of Plato:[9] That he who is discoursing about men should look also at earthly things as if he viewed them from some higher place; should look at them in their assemblies, armies, agricultural labours, marriages, treaties, births, deaths, noise of the courts of justice, desert places, various nations of barbarians, feasts, lamentations, markets, a mixture of all things and an orderly combination of contraries.

Consider the past; such great changes of political supremacies. Thou mayest foresee also the things which will be. For they will certainly be of like form, and it is not possible that they should deviate from the order of the things which take place now: accordingly to have contemplated human life for forty years is the same as to have contemplated it for ten thousand years. For what more wilt thou see?

> "That which has grown from the earth, to the earth;
> But that which has sprung from heavenly seed,
> Back to the heavenly realms returns."[10]

This is either a dissolution of the mutual involution of the atoms, or a similar dispersion of the unsentient elements.

> "With food and drinks and cunning magic arts
> Turning the channel's course to 'scape from death."[11]
> "The breeze which heaven has sent
> We must endure, and toil without complaining."

Another may be more expert in casting his opponent; but he is not more social, nor more modest, nor better disciplined to meet all that happens, nor more considerate with respect to the faults of his neighbours.

Where any work can be done conformably to the reason which is common to gods and men, there we have nothing to fear: for where we are able to get profit by means of the activity which is successful and proceeds according to our constitution, there no harm is to be suspected.

Everywhere and at all times it is in thy power piously to acquiesce in thy present condition, and to behave justly to those who are about thee, and to exert thy skill upon thy present thoughts, that nothing shall steal into them without being well examined.

Do not look around thee to discover other men's ruling principles, but look straight to this, to what nature leads thee, both the universal nature through the things which happen to thee, and thy own nature through the acts which must be done by thee. But every being ought to do that which is according to its constitution; and all other things have been constituted for the sake of rational beings, just as among irrational things the inferior for the sake of the superior, but the rational for the sake of one another.

The prime principle then in man's constitution is the social. And the second is not to yield to the persuasions of the body, for it is the peculiar office of the rational and intelligent motion to circumscribe itself, and never to be overpowered either by the motion of the senses or of the appetites, for both are animal; but the intelligent motion claims superiority and does not permit itself to be overpowered by the others. And with good reason, for it is formed by nature to use all of them. The third thing in the rational constitution is freedom from error and from deception. Let then the ruling principle holding fast to these things go straight on, and it has what is its own.

Consider thyself to be dead, and to have completed thy life up to the present time; and live according to nature the remainder which is allowed thee.

Love that only which happens to thee and is spun with the thread of thy destiny. For what is more suitable?

In everything which happens keep before thy eyes those to whom the same things happened, and how they were vexed, and treated them as strange things, and found fault with them: and now where are they? Nowhere. Why then dost thou too choose to act in the same way? and why dost thou not leave these agitations which are foreign to nature, to those who cause them and those who are moved by them? and why art thou not altogether intent upon the right way of making use of the things which happen to thee? for then thou wilt use them well, and they will be a material for thee [to work on]. Only attend to thyself, and resolve to be a good man in every act which thou doest: and remember . . . . .[12]

Look within. Within is the fountain of good, and it will ever bubble up, if thou wilt ever dig.

The body ought to be compact, and to show no irregularity either in motion or attitude. For what the mind shows in the face by maintaining in it the expression of intelligence and propriety, that ought to be required also in the whole body. But all these things should be observed without affectation.

The art of life is more like the wrestler's art than the dancer's, in respect of this, that it should stand ready and firm to meet onsets which are sudden and unexpected.

Constantly observe who those are whose approbation thou wishest to have, and what ruling principles they possess. For then thou wilt neither blame those who offend involuntarily, nor wilt thou want their approbation, if thou lookest to the sources of their opinions and appetites.

Every soul, the philosopher says, is involuntarily deprived of truth; consequently in the same way it is deprived of justice and temperance and benevolence and everything of the kind. It is most necessary to bear this constantly in mind, for thus thou wilt be more gentle towards all.

In every pain let this thought be present, that there is no dishonour in it, nor does it make the governing intelligence worse, for it does not damage the intelligence either so far as the intelligence is rational or so far as it is social. Indeed in the case of most pains let this remark of Epicurus aid thee, that pain is neither intolerable nor everlasting, if thou bearest in mind that it has its limits, and if thou addest nothing to it in imagination: and remember this too, that we do not perceive that many things which are disagreeable to us are the same as pain, such as excessive drowsiness, and the being scorched by heat, and the having no appetite. When then thou art discontented about any of these things, say to thyself, that thou art yielding to pain.

Take care not to feel towards the inhuman, as they feel towards men.

How do we know that Telauges was not superior in character to Socrates? for it is not enough that Socrates died a more noble death, and disputed more skilfully with the sophists, and passed the night in the cold with more endurance, and that when he was bid to arrest Leon of Salamis, he considered it more noble to refuse, and that he walked in a swaggering way in the streets—though as to this fact óne may have great doubts if it was true.   But we ought to inquire, what kind of a soul it was that Socrates possessed, and if he was able to be content with being just towards men and pious towards the gods; neither idly vexed on account of men's villany, nor yet making himself a slave to any man's ignorance, nor receiving as strange anything that fell to his share out of the universal, nor enduring it as intolerable, nor allowing his understanding to sympathize with the affects of the miserable flesh.

Nature has not so mingled* [the intelligence] with the composition of the body, as not to have allowed thee the power of circumscribing thyself and of bringing under subjection to thyself all that is thy own; for it is very possible to be a divine man and to be recognized as such by no one. Always bear this in mind; and another thing too, that very little indeed is necessary for living a happy life.   And because thou hast despaired of becoming a dialectician and skilled in the knowledge of nature, do not for this reason renounce the hope of being both free and modest and social and obedient to God.

It is in thy power to live free from all compulsion in the greatest tranquillity of mind, even if all the world cry out against thee as much as they choose, and even if wild beasts tear in pieces the members of this kneaded matter which has grown around thee.   For what hinders the mind in the midst of all this from maintaining itself in tranquillity, and in a just judgment of all surrounding things, and in a ready use of the objects which are presented to it, so that the judgment may say to the thing which falls under its observation · This thou art in substance [reality], though in men's opinion thou mayest appear to be of a different kind; and the use shall say to that which falls under the hand: Thou art the thing that I was seeking; for to me that which presents itself is always a material for virtue both rational and political, and in a word, for the exercise of art, which belongs to man or God. For everything which happens has a relationship either to God or to man, and is neither new nor difficult to handle, but usual and apt matter to work on.

The perfection of moral character consists in passing every day as the last, and in being neither violently excited nor torpid nor playing the hypocrite.

The gods, who are immortal, are not vexed because during so long a time they must tolerate continually men such as they are and so many of them bad; and besides this, they also take care of them in all ways. But thou, who art destined to end so soon, art thou wearied of enduring the bad, and this too when thou art one of them?

It is a ridiculous thing for a man not to fly from his own badness, which is indeed possible, but to fly from other men's badness, which is impossible.

Whatever the rational and political [social] faculty finds to be neither intelligent nor social, it properly judges to be inferior to itself.

When thou hast done a good act and another has received it, why dost thou still look for a third thing besides these, as fools do, either to have the reputation of having done a good act or to obtain a return?

No man is tired of receiving what is useful. But it is useful to act according to nature. Do not then be tired of receiving what is useful by doing it to others.

The nature of the All moved to make the universe. But now either everything that takes place comes by way of consequence or [continuity]; or even the chief things towards which the ruling power of the universe directs its own movement are governed by no rational principle. If this is remembered it will make thee more tranquil in many things.[18]

NOTES

[1] This is corrupt
[2] The end of this section is unintelligible.
[3] Plato, Pol vi, 486.
[4] From the Bellerophon of Euripides.

⁵ From the Hypsipyle of Euripides. Cicero (Tuscul. III, 25.) has translated six lines from Euripides, and among them are these two lines,—

"Reddenda terræ est terra : tum vita omnibus
Metenda ut fruges   Sic jubet necessitas."

⁶ See Aristophanes, Acharnenses, v. 661
⁷ From the Apologia, c 16.
⁸ Plato, Gorgias, c. 68 (512). In this passage the text of Antoninus has ἰατέον which is perhaps right, but there is a difficulty in the words μὴ γὰρ τοῦτο μέν, το ζῆν ὁποσονδὴ χρόνον τόνγε ὡς ἀληθῶς ἄνδρα ἰατέον ἐστί, καὶ οὐ, etc.
⁹ It is said that this is not in the extant writings of Plato
¹⁰ From the Chrysippus of Euripides.
¹¹ The first two lines are from the Supplices of Euripides, v. 1110.
¹² This section is obscure, and the conclusion is so corrupt that it is impossible to give any probable meaning to it. It is better to leave it as it is than to patch it up, as some critics and translators have done.
¹³ It is not easy to understand this section. It has been suggested that there is some error in ἢ ἀλόγιστα, etc Some of the translators have made nothing of the passage, and they have somewhat perverted the words. The first proposition is, that the universe was made by some sufficient power A beginning of the universe is assumed, and a power which framed an order The next question is, How are things produced now; or, in other words, by what power do forms appear in continuous succession? The answer, according to Antoninus, may be this: It is by virtue of the original constitution of things that all change and succession have been effected and are effected And this is intelligible in a sense, if we admit that the universe is always one and the same, a continuity of identity; as much one and the same as man is one and the same, which he believes himself to be, though he also believes and can not help believing that both in his body and in his thoughts there is change and succession There is no real discontinuity then in the universe; and if we say that there was an order framed in the beginning and that the things which are now produced are a consequence of a previous arrangement, we speak of things as we are compelled to view them, as forming a series or succession; just as we speak of the changes in our own bodies and the sequence of our own thoughts. But as there are no intervals, not even intervals infinitely small, between any two supposed states of any one thing, so there are no intervals, not even infinitely small, between what we call one thing and any other thing which we speak of as immediately preceding or following it What we call time is an idea derived from our notion of a succession of things or events, an idea which is a part of our constitution, but not an idea which we can suppose to belong to an infinite intelligence and power. The conclusion then is certain that the present and the past, the production of present things and the supposed original order, out of which we say that present things now come, are one: and the present productive power and the so-called past arrangement are only different names for one thing. I suppose then that Antoninus wrote here as people sometimes talk now, and that his real meaning is not exactly expressed by his words There are certainly other passages from which, I think, that we may collect that he had notions of production something like what I have expressed
We now come to the alternative: "or even the chief things . . . . .

principle." I do not exactly know what he means by τὰ κυριώτατα "the chief," or, "the most excellent," or whatever it is. But as he speaks elsewhere of inferior and superior things, and of the inferior being for the use of the superior, and of rational beings being the highest, he may here mean rational beings. He also in this alternative assumes a governing power of the universe, and that it acts by directing its power towards these chief objects, or making its special, proper, motion towards them. And here he uses the noun (ὁρμή) "movement," which contains the same motion as the verb (ὥρμησε) "moved," which he used at the beginning of the paragraph when he was speaking of the making of the universe. If we do not accept the first hypothesis, he says, we must take the conclusion of the second, that the "chief thing towards which the ruling power of the universe directs its own movement are governed by no rational principle." The meaning then is, if there is a meaning in it, that though there is a governing power, which strives to give effect to its efforts, we must conclude that there is no rational direction of anything, if the power which first made the universe does not in some way govern it still. Besides, if we assume that anything is now produced or now exists without the action of the supreme intelligence, and yet that this intelligence makes an effort to act, we obtain a conclusion which can not be reconciled with the nature of a supreme power, whose existence Antoninus always assumes. The tranquillity that a man may gain from these reflections must result from his rejecting the second hypothesis, and accepting the first; whatever may be the exact sense in which the emperor understood the first. Or, as he says elsewhere, if there is no providence which governs the world, man has at least the power of governing himself according to the constitution of his nature, and so he may be tranquil, if he does the best that he can.

If there is no error in the passage, it is worth the labour to discover the writer's exact meaning, for I think that he had a meaning, though people may not agree what it was. If I have rightly explained the emperor's meaning in this and other passages, he has touched the solution of a great question.

BOOK VIII

THIS reflection also tends to the removal of the desire of empty fame, that it is no longer in thy power to have lived the whole of thy life, or at least thy life from thy youth upwards, like the philosopher; but both to many others and to thyself it is plain that thou art far from philosophy. Thou hast fallen into disorder then, so that it is no longer easy for thee to get the reputation of a philosopher; and thy plan of life also opposes it. If then thou hast truly seen where the matter lies, throw away the thought, How thou shalt seem to others, and be content if thou shalt live the rest of thy life in such wise as thy nature wills. Observe then what it wills, and let nothing else distract thee; for thou hast had experience of many wanderings without having found happiness anywhere; not in syllogisms nor in wealth, nor in reputation, nor in enjoyment, nor anywhere. Where is it then? In doing what man's nature requires. How then shall a man do this? If he has principles from which come his affects and his acts. What principles? Those which relate to good and bad: the belief that there is nothing good for man, which does not make him just, temperate, manly, free; and that there is nothing bad, which does not do the contrary to what has been mentioned.

On the occasion of every act ask thyself, How is this with respect to me? Shall I repent of it? A little time and I am dead, and all is gone. What more do I seek, if what I am now doing is the work of an intelligent living being, and a social being, and one who is under the same law with God?

Alexander and Caius[1] and Pompeius, what are they in comparison with Diogenes and Heraclitus and Socrates? For they were acquainted with things, and their causes [forms], and their matter, and the ruling principles of these men were conformable to their pursuits. But as to the

others, how many things had they to care for, and to how
many things were they slaves.

Consider that men will do the same things nevertheless,
even though thou shouldst burst.

This is the chief thing: Be not perturbed, for all things are
according to the nature of the universal; and in a little time
thou wilt be nobody and nowhere, like Hadrianus and
Augustus. In the next place having fixed thy eyes steadily
on thy business look at it, and at the same time remembering
that it is thy duty to be a good man, and what man's nature
demands, do that without turning aside; and speak as it
seems to thee most just, only let it be with a good disposition
and with modesty and without hypocrisy.

The nature of the universal has this work to do, to remove
to that place the things which are in this, to change them,
to take them away hence, and to carry them there. All
things are change, yet we need not fear anything new. All
things are familiar to us; but the distribution of them still
remains the same.

Every nature is contented with itself when it goes on its
way well; and a rational nature goes on its way well, when
in its thoughts it assents to nothing false or uncertain, and
when it directs its movements to social acts only, and
when it confines its desires and aversions to the things which
are in its power, and when it is satisfied with everything that
is assigned to it by the common nature. For of this common
nature every particular nature is a part, as the nature of the
leaf is a part of the nature of the plant; except that in the
plant the nature of the leaf is part of a nature which has not
perception or reason, and is subject to be impeded; but the
nature of man is part of a nature which is not subject to
impediments, and is intelligent and just, since it gives to
everything in equal portions and according to its worth,
times, substance, cause [form], activity and incident. But
examine, not to discover that any one thing compared with
any other single thing is equal in all respects, but by taking
all the parts together of one thing and comparing them with
all the parts together of another.

Thou hast not leisure [or ability] to read. But thou hast
leisure [or ability] to check arrogance: thou hast leisure to

be superior to pleasure and pain: thou hast leisure to be superior to love of fame, and not to be vexed at stupid and ungrateful people; nay even to care for them.

Let no man any longer hear thee finding fault with the court life or with thy own.

Repentance is a kind of self-reproof for having neglected something useful; but that which is good must be something useful, and the perfect good man should look after it. But no such man would ever repent of having refused any sensual pleasure. Pleasure then is neither good nor useful.

This thing, what is it in itself, in its own constitution? What is its substance and material? And what its causal nature [or form]? And what is it doing in the world? And how long does it subsist?

When thou risest from sleep with reluctance, remember that it is according to thy constitution and according to human nature to perform social acts, but sleeping is common also to irrational animals. But that which is according to each individual's nature is also more peculiarly its own, and more suitable to its nature, and indeed also more agreeable.

Constantly and, if it be possible, on the occasion of every impression on the soul, apply to it the principles of Physics, of Ethics, and of Dialectics.

Whatever man thou meetest with, immediately say to thyself: What opinions has this man about good and bad? For if with respect to pleasure and pain and the causes of each, and with respect to fame and ignominy, death and life he has such and such opinions, it will seem nothing wonderful or strange to me, if he does such and such things; and I shall bear in mind that he is compelled to do so.

Remember that as it is a shame to be surprised if the figtree produces figs, so it is to be surprised if the world produces such and such things of which it is productive; and for the physician and the helmsman it is a shame to be surprised, if a man has a fever, or if the wind is unfavourable.

Remember that to change thy opinion and to follow him who corrects thy error is as consistent with freedom as it is to persist in thy error. For it is thy own, the activity which is exerted according to thy own movement and judgment, and indeed according to thy own understanding too.

If a thing is in thy own power, why dost thou do it? but if it is in the power of another, whom dost thou blame? the atoms [chance] or the gods? Both are foolish. Thou must blame nobody. For if thou canst, correct that which is the cause; but if thou canst not do this, correct at least the thing itself; but if thou canst not do even this, of what use is it to thee to find fault? for nothing should be done without a purpose.

That which has died falls not out of the universe. If it stays here, it also changes here, and is dissolved into its proper parts, which are elements of the universe and of thyself. And these too change, and they murmur not.

Everything exists for some end, a horse, a vine. Why dost thou wonder? Even the sun will say, I am for some purpose, and the rest of the gods will say the same. For what purpose then art thou? to enjoy pleasure? See if common sense allows this.

Nature has had regard in everything no less to the end than to the beginning and the continuance, just like the man who throws up a ball What good is it then for the ball to be thrown up, or harm for it to come down, or even to have fallen? and what good is it to the bubble while it holds together, or what harm when it is burst? The same may be said of a light also.

Turn it [the body] inside out, and see what kind of thing it is; and when it has grown old, what kind of thing it becomes; and when it is diseased

Short lived are both the praiser and the praised, and the rememberer and the remembered: and all this in a nook of this part of the world; and not even here do all agree, no, not any one with himself; and the whole earth too is a point.

Attend to the matter which is before thee, whether it is an opinion or an act or a word.

Thou sufferest this justly for thou choosest rather to become good to-morrow than to be good to-day.

Am I doing anything? I do it with reference to the good of mankind. Does anything happen to me? I receive it and refer it to the gods, and the source of all things, from which all that happens is derived

Such as bathing appears to thee—oil, sweat, dirt, filthy water, all things disgusting—so is every part of life and everything.

Lucilla saw Verus die, and then Lucilla died. Secunda saw Maximus die, and then Secunda died. Epitynchanus saw Diotimus die, and then Epitynchanus died. Antoninus saw Faustina die, and then Antoninus died. Such is everything. Celer saw Hadrianus die, and then Celer died. And those sharp-witted men, either seers or men inflated with pride, where are they? for instance the sharpwitted men, Charax and Demetrius the Platonist and Eudæmon, and any one else like them. All ephemeral, dead long ago. Some indeed have not been remembered even for a short time, and others have become the heroes of fables, and again others have disappeared even from fables. Remember this then, that this little compound, thyself, must either be dissolved, or thy poor breath must be extinguished, or be removed and placed elsewhere.

It is a satisfaction to a man to do the proper works of a man. Now it is a proper work of a man to be benevolent to his own kind, to despise the movements of the senses, to form a just judgment of plausible appearances, and to take a survey of the nature of the universe and of the things which happen in it.

There are three relations [between thee and other things] : the one to the body which surrounds thee; the second to the divine cause from which all things come to all; and the third to those who live with thee.

Pain is either an evil to the body—then let the body say what it thinks of it—or to the soul; but it is in the power of the soul to maintain its own serenity and tranquillity, and not to think that pain is an evil. For every judgment and movement and desire and aversion is within, and no evil ascends so high.

Wipe out thy imaginations by often saying to thyself: now it is in my power to let no badness be in this soul, nor desire nor any perturbation at all; but looking at all things I see what is their nature, and I use each according to its value —Remember this power which thou hast from nature.

Speak both in the senate and to every man, whoever he

may be appropriately, not with any affectation: use plain discourse.

Augustus' court, wife, daughter, descendants, ancestors, sister, Agrippa, kinsmen, intimates, friends, Areius,[2] Mæcenas, physicians and sacrificing priests—the whole court is dead Then turn to the rest, not considering the death of a single man, but of a whole race, as of the Pompeii; and that which is inscribed on the tombs—The last of his race. Then consider what trouble those before them have had that they might leave a successor; and then, that of necessity some one must be the last. Again here consider the death of a whole race.

It is thy duty to order thy life well in every single act; and if every act does its duty, as far as is possible, be content; and no one is able to hinder thee so that each act shall not do its duty.

But something external will stand in the way—Nothing will stand in the way of thy acting justly and soberly and considerately—But perhaps some other active power will be hindered—Well, but by acquiescing in the hindrance and by being content to transfer thy efforts to that which is allowed, another opportunity of action is immediately put before thee in place of that which was hindered, and one which will adapt itself to this ordering of which we are speaking.

Receive [wealth or prosperity] without arrogance; and be ready to let it go.

If thou didst ever see a hand cut off, or a foot, or a head, lying anywhere apart from the rest of the body, such does a man make himself, as far as he can, who is not content with what happens, and separates himself from others, or does anything unsocial. Suppose that thou hast detached thyself from the natural unity—for thou wast made by nature a part, but now thou hast cut thyself off—yet here there is this beautiful provision, that it is in thy power again to unite thyself. God has allowed this to no other part, after it has been separated and cut asunder, to come together again. But consider the kindness by which he has distinguished man, for he has put it in his power not to be separated at all from the universal; and when he has been separated, he has allowed him to return and to be united and to resume his place as a part.

As the nature of the universal has given to every rational being all the other powers that it has,* so we have received from it this power also. For as the universal nature converts and fixes in its predestined place everything which stands in the way and opposes it, and makes such things a part of itself, so also the rational animal is able to make every hindrance its own material, and to use it for such purposes as it may have designed.

Do not disturb thyself by thinking of the whole of thy life. Let not thy thoughts at once embrace all the various troubles which thou mayest expect to befall thee: but on every occasion ask thyself, What is there in this which is intolerable and past bearing? for thou wilt be ashamed to confess. In the next place remember that neither the future nor the past pains thee, but only the present. But this is reduced to a very little, if thou only circumscribest it, and chidest thy mind, if it is unable to hold out against even this.

Does Panthea or Pergamus now sit by the tomb of Verus?[3] Does Chaurias or Diotimus sit by the tomb of Hadrianus? That would be ridiculous. Well, suppose they did sit there, would the dead be conscious of it? and if the dead were conscious, would they be pleased? and if they were pleased, would that make them immortal? Was it not in the order of destiny that these persons too should first become old women and old men and then die? What then would those do after these were dead? All this is foul smell and blood in a bag.

If thou canst see sharply, look and judge wisely,* says the philosopher.

In the constitution of the rational animal I see no virtue which is opposed to justice; but I see a virtue which is opposed to love of pleasure, and that is temperance.

If thou takest away thy opinion about that which appears to give thee pain, thou thyself standest in perfect security—Who is this self?—The reason—But I am not reason—Be it so. Let then the reason itself not trouble itself. But if any other part of thee suffers let it have its own opinion about itself.

HADRIAN'S TOMB. NOW THE CASTLE OF S. ANGELO ROME

Hindrance to the perceptions of sense is an evil to the animal nature. Hindrance to the movements [desires] is equally an evil to the animal nature. And something else also is equally an impediment and an evil to the constitution of plants. So then that which is a hindrance to the intelligence is an evil to the intelligent nature. Apply all these things then to thyself. Does pain or sensuous pleasure affect thee? The senses will look to that.—Has any obstacle opposed thee in thy efforts towards an object? if indeed thou wast making this effort absolutely [unconditionally, or without any reservation], certainly this obstacle is an evil to thee considered as a rational animal. But if thou takest into consideration the usual course of things, thou hast not yet been injured nor even impeded. The things however which are proper to the understanding no other man is used to impede, for neither fire, nor iron, nor tyrant, nor abuse, touches it in any way. When it has been made a sphere, it continues a sphere.

It is not fit that I should give myself pain, for I have never intentionally given pain even to another.

Different things delight different people. But it is my delight to keep the ruling faculty sound without turning away either from any man or from any of the things which happen to men, but looking at and receiving all with welcome eyes and using everything according to its value.

See that thou secure this present time to thyself: for those who rather pursue posthumous fame do not consider that the men of after time will be exactly such as these whom they can not bear now; and both are mortal. And what is it in any way to thee if these men of after time utter this or that sound, or have this or that opinion about thee?

Take me and cast me where thou wilt; for there I shall keep my divine part tranquil, that is, content, if it can feel and act conformably to its proper constitution. Is this change of place sufficient reason why my soul should be unhappy and worse than it was, depressed, expanded, shrinking, affrighted? and what wilt thou find which is sufficient reason for this?

Nothing can happen to any man which is not a human accident, nor to an ox which is not according to the nature of an ox, nor to a vine which is not according to the nature of a vine, nor to a stone which is not proper to a stone. If then there happens to each thing both what is usual and natural, why shouldst thou complain? For the common nature brings nothing which may not be borne by thee.

If thou art pained by any external thing, it is not this thing that disturbs thee, but thy own judgment about it: And it is in thy power to wipe out this judgment now. But if anything in thy own disposition gives thee pain, who hinders thee from correcting thy opinion? And even if thou art pained because thou art not doing some particular thing which seems to thee to be right, why dost thou not rather act than complain?—But some insuperable obstacle is in the way?—Do not be grieved then, for the cause of its not being done depends not on thee—But it is not worth while to live, if this can not be done—Take thy departure then from life contentedly, just as he dies who is in full activity, and well pleased too with the things which are obstacles.

Remember that the ruling faculty is invincible, when self-collected it is satisfied with itself, if it does nothing which it does not choose to do, even if it resist from mere obstinacy What then will it be when it forms a judgment about anything aided by reason and deliberately? Therefore the mind which is free from passions is a citadel, for man has nothing more secure to which he can fly for refuge and for the future be inexpugnable. He then who has not seen this is an ignorant man; but he who has seen it and does not fly to this refuge is unhappy.

Say nothing more to thyself than what the first appearances report. Suppose that it has been reported to thee that a certain person speaks ill of thee. This has been reported; but that thou hast been injured, that has not been reported. I see that my child is sick. I do see; but that he is in danger, I do not see. Thus then always abide by the first appearances, and add nothing thyself from within, and then nothing happens to thee. Or rather add something, like a man who knows everything that happens in the world.

A cucumber is bitter.—Throw it away.—There are briars in the road —Turn aside from them.—This is enough. Do not add, And why were such things made in the world? For thou wilt be ridiculed by a man who is acquainted with nature, as thou wouldst be ridiculed by a carpenter and shoemaker if thou didst find fault because thou seest in their workshop shavings and cuttings from the things which they make   And yet they have places into which they can throw these shavings and cuttings, and the universal nature has no external space; but the wondrous part of her art is that though she has circumscribed herself, everything within her which appears to decay and to grow old and to be useless she changes into herself, and again makes other new things from these very same, so that she requires neither substance from without nor wants a place into which she may cast that which decays.   She is content then with her own space, and her own matter and her own art.

Neither in thy actions be sluggish, nor in thy conversation without method, nor wandering in thy thoughts, nor let there be in thy soul inward contention nor external effusion, nor in life be so busy as to have no leisure.

Suppose that men kill thee, cut thee in pieces, curse thee. What then can those things do to prevent thy mind from remaining pure, wise, sober, just? For instance, if a man should stand by a limpid, pure spring, and curse it, the spring never ceases sending up potable water; and if he should cast clay into it or filth, it will speedily disperse them and wash them out, and will not be at all polluted. How then shalt thou possess a perpetual fountain [and not a mere well]? By forming* thyself hourly, to freedom, conjoined with contentment, simplicity, and modesty.

He who does not know what the world is, does not know where he is.   And he who does not know for what purpose the world exists, does not know who he is, nor what the world is.   And he who has failed in any one of these things could not even say for what purpose he exists himself. What then dost thou think of him who seeks the praise of those who applaud, of men who know not either where they are or who they are?

Dost thou wish to be praised by a man who curses himself thrice every hour? wouldst thou wish to please a man who does not please himself? Does a man please himself who repents of nearly everything that he does?

No longer let thy breathing only act in concert with the air which surrounds thee, but let thy intelligence also now be in harmony with the intelligence which embraces all things. For the intelligent power is no less diffused in all parts and pervades all things for him who is willing to draw it to him than the aërial power for him who is able to respire it.

Generally, wickedness does no harm at all to the universe; and particularly, the wickedness of one man does no harm to another. It is only harmful to him who has it in his power to be released from it, as soon as he shall choose.

To my own free will the free will of my neighbour is just as indifferent as his poor breath and flesh. For though we are made especially for the sake of one another, still the ruling power of each of us has its own office for otherwise my neighbour's wickedness would be my harm, which God has not willed in order that my unhappiness may not depend on another.

The sun appears to be poured down, and in all directions indeed it is diffused, yet it is not effused. For this diffusion is extension: Accordingly its rays are called Extensions [ἀκτῖνες] because they are extended [ἀπὸ τοῦ ἐκτείνεσθαι].[4] But one may judge what kind of a thing a ray is, if he looks at the sun's light passing through a narrow opening into a darkened room, for it is extended in a right line, and as it were is divided when it meets with any solid body which stands in the way and intercepts the air beyond; but there the light remains fixed and does not glide or fall off. Such then ought to be the out-pouring and diffusion of the understanding, and it should in no way be an effusion, but an extension, and it should make no violent or impetuous collision with the obstacles which are in its way; nor yet fall down, but be fixed and enlighten that which receives it. For a body will deprive itself of the illumination, if it does not admit it.

He who fears death either fears the loss of sensation or a different kind of sensation. But if thou shalt have no sensation, neither wilt thou feel any harm; and if thou shalt acquire another kind of sensation, thou wilt be a different kind of living being and thou wilt not cease to live.

Men exist for the sake of one another. Teach them then or bear with them.

In one way an arrow moves, in another way the mind. The mind indeed both when it exercises caution and when it is employed about inquiry, moves straight onward not the less, and to its object.

Enter into every man's ruling faculty; and also let every other man enter into thine.

NOTES

[1] Caius is Caius Julius Cæsar, the dictator; and Pompeius is Cneius Pompeius, named Magnus.

[2] Areius was a philosopher, who was intimate with Augustus.

[3] " Verus " is a conjecture of Saumaise, and perhaps the true reading.

[4] A piece of bad etymology.

BOOK IX

H E who acts unjustly acts impiously. For since the universal nature has made rational animals for the sake of one another to help one another according to their deserts, but in no way to injure one another, he who transgresses her will, is clearly guilty of impiety towards the highest divinity. And he too who lies is guilty of impiety to the same divinity; for the universal nature is the nature of things that are; and things that are have a relation to all things that come into existence.[1] And further, this universal nature is named truth, and is the prime cause of all things that are true. He then who lies intentionally is guilty of impiety inasmuch as he acts unjustly by deceiving; and he also who lies unintentionally, inasmuch as he is at variance with the universal nature, and inasmuch as he disturbs the order by fighting against the nature of the world; for he fights against it, who is moved of himself to that which is contrary to truth, for he had received powers from nature through the neglect of which he is not able now to distinguish falsehood from truth. And indeed he who pursues pleasure as good, and avoids pain as evil is guilty of impiety. For of necessity such a man must often find fault with the universal nature, alleging that it assigns things to the bad and the good contrary to their deserts, because frequently the bad are in the enjoyment of pleasure and possess the things which procure pleasure, but the good have pain for their share and the things which cause pain. And further, he who is afraid of pain will sometimes also be afraid of some of the things which will happen in the world, and even this is impiety. And he who pursues pleasure will not abstain from injustice, and this is plainly impiety. Now with respect to the things towards which the universal nature is equally affected—for it would not have made both, unless it was equally affected towards both—towards these they who wish to follow nature should be of the same mind with it, and equally affected. With respect to pain, then, and pleasure, or death and life, or honour and dishonour, which the universal nature employs equally, whoever is not equally affected is manifestly acting impiously. And I say that the universal nature employs them equally, instead of saying that they happen alike to those who are produced in continuous series and to those who come after them by virtue of a certain original movement of Providence, according to which it moved from a certain beginning to this ordering of things, having conceived certain principles of the things which were to be, and having determined powers productive of beings and of changes and of such like successions.

It would be a man's happiest lot to depart from mankind without having had any taste of lying and hypocrisy and luxury and pride. However to breathe out one's life when a man has had enough of these things is the next best voyage, as the saying is. Hast thou determined to abide with vice, and has not experience yet induced thee to fly from this pestilence? For the destruction of the understanding is a pestilence, much more indeed than any such corruption and change of this atmosphere which surrounds us. For this corruption is a pestilence of animals so far as they are animals, but the other is a pestilence of men so far as they are men.

Do not despise death, but be well content with it, since this too is one of those things which nature wills. For such as it is to be young and to grow old, and to increase and to reach maturity, and to have teeth and beard and gray hairs, and to beget, and to be pregnant and to bring forth, and all the other natural operations which the seasons of thy life bring, such also is dissolution. This, then, is consistent with the character of a reflecting man, to be neither careless nor impatient nor contemptuous with respect to death, but to wait for it as one of the operations of nature. As thou now waitest for the time when the child shall come out of thy wife's womb, so be ready for the time when thy soul shall fall out of this envelope. But if thou requirest also a vulgar kind of comfort which shall reach thy heart, thou wilt be made best reconciled to death by observing the objects from which thou art going to be removed, and the morals of those with whom thy soul will no longer be mingled. For it is no way right to be offended with men, but it is thy duty to care for them and to bear with them gently; and yet to remember that thy departure will be not from men who have the same principles as thyself. For this is the only thing, if there be any, which could draw us the contrary way and attach us to life, to be permitted to live with those who have the same principles as ourselves. But now thou seest how great is the trouble arising from the discordance of those who live together, so that thou mayst say, Come quick, O death, lest perchance I, too, should forget myself.

He who does wrong does wrong against himself. He who acts unjustly acts unjustly to himself, because he makes himself bad.

He often acts unjustly who does not do a certain thing; not only he who does a certain thing.

Thy present opinion founded on understanding, and thy present conduct directed to social good, and thy present disposition of contentment with everything which happens*— that is enough.

Wipe out imagination: check desire: extinguish appetite: keep the ruling faculty in its own power.

Among the animals which have not reason one life is distributed; but among reasonable animals one intelligent soul is distributed: just as there is one earth of all things which are of an earthy nature, and we see by one light, and breathe one air, all of us that have the faculty of vision and all that have life.

All things which participate in anything which is common to them all move towards that which is of the same kind with themselves Everything which is earthly turns towards the earth, everything which is liquid flows together and everything which is of an aerial kind does the same, so that they require something to keep them asunder, and the application of force. Fire indeed moves upwards on account of the elemental fire, but it is so ready to be kindled together with all the fire which is here, that even every substance which is somewhat dry, is easily ignited because there is less mingled with it of that which is a hindrance to ignition. Accordingly then everything also which participates in the common intelligent nature moves in like manner towards that which is of the same kind with itself, or moves even more. For so much as it is superior in comparison with all other things, in the same degree also is it more ready to mingle with and to be fused with that which is akin to it. Accordingly among animals devoid of reason we find swarms of bees, and herds of cattle, and the nurture of young birds, and in a manner, loves; for even in animals there are souls, and that power which brings them together is seen to exert itself in the superior degree, and in such a way as never has been observed in plants nor in stones nor in trees. But in rational animals there are political communities and friendships, and families and meetings of people; and in wars, treaties and armistices. But in the things which are still superior, even though they are separated from one another, unity in a manner exists, as in the stars. Thus the ascent to the higher degree is able to produce a sympathy even in things which are separated. See, then, what now takes place For only intelligent animals have now forgotten this mutual desire and inclination, and in them alone the property of flowing together is not seen. But still though men strive to avoid [this union], they are caught and held by it, for their nature is too strong for them; and thou wilt see what I say if thou only observest. Sooner, then, will one find anything earthy which comes in contact with no earthy thing than a man altogether separated from other men.

Both man and God and the universe produce fruit; at the proper seasons each produce it. But if usage has especially fixed these terms to the vine and like things, this is nothing. Reason produces fruit both for all and for itself, and there are produced from it other things of the same kind as reason itself.

If thou art able, correct by teaching those who do wrong; but if thou canst not, remember that indulgence is given to thee for this purpose. And the gods, too, are indulgent to such persons; and for some purposes they even help them to

31

get health, wealth, reputation; so kind they are. And it is in thy power also; or say, who hinders thee?

Labour not as one who is wretched, nor yet as one who would be pitied or admired: but direct thy will to one thing only, to put thyself in motion and to check thyself, as the social reason requires.

To-day I have got out of all trouble, or rather I have cast out all trouble, for it was not outside, but within and in my opinions

All things are the same, familiar in experience, and ephemeral in time, and worthless in the matter. Everything now is just as it was in the time of those whom we have buried.

Things stand outside of us, themselves by themselves, neither knowing aught of themselves, nor expressing any judgment. What is it, then, which does judge about them? The ruling faculty.

Not in passivity, but in activity lie the evil and the good of the rational social animal, just as his virtue and his vice lie not in passivity, but in activity.

For the stone which has been thrown up it is no evil to come down, nor indeed any good to have been carried up.

Penetrate inwards into men's leading principles, and thou wilt see what judges thou art afraid of, and what kind of judges they are of themselves.

All things are changing: and thou thyself art in continuous mutation and in a manner in continuous destruction, and the whole universe too.

It is thy duty to leave another man's wrongful act there where it is.

Termination of activity, cessation from movement and opinion, and in a sense their death, is no evil. Turn thy thoughts now to the consideration of thy life, thy life as a child, as a youth, thy manhood, thy old age, for in these also every change was a death. Is this anything to fear? Turn thy thoughts now to thy life under thy grandfather, then to thy life under thy mother, then to thy life under thy father; and as thou findest many other differences and changes and terminations, ask thyself, Is this anything to fear? In like manner, then, neither are the termination and cessation and change of thy whole life a thing to be afraid of.

Hasten [to examine] thy own ruling faculty and that of the universe and that of thy neighbour: thy own that thou mayst make it just: and that of the universe, that thou mayst remember of what thou art a part; and that of thy neighbour, that thou mayst know whether he has acted ignorantly or with knowledge, and that thou mayst also consider that his ruling faculty is akin to thine.

As thou thyself art a component part of a social system, so let every act of thine be a component part of a social life. Whatever act of thine then has no reference either immediately or remotely to a social end, this tears asunder thy life, and does not allow it to be one, and it is of the nature of a mutiny, just as when in a popular assembly a man acting by himself stands apart from the general agreement.

Quarrels of little children and their sports, and poor spirits carrying about dead bodies [such is everything]; and so what is exhibited in the representation of the mansions of the dead strikes our eyes more clearly.

Examine into the quality of the form of an object, and detach it altogether from its material part, and then contemplate it; then determine the time, the longest which a thing of this peculiar form is naturally made to endure.

Thou hast endured infinite troubles through not being contented with thy ruling faculty, when it does the things which it is constituted by nature to do. But enough* [of this].

When another blames thee or hates thee, or when men say about thee anything injurious, approach their poor souls, penetrate within, and see what kind of men they are. Thou wilt discover that there is no reason to take any trouble that these men may have this or that opinion about thee. However thou must be well disposed towards them, for by nature they are friends. And the gods too aid them in all ways, by dreams, by signs, towards the attainment of those things on which they set a value.*

The periodic movements of the universe are the same, up and down from age to age. And either the universal intelligence puts itself in motion for every separate effect, and if this is so, be thou content with that which is the result of its activity; or it puts itself in motion once, and everything else comes by way of sequence in a manner; or indivisible elements are the origin of all things.—In a word, if there is a god, all is well; and if chance rules, do not thou also be governed by it.

Soon will the earth cover us all: then the earth, too, will change, and the things also which result from change will continue to change for ever, and these again for ever. For if a man reflects on the changes and transformations which follow one another like wave after wave, and their rapidity, he will despise everything which is perishable.

The universal cause is like a winter torrent: it carries everything along with it. But how worthless are all these poor people who are engaged in matters political, and, as they suppose, are playing the philosopher! All drivellers. Well then, man: do what nature now requires. Set thyself in motion, if it is in thy power, and do not look about thee to see if any one will observe it; nor yet expect Plato's Republic: but be content if the smallest thing goes on well, and consider such an event to be no small matter. For who can change men's opinions? and without a change of opinions what else is there than the slavery of men who groan while they pretend to obey? Come now and tell me of Alexander and Philippus and Demetrius of Phalerum. They themselves shall judge whether they discovered what the common nature required, and trained themselves accordingly. But if they acted like tragedy heroes, no one has condemned me to imitate them. Simple and modest is the work of philosophy. Draw me not aside to insolence and pride.

Look down from above on the countless herds of men and their countless solemnities, and the infinitely varied voyagings in storms and calms, and the differences among those who are born, who live together, and die. And consider, too, the life lived by others in olden time, and the life of those who will live after thee, and the life now lived among barbarous nations, and how many know not even thy name, and how many will soon forget it, and how they who perhaps now are praising thee will very soon blame thee, and that neither a posthumous name is of any value, nor reputation, nor anything else.

Let there be freedom from perturbations with respect to the things which come from the external cause; and let there be justice in the things done by virtue of the internal cause, that is, let there be movement and action terminating in this, in social acts, for this is according to thy nature.

Thou canst remove out of the way many useless things among those which disturb thee, for they lie entirely in thy opinion; and thou wilt then gain for thyself ample space by comprehending the whole universe in thy mind, and by contemplating the eternity of time, and observing the rapid change of every several thing, how short is the time from birth to dissolution, and the illimitable time before birth as well as the equally boundless time after dissolution.

All that thou seest will quickly perish, and those who have been spectators of its dissolution will very soon perish too. And he who dies at the extremest old age will be brought into the same condition with him who died prematurely.

What are these men's leading principles, and about what kind of things are they busy, and for what kind of reasons do they love and honour? Imagine that thou seest their poor souls laid bare. When they think that they do harm by their blame or good by their praise, what an idea!

Loss is nothing else than change. But the universal nature delights in change, and in obedience to her all things are now done well, and from eternity have been done in like form, and will be such to time without end. What, then, dost thou say? That all things have been and all things always will be bad, and that no power has ever been found in so many gods to rectify these things, but the world has been condemned to be bound in never ceasing evil?

The rottenness of the matter which is the foundation of everything! water, dust, bones, filth: or again, marble rocks, the callosities of the earth; and gold and silver, the sediments; and garments, only bits of hair; and purple dye, blood; and everything else is of the same kind. And that which is of the nature of breath is also another thing of the same kind, changing from this to that.

Enough of this wretched life and murmuring and apish tricks. Why art thou disturbed? What is there new in this? What unsettles thee? Is it the form of the thing? Look at it. Or is it the matter? Look at it But besides these there is nothing Towards the gods, then, now become at last more simple and better. It is the same whether we examine these things for a hundred years or three.

If any man has done wrong, the harm is his own. But perhaps he has not done wrong.

Either all things proceed from one intelligent source and come together as in one body, and the part ought not to find fault with what is done for the benefit of the whole: or there are only atoms, and nothing else than mixture and dispersion. Why, then, art thou disturbed? Say to the ruling faculty, Art thou dead, art thou corrupted, art thou playing the hypocrite, art thou become a beast, dost thou herd and feed with the rest?[2]

Either the gods have no power or they have power. If, then, they have no power, why dost thou pray to them? But if they have power, why dost thou not pray for them to give thee the faculty of not fearing any of the things which thou fearest, or of not desiring any of the things which thou desirest, or not being pained at anything, rather than pray that any of these things should not happen or happen? for certainly if they can co-operate with men, they can co-operate for these purposes. But perhaps thou wilt say, the gods have placed them in thy power. Well, then. is it not better to use what is in thy power like a free man than to desire in a slavish and abject way what is not in thy power? And who has told thee that the gods do not aid us even in the things which are in our power? Begin, then, to pray for such things, and thou wilt see. One man prays thus: How shall I be able to lie with that woman? Do thou pray thus: How shall I desire to lie with her? Another prays thus: How shall I be released from this? Another prays: How shall I not desire to be released? Another thus: How shall I not lose my little son? Thou thus: How shall I not be afraid to lose him? In fine, turn thy prayers this way, and see what comes.

Epicurus says, In my sickness my conversation was not

about my bodily sufferings, nor, says he, did I talk on such subjects to those who visited me; but I continued to discourse on the nature of things as before, keeping to this main point, how the mind, while participating in such movements as go on in the poor flesh, shall be free from perturbations and maintain its proper good. Nor did I, he says, give the physicians an opportunity of putting on solemn looks, as if they were doing something great, but my life· went on well and happily. Do, then, the same that he did both in sickness, if thou art sick, and in any other circumstances; for never to desert philosophy in any events that may befall us, nor to hold trifling talk either with an ignorant man or with one unacquainted with nature, is a principle of all schools of philosophy; but to be intent only on that which thou art now doing and on the instrument by which thou doest it.

When thou art offended with any man's shameless conduct, immediately ask thyself, Is it possible, then, that shameless men should not be in the world? It is not possible. Do not, then, require what is impossible. For this man also is one of those shameless men who must of necessity be in the world Let the same considerations be present to thy mind in the case of the knave, and the faithless man, and of every man who does wrong in any way. For at the same time that thou dost remind thyself that it is impossible that such kind of men should not exist, thou wilt become more kindly disposed towards every one individually. It is useful to perceive this, too, immediately when the occasion arises, what virtue nature has given to man to oppose to every wrongful act. For she has given to man, as an antidote against the stupid man, mildness, and against another kind of man some other power. And in all cases it is possible for thee to correct by teaching the man who is gone astray: for every man who errs misses his object and is gone astray. Besides wherein hast thou been injured? For thou wilt find that no one among those against whom thou art irritated has done anything by which thy mind could be made worse. but that which is evil to thee and harmful has its foundation only in the mind And what harm is done or what is there strange, if the man who has not been instructed does the acts of an uninstructed man? Consider whether thou shouldst not rather blame thyself, because thou didst not expect such a man to err in such a way. For thou hadst means given thee by thy reason to suppose that it was likely that he would commit this error, and yet thou hast forgotten and art amazed that he has erred. But most of all when thou blamest a man as faithless or ungrateful, turn to thyself. For the fault is manifestly thy own, whether thou didst trust that a man who had such a disposition would keep his promise, or when conferring thy kindness thou didst not confer it absolutely, nor yet in such way as to have received from thy very act all the profit. For what more dost thou want when thou hast done a man a service? art thou not content that thou hast done something conformable to thy nature, and dost thou seek to be paid for it? just as if the eye demanded a recompense for seeing, or the feet for walking. For as these members are formed for a particular purpose, and by working according to their several constitutions obtain what is their own; so also as man is formed by nature to acts of benevolence, when he has done anything benevolent or in any other way conducive to the common interest, he has acted conformably to his constitution, and he gets what is his own.

NOTES

[1] " As there is not any action or natural event, which we are acquainted with, so single and unconnected as not to have a respect to some other actions and events, so, possibly each of them, when it has not an immediate, may yet have a remote, natural relation to other actions and events, much beyond the compass of this present world." Again: "Things seemingly the most in significant imaginable, are perpetually observed to be necessary conditions to other things of the greatest importance, so that any one thing whatever, may, for aught we know to the contrary, be a necessary condition to any other."—Butler's Analogy, Chap. 7 See all the chapter.
[2] There is some corruption at the end of this section: but I think that the translation expresses the emperor's meaning Whether intelligence rules all things or chance rules, a man must not be disturbed. He must use the power that he has, and be tranquil.

BOOK X

WILT thou, then, my soul, never be good and simple and one and naked, more manifest than the body which surrounds thee? Wilt thou never enjoy an affectionate and contented disposition? Wilt thou never be full and without a want of any kind, longing for nothing more, nor desiring anything, either animate or inanimate, for the enjoyment of pleasures? nor yet desiring time wherein thou shalt have longer enjoyment, or place, or pleasant climate, or society of men with whom thou mayst live in harmony? but wilt thou be satisfied with thy present condition, and pleased with all that is about thee, and wilt thou convince thyself that thou hast everything and that it comes from the gods, that everything is well for thee, and will be well whatever shall please them, and whatever they shall give for the conservation of the perfect living being,[1] the good and just and beautiful, which generates and holds together all things, and contains and embraces all things which are dissolved for the production of other like things? Wilt thou never be such that thou shalt so dwell in community with gods and men as neither to find fault with them at all, nor to be condemned by them?

Observe what thy nature requires, so far as thou art governed by nature only: then do it and accept it, if thy nature, so far as thou art a living being, shall not be made worse by it. And next thou must observe what thy nature requires so far as thou art a living being. And all this thou mayst allow thyself, if thy nature, so far as thou art a rational animal, shall not be made worse by it. But the rational animal is consequently also a political [social] animal. Use these rules, then, and trouble thyself about nothing else.

Everything which happens either happens in such wise as thou art formed by nature to bear it, or as thou art not formed by nature to bear it. If, then, it happens to thee in such way as thou art formed by nature to bear it, do not complain, but bear it as thou art formed by nature to bear it. But if it happens in such wise as thou art not formed by nature to bear it, do not complain, for it will perish after it has consumed thee. Remember, however, that thou art formed by nature to bear everything, with respect to which it depends on thy opinion to make it endurable and tolerable, by thinking that it is either thy interest or thy duty to do this.

If a man is mistaken, instruct him kindly and show him his error. But if thou art not able, blame thyself, or blame not even thyself.

Whatever may happen to thee, it was prepared for thee from all eternity; and the implication of causes was from eternity spinning the thread of thy being, and of that which is incident to it.

Whether the universe is [a concourse of] atoms, or nature [is a system], let this first be established, that I am a part of the whole which is governed by nature; next, I am in a manner intimately related to the parts which are of the same kind with myself. For remembering this, inasmuch as I am a part, I shall be discontented with none of the things which are assigned to me out of the whole; for nothing is injurious to the part, if it is for the advantage of the whole. For the whole contains nothing which is not for its advantage; and all natures indeed have this common principle, but the nature of the universe has this principle besides, that it can not be compelled even by an external cause to generate anything harmful to itself. By remembering, then, that I am a part of such a whole, I shall be content with everything that happens. And inasmuch as I am in a manner intimately related to the parts which are of the same kind with myself, I shall do nothing unsocial, but I shall rather direct myself to the things which are of the same kind with myself, and I shall turn all my efforts to the common interest, and divert them from the contrary. Now, if these things are done so, life must flow on happily, just as thou mayst observe that the life of a citizen is happy, who continues a course of action which is advantageous to his fellow-citizens, and is content with whatever the state may assign to him.

The parts of the whole, everything, I mean, which is naturally comprehended in the universe, must of necessity perish; but let this be understood in this sense, that they must undergo change. But if this is naturally both an evil and a necessity for the parts, the whole would not continue to exist in a good condition, the parts being subject to change and constituted so as to perish in various ways. For whether did nature herself design to do evil to the things which are parts of herself, and to make them subject to evil and of necessity fall into evil, or have such results happened without her knowing it? Both these suppositions, indeed, are incredible. But if a man should even drop the term Nature [as an efficient power], and should speak of these things as natural, even then it would be ridiculous to affirm at the same time that the parts of the whole are in their nature subject to change, and at the same time to be surprised or vexed as if something were happening contrary to nature, particularly as the dissolution of things is into those things of which each thing is composed. For there is either a dispersion of the elements out of which everything has been compounded, or a change from the solid to the earthy and from the airy to the aerial, so that these parts are taken back into the universal reason, whether this at certain periods is consumed by fire or renewed by eternal changes. And do not imagine that the solid and the airy part belong to thee from the time of generation. For all this received its accretion only yesterday and the day before, as one may say, from the food and the air which is inspired. This, then, which has received [the accretion], changes, not that which thy mother brought forth. But suppose that this [which thy mother brought forth] implicates thee very much with that other part, which has the peculiar quality [of change], this is nothing in fact in the way of objection to what is said.[2]

When thou hast assumed these names, good, modest, true, rational, a man of equanimity, and magnanimous, take care that thou dost not change these names; and if thou shouldst lose them, quickly return to them. And remember that the term Rational was intended to signify a discriminating attention to every several thing and freedom from negligence; and that Equanimity is the voluntary acceptance of the things which are assigned to thee by the common nature; and that Magnanimity is the elevation of the intelligent part above the pleasurable or painful sensations of the flesh, and above that poor thing called fame, and death, and all such things. If, then, thou maintainest thyself in the possession of these names, without desiring to be called by these names by others, thou wilt be another person and wilt enter on another life. For to continue to be such as thou hast hitherto been, and to be torn in pieces and defiled in such a life, is the character of a very stupid man and one overfond of his life, and like those half-devoured fighters with wild beasts, who though covered with wounds and gore, still entreat to be kept to the following day, though they will be exposed in the same state to the same claws and bites [3] Therefore fix thyself in the possession of these few names: and if thou art able to abide in them, abide as if thou wast removed to certain islands of the Happy.[4] But if thou shalt perceive that thou fallest out of them and dost not maintain thy hold, go courageously into some nook where thou shalt maintain them, or even depart at once from life, not in passion, but with simplicity and freedom and modesty, after doing this one [laudable] thing at least in thy life, to have gone out of it thus. In order, however, to the remembrance of these names, it will greatly help thee, if thou rememberest the gods, and that they wish not to be flattered, but wish all reasonable beings to be made like themselves; and if thou rememberest that what does the work of a fig-tree is a fig-tree, and that what does the work of a dog is a dog, and that what does the work of a bee is a bee, and that what does the work of a man is a man.

Mimi,[5] war, astonishment, torpor, slavery, will daily wipe out those holy principles of thine. *How many things without studying nature dost thou imagine, and how many dost thou neglect? But it is thy duty so to look on and so to do every thing, that at the same time the power of dealing with circumstances is perfected, and the contemplative faculty is exercised, and the confidence which comes from the knowledge of each several thing is maintained without showing it, but yet not concealed. For when wilt thou enjoy simplicity, when gravity, and when the knowledge of every

several thing, both what it is in substance, and what place
it has in the universe, and how long it is formed to exist and
of what things it is compounded, and to whom it can belong,
and who are able to give it and take it away?

A spider is proud when it has caught a fly, and another
when he has caught a poor hare, and another when he has
taken a little fish in a net, and another when he has taken
wild-boars, and another when he has taken bears, and another when he has taken Sarmatians. Are not these robbers, if thou examinest their opinions?[6]

Acquire the contemplative way of seeing how all things
change into one another, and constantly attend to it, and
exercise thyself about this part [of philosophy]. For nothing is so much adapted to produce magnanimity. Such a
man has put off the body, and he sees that he must, no one
knows how soon, go away from among men and leave everything here, he gives himself up entirely to just doing in all
his actions, and in everything else that happens he resigns
himself to the universal nature. But as to what any man
shall say or think about him or do against him, he never
even thinks of it, being himself contented with these two
things, with acting justly in what he now does, and being
satisfied with what is now assigned to him; and he lays aside
all distracting and busy pursuits, and desires nothing else
than to accomplish the straight course through the law,[7] and
by accomplishing the straight course to follow God.

What need is there of suspicious fear, since it is in thy
power to inquire what ought to be done? And if thou seest
clear, go by this way content, without turning back: but if
thou dost not see clear, stop and take the best advisers. But
if any other things oppose thee, go on according to thy powers with due consideration, keeping to that which appears
to be just. For it is best to reach this object, and if thou
dost fail, let thy failure be in attempting this. He who
follows reason in all things is both tranquil and active at the
same time, and also cheerful and collected.

Inquire of thyself as soon as thou wakest from sleep
whether it will make any difference to thee, if another does
what is just and right. It will make no difference.

Thou hast not forgotten, I suppose, that those who assume

arrogant airs in bestowing their praise or blame on others, are such as they are at bed and at board, and thou hast not forgotten what they do, and what they avoid and what they pursue, and how they steal and how they rob, not with hands and feet, but with their most valuable part, by means of which there is produced, when a man chooses, fidelity, modesty, truth, law, a good dæmon [happiness]?

To her who gives and takes back all, to Nature, the man who is instructed and modest says, Give what thou wilt; take back what thou wilt. And he says this not proudly, but obediently and well pleased with her.

Short is the little which remains to thee of life. Live as on a mountain. 'For it makes no difference whether a man lives there or here, if he lives everywhere in the world as in a state [political community]. Let men see, let them know a real man who lives according to nature. If they can not endure him, let them kill him. For that is better than to live thus [as men do].

No longer talk at all about the kind of man that a good man ought to be, but be such.

Constantly contemplate the whole of time and the whole of substance, and consider that all individual things as to substance are a grain of a fig, and as to time, the turning of a gimlet.

Look at every thing that exists, and observe that it is already in dissolution and in change, and as it were putrefaction or dispersion, or that everything is so constituted by nature as to die.

Consider what men are when they are eating, sleeping, generating, easing themselves and so forth. Then what kind of men they are when they are imperious* and arrogant, or angry and scolding from their elevated place. But a short time ago to how many they were slaves and for what things: and after a little time consider in what a condition they will be.

That is for the good of each thing, which the universal nature brings to each. And it is for its good at the time when nature brings it.

"The earth loves the shower;" and "the solemn æther loves;" and the universe loves to make whatever is about to be. I say then to the universe, that I love as thou lovest. And is not this too said, that "this or that loves [is wont] to be produced?"[8]

Either thou livest here and hast already accustomed thyself to it, or thou art going away, and this was thy own will; or thou art dying and hast discharged thy duty. But besides these things there is nothing. Be of good cheer, then.

Let this always be plain to thee, that this piece of land is like any other; and that all things here are the same with things on the top of a mountain, or on the sea-shore, or wherever thou choosest to be. For thou wilt find just what Plato says, Dwelling within the walls of a city as in a shepherd's fold on a mountain. [The three last words are omitted in the translation.][9]

What is my ruling faculty now to me? and of what nature am I now making it? and for what purpose am I now using it? is it void of understanding? is it loosed and rent asunder from social life? is it melted into and mixed with the poor flesh so as to move together with it?

He who flies from his master is a runaway; but the law is master, and he who breaks the law is a runaway. And he also who is grieved or angry or afraid,* is dissatisfied because something has been or is or shall be of the things which are appointed by him who rules all things, and he is Law, and assigns to every man what is fit. He then who fears or is grieved or is angry is a runaway.[10]

A man deposits seed in a womb and goes away, and then another cause takes it, and labours on it and makes a child. What a thing from such a material! Again, the child passes food down through the throat, and then another cause takes it and makes perception and motion, and in fine life and strength and other things; how many and how strange! Observe then the things which are produced in such a hidden way, and see the power just as we see the power which carries things downwards and upwards, not with the eyes, but still no less plainly.

Constantly consider how all things such as they now are, in time past also were, and consider that they will be the same again. And place before thy eyes entire dramas and stages of the same form, whatever thou hast learned from thy experience or from older history; for example, the whole court of Hadrianus, and the whole court of Antoninus, and the whole court of Philippus, Alexander, Crœsus; for all those were such dramas as we see now, only with different actors.

Imagine every man who is grieved at anything or discontented to be like a pig which is sacrificed and kicks and screams.

Like this pig also is he who on his bed in silence laments the bonds in which we are held.   And consider that only to the rational animal is it given to follow voluntarily what happens; but simply to follow is a necessity imposed on all.

Severally on the occasion of everything that thou doest, pause and ask thyself, if death is a dreadful thing because it deprives thee of this.

When thou art offended at any man's fault, forthwith turn to thyself and reflect in what like manner thou dost err thyself; for example, in thinking that money is a good thing, or pleasure, or a bit of reputation, and the like.   For by attending to this thou wilt quickly forget thy anger, if this consideration also is added, that the man is compelled: for what else could he do? or, if thou art able, take away from him the compulsion.

When thou hast seen Satyron[11] the Socratic,* think of either Eutyches or Hymen, and when thou hast seen Euphrates, think of Eutychion or Silvanus, and when thou hast seen Alciphron think of Tropæophorus, and when thou hast seen Xenophon think of Crito[12] or Severus, and when thou hast looked on thyself, think of any other Cæsar, and in the case of every one do in like manner.   Then let this thought be in thy mind, Where then are those men?   Nowhere, or nobody knows where.   For thus continuously thou wilt look at human things as smoke and nothing at all; especially if thou reflectest at the same time that what has once changed will never exist again in the infinite duration of time.   But thou, in what a brief space of time is thy existence?   And why art thou not content to pass through this short time in an orderly way?   What matter and opportunity [for thy activity] art thou avoiding?   For what else are all these things, except exercises for the reason, when it has viewed

carefully and by examination into their nature the things
which happen in life? Persevere then until thou shalt have
made these things thy own, as the stomach which is strengthened makes all things its own, as the blazing fire makes flame
and brightness out of everything that is thrown into it.

Let it not be in any man's power to say truly of thee that
thou art not simple or that thou art not good; but let him
be a liar whoever shall think anything of this kind about
thee; and this is altogether in thy power. For who is he
that shall hinder thee from being good and simple? Do
thou only determine to live no longer, unless thou shalt be
such. For neither does reason allow [thee to live], if thou
art not such.

What is that which as to this material [our life] can be
done or said in the way most conformable to reason. For
whatever this may be, it is in thy power to do it or to say
it, and do not make excuses that thou art hindered. Thou
wilt not cease to lament till thy mind is in such a condition
that, what luxury is to those who enjoy pleasure, such shall
be to thee, in the matter which is subjected and presented
to thee, the doing of the things which are conformable to
man's constitution; for a man ought to consider as an enjoyment everything which it is in his power to do according
to his own nature. And it is in his power everywhere.
Now, it is not given to a cylinder to move everywhere by
its own motion, nor yet to water nor to fire, nor to anything
else which is governed by nature or an irrational soul,
for the things which check them and stand in the way are
many. But intelligence and reason are able to go through
everything that opposes them, and in such manner as they
are formed by nature and as they choose. Place before thy
eyes this facility with which the reason will be carried
through all things, as fire upwards, as a stone downwards, as
a cylinder down an inclined surface, and seek for nothing
further. For all other obstacles either affect the body only
which is a dead thing; or, except through opinion and the yielding of the reason itself, they do not crush nor do any harm of
any kind; for if they did, he who felt it would immediately
become bad. Now, in the case of all things which have
a certain constitution, whatever harm may happen to any

of them, that which is so affected becomes consequently worse; but in the like case, a man becomes both better, if one may say so, and more worthy of praise by making right use of these accidents.   And finally remember that nothing harms him who is really a citizen, which does not harm the state; nor yet does anything harm the state, which does not harm law [order] ; and of these things which are called misfortunes not one harms law.   What then does not harm law does not harm either state or citizen.

To him who is penetrated by true principles even the briefest precept is sufficient, and any common precept, to remind him that he should be free from grief and fear.   For example—

> "Leaves, some the wind scatters on the ground—
> So is the race of men."[1]

Leaves, also, are thy children; and leaves, too, are they who cry out as if they were worthy of credit and bestow their praise, or on the contrary curse, or secretly blame and sneer; and leaves, in like manner, are those who shall receive and transmit a man's fame to after times   For all such things as these "are produced in the season of spring," as the poet says; then the wind casts them down, then the forest produces other leaves in their places.   But a brief existence is common to all things, and yet thou avoidest and pursuest all things as if they would be eternal.   A little time, and thou shalt close thy eyes; and him who has attended thee to thy grave another soon will lament.

The healthy eye ought to see all visible things and not to say, I wish for green things; for this is the condition of a diseased eye.   And the healthy hearing and smelling ought to be ready to perceive all that can be heard and smelled. And the healthy stomach ought to be with respect to all food just as the mill with respect to all things which it is formed to grind.   And accordingly the healthy understanding ought to be prepared for everything which happens; but that which says, Let my dear children live, and let all men praise whatever I may do, is an eye which seeks for green things, or teeth which seek for soft things.

There is no man so fortunate that there shall not be by him when he is dying some who are pleased with what is going to happen.[14] Suppose that he was a good and wise man, will there not be at last some one to say to himself, Let us at last breathe freely being relieved from this schoolmaster? It is true that he was harsh to none of us, but I perceived that he tacitly condemns us.—This is what is said of a good man. But in our own case how many other things are there for which there are many who wish to get rid of us. Thou wilt consider this then when thou art dying, and thou wilt depart more contentedly by reflecting thus: I am going away from such a life, in which even my associates in behalf of whom I have striven so much, prayed, and cared, themselves wish me to depart, hoping perchance to get some little advantage by it. Why then should a man cling to a longer stay here? Do not however for this reason go away less kindly disposed to them, but preserving thy own character, and friendly and benevolent and mild, and on the other hand not as if thou wast torn away; but as when a man dies a quiet death, the poor soul is easily separated from the body, such also ought thy departure from men to be, for nature united thee to them and associated thee. But does she now dissolve the union? Well, I am separated as from kinsmen, not however dragged resisting, but without compulsion; for this too is one of the things according to nature.

Accustom thyself as much as possible, on the occasion of anything being done by any person, to inquire with thyself, For what object is this man doing this? but begin with thyself, and examine thyself first.

Remember that this which pulls the strings is the thing which is hidden within: this is the power of persuasion, this is life, this, if one may so say, is man. In contemplating thyself never include the vessel which surrounds thee and these instruments which are attached about it. For they are like to an axe, differing only in this that they grow to the body. For indeed there is no more use in these parts without the cause which moves and checks them than in the weaver's shuttle, and the writer's pen, and the driver's whip.

NOTES

[1] That is, God, as he is defined by Zeno. But the confusion between gods and God is strange
[2] The end of this section is perhaps corrupt. The meaning is very ob-

scure   I have given that meaning which appears to be consistent with the whole argument. The emperor here maintains that the essential part of man is unchangeable, and that the other parts, if they change or perish, do not affect that which really constitutes the man.

³ See Seneca, Epp. 70, on these exhibitions which amused the people of those days. These fighters were the Bestiarii, some of whom may have been criminals, but even if they were, the exhibition was equally characteristic of the depraved habits of the spectators.

⁴ The islands of the Happy or the Fortunatæ Insulæ are spoken of by the Greek and Roman writers. They were the abode of Heroes, like Achilles and Diomedes, as we see in the Scolion of Harmodius and Aristogiton. Sertorius heard of the islands at Cadiz from some sailors who had been there, and he had a wish to go and live in them and rest from his troubles. (Plutarch. Sertorius, c. 8) In the Odyssey, Proteus told Menelaus that he should not die in Argos, but be removed to a place at the boundary of the earth where Rhadamanthus dwelt. (Odyssey, IV, 565.)

> "For there in sooth man's life is easiest:
> Nor snow nor raging storm nor rain is there,
> But ever gently breathing gales of Zephyr
> Oceanus sends up to gladden man."

It is certain that the writer of the Odyssey only follows some old legend without having any knowledge of any place which corresponds to his description. The two islands which Sertorius heard of may be Madeira and the adjacent island. Compare Pindar, Ol. II, 129

⁵ Corais conjectured μῖσος "hatred" in place of Mimi, Roman plays in which action and gesticulation were all or nearly all.

⁶ Marcus means to say that conquerors are robbers. He himself warred against Sarmatians, and was a robber, as he says, like the rest.

⁷ By the law, he means the divine law, obedience to the will of God

⁸ These words are from Euripides. They are cited by Aristotle, Ethic. Nicom. VIII, I. Athenæus (XIII, 296.) and Stobæus quotes seven complete lines beginning ἐρᾷ μὲν ομβρου γαῖα. There is a similar fragment of Æcschylus, Danaides, also quoted by Althenæus.

It was the fashion of the Stoics to work on the meanings of words. So Antoninus here takes the verb φιλεῖ, "loves," which has also the sense of "is wont," "uses," and the like. He finds in the common language of mankind a philosophical truth, and most great truths are expressed in the common language of life; some understand them, but most people utter them without knowing how much they mean.

⁹ Plato Theæt. 174 D E. But compare the original with the use that Antoninus has made of it.

¹⁰ Antoninus is here playing on the etymology of νόμος, law, assignment, that which assigns (νέμει) to every man his portion.

¹¹ Nothing is known of Satyron or Satyrion; nor, I believe, of Eutyches or Hymen Euphrates is honourably mentioned by Epictetus. Pliny speaks very highly of him He obtained the permission of the Emperor Hadrian to drink poison, because he was old and in bad health.

¹² Crito is the friend of Socrates; and he was, it appears, also a friend of Xenophon. When the emperor says "seen" (ἰδών) he does not mean with the eyes.

¹³ Homer, Il. VI, 146.

¹⁴ He says κακόν, but as he affirms in other places that death is no evil, he must mean what others may call an evil, and he means only "what is going to happen."

BOOK XI

THESE are the properties of the rational soul: it sees itself, analyses itself, and makes itself such as it chooses; the fruit which it bears itself enjoys—for the fruits of plants and that in animals which corresponds to fruits others enjoy—it obtains its own end, wherever the limit of life may be fixed. Not as in a dance and in a play and in such like things, where the whole action is incomplete, if anything cuts it short; but in every part and wherever it may be stopped, it makes what has been set before it full and complete, so that it can say, I have what is my own. And further it traverses the whole universe, and the surrounding vacuum, and surveys its form, and it extends itself into the infinity of time, and embraces and comprehends the periodical renovation of all things, and it comprehends that those who come after us will see nothing new, nor have those before us seen anything more, but in a manner he who is forty years old, if he has any understanding at all, has seen by virtue of the uniformity that prevails all things which have been and all that will be This too is a property of the rational soul, love of one's neighbour, and truth and modesty, and to value nothing more than itself, which is also the property of Law.[1] Thus then right reason differs not at all from the reason of justice.

Thou wilt set little value on pleasing song and dancing and the pancratium, if thou wilt distribute the melody of the voice into its several sounds, and ask thyself as to each, if thou art mastered by this; for thou wilt be prevented by shame from confessing it: and in the matter of dancing, if at each movement and attitude thou wilt do the same; and the like also in the matter of the pancratium. In all things, then, except virtue and the acts of virtue, remember to apply thyself to their several parts, and by this division to come to value them little · and apply this rule also to thy whole life.

What a soul that is which is ready, if at any moment it must be separated from the body, and ready either to be extinguished or dispersed or continue to exist; but so that this readiness comes from a man's own judgment, not from mere obstinacy, as with the Christians,[2] but considerately and with dignity and in a way to persuade another, without tragic show.

Have I done something for the general interest? Well then I have had my reward. Let this always be present to thy mind, and never stop [doing such good].

What is thy art? to be good And how is this accomplished well except by general principles, some about the nature of the universe, and others about the proper constitution of man?

At first tragedies were brought on the stage as means of reminding men of the things which happen to them, and that it is according to nature for things to happen so, and that, if you are delighted with what is shown on the stage, you should not be troubled with that which takes place on the larger stage. For you see that these things must be accomplished thus, and that even they bear them who cry out[3] "O Cithæron " And, indeed, some things are said well by the dramatic writers, of which kind is the following especially :—

> "Me and my children if the gods neglect,
> This has its reason too."

And again—

> "We must not chafe and fret at that which happens."

And—

> "Life's harvest reap like the wheat's fruitful ear."

And other things of the same kind.

After tragedy the old comedy was introduced, which had a magisterial freedom of speech, and by its very plainness of speaking was useful in reminding men to beware of insolence; and for this purpose too Diogenes used to take from these writers.

But as to the middle comedy which came next, observe

what it was, and again, for what object the new comedy was introduced, which gradually sunk down into a mere mimic artifice. That some good things are said even by these writers, everybody knows : but the whole plan of such poetry and dramaturgy, to what end does it look !

How plain does it appear that there is not another condition of life so well suited for philosophizing as this in which thou now happenest to be.

A branch cut off from the adjacent branch must of necessity be cut off from the whole tree also. So too a man when he is separated from another man has fallen off from the whole social community. Now as to a branch, another cuts it off, but a man by his own act separates himself from his neighbour when he hates him and turns away from him, and he does not know that he has at the same time cut himself off from the whole social system. Yet he has this privilege certainly from Zeus who framed society, for it is in our power to grow again to that which is near to us, and again to become a part which helps to make up the whole. However, if it often happens, this kind of separation, it makes it difficult for that which detaches itself to be brought to unity and to be restored to its former condition. Finally, the branch, which from the first grew together with the tree, and has continued to have one life with it, is not like that which after being cut off is then ingrafted, for this is something like what the gardeners mean when they say that it grows with the rest of the tree, but* that it has not the same mind with it.

As those who try to stand in thy way when thou art proceeding according to right reason, will not be able to turn thee aside from thy proper action, so neither let them drive thee from thy benevolent feelings towards them, but be on thy guard equally in both matters, not only in the matter of steady judgment and action, but also in the matter of gentleness towards those who try to hinder or otherwise trouble thee. For this also is a weakness, to be vexed at them, as well as to be diverted from thy course of action and to give way through fear; for both are equally deserters from their posts, the man who does it through fear, and the man who is alienated from him who is by nature a kinsman and a friend.

There is no nature which is inferior to art, for the arts imitate the natures of things. But if this is so, that nature which is the most perfect and the most comprehensive of all natures, can not fall short of the skill of art. Now all arts do the inferior things for the sake of the superior; therefore the universal nature does so too. And, indeed, hence is the origin of justice, and in justice the other virtues have their foundation: for justice will not be observed, if we either care for middle things [things indifferent], or are easily deceived and careless and changeable.

If the things do not come to thee, the pursuits and avoidances of which disturb thee, still in a manner thou goest to them. Let then thy judgment about them be at rest, and they will remain quiet, and thou wilt not be seen either pursuing or avoiding.

The spherical form of the soul maintains its figure, when it is neither extended towards any object, nor contracted inwards, nor dispersed nor sinks down, but is illuminated by light, by which it sees the truth, the truth of all things and the truth that is in itself.

Suppose any man shall despise me. Let him look to that himself. But I will look to this, that I be not discovered doing or saying anything deserving of contempt. Shall any man hate me? Let him look to it. But I will be mild and benevolent towards every man, and ready to show even him his mistake, not reproachfully, nor yet as making a display of my endurance, but nobly and honestly, like the great Phocion, unless indeed he only assumed it. For the interior [parts] ought to be such, and a man ought to be seen by the gods neither dissatisfied with anything nor complaining. For what evil is it to thee, if thou art now doing what is agreeable to thy own nature, and art satisfied with that which at this moment is suitable to the nature of the universe, since thou art a human being placed at thy post in order that what is for the common advantage may be done in some way?

Men despise one another and flatter one another; and men wish to raise themselves above one another, and crouch before one another.

How unsound and insincere is he who says, I have determined to deal with thee in a fair way.—What art thou doing,
man? There is no occasion to give this notice. It will soon
show itself by acts. The voice ought to be plainly written
on the forehead. Such as a man's character is,* he immediately shows it in his eyes, just as he who is beloved forthwith reads everything in the eyes of lovers. The man who
is honest and good ought to be exactly like a man who smells
strong, so that the bystander as soon as he comes near him
must smell whether he choose or not. But the affectation of
simplicity is like a crooked stick.⁴ Nothing is more disgraceful than a wolfish friendship [false friendship]. Avoid
this most of all. The good and simple and benevolent
show all these things in the eyes, and there is no mis-
taking.

As to living in the best way, this power is in the soul,
if it be indifferent to things which are indifferent. And it
will be indifferent, if it looks on each of these things separately and all together, and if it remembers that not one of
them produces in us an opinion about itself, nor comes to us;
but these things remain immovable, and it is we ourselves
who produce the judgments about them, and, as we may say,
write them in ourselves, it being in our power not to write
them, and it being in our power, if perchance these judgments
have imperceptibly got admission to our minds, to wipe them
out; and if we remember also that such attention will only be
for a short time, and then life will be at an end. Besides,
what trouble is there at all in doing this? For if these
things are according to nature, rejoice in them, and they will
be easy to thee: but if contrary to nature, seek what is conformable to thy own nature, and strive towards this, even
if it bring no reputation; for every man is allowed to seek
his own good.

Consider whence each thing is come, and of what it consists,* and into what it changes, and what kind of a thing
it will be when it has changed, and that it will sustain no
harm.

[If any have offended against thee, consider first]: What
is my relation to men, and that we are made for one another;
and in another respect, I was made to be set over them, as a

ram over the flock or a bull over the herd. But examine the matter from first principles, from this · If all things are not mere atoms, it is nature which orders all things: if this is so, the inferior things exist for the sake of the superior, and these for the sake of one another.

Second, consider what kind of men they are at table, in bed, and so forth: and particularly, under what compulsions in respect of opinions they are; and as to their acts, consider with what pride they do what they do.

Third, that if men do rightly what they do, we ought not to be displeased; but if they do not right, it is plain that they do so involuntarily and in ignorance. For as every soul is unwillingly deprived of the truth, so also is it unwillingly deprived of the power of behaving to each man according to his deserts. Accordingly men are pained when they are called unjust, ungrateful, and greedy, and in a word wrong-doers to their neighbours.

Fourth, consider that thou also doest many things wrong, and that thou art a man like others; and even if thou dost abstain from certain faults, still thou hast the disposition to commit them, though either through cowardice, or concern about reputation or some such mean motive, thou dost abstain from such faults.

Fifth, consider that thou dost not even understand whether men are doing wrong, or not, for many things are done with a certain reference to circumstances. And in short, a man must learn a great deal to enable him to pass a correct judgment on another man's acts.

Sixth, consider when thou art much vexed or grieved, that man's life is only a moment, and after a short time we are all laid out dead.

Seventh, that it is not men's acts which disturb us, for those acts have their foundation in men's ruling principles, but it is our own opinions which disturb us. Take away these opinions then, and resolve to dismiss thy judgment about an act as if it were something grievous, and thy anger is gone. How then shall I take away these opinions? By reflecting that no wrongful act of another brings shame on thee: for unless that which is shameful is alone bad, thou also must of necessity do many things wrong, and become a robber and everything else.

Eighth, consider how much more pain is brought on us by the anger and vexation caused by such acts than by the acts themselves, at which we are angry and vexed.

Ninth, consider that a good disposition is invincible, if it be genuine, and not an affected smile and acting a part. For what will the most violent man do to thee, if thou continuest to be of a kind disposition towards him, and if, as opportunity offers, thou gently admonishest him and calmly correctest his errors at the very time when he is trying to do thee harm, saying, "Not so, my child: we are constituted by nature for something else: I shall certainly not be injured, but thou art injuring thyself, my child."—And show him with gentle tact and by general principles that this is so, and that even bees do not do as he does, nor any animals which are formed by nature to be gregarious. And thou must do this neither with any double meaning nor in the way of reproach, but affectionately and without any rancour in thy soul; and not as if thou wert lecturing him, nor yet that any bystander may admire, but either when he is alone, and if others are present[5] . . . . .

Remember these nine rules, as if thou hadst received them as a gift from the Muses, and begin at last to be a man while thou livest.   But thou must equally avoid flattering men and being vexed at them, for both are unsocial and lead to harm. And let this truth be present to thee in the excitement of anger, that to be moved by passion is not manly, but that mildness and gentleness, as they are more agreeable to human nature, so also are they more manly; and he who possesses these qualities possesses strength, nerves, and courage, and not the man who is subject to fits of passion and discontent. For in the same degree in which a man's mind is nearer to freedom from all passion, in the same degree also is it nearer to strength: and as the sense of pain is a characteristic of weakness, so also is anger.   For he who yields to pain and he who yields to anger, both are wounded and both submit.

But if thou wilt, receive also a tenth present from the leader of the [Muses, Apollo], and it is this—that to expect

bad men not to do wrong is madness, for he who expects this
desires an impossibility.   But to allow men to behave so to
others, and to expect them not to do thee any wrong, is irrational and tyrannical.

There are four principal aberrations of the superior faculty
against which thou shouldst be constantly on thy guard, and
when thou hast detected them, thou shouldst wipe them out
and say on each occasion thus : this thought is not necessary :
this tends to destroy social union : this which thou art going
to say comes not from the real thoughts; for thou shouldst
consider it among the most absurd of things for a man not to
speak from his real thoughts.   But the fourth is when thou
shalt reproach thyself for anything, for this is an evidence
of the diviner part within thee being overpowered and yielding to the less honourable and to the perishable part, the
body, and to its gross pleasures.

Thy aerial part and all the fiery parts which are mingled
in thee, though by nature they have an upward tendency, still
in obedience to the disposition of the universe they are overpowered here in the compound mass [the body].   And also
the whole of the earthly part in thee and the watery, though
their tendency is downward, still are raised up and occupy a
position which is not their natural one.   In this manner then
the elemental parts obey the universal, for when they have
been fixed in any place perforce they remain there until again
the universal shall sound the signal for dissolution.   Is it
not then strange that thy intelligent part only should be disobedient and discontented with its own place?   And yet no
force is imposed on it, but only those things which are conformable to its nature : still it does not submit, but is carried
in the opposite direction.   For the movement towards injustice and intemperance and to anger and grief and fear is
nothing else than the act of one who deviates from nature.
And also when the ruling faculty is discontented with anything that happens, then too it deserts its post : for it is constituted for piety and reverence towards the gods no less than
for justice.   For these qualities also are comprehended under
the generic term of contentment with the constitution of
things, and indeed they are prior[6] to acts of justice.

He who has not one and always the same object in life,

can not be one and the same all through his life. But what I have said is not enough, unless this also is added, what this object ought to be. For as there is not the same opinion about all the things which in some way or other are considered by the majority to be good, but only about some certain things, that is, things which concern the common interest; so also ought we to propose to ourselves an object which shall be of a common kind [social] and political. For he who directs all his own efforts to this object, will make all his acts alike, and thus will always be the same.

Think of the country mouse and of the town mouse, and of the alarm and trepidation of the town mouse.[7]

Socrates used to call the opinions of the many by the name of Lamiæ, bugbears to frighten children.

The Lacedæmonians at their public spectacles used to set seats in the shade for strangers, but themselves sat down anywhere.

Socrates excused himself to Perdiccas[8] for not going to him, saying, It is because I would not perish by the worst of all ends, that is, I would not receive a favour and then be unable to return it.

In the writing of the [Ephesians] there was this precept, constantly to think of some one of the men of former times who practised virtue.

The Pythagoreans bid us in the morning look to the heavens that we may be reminded of those bodies which continually do the same things and in the same manner perform their work, and also be reminded of their purity and nudity. For there is no veil over a star.

Consider what a man Socrates was when he dressed himself in a skin, after Xanthippe had taken his cloak and gone out, and what Socrates said to his friends who were ashamed of him and drew back from him when they saw him dressed thus.

Neither in writing nor in reading wilt thou be able to lay down rules for others before thou shalt have first learned to obey rules thyself. Much more is this so in life.

A slave thou art: free speech is not for thee.

———And my heart laughed within.[9]

And virtue they will curse speaking harsh words.[10]

To look for the fig in winter is a madman's act: such is he
who looks for his child when it is no longer allowed.[11]

When a man kisses his child, said Epictetus, he should
whisper to himself, "To-morrow perchance thou wilt die"—
But those are words of bad omen—"No word is a word of
bad omen," said Epictetus, "which expresses any work of
nature; or if it is so, it is also a word of bad omen to speak
of the ears of corn being reaped."

The unripe grape, the ripe bunch, the dried grape all are
changes, not into nothing, but into something which exists
not yet.[12]

No man can rob us of our free will.[13]

Epictetus also said, a man must discover an art [or rules]
with respect to giving his assent; and in respect to his movements he must be careful that they be made with regard to
circumstances, that they be consistent with social interests,
that they have regard to the value of the object; and as to
sensual desire, he should altogether keep away from it; and
as to avoidance [aversion] he should not show it with respect to any of the things which are not in our power.

The dispute then, he said, is not about any common matter, but about being mad or not.

Socrates used to say, What do you want? Souls of
rational men or irrational?—Souls of rational men—Of
what rational men? Sound or unsound?—Sound—Why
then do you not seek for them?—Because we have them—
Why then do you fight and quarrel?

NOTES

[1] Law is the order by which all things are governed.
[2] This is the only passage in which the emperor speaks of the
Christians. Epictetus (IV, 7,) names them Galilæi
[3] Sophocles, Œdipus Rex.
[4] Instead of σκάλμη Saumaise reads σκαμβή. There is a Greek proverb, σκαμβὸν ξύλον οὐδέποτ' ὀρθόν: "You cannot make a crooked
stick straight "
  The wolfish friendship is an allusion to the fable of the sheep and
the wolves
[5] It appears that there is a defect in the text here
[6] The word πρεσβύτερα, which is here translated "prior" may also
mean "superior;" but Antoninus seems to say that piety and reverence
of the gods precede all virtues, and that other virtues are derived from
them, even justice, which in another passage (XI, 10) he makes the
foundation of all virtues. The ancient notion of justice is that of giving

to every one his due. It is not a legal definition, as some have supposed, but a moral rule which law can not in all cases enforce Besides law has its own rules, which are sometimes moral and sometimes immoral, but it enforces them all simply because they are general rules, and if it did not or could not enforce them, so far law would not be law Justice, or the doing what is just, implies a universal rule and obedience to it, and as we all live under universal law, which commands both our body and our intelligence, and is the law of our nature, that is the law of the whole constitution of man, we must endeavour to discover what this supreme law is It is the will of the power that rules all. By acting in obedience to this will, we do justice, and by consequence everything else that we ought to do.

⁷ The story is told by Horace in his Satires (II, 6), and by others since, but not better.

⁸ Perhaps the emperor made a mistake here, for other writers say that it was Archelaus, the son of Perdiccas, who invited Socrates to Macedonia.

⁹ Od. IX 413.

¹⁰Hesiod, Works and Days, 184.

¹¹Epictetus, III, 24, 87.

¹²Epictetus, III, 24.

¹³Epictetus, III, 22, 105.

BOOK XII.

ALL those things at which thou wishest to arrive by a circuitous road, thou canst have now, if thou dost not refuse them to thyself. And this means, if thou wilt take no notice of all the past, and trust the future to providence, and direct the present only conformably to piety and justice. Conformably to piety, that thou mayst be content with the lot which is assigned to thee, for nature designed it for thee and thee for it. Conformably to justice, that thou mayst always speak the truth freely and without disguise, and do things which are agreeable to law and according to the worth of each. And let neither another man's wickedness hinder thee, nor opinion nor voice, nor yet the sensations of the poor flesh which has grown about thee; for the passive part will look to this. If then, whatever the time may be when thou shalt be near to thy departure, neglecting everything else thou shalt respect only thy ruling faculty and the divinity within thee, and if thou shalt be afraid not because thou must some time cease to live, but if thou shalt fear never to have begun to live according to nature—then thou wilt be a man worthy of the universe which has produced thee, and thou wilt cease to be a stranger in thy native land, and to wonder at things which happen daily as if they were something unexpected, and to be dependent on this or that.

God sees the minds (ruling principles) of all men bared of the material vesture and rind and impurities. For with his intellectual part alone he touches the intelligence only which has flowed and been derived from himself into these bodies. And if thou also usest thyself to do this, thou wilt rid thyself of thy much trouble. For he who regards not the poor flesh which envelopes him, surely will not trouble himself by looking after raiment and dwelling and fame and such like externals and show.

The things are three of which thou art composed, a little body, a little breath, [life], intelligence. Of these the first two are thine, so far as it is thy duty to take care of them; but the third alone is properly thine. Therefore if thou shalt separate from thyself, that is, from thy understanding, whatever others do or say, and whatever thou hast done or said thyself, and whatever future things trouble thee because they may happen, and whatever in the body which envelopes thee or in the breath [life], which is by nature associated with the body, is attached to thee independent of thy will, and whatever the external circumfluent vortex whirls round, so that the intellectual power exempt from the things of fate can live pure and free by itself, doing what is just and accepting what happens and saying the truth: if thou wilt separate, I say, from this ruling faculty the things which are attached to it by the impressions of sense, and the things of time to come and of time that is past, and wilt make thyself like Empedocles' sphere,—

"All round, and in its joyous rest reposing:"[1]

and if thou shalt strive to live only what is really thy life, that is, the present—then thou wilt be able to pass that portion of life which remains for thee up to the time of thy death, free from perturbations, nobly, and obedient to thy own dæmon [to the god that is within thee].

I have often wondered how it is that every man loves himself more than all the rest of men, but yet sets less value on his own opinion of himself than on the opinion of others. If then a god or a wise teacher should present himself to man and bid him to think of nothing and to design nothing which he would not express as soon as he conceived it, he could not endure it even for a single day. So much more respect have we to what our neighbours shall think of us than to what we shall think of ourselves.

How can it be that the gods after having arranged all things well and benevolently for mankind, have overlooked this alone, that some men and very good men, and men who, as we may say, have had most communion with the divinity,

33

and through pious acts and religious observances have been most intimate with the divinity, when they have once died should never exist again, but should be completely extinguished?

But if this is so, be assured that if it ought to have been otherwise, the gods would have done it. For if it were just, it would also be possible; and if it were according to nature, nature would have had it so. But because it is not so, if in fact it is not so, be thou convinced that it ought not to have been so:—for thou seest even of thyself that in this inquiry thou art disputing with the deity; and we should not thus dispute with the gods, unless they were most excellent and most just;—but if this is so, they would not have allowed anything in the ordering of the universe to be neglected unjustly and irrationally.

Practise thyself even in the things which thou despairest of accomplishing. For even the left hand, which is ineffectual for all other things for want of practice, holds the bridle more vigorously than the right hand; for it has been practised in this.

Consider in what condition both in body and soul a man should be when he is overtaken by death; and consider the shortness of life, the boundless abyss of time past and future, the feebleness of all matter.

Contemplate the formative principles [forms] of things bare of their coverings; the purposes of actions; consider what pain is, what pleasure is, and death, and fame; who is to himself the cause of his uneasiness; how no man is hindered by another; that everything is opinion.

In the application of thy principles thou must be like the pancratiast, not like the gladiator; for the gladiator lets fall the sword which he uses and is killed; but the other always has his hand, and needs to do nothing else than use it.

See what things are in themselves, dividing them into matter, form, and purpose

What a power man has to do nothing except what god will approve, and to accept all that god may give him.

With respect to that which happens conformably to nature, we ought to blame neither gods, for they do nothing wrong either voluntarily or involuntarily, nor men, for they do nothing wrong except involuntarily. Consequently we should blame nobody.

How ridiculous and what a stranger he is who is surprised at anything which happens in life.

Either there is a fatal necessity and invincible order, or a kind providence, or a confusion without a purpose and without a director. If then there is an invincible necessity, why dost thou resist? But if there is a providence which allows itself to be propitiated, make thyself worthy of the help of the divinity. But if there is a confusion without a governor, be content that in such a tempest thou hast in thyself a certain ruling intelligence. And even if the tempest carry thee away, let it carry away the poor flesh, the poor breath, everything else; for the intelligence at least it will not carry away.

Does the light of the lamp shine without losing its splendour until it is extinguished; and shall the truth which is in thee and justice and temperance be extinguished [before thy death]?

When a man has presented the appearance of having done wrong, [say,] How then do I know that this is a wrongful act? And if he has done wrong, how do I know that he has not condemned himself? and so this is like tearing his own face Consider that he, who would not have the bad man do wrong, is like the man who would not have the fig-tree to bear juice in the figs and infants to cry and the horse to neigh, and whatever else must of necessity be. For what must a man do who has such a character? If then thou art irritable,* cure this man's disposition.

If it is not right, do not do it: if it is not true, do not say it. [For let thy efforts be.—][2]

In everything always observe what the thing is which produces for thee an appearance, and resolve it by dividing it into the formal, the material, the purpose, and the time within which it must end.

Perceive at last that thou hast in thee something better and more divine than the things which cause the various affects, and as it were pull thee by the strings. What is there now in my mind? is it fear, or suspicion, or desire, or anything of the kind?

First, do nothing inconsiderately, nor without a purpose.

Second, make thy acts refer to nothing else than to a social end.

Consider that before long thou wilt be nobody and nowhere, nor will any of the things exist which thou now seest, nor any of those who are now living For all things are formed by nature to change and be turned and to perish in order that other things in continuous succession may exist.

Consider that everything is opinion, and opinion is in thy power. Take away then, when thou choosest, thy opinion, and like a mariner, who has doubled the promontory, thou wilt find calm, everything stable, and a waveless bay.

Any one activity whatever it may be, when it has ceased at its proper time, suffers no evil because it has ceased; nor he who has done this act, does he suffer any evil for this reason that the act has ceased. In like manner then the whole which consists of all the acts, which is our life, if it cease at its proper time, suffers no evil for this reason that it has ceased; nor he who has terminated this series at the proper time, has he been ill dealt with. But the proper time and the limit nature fixes, sometimes as in old age the peculiar nature of man, but always the universal nature, by the change of whose parts the whole universe continues ever young and perfect. And everything which is useful to the universal is always good and in season. Therefore the termination of life for every man is no evil, because neither is it shameful, since it is both independent of the will and not opposed to the general interest, but it is good, since it is seasonable and profitable to and congruent with the universal. For thus too he is moved by the deity who is moved in the same manner with the deity and moved towards the same things in his mind.

These three principles thou must have in readiness. In the things which thou doest do nothing either inconsiderately or otherwise than as justice herself would act; but with respect to what may happen to thee from without, consider that it happens either by chance or according to providence, and thou must neither blame chance nor accuse providence Second, consider what every being is from the seed to the time of its receiving a soul, and from the reception of a soul to the giving back of the same, and of what things every being is compounded and into what things it is resolved. Third, if thou shouldst suddenly be raised up above the earth, and shouldst look down on human things, and observe the variety of them how great it is, and at the same time also shouldst see at a glance how great is the number of beings who dwell all around in the air and the æther, consider that as often as thou shouldst be raised up, thou wouldst see the same things, sameness of form and shortness of duration. Are these things to be proud of?

Cast away opinion: thou art saved. Who then hinders thee from casting it away?

When thou art troubled about anything, thou hast forgotten this, that all things happen according to the universal nature; and forgotten this, that a man's wrongful act is nothing to thee; and further thou hast forgotten this, that everything which happens, always happened so and will happen so, and now happens so everywhere; forgotten this too, how close is the kinship between a man and the whole human race, for it is a community, not of a little blood or seed, but of intelligence. And thou hast forgotten this too, that every man's intelligence is a god, and is an efflux of the deity; and forgotten this, that nothing is a man's own, but that his child and his body and his very soul came from the deity; forgotten this, that everything is opinion; and lastly thou hast forgotten that every man lives the present time only, and loses only this.

Constantly bring to thy recollection those who have complained greatly about anything, those who have been most conspicuous by the greatest fame or misfortunes or enmities or fortunes of any kind: then think where are they all now? Smoke and ash and a tale, or not even a tale. And let there be present to thy mind also everything of this sort, how Fabius Catullinus lived in the country, and Lucius Lupus in his gardens, and Stertinius at Baiæ, and Tiberius at Capreæ and Velius Rufus [or Rufus at Velia]; and in fine think of the eager pursuit of anything conjoined with pride; and how worthless everything is after which men violently strain; and how much more philosophical it is for a man in the opportunities presented to him to show himself just, temperate, obedient to the gods, and to do this with all simplicity: for the pride which is proud of its want of pride is the most intolerable of all.

To those who ask, Where hast thou seen the gods or how dost thou comprehend that they exist and so worshipest them, I answer, in the first place, they may be seen even with the eyes;[3] in the second place neither have I seen even my own soul and yet I honour it. Thus then with respect to the gods, from what I constantly experience of their power, from this I comprehend that they exist and I venerate them.

The safety of life is this, to examine everything all through, what it is itself, what is its material, what the formal part; with all thy soul to do justice and to say the truth. What remains except to enjoy life by joining one good thing to another so as not to leave even the smallest intervals between?

There is one light of the sun, though it is interrupted by walls, mountains, and other things infinite. There is one common substance, though it is distributed among countless bodies which have their several qualities. There is one soul, though it is distributed among infinite natures and individual circumscriptions [or individuals]. There is one intelligent soul, though it seems to be divided. Now in the things which have been mentioned all the other parts, such as those which are air and matter, are without sensation and have no fellowship: and yet even these parts the intelligent principle holds together and the gravitation towards the same. But intellect in a peculiar manner tends to that which is of the same kin, and combines with it, and the feeling for communion is not interrupted.

What dost thou wish? to continue to exist? Well, dost thou wish to have sensation? movement? growth? and then again to cease to grow? to use thy speech? to think? What is there of all these things which seems to thee worth desiring? But if it is easy to set little value on all these things, turn to that which remains, which is to follow reason and god. But it is inconsistent with honouring reason and god to be troubled because by death a man will be deprived of the other things.

How small a part of the boundless and unfathomable time is assigned to every man? for it is very soon swallowed up

in the eternal. And how small a part of the whole substance? and how small a part of the universal soul? and on
what a small clod of the whole earth thou creepest? Reflecting on all this consider nothing to be great, except to act as
thy nature leads thee, and to endure that which the common
nature brings.

How does the ruling faculty make use of itself? for all
lies in this. But everything else, whether it is in the power
of thy will or not, is only lifeless ashes and smoke.

This reflection is most adapted to move us to contempt
of death, that even those who think pleasure to be a good and
pain an evil still have despised it.

The man to whom that only is good which comes in
due season, and to whom it is the same thing whether he has
done more or fewer acts conformable to right reason, and to
whom it makes no difference whether he contemplates the
world for a longer or a shorter time—for this man neither is
death a terrible thing.

Man, thou hast been a citizen in this great state [the
world]: what difference does it make to thee whether for
five years [or three]? for that which is conformable to the
laws is just for all. Where is the hardship then, if no tyrant
nor yet an unjust judge sends thee away from the state, but
nature who brought thee into it? the same as if a praetor who
has employed an actor dismisses him from the stage—"But
I have not finished the five acts, but only three of them"—
Thou sayest well, but in life the three acts are the whole
drama; for what shall be a complete drama is determined by
him who was once the cause of its composition, and now of
its dissolution: but thou art the cause of neither. Depart
then satisfied, for he also who releases thee is satisfied.

NOTES

¹ The verse of Empedocles is corrupt in Antoninus. It has been restored by Peyron from a Turin manuscript, thus:

Σφαῖρος κυκλοτερής μονίῃ περιγηθέϊ γαίων.

² There is something wrong here, or incomplete.
³ " Seen even with the eyes." It is supposed that this may be explained by the Stoic doctrine, that the universe is a god or living being
(IV, 40), and that the celestial bodies are gods (VIII, 19). But the em-

peror may mean that we know that the gods exist, as he afterwards states it, because we see what they do; as we know that man has intellectual powers, because we see what he does, and in no other way do we know it. This passage then will agree with the passage in the Epistle to the Romans (1 *v* 20), and with the Epistle to the Colossians (1 *v.* 15), in which Jesus Christ is named "the image of the invisible god;" and with the passage in the Gospel of St. John (XIV *v.* 9).

Gataker, whose notes are a wonderful collection of learning, and all of it sound and good, quotes a passage of Calvin which is founded on St. Paul's language (Rom. 1 *v.* 20) : "God by creating the universe [or world, mundum], being Himself invisible, has presented Himself to our eyes conspicuously in a certain visible form" He also quotes Seneca (De Benef. IV c. 8) : "Quocunque te flexeris, ibi illum videbis occurrentem tibi: nihil ab illo vacat, opus suum ipse implet." Compare also Cicero, De Senectute (c. 22), Xenophon's Cyropaedia (VIII, 7), and Mem. IV, 3; also Epictetus, 1, 6, de Providentia. I think that my interpretation of Antoninus is right.

(1)

THE END.